Be Hidden Love

Love with inspiration from Rumi's wisdom

A true love story written by:

Y. Josephson

(Edited by: Catherine Suchowij)

TITLE Copyright © 2014 by Yousef Josephson.

All rights reserved. Printed in the United States of America. No part of this book may be used or reproduced in any manner whatsoever without written permission except in the case of brief quotations embodied in critical articles or reviews.

This book is a work of fiction. Names, characters, businesses, organiza- tions, places, events and incidents either are the product of the author's imagination or are used fictitiously. Any resemblance to actual persons, living or dead, events, or locales is entirely coincidental.

For information contact; address www.behiddenlove.com

Book and Cover design by Adeeb

ISBN: 978-0-692-30983-4

First Edition: October 2014

10 9 8 7 6 5 4 3 2 1

CONTENTS

CONTENTS iv
CHAPTER 1 *The Meeting* 1
CHAPTER 2 *The Camping Trip* 29
CHAPTER 3 *Assa* 43
CHAPTER 4 *School Matters* 63
CHAPTER 5 *Summer in Tehran, 1975* 88
CHAPTER 6 *A Trip North* 111
CHAPTER 7 *The Bus Trip* 148
CHAPTER 8 *Meetra* 180
CHAPTER 9 *Our Daily Lives* 262
CHAPTER 10 *For The Love of Rumi* 301
CHAPTER 11 *A New Year* 344
CHAPTER 12 *The Party* 379
CHAPTER 13 *Shared Stories* 412
CHAPTER 14 *Back to Shiraz* 449
CHAPTER 15 *Rumi Nights* 492
CHAPTER 16 *Keys* 555
CHAPTER 17 *Mama* 582
CHAPTER 18 *Nasty Business* 604

Dedication

     I tried to dedicate this book to someone such as my love or my folks. But I couldn't; this is not my book, her book or your book to dedicate to just one person. This is our book, our history, and our way to tell our history. So, I will just say thanks to the people who were involved in our life and our love.

I owe a lot of thanks to so many people, but unfortunately, I don't have that much room, so I will start with my folks and go from there.

First I have to thank my folks for everything; especially for teaching me love and how to be in love. They married with love and they lived together with love for close to sixty years. So I thank you both from bottom of my heart for the love you gave me and the things you taught me. You didn't get involved in my personal life. Yes, I knew that you knew and you knew that I knew you knew. But you never brought it up, instead you gave me advice that was more precious than diamonds and I knew it. You both did bear with me and loved me so much for the sake of love. For that I thank you. Finally I thank you for everything you did for me and for the love you knew existed, even though you didn't know whom it was. My Love loved you so much and she always turned my anger away from you, protecting you and she was always right.

Next I have to thank my dear friend, Assa, very much because if it weren't for him, I would never have met her in the first place. He was a good friend, buddy and a good listener. We had much fun together when we were in high school. I hope that God will be with him and love him.

Next, my thanks go to my sweetie, my baby, Meetra. I owe her a million thanks, because if she didn't invite me to her party I wouldn't have had the chance to meet my Love. She was my friend, my secret-keeper, my helper and my advisor. She helped me a lot; during the time I really needed it. She knew everything from the first moment but she supported us throughout the years. Meetra stood up to her brother, Assa, on my behalf and for us both. She taught me to feel how daddies feel toward their daughters. She called me daddy and she really meant it. I love her as a daddy from bottom of my heart and I missed her so much especially as the young woman she was. She was a look-alike to her mother. God bless both of you and I thank you for everything you have done for me and I am so sorry I couldn't be there for you. Sorry my baby.

Next I have to thank to all my nephews and my niece. My two nephews were with me during that time and they were very helpful. My older nephew especially helped me a lot in that time and this time in writing this story. Unfortunately I cannot talk to my younger one because I lost him. God be with him and I am sure he is in a good place. God bless my older nephew and God help him, he is fantastic guy and he is a ""lovey"" guy too. I have to thank my other nephew Mr. Dr. because if he wasn't there for me during that time I wouldn't be able to write this book at all God bless him and help him. And my little niece, she helped a lot with the taping and arranging the computer I thank her very much because without her this would be very difficult.

Next is my late oldest brother. When he passed away, his loss was very hard on me. I have to thank him for what he did for me. He was my brother, father, friend, helper and companion. I know he is in a good place, God be with him and bless him.

Next is my sister in law and my second brother. She worked very hard to teach me English, when I was living with them in early 1980's. My sister in law had the power of patience for teaching me English, and it reminded me of the time when Mahsa made such an effort to tutor me in high school. Sister in law was a really fantastic lady and very good friend to me. I will never ever forget what she did for me. Their kids really have been like my own; I thank you, for that much friendship and love. My brother did fantastic job to be close to me as much as he could. He let me have everything including his own kid. I thank you, too and hope one day all of us be together again as one big happy family. I hoped in that time I could have had her with me so you could see what I was talking about and how much I had really lost.

Last, but not least is my oh-so-dear, dear, dear spirit, soul mate and love, Mahsa. I cannot properly thank her because words are too small for everything she did. I wish to find a word for it to tell her. She was everything and everyone to me. She was my soul, spirit and love. She was every inch of my body. She was my bone, flesh and blood. She was my mom, sister, brother, father, uncle, aunt, cousins, nephews and nieces all in one. She was my love, lover, wife, companion, friend, and most importantly she was my teacher. She taught me how to kiss, how to be a fantastic lover. She taught me things that nobody else could teach me. She could be so serious and hard when she was tutoring me for my school lessons and at the same time she was an Angel next to me. Yes I was just a high school student outside but she made me into a proud guy inside. On the outside I was someone's son but with her I was a man and in charge. She found me at the time I was so down and desperate to have a good friend. She showed me the road to heaven and brought me to the door of true love. She taught me how to look inside of myself and find the person I was meant to be. She taught me how to shape my personality and to be proud of who I am. And finally she showed me the world from her eyes and that was the most difficult thing she did.

I loved her more than anything in the world. Nothing was more important than her in my life and that is still true. She was so unique, so beautiful, so understanding; she was a real angel. She spoiled me with love; I cannot live with anybody else. She didn't just teach me, she showed me what love is. She was a mom who had two adult kids but she put me in charge and I can tell she loved me so much because she showed me (when you read this book you will learn that). I cannot think of anything that she didn't do, it's impossible. I cannot say she was the most beautiful woman on the planet, but she certainly was in my eyes. Her most beautiful features were her eyes and her hair. We did everything together and we went everywhere together. She was always smiling and she had such a beautiful smile. She didn't wear much makeup she did only little touch-ups but those would make her look like a queen. I loved her so much and she loved me more than I deserved.

I was living in the city of Shiraz, a city that is much known for its beautiful spring season. But I never paid attention. People would tell me to go look around and see the beauty, go to the gardens and the parks. From time to time I would go, but wouldn't see anything special; everything was so ordinarily to me. That was nothing for me to be excited about. Then something happened - I met her in first month of spring, and suddenly I began to notice what I had been missing. I always told myself my God Yousef, you lost big! She filled up everything I missed before and she showed me everything. My God everything was so beautiful then. It's like going to Vermont in the fall, there is so much beauty all around. Go with your love so then you might understand what I mean. I never went there with my love, but in spirit, I've been there. It was like I was someplace else with my love and I looked like it too. What can I tell you about her? She was taller than me. I was 5.7 and she was 5.9 ½ and that was a grace and beauty about her. She was what she was and she was an angel. Yes she was! I found myself through her and she showed me every corner of myself. She was a giver such as I. Together we gave everything, yes everything, to each other and become each other's lover. Maybe I could use different word instead of lover but lover has a feeling to it I can't feel it in any other word, so that's why I use it.

So my love, may God be with you, help you, bless you and keep you alive. I love you so much, more than anything or what anyone can imagine.

My love, see you when I see you.

I could not leave this section without expressing my immense gratitude to my editor; Catherine who painstakingly, with incredible patience, word-by-word worked on this book. Without her, this book could not have happened.

There is a term that is used in this book that is very important for the reader to understand. The Farsi (Persian) word is 'eshghi' pronounced esh-ghee; the closest English word would be 'lovey'. It has different meanings. The first is a term that someone would call another person who is dear to him/her, it denotes a fondness and familiarity between them, but not necessarily as lovers. For example: a woman might call her nephew 'lovey'.

The second use is to describe someone who is very passionate about love and life. This person might be seen as a romantic. In this book, people use 'lovey' to describe me in both senses of the word.

Yousef

Preface

All of the names in this book have been changed to protect the identity of those I care deeply about. This was also done in accordance with Mahsa's wishes.

I picked these names very carefully and because of their meanings in Farsi. It took me a long time to come up with these names and went through several changes before I found the ones I felt had the most meaning.

Mahsa means 'twin moon, twin sun'. The Sun was the symbol of the ancient Persian god, Mithras who was the god of love.

Meetra refers to the five angles of love as symbolized by red flowers. I reference this throughout the book by the bouquets of flowers with one white and five red flowers. I always used roses.

Assa refers to a man who is easy to get along with.

Many others I picked as they are used in both Farsi and English.

I hope that in reading this book, you might find your own hidden or remember your school sweetheart.

There are times that you may laugh or cry, or you might be confused. But as long as you understand what each of us was going through. You can find yourself sad reading one page, or hot by the next.

Perhaps you may find the road that leads to the door to your love or your lover's heart. I hope you enjoy Rumi's poetry and his wisdom. I hope you will learn how important you are as part of humanity. You will also discover how important family backgrounds are important in all of our lives.

Finally, this book will describe how important it is to deal with destiny and how each of us interprets it. I still try to understand the wisdom of both Rumi and Hafez. I have been a scholar of their works since I was fourteen, and thanks to my father, I have known about their poems since when I was a kid. I feel that the excerpt below best reflects my life.

Rumi "Divan -e Shams-e Tabriz": Gazal # 1768

My life result is not out of these three words

I was without spirit, passion or fire inside

Then spirits took over and made a fire too hot as to burn me and make my soul

Spirit burned more and more until it turned me into ashes of love

So, that I became pure love such as love and lover in one

<u>Y. Josephson</u>

The excerpt lines from starting Masnavi

بشنو از نی چون حکایت می کند   از جدائیها شکایت میکند

Listen to my heart voice when telling you the story,
The story of complaining about the separation of love.

کز نیستان تا مرا ببریده اند   از نفیرم مرد و زن نالیده اند

Since they separated me from land of heart and love,
Man and woman whined from my heart sound.

سینه خواهم شرحه شرحه از فراق   تا بگویم شرح درد اشتیاق

I need the heart to tell the story of the broken heart from separation
Then I will tell you the explanation of real pain of eagerness.

CHAPTER 1

The Meeting

I am honored to tell you a true story about love; that happened in early spring of 1975 in Shiraz, Iran. It all began with just a look, the look became love, love became spirit and soul, spirit and soul then became life.

I was sitting in a friend's home on the sofa drinking my tea. Suddenly I heard something, I turned my head to see what it was and there she was! Oh my God she was beautiful or something more than beautiful. She was like an angel or a princess. No, she was definitely 'Princess of the Angels'. She came down the stairs very slowly and came to where I was sitting. I got up to shake her hand and I kissed her hand too. What a hand it was I had just kissed - so beautiful and soft.

Y. JOSEPHSON

She said, "You must be Yousef". I said, "Yes Ma'm". My heart beat so fast and I felt like my body was on fire. It seemed that the room became too small for me to breathe and I felt my throat tighten. The lady who had brought me the tea came back and asked me, "Would you like more tea?" I answered, "Yes please, thank you." She added, "But we also have very good coffee too, if you like." I couldn't talk anymore. The Angel told her "Get us two coffees and we going to have them outside on the balcony." Then she took my hand and said, "Let's go out there my dear." I couldn't say anything, I just followed her to outside to balcony and we sat.

She was looking at me very closely and started talking. I still couldn't talk, but I looked into her eyes and my God they were so beautiful; like the deep ocean. The lady brought us our coffee and placed them on the table. As I reached for the coffee, my hand touched her hand. I didn't want to move my hand any further, so I used my other hand for the coffee. I didn't move the hand was touching her hand. My heart felt like it was going to explode, just like my blood pressure. When I looked at her, it seemed that her face was on fire. I could hear her heart beat as much as I heard mine. In that time my hand was next to hers as if they were stuck to each other. Suddenly I moved my hand on top of her hand and I don't know why and how I did it but I did it. After a minute she grabbed my hand with one hand and with other hand she grabbed my face and kissed me so deeply and I kissed her back. We sat back in our seats and my heartbeat settled down slowly. We started drinking our coffee and she began talking to me, but I had no idea what she was talking about. Suddenly I heard a voice saying, "He's here with mom." It was my friend, and his sister Meetra. He asked, "When are you joining the party?" I replied, "As soon as I finish talking with your mom." He turned to Meetra saying, "O.K. let's go in, he's talking now he will be there later."

She called to the lady, "Mama." the lady who served me tea came up. She told her to please replace this coffee with Turkish coffee. Mama said, "Yes Ma'm", and left. In no time she returned with the Turkish coffee but it was in a big mug, not like other places that only use small cups. After Mama left, she turned to me and suggested that we walk through the side garden. Still speechless, I went with her, I felt like I didn't have any control at all; she stole my heart since I saw her at the top of the stairs. We got to the side garden and in middle of it that was a walkway about seven to eight feet wide. We went until the end. We sat on the wooden bench and finished our coffee. I turned and look at her eyes - my God they were so beautiful, like a most beautiful flower only God could create. She had long, wavy hair that was gorgeous. I reached out and touched her hair, stroking it. Then I kissed her, she embraced me and held me to herself and I let her. I said, "Sorry, I should not have done that!' She replied, "Its O.K. it is from both of us. I feel like I don't have any control over what I'm doing either." I told her, "Your eyes are so beautiful, especially in full moonlight. They could kill me in a second!" We sat and gazed into each other's eyes without any more talk or movement. Then after some time, we started kissing again and looking into each other's eyes, then kissing again. After a while, we started back to the balcony. We sat there and Mama brought us more coffee. We stared at each other like crazy; just looking at each other in silence and drinking that coffee. When we finished, she asked me "What are you going to do tonight?" I didn't know what to say. Looking deeply into my eyes, she said "I mean, would you like to stay here with me tonight?" I said, "Yes!" without giving any further thought. I told her that I had to make a telephone call. She said, "You have to get to my room first, on right side of the bed are two phones, use the blue one, it's O.K." Then she told me "Let's go to the party first and stay there for a while. Then I will excuse us; just tell them you have to go home. I will take you to the door. You run upstairs to the first big door that is mine. Go in and get into the closet. Stay there until I come and get you and then you can make your call from there."

We went to the party and I stayed for an hour and had some dinner. Then I said good-bye to Assa and Meetra and told them I knew how to get out. Mahsa came up and said I will show him out. We went to the door and when she opened the door, I ran upstairs and went into her room. She closed the door and went back to the party. I closed the door, and then called one of my friends to ask if he would call my home and tell my family that I am at his house and will stay there for the night. I told him that I would call later and explain everything. He said that he would call my parents. I hung up and went into that closet like she said and waited there.

BE HIDDEN LOVE

While I was in the closet, I started thinking 'how I got here, what am I doing and where am I?' Then I remembered; one day I was very down and upset about my life. I didn't have much and I felt so alone and lonely. The only place I felt most comfortable was the grave of the great Hafez. One day I went there and I got a Hafez book from a guy there and his name was Hafez too. I was reading poetry to myself for a while then suddenly a voice said, "Read louder!" I looked up and saw that it was my friend, Assa, my buddy from school. He understood me and was a great companion for conversation. We were in the same grade. He was with a beautiful girl; so I got up and hugged him and he introduced me to his sister, Meetra. I kissed her hand and asked them to sit with me. I opened the Hafez book, gave it to Assa and told him to read because he had a very nice voice for reciting poetry. He read the whole poem then he handed the book back to me and said, "Now you read it the way you understand it." I looked at the poem for a couple of times then I started reciting. After I finished he told his sister "Do you see that son-of-a-gun, how beautiful he read that? The only thing he has to do read it couple times first!" We were talking and having fun when Mr. Hafez came and told me "Mr., don't you want to go home? I have to close in here." I said, "I am so sorry!" I put some money on the book and told him "This is for your tea." and we got out of there. While we were going down the stairs, Meetra looked at me and said "I have a party next week and I would love to have you there." I said "Thank you, but I cannot. I don't go to parties at all. I'm so sorry." My family was very strict. Then Assa told me "What an idiot you are! I never heard her invite anyone like that and you tell her you cannot come?" He told his sister "Don't worry, my dear, he will be there. If I have to, I will go and drag him. I promise he will be there." Then something forced me to say "O.K. I will be there." Then Assa said to Meetra, "I told you he will come." All that week I really had difficulty with myself about going. How much do you want to go somewhere when you don't know anybody? But I made a promise, and when the day arrived and I went. So that's how I got there in the first place.

I was deep in those thoughts when she opened the door and said that I could come out. I got out but I didn't know what to do because she was the first woman I was alone with. She asked me "Do you drink at all? I know you don't drink in public, but how about here?" I said "No, thank you." She asked, "Then what you do for fun?" I didn't say to anything at first, so she said "It's O.K. you can tell me what you do." I felt completely powerless in front of her, so I told her that I would smoke from time to time. She wanted to know what I smoke. I showed her what I had. "Wow, strong but classic!" she exclaimed. She instructed me go to the closet to pick out something to wear. I chose a pair of raw silk pajamas to be more relaxed. After I had changed, she took me to another room that was much smaller compared to the bedroom that was like a sitting room where everything was there. We sat and smoked together. Then she embraced me, kissed me and caressed me and asked, "Is it really?" I asked, surprised, "How did you know that?" She simply answered, "I just know, but don't worry about that, we will learn together. I am as much a beginner as you are."

She was like a princess or an angel. I couldn't decide, but she couldn't be anything else, so she must be a 'Princess of the Angels'. No question about that. She kissed me hard and deep and then went deeper than before. I tried to kiss her like that in return, but I failed. She taught me how to kiss a woman - a love such as herself. She taught me to first listen and breathe. I kissed her back hard and deep for moment. After some time, she lay down on the bed and said to me, "Before you come to our bed, you have to promise me four things." Eagerly I said, "I promise to you." She stopped me, "You don't even know what I am going to ask? I assured her, "Whatever it is that you want, then that is what you shall have. Your wish is my command!" Then she told me the four promises.

1- Never ever lie to me.
2- Never ever cheat on me.
3- Never ever keep any secrets from me.
4- Never ever, EVER look at my daughter.

I said "Done." then I put my left hand over my heart and swore by my heart and for the love of God to keep those promises.

Then I said, "I would love to start from the 4th one. What fool or idiot would exchange a diamond for 24-karat gold? You are my beautiful diamond, how could I do that to you? Yes, your daughter is a red line and so is any other woman."

"I swear to never ever lie to you or cheat on you. I do not have anything to keep from you. If my heart is right then you are everything to me and you will be my secret."

Then she said, "Come to bed my love!" and I did so. She started to kiss me then opened the buttons of my top and suddenly she asks me "How do you feel?" I didn't know what to say and she said, "It is O.K. you are a lover boy aren't you? Oh my God you are full of love!" Then she massaged my chest and held my hand and all the while, she was kissing me nonstop and I kissed her back. Then we began making love and what a beautiful love making it was! She held onto me very tightly and then started switching positions. Then after we both reached orgasm she said "You are amazing in lovemaking!" and she put her face on my chest and with her hand massaging my body. I don't know how much time had passed. We started kissing again and began making love for the second time and this time it took much longer for both of us to reach climax. We lay holding each other; I put my head on her shoulder and she put her face on my chest as before.

The sky started to show the colors of dawn and we still hadn't slept. After a while I got up and put on my clothes. She watched me and asked "Where you going so early?" I replied, "Normally if I am up at this time, I like to go for lamb stew at a shop near my school." She said "I would love to come with you; I haven't been to such a place." I said, "O.K. then let's go!" She warned me first, "Don't go down the stairs with your shoes on. We need to be quiet." I said "O.K." We drove to that shop and ate lamb stew. Then we walked through the allies and by seven thirty A.M we kissed each other. She then said, "My God you are really in love!" I smiled and said, "From the moment I saw you. You took my heart and stole my soul." She looked deep into my eyes and exclaimed, "My God, you are really something!" She kissed me then I said, "I love you so much." "Shut up and do not say anything more about it. She snapped. Then "See you later alligator." and she left.

I headed to school, when I ran into my friend who worked for the school. He was surprised to see me that early. I told him that I didn't sleep at all last night and he could see it in my eyes. He said, "Go to my room and sleep on my bed at least for an hour." I did so but instead, slept for two hours and felt a little better. I went to my classes, but couldn't concentrate. I finished the classes and went home. As soon as I got home my mom wanted to know what was wrong. I said, "It's nothing, I just didn't sleep last night and now I have headache. I am going to bed and I don't think I will be going to school this afternoon." My mom gave me a pill for the headache but I didn't take it. I went to bed as soon as I pulled my clothes off and don't remember anything except the dreams I had.

Day after day passed; and I couldn't bring myself to call her because I was so afraid she hang up on me or say "Look, it was just one night and we had fun. Don't call me again." And so on………………………….. After the fourth day just after lunch, as my father was about to start afternoon prayers, the phone rang twice. He picked up the phone but no one was there. Then phone rang again, this time only once. My father was in the middle of his prayers, so I turned off his phone ringer, went to my room and called her. Yes it was she!!! When she answered, I said hi. But she was very angry and demanded to know why I hadn't called her. I said, "I cannot talk now but I have to see you then I can explain everything." She said "You better have a good reason. Let us meet later today around six thirty to seven P.M." I said "Fine do you know Táchira Bar and Grill?" She said yes, I said "Then I will see you at Táchira." She said, "See you." I had to go back to school in the afternoon, so I changed into nicer clothes.

After school I went to my friend's house and went in through the front, stayed for about an hour and then left from the back entrance. I stopped by a florist and got some roses; five red and one big white one. I hailed a cab and told him go to Táchira. He started talking and was playing a tape of some very Old Iranian classical music. When he tried to change the tape I asked him if is possible to please leave it on and he said sure. I got to Táchira by 6:30 P.M. and she wasn't there yet. I went to the garden to wait until she arrived. After about five minutes I went upstairs and saw her next to the window behind a small wall. When I got to the table, I said "Hi sweetie!" She replied "Hi. You better have a good reason."

Then I gave her the flowers, she said "Thanks, but you have to talk to me. Why you didn't call?" I said one word "Afraid." "Of what?" she asked. I said "Of you and how you might react." I continued "Do you know how many times I tried to call you, but then would hang up the phone? More than hundred times and do you know what I went through these past four days? And I know you had as hard a time as me."

She ordered coffee for both of us and she started to talk. "What did you think; that I don't have any feelings? Now you know I do have feelings. From the first time I saw you I fell in love with you. I never had this feeling before for anybody; not even for my late husband. I don't know what it was in your eyes that affected me that much. But I fell in love with you just like that. It's crazy!" I added, "I am too!" She said "I've know that since that morning in that alley, your eyes told me everything and that's why I was so mad at you. Now I know exactly how you're feeling, because I feel the same way." She moved to sit next to me, kissed me and said, "I'm sorry baby, my love. We are the same."

She ordered more coffee with cream cheese pie. As we were enjoying the coffee and pie, music starts playing; some songs from the 60's. She took my hand and leads me to the dance floor. We danced for two songs and then we went back to our table and finished coffee and pie. I told her "I am very sorry, I really didn't mean to make you upset. I don't want to see you upset again. You are my Angel and to see you upset drives me crazy." She took my hand and held my face with her other hand and said "We have to get to know each other much better." We asked for the bill and I paid for it.

We went down to the garden to discover that it was sunset. The sky was so beautiful as we walked through the garden. I told her "You see how beautiful the blossoms are? You can probably get high from the smell." She said yes I then told her "This is all because of you. You made this happen because this garden has always been here, but I didn't have this feeling, until now." She cut me off "Don't talk like this!" and she put her head on my shoulder and started to cry. I lifted her head and the tears on her face were like diamonds. I kissed her and took the tears with my lips and told her "Don't cry! Those diamonds are worth more than this." She gazed at me and kissed me, saying "You are crazy and I love you very much just for that." As the spring sky slowly darkened, we were still holding each other and kissing.

We made our way back to the car and as she started driving, she asked, "Where should we go?" I said, "Would you like to go to a movie?" She said "Yes, but which one?" I suggested that we go to Aryana Cinema, a dome-style theater. I got out buying the tickets while she parked the car; I went to the ticket booth and saw my friend who worked there. I told him "Do me a favor and give me two tickets in the corner of the last row." He said "For sure. Which side?" I said, "Right if you have." He said fine and gave me two tickets and we went in. The theater was almost empty. We got to our seat just after a few minutes movie started. It was a French movie that we knew nothing about. But we didn't come to see the movie; we came to be alone together. I started massaging her back and then slipped my hand under her t-shirt and massaged her back and shoulders. All the while she held my other hand very tight and kissed me from time to time. Then she moved my hand from back to the front shoulder and she started rubbing my lap. We had a wonderful time in there and as soon as the movie finished, we ran out and went to the car got in and drove out. I told her to make U-turn and go west.

We reached Alam Square, parked the car and went to the west side because on that side there was a garden on right and the river on the left and that would be safe for us. As we walked west, it was completely dark with only one light on far away. We stopped at a very big maple tree we lay on the ground underneath it. She held me against the tree and we gazed into each other's eyes as she caressed my face and I played with her silky hair. We started kissing passionately and she whispered to me, "Do you want to make love with me?" I was surprised, "Right here?" "Yes." She said "Right here. I miss you so much." I had missed her so much too. I began kissing her neck and unbuttoned her dress and began kissing her chest. Then she started making love to me in such a way I will never ever forget. She took me so high I thought 'I am in Heaven' and she didn't stop until we were both soaring together. Throughout all this, we kept eye contact; but that lovemaking was amazing and it seemed to form the bond of the love we felt with each other. In the end she grabs my shoulder and brought her head down and kissed me. It was such a different feeling that I never experienced before.

We headed back to the car when we heard a sound behind us. It was a guy with an old bicycle, he told us, "Hope you have a good time." We told him thanks, and continued waking toward the car. We got there she lay on the car and kissed me again. I forgot to tell you she was taller than me. Don't ask how much taller, but we made it work anyway. She started to get in the car and said, "See you later." then I said "…alligator." She started the car as I just stood there, looking at her. Suddenly, I lost all control and began to cry. She opened the door, got out of the car and held my face and kissed me. She asked, "Why are you crying? We will see each other very soon! I will call you as soon as I can; remember two rings then one ring. You will know it is me." She got back in the car and left. I just stood there watching her car disappear and suddenly another car stopped for me. It was a cab. I told him where am I going and the driver said "Get in." I don't remember how we got there but we did. I paid him including the tip and he said, "This is too much!" "It is O.K." I told him. He thanked me and left.

I came home and met my mom who was in the yard. I said hi to her, and she looked at me very closely and asked, "What happened to you your face? It is a little red and your voice is different!" I told her "That's what happens when you always say 'God bless you'. And today he did." I then said to her "Good night, I have to go up and sleep. I am very tired." She knew that I didn't want to talk; she was a very smart woman.

She said, "Good night and God bless you my son." I got to my room, changed out of my clothes, then turned off the light and got into bed. Was I able to go to sleep? No. All I could do was keep reliving the past four, five hours I spent with her; especially that last hour! My body was hot and my mind was totally with her. I had her scent all over my hands, up to the elbows. "My God!" I said, "I smell of her." I took one of my pillows, put my hand around it next to my nose and held it there. I relished this solitude alone with my love. I know that I am not alone anymore; she is with me for the rest of my life.

That Next morning I got up very early. It was time for morning prayers. My father was in the yard when I came down. He was surprised to see me. I said good morning to him and he answered, "Good morning my son, are you joining me for morning prayers?" When I said yes, he looked pleased and said "God bless you son." I washed my face and hands, and then went to my room. As I did morning prayers, I talked to my God very personally and thanked him for all he gave me. But I couldn't believe that I deserved that much. After my prayers, I went back to bed and before long, my mom was calling me to get up and I got up quickly that day. I ate breakfast and went to school.

School was different for me today. I raptly listened to the teacher and memorized whatever was said. That was hard work, but I had to do it. After class, I went home for lunch. Shortly after lunch, the phone rang, but it wasn't her. Minutes later, the phone rang again: twice then once. That was she! I washed my plate and did some other chores. Quickly I went to my room and called her. I said "Hi sweetheart!" She answered, "Hi my love, can you talk?" I said "Not now, but I will call you back in about ten to fifteen minutes." so we said bye to each other and hung up. I changed my clothes and went to my father's room. My mom said, "It's early." I told her that I have an important class that I did not want to be late for. She was surprised, "Are you O.K.?" I said "Yes, why?" and she said "You and an early important class; that must be something!" Then she asked if I wanted tea and I said "No thanks, I am late." and then I said good-bye and left, I don't know how fast I walked to Main Street to find a payphone, then I called her.

My sweet love talked about last night and when she went to bed. "I took your pajamas to bed with me so I could feel you next to me. They still had your scent on them and I went to sleep with it. I then told her about my night and then asked, "What are you doing tonight?" She said, "I am free." I said "Can I meet you somewhere outside?" "Sure, how about Rose square? It's next to the airport." I said "Oh yes, that Rose. What time?" she said to meet at 6:30 P.M I said that I would be there and we kissed each other 'bye' over the phone and hung up.

I went to my afternoon classes and listened to the lessons very carefully. That was a totally different experience for me. It was like a tape recorder in my head - yes it was exactly like that. School finished by 4:30 and I had plenty of time to kill, so I went to a market next to the school to buy a pack of cigarettes, but before handing me the pack, he grabbed my hand and looked at the palm. He told me "This is your tea 'lovey' boy, drink and go to your love." I just stared at him and sat down beside the counter. I had a good amount of time left, and he knew I wanted to know more. He started reading a poem and I closed my eyes to feel the sound of that poem with all my bones and blood. Suddenly he stopped and asked me "Do you know where this is from?" I said, "Sure, it's by Rumi." He nodded "Very good, my boy. But did you feel it?" "Oh yes," I said, "deep down. He took my cup and filled up then gave it to me and he said, "Drink my son. She loves you very much as much as you love her. Drink and go to your love and don't be late!" I tried to pay him, but he refused to take any money, just saying, "Next time my boy, next time." I shook his hand and left. I thought that he was very wise and perhaps he didn't have much education, but he knew a lot of things.

As I set out to meet my love, I kept thinking about the shopkeeper. I caught a cab and went to Rose; I waited across the street until she came, some 20 minutes later. She saw me, stopped the car and said, "Get in. Let's go." "Where are we going?" I asked. She replied, "Sit back and relax. We are going to see a friend of mine. Don't worry, everything will be O.K." She drove around the airport and we could see all the planes. Suddenly she grasped my shoulder with her right hand and pulled me close by her side. I put my head on her shoulder and she began stroking my hair and my face. We started talking some 'sweet talk'. Then I kissed her neck and part of her shoulder then she said, "Do you want to drive - do you?" "No!" I answered. "I cannot drive because you will drive me crazy when you kiss me like that!" she said. She started laughing and kissed me, saying "I love you my 'chubby'!" We drove past the police station, until she finally pulled into a driveway, behind a pickup truck. We got out of the car and she started calling someone, "Ali, Ali, Ali!" A man appeared and waved, walking toward us. He took his gloves off and hugged Mahsa, and then shook my hand. Mahsa gave introductions. Gesturing to me, "This is the Yousef, you wanted to meet him." Ali hugged me and said, "Welcome to the family!" I said "Thank you." Mahsa told me 'This is Ali, one of my buddies." Ali said "Let's go home, give me five to ten minutes, then I will come with you." She said, "We will go across the street and I will show him my land." Ali said "O.K." We crossed the street and she showed me her land and told me "Next year Ali wants to get a guy in here to work on it." She wanted to know what I thought about that. I said "I don't know anything about land or how that work is done, but I think it's a good thing to do."

Ali came back out; got into his old pickup and told us to follow him. We eventually arrived at a beautiful house out in the middle of nowhere. Ali got out before us and opened a large gate and we followed him inside. We got out of the car and she hold my hand very tightly as we entered his house. The house was designed in a country style right down to the furniture. Ali asked me if I would like a drink, but Mahsa told him "Yousef, doesn't drink, please make us some coffee." He brought us each a cup while he had a beer. He then asked us "What are you guys doing here?" Mahsa explained that we were planning to go to Rose and she thought perhaps he might want to join us. "And since you wanted to meet Yousef, I thought it was a good idea to come to you first and we could all go there together." Ali agreed, saying, "That is a wonderful idea. I would love to come with you." As we were finishing our drinks, he said "Give me five minutes, so I can get ready." We said 'Fine, take your time; we are not in a hurry."

Mahsa and I went outside, it was near sunset and sky looked like it was on fire. It was absolutely beautiful! I turned to her "Don't even try to tell me not to be romantic! This is all because of you." Then I started kissing her and she hugged me tight and wrapped her fingers in my hair as she gave me a single kiss and held me in her arms. Ali came out and called out, "it's nice isn't?" I answered back "Very nice especially if you are next to her." Mahsa laughed saying "I told you he is romantic and crazy!" Ali paused, "Romantic yes, but crazy? I don't think so, he knows what he has." Still laughing she said, "Let's move it, both of you crazy guys!" We got into our vehicles and drove to the Rose.

We got there quickly and went inside. I headed to the restroom, washed my hands and joined them at the table. By the time I returned, Mahsa had already ordered drinks and dinner, which made life easy for me. In no time they brought

Ali his beer and our coffee. I asked if they have hot bread, he said yes so I ordered bread and butter. When the waiter returned back with that, I started in on the bread and butter with my coffee and they did the same. The food arrived and there were three different entrees for us to share. We were eating and talking about anything and everything. Suddenly I looked at my watch and was dismayed to see that it was past ten. I turned to Mahsa and said, "It is after ten already and I must get home!" She said, "Let's go then." and called the waiter for the bill that he brought quickly and she paid. We got out, said bye to Ali and drove back into the city. When we arrived at the first square in city I told her "I will get out here and you can go straight home." "No," she argued, "let me take you home." Giving in, I said "Sure, why not." She laughed and added, "One day when you get home, I will be there; and then what will you do?" I replied "I would say 'hi' and shake hands with you." Still laughing, she said, "We will see!" I got out and helped her to put the top up and told her to close all the windows and lock all her doors. She asked why and I told her "This area is not safe for you and for your car. I am afraid for you." She looked lovingly at me and said "Thanks Chubby!" She kissed me and left.

I caught a cab and went home. I got in at quarter to 11, which meant 'on time'. My mom made me dinner that night so I had to eat again. It was a stew made with dark red beans. It was one of my favorites. I ate the stew with some smashed beans and toasted bread, but I left some for tomorrow. Then she made me some tea. After my second dinner, I went to my room and got into bed. But there was no sleep. All I could think about was her and our night together.

When I finally fell asleep, all my dreams were of her. I got up the next morning at the sound of my mom's voice "Get up, get up – you are late for school!" I said "O.K.! O.K.! I am up!" I went down, washed up and got some breakfast. I said bye to everybody and got to school late as always. Late was my middle name. As I entered the classroom, the teacher looked at me and said, "Oh, it's you. Come on in, have a seat and tell me why you come in late every day." "Sorry," I said, "You know how far I come." Then he said, "Please try to come on time!" I said that I would. The teacher continued with the class until the break. When break time started everybody went out and as I started to leave, he called me back asking "What's wrong with you? You have never been so soft spoken to any of us." I said that there was nothing wrong. The teacher looked at me very closely and ventured "Is there someone special in your life?" I said "I will talk to you later." He smiled and said "O.K. go have fun."

When I came out of the classroom, some of my classmates came up to me see what the matter was with me today. I told them that I didn't sleep last night and just didn't want to argue with him. You don't know that much about me; but in school I had total power and the school authorities didn't want to mess with me. It was not so much that they were afraid of me, but because of my father and his notoriety. I knew that and used it to my advantage. So I was able to get away with a lot of stuff.

My next class was literature. The teacher started reading a poem and explaining its meaning. But I disagreed. I raised my hand and asked him whether he was translating it from a philosophical or Gnostic perspective. He said, "O.K. but you have to listen well!" When he started his translation, oh my God he took us to a level of understanding that was so high that I didn't want to come back down! But unfortunately the time was up and he had to let us go. School was finished for the morning and everybody went home for lunch. I stayed with the teacher for a while and he said to me "What was wrong with you? The others don't understand!" I said "I know, but did you see them while you were reading?" "Yes" he answered. I went on "Did you see how they were so crushed and crying. Why would you guys want to take that understanding away from them? Give it to them they will be so different; you couldn't imagine. He argued, "Well we are behind in the lesson book, I told him to screw the book, give the students what they want. After some consideration, the teacher asked "And how will you answer on your exam?" I smiled "What do you think?" "My apologies," he added, "That was the wrong question. You will get an A in this class. Now go have fun!"

I went home to have lunch and tea and then I waited for my parents to go to sleep. Normally, I would go to the theater and see a couple of movies in the afternoon. That was what we did in Shiraz. But today I didn't want to go to the movies.

I wanted to go and see her - only her. I called her around 2:30 and followed the same code: two rings then one ring. Mahsa called me right back and said "Hi my Chubby love. How are you?" I happily responded, "Now I am very good and couldn't be better than this!" I asked her how she was and she replied "Same as you my love, same as you." I asked her what her plans were for the day and she said "The kids are home until four, four-thirty then they are going to a party and won't be coming home until late. Why don't you come on over after five?" I said "I will my sweetie, I will!" I lay on my bed until quarter after four, and then I put on my suit. As I went to leave, my mom saw me and asked me "Are you going out?" I told her yes, but that I would be back not too late. She then said "God bless you!" and I left my home to go to my love's home.

When I arrived, I was too early and had to wait until they left the house. I waited about thirty minutes, until I saw them leave. Just to be safe, I waited fifteen minutes more and then went up and rang the bell. An older lady opened the door and said, "Good afternoon, come in. Would you like coffee or tea?" I smiled "Definitely your coffee!" She said, "I will make some for you both. She is upstairs, I will call her." After a short time, Mahsa came down as beautiful as first time I saw her. I was sitting on the same sofa. I got up, walked over to her and grabbed her in my arms. She held me hard and kissed me. Oh that kiss was unbelievable and unforgettable! We went outside to the balcony and the lady brought us each a double coffee.

Y. JOSEPHSON

I started telling her about the dream I had the night before and that it was all about her. Then I said, "I saw today how you came down the stairs exactly the same way as the night I first saw you." "Yes, I always come down the same way." She admitted, "Because I am afraid that I might fall down. She paused, "I had dreams about you almost every night since that first night. Sometimes I wake up wet from sweating and I have to take a pill so I can get back to sleep again." We finished our coffee and went upstairs to her bedroom and stepped out on the balcony outside her room. We held each other as we talked.

After some time, I told her about my literature class this afternoon. Then I brought out two books; one Rumi and the other Hafez. I told her that the amazing thing was that these two men two centuries apart were saying exactly the same thing only with slightly different words. Is it not amazing? I gave her copies of each poem that I wrote by my own hand. She took the papers and began reading them. Amazed, she asked me "Did you find these two, put them next to each other or not? Did it really happen when you opened these books?" "No" I said. "I opened the books and poems were there. I swear to you this is the truth. I am not that good at matching such things together." Suddenly she hugged and kissed me, saying, "I love you my Chubby very much!" We sat a while longer on the balcony just holding each other. We went inside and I asked "Would you like a massage?" She said hesitated, but I said, "You don't need to take off your T-shirt." She lay on bed and I started massaging all along her back, shoulders and down to her hands. I asked her "Are you relaxed?" She replied, "Yes thank you Chubby I won't ever forget this." Then I remembered to ask her about the tape she was playing before. She pointed it out on a nearby shelf. I asked her for a tape player and she told me that it should be there in the same place. I found them both, put the tape in the player and pushed the start button. As the music started to play, I went back to the balcony, kissed her hand and asked her for a dance. She kissed me and added, "Sure, you owed me a dance anyway from that party." We started to dance and she asked me "Do you know any jazz dances?" I said "No I don't." Then she said, "Now you will learn." She told me to relax and just follow her steps and watch her hands.

She took my waist, wrapped my fingers with hers and started moving. But she did it very slowly so I could follow her steps and her hand movements. We danced almost entire duration of that one-hour tape. When the music ended, we still stood, holding each other and kissing, I cannot fully explain the feelings I felt after dancing with her so closely for one full hour. How our bodies felt moving together and sharing body language was really amazing. We headed downstairs, holding hands. Mahsa walked me to the front door when Mama (the lady who served me coffee before) asked if I wanted to stay for dinner. I promised to stay next time. Mahsa then said, "See you later alligator." and I replied, "See you later." and turned to go, but before I get to the front gate, I looked back at her again. As soon as I turned she ran toward me and hugged me hard and kissing me again, said, "I was waiting for you to do that! I love you my Chubby boy."

I got home and went straight to my room and changed clothes. Then I went to my father's room to say hi and eat dinner. After we finished, I said good night but before I could leave the room my father asked me to wait. He told me to have a seat next to him; he looked closely at me and started talking about a lot of different things. He said to me "My son, the world and life you see now is not as clean as you might think. Things are often very hard and dirty. You have to watch yourself with many things." After pausing, he continued, "Do you have anything to tell me that I should know?" I said, "No, everything is O.K." He then wished me a goodnight and added "God bless you." and I went back to my room.

Yes my room, my private place to think, my place where I could feel, touches and smell her. The room I used to hate has now become the place I love. In there I could physically feel, touch and hold her in my arms. Yes I could see up and down her entire body; specially those ocean-blue eyes and her silky auburn hair. Those were her features I was most in love with.

So I got to that room, turned on my stereo and put on a set of headphones. I turned off the light and played the tape I got from her and climbed into bed. Listening to that music took me back to afternoon we spent in her bedroom. The dancing and all the rest of those memories; what the afternoon it was! I don't think I could ever forget it for rest of my life. I don't remember when I fell to sleep because the dreams followed the feelings and the next thing I knew was the sound of my mom's voice "Get up, get up. You're late again!"

I got up, went downstairs and washed up. I went to my father's room for breakfast. After breakfast and tea, I went to my room and changed, then came back say bye to everybody and headed off to school. I got there late, same as always. I knocked on the door and went in. That day I had three classes and during each I made some comments to disrupt the lessons. I had the whole class laughing. I did that because I didn't want anybody to think Yousef has changed or died and to show my classmates that I was still in charge.

I went home for lunch and tea. Afterward, I called one of my friends who had a very mature sounding voice and asked him to call my home in two hours to tell my mom that he was from a very important program. He said, "That's all? You are a son of a gun!" I told him "Yes that's all, my son!" He laughed and said "Yeah, O.K. I will call in two hours." I said "Thanks!" I went to my afternoon classes and then walked home. I went to my room and started reading my schoolbooks. The time flew so fast and before I knew it, I heard my mom calling that dinner was ready. I checked my watch and it was about ten. I went to my father's room for dinner and tea. Then I said "Good night. I am going to study some more." My father looked pleased and said "I think you want to pass the spring exams with good grades this year. Very good my son!" I said "I will try my best this year." I went back to my room. I study some more until about midnight then I turned the stereo on and plugged in the headphones. I turned off the light, playing the same tape as last night and went to bed.

I held my pillow and imagined her next to me. I could feel her whole body especially her lips and her beautiful hands all over me. I imagined us dancing. I still don't know how I fell to sleep because reality, feelings and dreams came over me one after another and sometimes they all blended together making it hard to tell any of them apart. The next morning again, I awoke to my mom's voice, had breakfast, went to school and came back home.

CHAPTER 2

The Camping trip

Two days went by and by the third day I was really going crazy! I didn't know what to do. That afternoon, while I was eating lunch, the phone rang twice then once. That was her!!! I waited and in good time I called her, she picked up the phone and said "Hi sweetie. I'm sorry that I didn't call you sooner. What are you doing this weekend?" I answered "Hi sweetie, I have no plans." "Good: she said "I want to pick you up Thursday. Can you do something about that?" I assured that I could, but needed to know what time. She said I'll let you know tomorrow." We talked about other things and then we kissed and said 'See you later alligator' and hung up.

I was so happy to hear her voice and my body felt warmer. I changed clothes and as I was leaving to go back to school, my mom stopped me saying "I'm sorry, I forgot to tell you that somebody from the Red Cross called for you about a weekend camp." She apologized again. I said "That is no problem and thank you. I will call him back." I said bye and left for school.

I came back early like the previous two nights and started to study a lesson I was behind on. At about nine I called my friend to thank him and we talked for a few minutes. After that I went to my father's room and I told my mom I called the guy from the Red Cross. There was to be an exercise camp beginning on Thursday that would last until Saturday. My father wanted to know if this camp was just exercise or a real camp. I assured him that it was just exercise. I had dinner and tea than went back to my room study some more before going to bed.

The next day was Wednesday, I went to school and came back home for lunch. The phone rang twice then once signaling that was her. I went to my room and called her back. After a couple of quick 'hellos', she instructed me to meet her tomorrow at Alam Square at one-thirty. The same as every other day I went to my afternoon classes then after school, I went to visit my elder sister and took her oldest son to a city park. We stayed there all evening reading poems from Hafez and then we wrote some poems by ourselves. We exchanged poems and offered corrections where needed. Then between nine-thirty and ten, we got back to my sister's house. I called my mom to tell her that I was with my sister and that I would stay for dinner. My mom said "O.K. but just be careful and get home soon." I promised that I would. After dinner, my nephew asked me "How is she?" I didn't understand, "What do you mean?" I asked. He said "I could tell from your poem that you are in love." So I asked him in return, "Are you in love?" He said "Why are you asking me that?" I explained that you have to be in love in order to know that somebody else is in love. He admitted "Yes I am." So I confessed "I am too, but I can't tell you who she is." My nephew asked if she was in Shiraz. I told him no and do not ask any more questions. Then I said bye to everybody and left for home. I got in after eleven and went to my father to say good night. Then I went to my room, turned on that tape and went to sleep.

Thursday is finally here! I packed up my sleeping bag and clothes for two days and put on my suit. I said bye to everybody and went to school. My classes finished at ten-thirty; I had a lot of time to kill and didn't want to stay in the streets, so I went to my sister's. Her house was very close to the school. She was surprised to see me and wanted to know what I was doing here. I told her about the camp and stayed there until 12:30. I walked over to Alam Square to meet Mahsa. She arrived soon after, I put my stuff in the back and she drove out of town. I asked her where we were going. She said "We are going to see couple of my friends. Don't worry, everything will be fine." After driving for some time, she pulled over suddenly to a little parking area off of the road. She took my head in her hands and kissed me. We moved the seat back until it was flat and held each other, kissing. I had really missed her and she said she missed me so much too.

After a little while, we moved the seat upright, she started the car and drove until we got to a large wooden garden gate. As she pulled up to the door, she blew the horn a couple of times and someone opened the door.

We drove into a courtyard and got out of the car. I went to her side and she took my hand. We walked up to a group of people and Mahsa said "Here you go, this is Yousef. He's the one you wanted to meet." First Mo' (short for Mohammad) came up to me and gave me a hug saying "Welcome to the family!" He was followed by his wife, Mary who also hugged me. I recognized Ali and shook his hand. They were sitting outside under very large and wide walnut tree. They started teasing me about coming dressed up in a suit. Laughing, Mahsa said "Let him change!" I went to the car, took my stuff and went inside to put on jeans and a T-shirt. I came back out, feeling more comfortable and sat next to Mahsa. They invited us to go to the other side of the house. We followed the sidewalk until we got to a beautiful brick floor patio. It was a very large, spacious area about 20 X 20 square feet.

Adding to the beauty of the area, were four huge walnut trees, much like the one in the front yard. Their branches created a canopy of shade above the patio. There were two rugs on the floor and a barbeque on the other side. I saw Mahsa talking to Mary and they disappeared heading to the front of the cottage. Shortly, Mahsa returned holding a bag and Mary had wine glasses.

Mahsa opened the bag and took out a bottle. Mary exclaimed, "Son of a gun! Where did you get that?" Mahsa gave a big grin saying "I have my ways." I went over to Mahsa to look at the bottle when I saw the 'Khollar' label. Amazed, I said "Where DID you get that? This is most expensive wine in the whole country! This is only for export and the royal family. How were you able to get it?" She admitted, "O.K. I ordered that one from a friend." She opened the bottle and filled all the glasses. Everyone toasted to us, and then she and I toasted them in return. Ali leaned over to Mahsa "You told me he doesn't drink, but he knows about that one better than me at least." She shrugged "I don't know. You will have to ask him." Then Ali looked over at me and I replied "It's my job to know these things. But normally I do not drink in Shiraz."

As we enjoyed the wine, Mo', Ali and I started preparing kebabs for lunch. In about an hour, the kebabs were ready and Mahsa opened the second bottle. We sat and enjoyed the meal and excellent wine. After we finished, Ali grabbed a pillow and laid down to rest. Mary and Mo' went inside to their room. Mahsa and I went to the car; took out our sleeping bags and wandered down to the far end of the garden.

We found a nice grassy area, opened the sleeping bags and lay next to each other. While lying there, we looked up at the sky, listened to the sound of the rustling leaves and felt the breeze as it came from the west. The feeling was absolute, just perfect. Mahsa spoke, "I had a dream moments ago that when the time is right and we want to get married, I would love to be someplace like this and with only a few close friends and family around us." I laughed and she said "Why are you laughing?" I answered, "The people you mentioned would be over three hundred." "Oh well" she stated, "then we have two choices." I asked her "Don't you want classy and fancy, with a long white dress and me with a tuxedo and black tie?" "No" she declared "I want it to be as simple as possible." I said "I agree with you, it is a waste of time and money. We will do it differently." She kissed me and pulled my T-shirt up and kissed my chest. Then she rested her face on my chest and I buried my face in her silky hair and played with it. I don't know how long we stayed there in the same position.

After some time, Mahsa raised her beautiful head and kissed me saying, "I will never forget this time. It is like you have taken me back to my early teens. Thank you! You make my dreams and fantasies from long ago, come true." I smiled at her "You're welcome, any time. I am yours." We got up, picked up the sleeping bags and went back to the front of the cottage. When we got there Mary and Mo' had just came out and asked us if we had seen Ali. Mahsa said "He is still asleep on the patio." Mary called out to him, "Ali, Ali wake up, it's late." and Ali got up. He came out to the front and complained to me "You see? They won't even let you sleep. That's why I don't want to get married!"

We sat around the table trying to decide what to do that night. Finally, we looked to Mo' for help. He suggested "The only place I know is very good. It is chicken place."

Everybody said yes. He added "It is too soon to go there now. Let's have a drink." They brought out all kinds of stuff, I fixed a vodka lime for myself, Mahsa tasted it and liked it, and so I gave her mine and made another for myself. Two hours later, Mo' said "O.K. now it's time!" and everybody piled into his early 70's model Chevy Blazer. When we got to the chicken place, we had doubts. The outside wasn't very clean, but the inside was much better. The waiter took us out on the roof that was beautiful. Mo' told the guy 'the usual'. He brought us cold water and after twenty-five minutes he brought out the chicken. It looked roasted to perfection and tasted wonderful. We ate and had tea. We headed back to Mary and Mo's place and went out to the garden. We played cards for a while until none of us could keep our eyes open. That was time for bed.

Mary and Mo' gave us their bedroom and there was no changing their minds. Mahsa told me to let it be, so we said good night and got ready for bed. We changed our clothes; and she brought me those silk pajamas and a silky nightgown for herself. We opened the window to the sound the westerly breeze rustling through the trees. We stood at the window enjoying the evening for a few minutes, then Mahsa told me she was cold. But the way she said it, I understood exactly what she meant. I asked her "Are you sure?" She answered "Yes, we will be quiet." I took her in my arms, there next to the window and started kissing her. First I took her rob off. Then I pushed the straps of her nightgown from her shoulders. It fell soundlessly to the floor. Oh my God she was beautiful! She took my pajama top off and held me to her - chest to breast and kissed me. We stood there for a little while longer, and then moved to the bed. She pushed me onto the bed, sat on my tummy and gave me a little massage. Then she began a body-to-body massage, stripped off my pajama bottoms so we were totally naked. We started making love trying to be as quiet as possible. What a night that was! We explored every inch of each other's bodies, fully enjoying ourselves. Our love making lasted about two hours and after that we held each other so tightly and fell asleep.

We woke to the sound of Ali's voice "Wake up 'lovey guy'. Wake up! It is almost noon!" When we opened our eyes and gazed into each other's face and she had this beautiful smile that worth millions. She kissed me saying "Good morning my chubby love!" That would be the first time she told me that during our mornings in bed together. I kissed her and said "Good morning Honey Bunch!" She smiled again and said "I love that." "What did you like?" I asked, and she answered, "That word 'Honey Bunch'. It's beautiful and I really love that." Then I said "You're welcome anytime."

We got out of bed and washed up. We came out and said good morning to everybody and sat down next to each other. Mo' had prepared an excellent breakfast with hot bread from the village, fresh eggs and Iranian feta cheese; all totally organic. I got a glass of hot tea first then began eating. I had a second glass of tea and felt like I couldn't move after all that delicious food.

After breakfast we started discussing where we should go for the day. Mahsa suggested that we go for a picnic and everybody thought that was a great idea. The trouble was that we didn't have anything to cook with. So we had to go to the village and buy things there. We bought different kinds of melons, cucumber, tomatoes, yogurt and cheeses and some fresh, hot bread. Then we followed a road out of town until it turned from asphalt to dirt. After a while, Mo' stopped at a gorgeous place. We got out of the car and quickly became dizzy with the view. On both sides of the road, the area was full of wild poppies in different colors. In their midst was every other kind of other wildflower.

The smell from all those flowers made us high; as if we had smoked some weed. We put down some blankets and laid on them. We had to watch out for scorpions, however. We relaxed for a little while and then prepared lunch. After lunch, Ali fell asleep, Mary and Mo' were lying next to each other, while Mahsa and I sat on our blanket holding each other. We looked at those beautiful flowers and enjoyed our time together. The weather was like early spring when you could enjoy sitting under the sun and not feel too hot. We sat holding each other and sometimes kissing, but most the time her head was on my shoulder. I was stroking her silky hair and she massaged my back, I will never forget that afternoon picnic ever. We stayed the whole day, but just before nightfall, Mo' said that we had better leave soon because after dark the area is very dangerous. So we packed up our stuff and put it in the car and headed back to Mary and Mo's. On the way, the countryside was so beautiful especially near sunset. We got back to the cottage and garden. After about twenty minutes, Mahsa asked me if I wanted to go. "Sure," I said "if it's O.K. with you." She said "Let's go then." We put our stuff in her car and said good-bye to everybody and we headed back to Shiraz. She didn't drive fast and we started talking. I asked her how Mary and Mo' got married. She told me that they were students at the same university. Mary was a junior and Mo' was a senior. They dated for quite some time and they fell in love with each other. They got married despite the fact that neither of their parents would agree to the marriage. But in the end, their families finally accepted it. I then asked about Ali. Mahsa shook her head and said that he has some difficulties from what he sees in his folk's lives. He thinks that marriage is always just a fight. So he doesn't want any part of it. Then I said, maybe that is the right choice for him and maybe he shouldn't get married, but she didn't agree with me.

We got to town; she asked me if I wanted to stop for coffee? I said "Sure, do you know any place that will be safe and private?" Mahsa said "Yes, I know a place, let's go there." We got to the coffee place, but first she called home to check in and find out who is home and who is out. Mama answered and told her nobody is home. Meetra was staying with friend for the night and Assa went out of town and would be back tomorrow. Mahsa said thanked Mama, hung up the phone, told me the news and asked "Do you want to have coffee here or at home? I said "I would prefer to go home." "So let's go!" she said. As we left, Mahsa tipped the doorman for using the phone and he thanked her. We went home and knocked on the door. Mama opened the door and hugged us saying "Welcome home!" We went out to the balcony and she brought us double Turkish coffees. I thanked her and asked if she could get me a glass of ice water. Mana said "Sure but it's not that icy, is that O.K.?" I said "Yes, sure thank you." In no time she brought me the water and I drank it down in one gulp. Mama turned to Mahsa and asked, "What did this poor guy have?" Mahsa laughed and said "Nothing only one glass of wine, that's it." Mama went back inside, while Mahsa and I talked for a while. Mama came out again and asked "What would you like for dinner?" I said something light, hot and delicious. Mama said "You must be hungry; I will fix something for the pretty "lovey" boy!" Mahsa laughed and Mama left to prepare dinner.

Mahsa said "Mama has taken to you very well my chubby." She continued to tell me about Mama. She was

Mahsa's nanny and Mahsa grow up under her care. When Mahsa got married and moved to London, Mama went with her. Now she is in Shiraz, taking of Mahsa and her two children. Mahsa loved her very much and they were very close.

Twenty minutes later, Mama brought us a wonderful dinner with chicken, vegetables and homemade bread. We ate heartily. Mahsa drank milk and I had water. After dinner Mahsa turned to me and said "Let's go up." I asked Mama to please wake me up by seven, seven-thirty at the latest. She said that she would. We said good-night and went upstairs.

We went up to the bed room, took showers and turning off the lights, got into bed. I wrapped her in my arms, with her head on my shoulder. I felt something wet and reached out to touch her face. Yes I was right, she was crying. I asked her what the matter was. She told me "These are happy tears. You know that for such a long time I didn't have anybody's shoulder to lay my head upon. Nor did I have anybody to talk to or to share these feelings with. But now I have you for all these things, plus I love you to death." I squeezed her tightly and kissed her, saying "I am here or any place you want me to be and I love you unconditionally. I am a fighter and I will fight for my love no matter what." She moved from her side and sat on my tummy and put her hands on my shoulders and looked deep into my eyes. I could see her eyes very well despite the dark and so could she. She said "Look into my eyes." I said "I am." She said 'No, close your eyes then look at me." I was confused, "What?" "Please do it!" she persisted. So I closed my eyes and then she said "I am going to close my eyes too. Let's look deep inside of each other. She moved closer and closer; each time I could see her better and more clearly and I could feel her breathing. Then suddenly she said "Yousef can you repeat what you just said?" I said "Yes. I told you I am yours, I am here or any place you want me to be and I love you unconditionally to death. I told you I am a fighter and I will fight for my love no matter what." She gently opened my eyes with her hand and put her beautiful lips to mine and kissed me with all the love and energy she had. Then she held my face and we locked eyes. She told me "I will never leave you alone my chubby love." I answered her "I don't think death can separate me from you, because death is not powerful enough to keep us apart." I continued "We will be as a one, one soul in two bodies but we will have to work on it." I quoted Rumi "'First we are raw, than we have to be warmed up, then we cook and then we have to burn. When you are burned, you become ashes. Love has to drop the tear of love on those ashes. Then we rise up from root of the love, and from there we will be unbeaten and can live forever with each other.'" I finished, "Death cannot part us anymore, because we are not just body, we are soul." Afterwards she turned back onto her side and rested her head on my chest and I placed my head over her shoulder and we twined our legs together like a chain and we fell asleep. I woke up at the sound of Mama's voice saying "It is seven o'clock." As I went to the closet to get dressed, Mahsa moved to my side of the bed, reaching for me. When she discovered that I wasn't there she called me "Chubby, where are you?" I said "I am changing, I have to go." "Come back here!" She demanded. I answered, "I will when I am finished." I went over to the bed, she wrapped her arms around my neck and kissed me saying "Have a nice day in school Chubby." I kissed her back and went downstairs, got the car keys from Mama and got my stuff from the car. I gave the keys back to her and she called a cab for me. I got home by seven-thirty.

CHAPTER 3

Assa

When I got in, everybody was up. I said hi and my mom said "I was so worried! You said that you would be home yesterday." I said "No, I said maybe Friday or Saturday." But my mom said "It is O.K. you are home now and that is what's important." I went to my room and put my things away, ate the breakfast and headed out to school. Days passed and on the third day, I still hadn't heard from her. One afternoon after school, I stopped by her house. I kept my distance and saw her with the kids, so I knew she was O.K. I went down an alley before they could spot me. Then I went home. That night I told myself 'Yousef you are stronger than this. Maybe she had some problems and couldn't call. You have to wait - she will call. She will call.' I kept telling myself that.

Day after day passed and every time the phone would ring, I thought 'It is her!' but it wasn't so. Nothing happened until Thursday afternoon phone rang twice then once. I called her immediately, when she picked up the phone, I said "Hi sweetie!" "Hi," she said "Can you come here right away?" I said "Yes, I will be there as soon as possible." I put my jeans and T- shirt and left the house.

I don't remember how fast I got there but it was fast enough. I rang the bell and Mahsa opened the door. I could tell by her face that something was wrong. I turned to my left and suddenly something very heavy struck my face. For a couple of minutes, I couldn't see well. Then I saw Assa standing there. He started calling me every name he knew and then said "I will kill you!" I just stood there and let him talk as much as he wanted and he kept on going and called me more names. After a while, I said quietly "Are you finished?" He exploded No, I have only just begun!" So I let him talk some more until he started repeating himself. I tried to cut him off "Enough, you are just repeating yourself now…" Assa just kept talking over me. Suddenly I lost my temper and shouted at the top of my voice, "Shut the fuck up!" He froze in mid insult, shocked. "Enough is enough." I said, calming down a little. "You made your point, now it's my turn to explain. First of all, nobody planned this, it just happened. Don't you remember that day at the grave

BE HIDDEN LOVE

of Hafez? I told you that I could not come to that party. But you and Meetra forced me to come. I have never gone to any mixed party in Shiraz because my family name is more important than just some party." I continued "I don't know why I agreed to come, but I guess it was destiny. Yes, we fell in love from the first moment we saw each other and that was beyond anybody's control." I was not finished "Yes I love her to death and I will do anything for her! If you kick me out of this house, tell me not to come back and if she agrees with it, I will not just leave this house I will leave this city. This is up to you, but remembers, if you do this, you will destroy three lives.

First: my life without her is nothing and I am dead, because she is all my life now, and without her I am totally destroyed.

Second: you will destroy your mom's life too because I know how much she cares about me and she never be the same person again. She found a life with me and nobody can do anything to change that.

Third: you definitely will destroy your own life because you will always remember what you had done and you will never forgive yourself for destroying our lives and yours.

Now it is totally up to you. If you really want to kill

me then I will give you a knife because dying by my love's son's hand is really an honor. And I want that honor.

Meetra from top of the stairs shouted at Assa "You are so stupid! You don't know about anything except going out with girls. They don't even know you but they go out with you because you spend money on them" Just once, stop doing that and see how many friend you really have. Don't be so selfish. Look at mom, all her life she has always put you and me before herself." Meetra went on, "She has never gone out and has never had anybody at home. She sacrificed all her life for us and now she has finally found love. Look at her! She's happy and looks so much younger than she did a month ago. She is an adult, and can decide for herself. Yes maybe Yousef is younger than her but he brought joy and happiness to her. What more could we want for our own mother? Yes maybe this relationship is wrong, but love doesn't ask how old they are, just like death. Love happens and can come to you in matter of seconds. What you want to do? Kill everybody? Think twice then act one time."

Assa sat down in a chair and said nothing. After about five or ten minutes when he became aware that all eyes were fixed on him; he got up and said "Sorry everybody, but I really cannot see Yousef with my mom at least while I am home." Assa continued, "No I won't kill you; you are still my friend." I walked over to him and grabbed him in a bear-hug, telling him "You have every right to be mad at me. But this isn't anybody's fault. I see you as my younger brother, and always will."

Mahsa got up from the stairs where she had been sitting and threw her arms around him saying, "I love you baby, nothing will ever change that. Both of them started crying and kissing each other. After they had both calmed down, Masha asked him if he would join us outside for tea. But Assa just shook his head and said, "I am late for a party and I won't be back until late." We shook hands, he just looked at me and said "See you around." and left the house.

Mahsa took a deep breath and just looked at me. I went to her I held her saying, "I am so sorry, it's all my fault. I really am sorry." She kissed me and said "No baby I am the one who is sorry. Assa stormed out of the house and came back in no time. His face was so red; I never saw him like this before." She went on "He paced back and forth and then he told me call that son of a …….. to come over here. First I didn't know what's he talking about, so I asked him 'Who are you talking about?' He yelled 'that… Yousef!' then I knew what this was all is about." Mahsa continued, "I said 'What do you want him for? This is not his

47

fault!' Then he starts shouting and calling you all those names. Then he forced me to call you while he listened in from the other phone."

We walked out to the balcony arm in arm, when Meetra came out and joined us. She said "I am sorry too for Assa's behavior." I told her that she has nothing to be sorry for, adding, "Assa was right in his own way, but as you said, love doesn't know any social or age limitations and love doesn't follow any rules either. So don't worry, life goes on and everything will be O.K."

Mama came out with three double Turkish coffees and said "Assa is crazy, I told you that." and then left. Mahsa and I began smoking and suddenly Meetra asked Mahsa "Can I have one? I really need it." Mahsa looked at her in surprise and gave her one and asked, "How long you are smoking?" Meetra answered, "I don't smoke everyday only on special days like this." Mahsa agreed and said it was O.K.

As we were drinking our coffee, I asked Meetra "How long have you known about us?" Meetra confessed "From first night when you guys were kissing each other out here. And when you walked in the garden and sat on the bench. Also whenever you spend the night here; I look at mom every day and see her so happy. That was enough for me. Mahsa and I smoked two or three cigarettes in a row and started on our second coffee. Meetra turned to Mahsa and said "I'm sorry mommy, I have to go now. I wish I didn't have to go but this party was arranged two weeks ago." Mahsa told her "No, please go and thank you for what you've done and your speech. Meetra smiled and said "You're welcome, any time for you two."

Meetra changed clothes, said bye to us and went out to her party. Mahsa and I were still sitting outside, smoking. Then saw my face and came to my side to get a closer look and said "Oh my God!" She ran to her bedroom and brought three lotions. When she touched my face for the first time, it hurt a lot and she said "My babe, it will be O.K. in a second." She applied one lotion after another to my aching swollen face and all the while, she was stroking my hair and sometimes kissing me, saying "I am sorry my Chubby. I love you so much."

After she finished doctoring my face she began talking. She started by thanking me. "What for?" I asked her, "I really didn't do anything." She corrected me, "You did a lot. First, you didn't get angry right away. You let Assa speak his mind. That showed how much you respect him. Plus, your speech showed so much support for me. That was a great deal what you did for me." I told her "For our love, that is nothing and as I said before, I will say again; I will die for you, my Honey Bunch. To me it was nothing." She hugged and kissed me, saying "Then I wasn't wrong." I was right in thinking that you are the one I have been waiting for this all my life!" Mama came back out and asked if we wanted anything. Mahsa said "Please bring us something very delicious and fresh tea." Mama said sure and left.

I then asked Mahsa if she could help me. She looked puzzled "Whatever you want Chubby, just name it." I told her "I need help with some of my school subjects. "Sure!" she said, "I would love to help you, but in what subjects?" I replied "Physics, math and one more."

Mahsa asked "When do you want to start?" I said, surprised, "Are you sure?" She said "Yes absolutely!" Excited, I said "Let me talk to the school about not coming in on Sundays. Then maybe we can start on Sunday." "That's my Chubby!" she encouraged, "And you will pass everything in the spring. Don't worry." I told her that I was 90% sure that we would start Sunday and that we would have time to finish everything. I thanked her for doing this and she said "Don't mention it."

She was holding me when Mama brought cream cheese pie and fresh hot tea. Mahsa said "This is my Mama. She knows exactly what I want. I love you

Mama!" Mama smiled at her and replied, "I love you too my baby." We finished the pie and tea; then she turned to me saying, "Let's go up." She took my hand and led me upstairs to the bedroom.

Once we were inside, she examined my face again and gave me little massage on the area. She said "I can't curse him, you know that?" I agreed "Yes I know and you don't need to because it's really nobody's fault." Mahsa embraced me again, kissed me hard and said "This is love and I love you Chubby."

She removed my t-shirt, very slowly then pushed me onto the bed. Her body felt so very hot as she took her t-shirt and bra off. She held me very tight and began to give me a body-to-body massage. Oh my God - the feeling was unimaginable! She took me so high and put me on a cloud. She could be as strong as steel, yet soft as goose down and could take me as high and as far as the moon. My body became hotter than fire and burned like pieces of old dry fire wood. She was holding onto me and moving me from left to right; up then down. She was sticking to me as though we were glued together. There are no words in existence that can describe my feelings from this experience. That night and that time whenever she tried to move from me; it felt exactly like she was taking part of my body with her. I held her back because it was hurting me so badly and we remained stuck to each other for what seemed to be forever. This went on until we both were satisfied and were finally able to relax. We still held each other until we could separate from each other. Then she turned to her side, lying against me, put her head on my chest and kissed me again and again. She said "I love you so very much!" I buried my face in her golden brown hair and kissed her neck replying in kind, "I love you Honey Bunch! I love you unbelievably and unconditionally." I kissed her over and over.

We lay like that for quite some time. She got up and got a damp cloth to wash my face and applied more lotion to my face, while saying "Let this stay on your face until you are ready to go. Then I will fix your face for you." We went back downstairs and out to the balcony. There we sat while Mama brought us Turkish coffee and some sweets. We both lit cigarettes and found it funny to discover that we smoke the same brand. Mama came back out and asked "Does my 'lovey' boy want to stay for dinner tonight?" I sight "I wish I could, but my folks don't know where the hell I am. No thank you but I have to go. Next time my dear." It was eight-thirty when Mahsa called a cab for me. I say bye to Mama and hugged Mahsa. As I got ready to leave, I told her "If you love me, please forget what happened here today because the past is the past. We can't change anything, and it will only make ourselves miserable. It's best to just forget all about it." Then I kissed her good-bye. The cab was waiting, so I got in and went home.

I got in by nine o'clock and said "Hi I'm home." My mom looked surprised and said, "It's early for you to come home. Where have you been?" I gestured with my hand for her come to my room and she did. I told her "It is Thursday normally I go to the movies as you know and I always come home at this time. This is not new." "I'm sorry," she said "I totally forgot about that, but you always tell me before you go." "You are right." I admitted, "But you were asleep I didn't want to wake you up and I am sorry." Then I asked my mom about father and she reassured me, saying "I already took care of that." I said "Thanks, you are an angel!" She left my room so I could change clothes and go to my father's room.

My mom made me very nice dish from the southern region because she knew I loved it. I ate dinner with them and had some tea. Then I picked up a book of Rumi, sat next to my father and read some poems. Now came the time of challenges as my father was really a master of this and he started explaining to me the meanings of each line in those poems: literal, philosophical and Gnostic. He knew how interested I was in understanding these meanings, especially the last two. Sometimes I would ask a question and he would continue arguing on some word and sometimes he would agree with my point. There were other times he would stick to whatever it was that he believed. On that particular night our debates took us well after midnight until my mom interrupted us "That's enough. You two can continue arguing tomorrow for however long you want. But now is time for bed!" My father told me to write a note to remind us where we left off until then next time when we could continue from there. I said that I would. We said 'Goodnight and God bless' and I went to my room.

I got to my room but wasn't ready for sleep. I hate the school books; not my other books, I turned my passion for learning over to Rumi and Hafez. I opened those books and also some others who were still alive, but their styles were so different from the classical ones. I sat on the floor in the midst of all these books, going from one to another and returning to Rumi. I read one of his love poems and then turned to Hafez — oh my God! I discovered that one of his beautiful poems in particular was so very similar to one of Rumi's. I went through each book, one after another and was amazed at what I discovered. That night was truly a night for love. I read until three-thirty in the morning then went to bed to dream about her and her love until morning.

My uncle was tapping my shoulder saying "Yousef wake up. It is almost noon - wake up!" I opened my eyes and said hi to him and told him that I went to sleep late. He said "I see that, look at all those books on the floor. Did you read them all?" I answered him, "Yes I did." He looked surprised. Then he took a book from my shelf saying "I must talk to my brother about this. This is not a book, you should be reading; at least not now." "Why not now?" I wanted to know, "That book is mine." But he didn't listen to me and took the book. I got up and went downstairs, washed up and went to my father. I walked into the room while my uncle was talking with my father. Turning to me, my uncle said "I think that I should keep this book until the time comes when you can better understand it." I told him that if he wanted that book, he could have it, because I had more anyway. "Nobody tells me what I can and cannot read." I added, "This is up to me and me only and you see that my father doesn't even force me." My uncle got so upset and told me "I will take this book anyway; it is not good for you." I responded to him, "How do you know what is good for me? You don't even know what is good for yourself!" At that point, my father cut me off sternly "You shouldn't talk to your uncle like this!" Without another word, I left the room but listened to them from the other room. My father told my uncle "You are not supposed to take anything out of his room. You could have come to me about it and I would talk to him. That would have solved the problem. If Yousef has not already read that book, he most definitely will now! Don't forget, he has our father's blood."

I headed back up to my room and my mom called to me asking, "Don't you want any breakfast or tea?" Changing my mind, I went down, got a plate of food and some tea and went to my room. I then dialed Mahsa's number: twice, then once. When she answered, I said "Hi sweetie!" She said "Hi is anything wrong?" "No." I assured her, "Except that I miss you so much and I want to know if everything is O.K." She reassured me in return "Everything is O.K. Where are you?" I said "I am home but will go out later." She told me to call her around five, saying "I miss you so much, but I have to go now."

After my uncle left, I asked my father "What was he talking about? Do you know which book he is talking about?" "Oh, that book!" my father started laughing and said "It is O.K." then he became serious. "But you shouldn't talk to your uncle like that." I stood my ground "But you know that what I said was the truth." He didn't want to say anything more. He finished by telling me "Just be careful son, not to always say everything you mean."

I went to help my mom and our maid make lunch and take it to my father. I went to my room to see what else my uncle might have taken and was relieved to find that he only took that book. After lunch and tea, I told my mom that I was going out to see a movie, then visit a friend and that I would be back before ten. She told me "Take care of yourself and God bless you."

I went to see a movie then called Mahsa around five o'clock, using the same code: twice then once and let it ring. She picked up and said "Yes my Chubby, come here as soon as you can, there is nobody home." I caught a cab and got there right away.

I rang the bell and she opened the door. She hugged and kissed me; then looked at my face saying "Thank God it looks so much better than yesterday." Then she took me out to the balcony and asked "Would you like tea or coffee?" Then she suggested something different. "You will like this coffee, it's Italian." She went to the kitchen and fixed me a coffee. After about ten minutes, she brought the coffee. And she was right, it was really good. I lit two cigarettes and gave her one. We sat smoking and drinking our coffee. Oh my God what a feeling that was; sitting next to each other on that balcony. I ask her if anything else happened when Assa got home. She answered, "I didn't see him last night, but this morning when I came down for breakfast he came in and asked Mama to make him some breakfast. We started taking first and he said 'I am very sorry for what I did and said yesterday, but I was so mad because it was in such a bad way that I found out. I had to find out from someone else. I wish you guys would have told me yourselves. Maybe it would have been much better than the way I heard it.'" Mahsa continued, "I asked him how he found out. He said 'I went to a friend's home, and another guy was there. A guy who knew us said that last Friday night he saw my mom with some young guy. Then he asked me who he was, a gigolo? After that I don't know what happened. I tried to remember everything that has happened recently. It took me a little time to find out who the mystery guy was; but I started putting everything together and Yousef's name came up. I didn't want to believe it but soon found out that it was true. You know the rest.'" Mahsa paused, "Assa asked me if you came on to me. 'Tell me the truth!' he demanded. So I told him exactly what happened. Then he asked me, 'Are you absolutely certain that this is what happened?' I told him 'I swear on my life. You know that this is more important than anything else to me. And understand that I told you exactly what happened.' Then after I told him everything exactly as it happened. Assa said 'I have to apologize to Yousef, but I can't.' I told him what you told me, then he said 'Then I don't need to tell him. I said, 'No you don't; he is a good friend.' And Assa agreed to that."

I held her close, saying "I am very sorry that you got caught in such a difficult situation, and I know how you feel." She smiled, "I know you know and that's why I love you and stay with you, because you understand me better than anybody else. You know and understand me in this short time better than my own brother."

She took my hand and led me to the back of the house; a place I had never seen before. We walked into a beautiful garden that was so big you could not see the end of it. We walked until we got to a patio with a brick floor, like what Mary and Mo' had at their place. We stopped when she threw her arms around me and started kissing me, saying "I wanted to bring you here before, but couldn't. Now for first time I have someone…… for myself. I wanted to show you this; I made this part by myself. I mean - by hand, but I had a little help, Ali and Mo' helped me with it. She fell silent and held and kissed me. I hugged her tight and started stroking her hair and her ears. I kissed her neck and shoulders. Oh my God! She smelled like wildflowers and Jasmine. That smell drove me crazy. I picked her up and buried my face in her breast, inhaling deeply the intoxicating scent of her. I began kissing her chest then put her down. She grabbed my hand and we ran back to the house, to the balcony and then dashed upstairs to the bedroom. As soon as we got in the room, she pulled my shirt apart, stripped off my T-shirt and pushed me to the bed.

Note: Before I go further: I must explain that every time we made love, Mahsa took me to a different place, this is not so much as physical, but mental, spiritual and emotional and we experienced these different feelings together. Please bear this in mind as you read on.

She took off her robe and silk nightgown as I took off my jeans. Then she jumped on me and kissed me all over my body. Oh my God! I had never experienced this before. As we made love, she took me out of this world and we went so high that we could reach out and touch the stars. We became so hot like fire itself. We sweat and got so wet it was like we were in a pool. We moved around each other like we were in outer space. She turned me around and moved me up and down and it felt as if we were floating on goose feathers over the earth. I could see the beauty of the land below us. Then she locked her legs around me and rubbed her feet up and down my lover back. Oh my Jesus, it felt so good! Suddenly it felt like all the blood drained from my body but at the same time I tasted like I had drunk the sweetest water ever. The combination of these two sensations drove me nuts. I held her so tightly like we are one unit and we couldn't be separated. We stayed that position for several minutes, and then she moved to her side, putting her face on my chest, while I stroked her hair and kissed her neck. We didn't want to move at any cost. So we just laid there and she spoke, "Thank you Chubby for giving me my old life back. I am so happy that I can share my teen years that I missed with you. You took me back to a time that was even before I got married. With you I feel alive again and I don't want to miss this at any price. I love you so much!" I replied, "Honey Bunch, you have given me back my lost soul. I don't know what I would do without you. I don't want to miss this for anything or at any cost either." Then we kissed each other, got up from the bed and dressed.

We went downstairs to the kitchen and Mama was there. We said hi to Mama and she greeted us in return. Then she asked me if I would stay for dinner. I shook my head and told her "I would love to but can't, maybe next time." Mama turned to Mahsa saying "I see you made coffee for 'Lovey'. Do you guys want anymore?" We both answered together "Yes, thank you!" Mama asked us which one we would like and Mahsa replied "Turkish is better now." We went outside to the balcony and lit cigarettes. A few minutes later, Mama brought us our coffee saying "Bon appetite!" We said "Thank you dear." and she left. We sat close to each other and time to time we kissed. We finished the coffee with two more smokes. Then I took her in my arms. Mahsa said "It is after nine, don't you have to go?" "Yes" I said "I have to go, but my heart will stay here in this house with you. Do you know that?" She said "Yes I know." then kissed me and told Mama to call for a cab. As we left the balcony and headed to the door, I said bye to Mama and thanked her for the coffee. She smiled and said "You're welcome. For you, any time." Mahsa and I got to the door and we start kissing and I said "See you Sunday, Alligator." She replied "Yes, I will see you. But be prepared, I will kick your butt. I will kill you Chubby!" Laughing, I said "I would love to see that!" We kissed again and held that kiss until we heard the cab's horn. She opened the door for me, but as I went out, I looked back several times and she threw me kisses from the door until I got in the cab.

CHAPTER 4

School Matters

I got home safely before ten o'clock. I had dinner with my father and then went to my room. I turned off the light and dumped myself into bed. It was like a movie from that afternoon, replaying over and over in my head. I couldn't get to sleep. I could stay up all night and be a mess the next day, or try to get some sleep. I went to my mom's room and got a Valium. After taking it, I became light-headed and quickly fell asleep, but what a sleep it was! I dreamt of her all night then awoke at the sound of my mom's voice calling, "You are late, wake up!" I washed up, had breakfast with my father and headed to school. After morning classes, I went to the principal's office to talk to him about my arrangement with Mahsa. I informed him that I would not be coming to school for next fifteen to twenty days because I had gotten a private teacher and would work exclusively with him. The principal disagreed by telling me I can't do that and it is not possible. I explained to him that it is important to for me to work this way. I promised to return with good grade except in English. Then I told him that he could do anything he wanted to punish me if I don't get those good marks. He shook my hand and said "You've got a deal, now go and study." I went home for lunch and came back to school in the afternoon. After classes were finished, I returned to the principal's office and reminded him then I would not be coming to school from tomorrow until final exams. He said "Good luck!" I left the school and went to a newspaper stand at the traffic light and called her. I informed her that everything is set and at what time should I be there? She told me after nine-thirty and I said "O.K. I will be there." We said bye to each other and I went home. I started reviewing my books. I started with biology and studied all evening. I had dinner with my father and he was so happy to see me study because this was something that they hardly saw. He said to me "You are going to do very well this year! I think you will pass all the spring finals." I replied "I will do my best to make it happen this year." After dinner, I left my father, went back to my room, started in again and continued studying my books. After several hours of studying, I went to bed and fell asleep quickly that night. I woke up the same as any other day and left the house, but today I didn't go to school, I went to my other (Mahsa's) house today.

I got there before nine-thirty and knocked on the door. Mama opened the door and I heard Mahsa's voice "I am here in the kitchen." I walked in and she was eating her breakfast. She asked if I had mine yet. I said "Yes thank you, but may I have a cup of tea or coffee?" She said "Sure, which one would you prefer?" I answered, "Coffee if you have." Mama brought me a coffee. We went outside to the balcony to drink our coffee and smoke. After we finished, Mahsa looked at me and said "Well, well, well. Did you bring everything I asked?" "Yes, Ma'am!" I gave her my textbooks and my notes. She looked at the notes, and asked, "Do you have a pen?" I said yes and she instructed me, "Write down exactly what I tell you." I told her "I would prefer you to explain the subject to me; it is the best way for me to understand. Then you ask me a question about it. If I don't answer correctly, then I will write down whatever you say." She looked down at the book again and said, "The first chapter is very short, if you can pass that section, we will go on. Deal?" I agreed "Deal!" She started lecturing and explained each lesson very clearly and slowly. After the first chapter, she quizzed me and I answered all of them quickly and correctly. Mahsa gazed at me in surprise and asked "Did you study that chapter last night to surprise me?" I answered her honestly "No, I didn't study that book at all." "This is amazing!" She exclaimed, "Do you have a photographic memory?" I shrugged "Sort of. I can remember anything I see or hear." She reaffirmed her discovery "You do have a photographic memory. Oh my God!"

We went on to complete two chapters that morning. Time passed quickly and it was already one o'clock and we took a break for lunch. During lunch Mahsa kissed me and asked "Do you really remember everything?" I answered, "Yes anything I see or hear I remember. But the only things I am bad with are names. I can't remember them at all except the ones I use often." She repeated again "Really, everything?" I turned to her and asked "What would you like to know? Do you want me to tell you everything we said and did? How about how everything looked in that garden from that weekend we spent with Mary and Mo'?" Astonished, she said "Really? You can remember all that?" "Yes, I can." I assured her, "Just ask me!" So she did ask me a few questions and I answered them exactly as I remembered them. Then she kissed me saying "I love you Chubby, you are amazing!" I smiled "Thank you but I am not that amazing, I am just a regular guy."

Around five-thirty I went home to study the other

books. I followed this routine every day except Fridays. On Fridays I studied at home during the day but sometimes I would go to see her if nobody was home. This went on until three or four days before the exams. On the last day while I studied with her, I told her "I have to get out of the city for the next three or four days." She said "I am free to do something about that for you." I said "Please do! I have to get away. I really need the break." "No problem." Mahsa said "Just find a way around your family and leave the rest to me." "O.K. I will." I replied.

I went home and went straight to my room to think hard about an excuse to get away. But I couldn't think of anything. I joined my father for dinner and tea and went back to my room again start to thinking again. I put on my headphones, listened to the tape Mahsa gave me and fell asleep.

When I woke up the next morning, I had the answer! I went down, washed up and went to my father's room for breakfast. I told my parents that I had to get out of town for the next few days because I am so tired. I need to relax, refresh my mind and get some fresh air before my exams. My mom asked "Where do you want to go?" I told them that I wanted to go to such and such a village with a couple of guys and come back on Friday afternoon. I kept saying that if I stay, I would really lose it and lose everything I worked so hard for. Then my father told me "Let me think about it and I will let you know." "O.K." I said and went back to my room. My mom knew I didn't like the answer my father gave and came up to me, saying "Don't worry, he will say yes. Just give him a little time to think about it. I was impatient "What does he need to think about? It's only two days! Two days won't kill anybody." My mom calmed me down, "Don't you worry about that, just make sure you will be O.K. and pass those damned exams! We will take care of the rest."

Two hours later, my mom called me, telling me to go to my father's room. When I entered the room, my father told me to sit and I obeyed him without a word. He began talking and went on for about a half an hour before he got to his point. He told me "Son, the world is not as good as you might think it is. I worry about you and who you are hanging out with. You know very well that all we have is our family name and nobody has the right to damage it." He added, "Tell me, man to man — promise me that you don't get involved with any of those things that could ruin our family, and that I won't have any problem with you ever." Without hesitation I answered my father, "I have told you before that you worry about me too much and as I have promised before I will promise again and again to you that I will never ever damage our name. And furthermore, I will stop anyone who might try." Smiling, my father gives me some money and told me "Use what you need and keep the rest." I thanked him and my mom and ran out of the room so I could change clothes. I told my mom "I am going out now and will not be back for lunch." and left the house.

I went to Main Street and found a phone. I called Mahsa and when she picked up; she asked "What do you have for me?" Excitedly, I said "We can go tomorrow!" She instructed me come over after eleven. I said "O.K. but doesn't that mean you don't want to see me today?" She said "No, where are you now?" "I am in the street at a payphone." I told her. "Then move your butt and get over here!" she ordered. I caught a cab and got there in a flash. I knocked on the door and she opened it herself. I stepped in and hugged her, saying "I really love you! You just know that everything will be O.K. It's all because of you and your spirit." Mahsa was puzzled, "What you mean?" I said "Only your spirit could make it happen. My father gave me permission to go, and I thank you." She hugged me back and said "You know, after I took a shower last night, I prayed for a long time asking God to give us permission to be together. And today I got my answer! Praise God!"

We went outside on the balcony. Mahsa brought me a cup of coffee and I asked "Where is Mama?" She answered "She had something to do, so she is off today." We took our coffee and went to the side garden the one we walked through on that first night. We walked to the end and sat down on the beach drinking and smoking. We talked for a little while. Then she glanced at her watch and asked me "Aren't you hungry?" I realized that I was hungry. "Then why you didn't say so?" she asked. I said "you were talking and that's enough for me." She kissed me and asked, "Do you like pizza?" "Sure." I said "I love it, the only thing I don't like are bell peppers." "Good." she said. We walked back to the house and she ordered the pizza. It arrived twenty minutes later and as soon as we got it we started eating like pigs! Hungry as we were, we still couldn't finish it, so she put the rest in the refrigerator. After eating, we went up to the bedroom and stayed there until about five-thirty. We went back downstairs and she called a cab for me. While we waited for the cab to arrive we started kissing, I said "I'll see you later." and she added "Alligator."

I had the cab drop me off at my sister's and I met up with my eldest nephew. We went to City Park and sat there reading some poems from Hafez and whatever else we had with us. We critiqued each other wherever our poems had some difficulty. By nine we got home and I called my parents to tell them where I was and that I would stay for dinner, then head home.

After dinner my nephew told me "I had hoped to come to your house Thursday night, but now you say you will not be in town. Can I come over after exams?" I said "Yes, and I am so sorry but this just came up, so will see each other after exams." Then he said "But you always leave next day for Tehran." I promised him "Not this year, I will go later." It was around ten and time for me to head home. I said good night to everybody and went home.

The first thing I did when I got home was to see my father and stayed for half an hour. Then went to my room and got ready for bed. I fell asleep very quickly and got up very early the next morning. I asked my mom, "Do you want green stew for breakfast?" She answered "It would be nice to have that one today." So I went first to the bakery for some fresh bread and then over to another shop for the green stew and brought them home. I saw my father in the yard and he greeted me saying "Aha! You got up early and went out to buy breakfast? That's new!" "Thank you!" I said and took everything inside and waited for father to come back for breakfast. After breakfast and tea, I went to my room to pack my stuff. I left the house by ten-thirty and got to my other house after eleven and we left for our trip by noon. Mahsa drove out to a hotel near Persepolis. We pulled up to the entrance, she went inside and got the room key. She came out and told the valet which unit we would be in. He took the key and our luggage to the suite and we followed him.

When we got in the room, I tipped him and he left. We opened the drapes and windows to take in the fabulous view. It was so beautiful! Removing our clothes, we lay on bed and I gave her a good, hard massage from neck to toes. Then I moved up to her head. I have to tell you about her hair! She had gorgeous auburn (brownish-gold) wavy hair that was just past her shoulders. It really added to her beauty. I gave a good massage to that beautiful head of hair. Then she got up and started to give me a massage in return. I started to protest "Leave it for later..." but she wouldn't listen and proceeded to give me a neck and head massage. She then asked if I wanted anything to eat or drink. I said that I could wait for dinner, but she called room service anyway and ordered coffee, tea and a snack, all of which they brought in no time. We took the tray of refreshments out to the balcony to enjoy with our cigarettes. Then after we finished, we went back to bed and napped for half an hour.

After that nap, we felt rested and refreshed so we went down to do some window shopping. Mahsa stopped in one shop where she saw something very nice. Taking my hand, she pulled me into that shop. She instructed the salesman to bring out a jacket and matching pants. She also picked out a T-shirt. The salesman brought out all the items and Mahsa asked me to try them on. I came out of the dressing room and saw in her eyes that she loved the set. As I went back to change into my own clothes, she told the guy to put my old clothes in the bag and he did. We left that shop and walked a little further down until she went into another shop, but I didn't follow her. She came out with a bag and we continued walking to see the rest of the shops. She didn't buy anything more. During all this time I was quiet and didn't say anything until we got back to our room.

Mahsa handed me the bag and said "This is yours Chubby." Then I got upset and demanded "Do you know what you are doing?" "Yes." she answered calmly, "I know what I am doing. I am doing what my heart has wanted to do all my life! Do you have a problem with that?" I calmed down "No, but this is too much!" "Is that why you didn't talk to me at all on the way back?" she inquired. I felt embarrassed "I am sorry, but I am not used to this." Mahsa wrapped her arms around me and kissed me saying "I know you are proud of not having money or wanting a lot of things, and I am proud of your pride." She continued "I am so sorry if you don't like them, we will take them back. And don't worry about it." She put her head on my shoulder and starts to cry. I held her close, kissed her and apologized, "I didn't know that you would be so upset. I am so sorry!" She said "It's not just that I love you so very much from bottom of my heart; I also did it for my heart and why would you want take that from me?" I kissed her again and again, telling her "I would never want to take your feelings away from you! I will keep all those things forever in my heart because comes from your heart." She stopped crying and kissed me saying, "Yes maybe the way I did it was wrong." I kissed her in turn and said "I thank you, my Honey Bunch! You are my Honey Bunch, aren't you?" Then she squeezed me so tightly and said "I love you more than ever. Yes more than ever. Yes I am your Honey Bunch and you are my Chubby." We stood for a long time, just kissing. Finally I said "I am going to take a shower." and went in. Suddenly I turned and saw her next to me in the shower. She announced "In here is where I will punish you!!" and she started hitting me on my back and shoulders. She grabbed the soap and began scrubbing me. We embraced and kissed for only a moment then continued washing each other. After that most refreshing shower, I shaved while she fixed her hair.

It took Mahsa nearly forty-five minutes to get ready and then she offered to fix my hair. Next was the decision of what to wear. I asked her what I should wear. But that was a stupid question, I should have known better! I had to wear the set she had just bought for me. Then she showed me two dresses and asked me to choose, both were nice but I picked one with a flared collar. She laughed saying, "You son of a gun! This is the more expensive one!" But I liked it, so that was the one she wore. We finished getting ready and went downstairs to restaurant. Mahsa asked the waiter to give us a table in a private corner and he seated us at a choice spot and brought us the wine list. Mahsa studied it carefully then chose one and instructed the waiter "Bring us this one and please make sure the year is correct." He returned five minutes later and presented the bottle to her. She nodded and he opened it. He poured her a little to test and she nodded again - O.K. The waiter then filled both of our glasses and placed the bottle in the ice bucket on the floor which Mahsa then pushed under the table saying "Thanks God that was white wine!" The waiter returned bringing us chips and dip along with some other things. We talked while enjoying our food and drinks. Mahsa spoke first, "O.K. we have been invited to a party tomorrow night. Will that be O.K? You are safe there so don't worry. We do have to go because in a way, you are the guest of honor!" Then we talked a little more about that afternoon and then the conversation turned more personal. Mahsa picked up the dinner menu and asked me what would want for dinner? I shrugged and said "I like seafood, meat and chicken." She laughed saying "That's all?" "Yes." I answered, "Why?" She called the waiter over and ordered two meals, he refilled our glasses and left to place our order. After forty minutes, they brought our food. My God, it looked and smelled fantastic! They set the food at the center of the table to be shared and gave both of us plates. The waiter asked if we needed anything else and Mahsa said "No, thank you." and they left us to enjoy our meal.

We enjoyed our meal immensely and resumed talking about anything and everything. During the course of our dinner, music started playing and we sat listening, enjoying it. After we finished our meal but we still had some wine left. Suddenly the DJ started playing some Italian music from the '60's; Mahsa turned to me and asked "Do you want to dance?" I smiled saying, "It would be my pleasure!" I got up, took her by the hand and we went to a corner and started dancing. We danced two songs then went back to our table. The waiter brought us the dessert list and we ordered cream cheese pie with coffee. Our dessert arrived five minutes later and was fantastic too. We stayed until midnight then went back up to our room.

When we got to our room, we changed clothes, washed up and got ready for bed. What a beautiful way to start that special night. After we both changed into our night clothes, we sat on the bed across from each other and gazed into each other's eyes, holding hands. That feeling started again in my body - I got so hot and I could feel the heat radiating from her hand. This was the first night we had just to ourselves; we didn't have to worry about anything. We started kissing and undressing each other very slowly and gently Oh my God! This was such a different feeling from any other time. We kissed each other from head to toe and began making love. What beautiful love play it was. Together we flew so high as if we could reach heaven! What a gorgeous time we had. We clung to each other and rolled around as if we were in our own private garden, how beautiful it that! We were free of all our cares; we were free to be together with our love. Yes we were free so that nobody could hold us down or tell us what to do. So we made love the way we wanted. We got so hot and sweaty like hell, but it was so nice to get wet from each other. You could say that we were crazy, but it is a wonderful kind of crazy. Slowly and sweetly we came back down to earth and the same as always, she rested her face on my chest and I put my head over hers and we curled up around each other and fell blissfully to sleep. And what a sleep it was; to be in the arms of my love and to feel her by my side.

We woke up around eleven o'clock, said good morning to each other and enjoyed a nice long morning kiss. As we washed up, Mahsa asked, "Do you want breakfast here or do you want to go down?" Smiling, I said "What do you think?" She picked up the phone and called room service and ordered breakfast. They brought up a tray that was piled with just about everything on it. We had a feast of eggs, fruit, milk, coffee and tea. We took the tray out to the balcony and enjoyed our breakfast out there in the morning sun. After breakfast, we went back to bed again and relaxed for another hour or so. Then we got up, took showers and packed up our stuff. Mahsa said, "Checkout is at four." But we only had about an hour left. So we went downstairs to the garden and spent the rest of our time there. We checked out of our hotel and then went to see one of the oldest temples in Iran. It was amazing to see such beauty and history. We walked around the site and admired what we saw. It was such a wonderful time we spent there. We headed back into town around eight and over to where the party was.

Mahsa went in first and then followed her after waiting fifteen minutes. As soon I entered, a guy came up to me and grabbed my hand, saying, "I thank you for coming!", then took me around and introduced me to everyone at the party. Oh my God! Everybody who was anybody was there! The governor, the mayor, and a man who was the head of a university; were all at this party! There was one fellow who I didn't know at all. I shook hands with everyone and when I got to the head of university and he offered me a seat for me. Every single person I met that evening asked me

BE HIDDEN LOVE

about my father. A little embarrassed, l each one that he is fine - thank you and nice to see you again. The head of university turned and asked me if I would like a drink. Quickly, I answered, "I don't drink." Pressing the matter he inquired, "You don't or you can't or you don't want to?" I replied, "All the above." He laughed, saying, "That's the right answer, my son!" A waiter passing by asked me "What would you like, Sir?" I told him tea or coffee is fine and he brought me some coffee. I felt that was O.K. I thought it was so funny; on one side of me was the head of university and the other side was the governor and they talked to me like I actually belonged there.

After a little while, I excused myself to go to the men's room, I passed by the entrance and saw Mahsa in the kitchen, and I entered from back to talk to her. She asked me if I wanted a drink I said "Are you crazy? In here? With all these people?" She said reassuringly, "Don't worry about it. Everybody had drinks, so they won't be able smell you." "Well" I said, "In that case, get me a double Scotch, no ice!" The waiter present exclaimed, "My God! You don't drink and you want that? I don't know what you might say if you have this drink!

I laughed saying "The exact same thing as before the drink." He fixed me the double Scotch and I downed it in a couple gulps and headed to the men's room.

When I came out, a man I met earlier was waiting. I apologized for taking so long and he said not to worry. I returned to the party to watch what was going on and to see what's going to happen because I didn't know where I was and what the party was really about. Suddenly everyone stood up and turned their attention to the entrance as an elderly lady walked in. To my surprise, everyone went up to her and kissed her hand, so I did the same. Mahsa was standing behind her and escorted her to a seat and as she sat, everyone rushed up to talk to her. The waiter then announced that it was time for dinner. As I waited for everyone to go to the dining area; the governor took my hand, give me a plate and instructed me to follow him. I didn't have any choice at that point except to join him for dinner. During the meal, I went into the other room and found Mahsa again. She took me to the elderly lady and introduced us. "This is *the* Yousef you wanted to meet." Turning to me, Mahsa said "This is my beautiful Auntie. I kissed her hand again and she looked at me closely, "So, you are the one who drove my daughter crazy aren't you?" Smiling, I told her "Well she drives me crazy too." She laughed saying, "That's a guy! Nice to see you son and welcome to the family." I said "Thank you Ma'am." After dinner, the guests, one by one, filed in to sit with her and talk.

I gave up my chair for the governor and moved a little

farther from the crowd and sat down. Shortly, Mahsa came and sat with me and we talked. She pointed people out of the crowd and told me who's who and explained what this party was all about. It was the twenty-first birthday of the guy who first came up to me when I arrived. After some time had passed, everyone went back to the dining room. An enormous cake decorated with candles was brought out and the man-of-the-honor walked up to me and took me to the head of the table next to him. After blowing out the candles, he turned and thanked me for our friendship. He then cut the cake and went around the room to talk to the other guests.

Mahsa and I stayed until everyone else had left. Then we went back to talk to Auntie. She hugged and kissed me, saying "Mahsa told me about you, but I thought she was exaggerating about you. But now I see that she didn't. You are the one she really needs." I replied "Thank you, but she is wonderful by herself that's why you see me this way." But auntie corrected me, "No you are a really good person and a gentleman. Just like your father. He's a very good man and we need him here." She turned to Mahsa, saying, "Your room is ready. Now I have to go and rest." We said good night to her, went upstairs and found our room. Oh my goodness, what a room it was! It was beautifully decorated and the bed alone was wonderful. We changed into our night clothes and got

81

into that amazing bed. Snuggling under the covers, we held each other and started kissing. Mahsa took off my t-shirt, pulled off her nightgown and rested her head on my chest. I laid my head on hers and wrapped my arms around her. She held my shoulder and we fell asleep.

We awoke around ten, washed up then went downstairs to the kitchen. Her auntie was nearly finished with her breakfast. She asked us to join her. The maid brought coffee and then left again to make breakfast for us. Auntie told us she had to go to a fund raising event that day, but asked if Mahsa would stay until she returned. Auntie turned to Mahsa, saying, "I need to talk to you." Mahsa replied, "Yes, I will be here."

The maid brought us breakfast and after we had finished, we took our tea and went out to the garden for a walk. We enjoyed our tea and cigarettes in the fresh morning air as we walked. This garden was much bigger than Mahsa's. She showed me around the entire grounds, and then we went in for lunch and a nap. Later that afternoon, she called a cab for me and we got ready by taking my stuff out of her car. I kissed her and asked her to pray for me. The exams started the next day. Mahsa kissed me, saying "Good luck my chubby, and may God be with you. You know that I will pray for you." The cab arrived and waited while we held each other. Letting go, she said "Come to the house after your exams." I promised that l would and then I left.

My first exam started on Saturday at nine-thirty. I told my mom that I would be going to stay with some guys and study a little more for next day's tests and that I would be home around six in afternoon. I also told her not to worry, that we would eat lunch somewhere. She said "Good luck and God bless!" By doing that, I was free every day after my exams so I could go to 'my other house' - the house I really loved very much. I liked my family's house well enough, but her house was something else entirely.

So, every day, I would knock on that door and she would open it, throw her arms around me and ask "How did it go today?" When I said, "Yes, it was okay." she would kiss me, saying "Yes chubby you did it, yes you did. Amen! We would go out on the balcony for coffee or tea and cigarettes. Sometimes we would go to the back garden and pick some fresh greens like basil, mint, tarragon, green onions, radishes and Iranian chives for the lunch. Mama would then use these ingredients to cook some very delicious dishes, either Iranian or foreign.

This was my schedule during exams. Sometimes, Mahsa and I would go upstairs, lie down on the bed and simply enjoy each other's company. We would hold each other and savor the shared body heat and breath. Those days we spent doing just that; we felt as if we were the very lightest of goose down and with the tiniest puff of air, we could float anywhere the breeze sent us. And sometimes, we hoped the breeze would take us to a magic land for lovers only; a place where one can be in love and be loved in return. It would be a place where no one is without love and everyone has their own special someone. Yes my dear readers, lying on the bed next to your love and just holding each other can be as fantastic and intimate as making love to that person. If you are really and deeply in love, believe me, it is possible to experience orgasm without sex. If we could do it, anyone can!

One particular day after we finished studying, Mahsa took me up to the bedroom, saying "I want to show you a movie." At that time we didn't have VHS; it was an 8 mm reel on a projector. She closed the drapes and started the movie - oh my God! It was her wedding movie but without sound. She was so young and beautiful and classy. She was like an angel. The movie was about thirty minutes long and as we watched; it all seemed so romantic and so good. But there was definitely something missing. I watched very closely and realized that there was no expression from her; especially as they danced. There wasn't any emotion in that dance. She told me later on that she wasn't in love with him, but tried her best to at least like him as much as she could.

After the last exam, I stayed with her until five-thirty and told her "I am free for the summer now. When do you think we can go to Tehran?" She shook her head and said "I cannot go this week, I have something to do, but maybe we can go next week. I will let you know which day." I said O.K. and I left her house and went home.

Everyone was happy with my exam scores. My mom asked me "When do you plan to go to Tehran?" I answered "I have something to do here first then maybe next week I'll go." Surprised, she said "It must be a very important thing to keep you here!" and I agreed. Three days after the completion of my exams, the principal called my father and give him the good news. I passed the exams with flying colors! I called Mahsa that afternoon and told her the good news; she started crying and sent me kisses over the phone, saying "Meet me tomorrow night!" Smiling, I said "Fine my sweetie, fine!" then I started crying too and we said 'See you later' to each other and hang up.

Later that day, I went to my sister's around six o'clock and shared the news with them. It was such good news that I had to tell everyone! My sister also asked me when I planned on going to Tehran and I told her the same thing that I told my mom. She too was shocked by that because normally I would leave for Tehran the day after my last exam and would never stay for the test results - ever. My nephews came down from their rooms and I told them the news; then told them to go put something on so we could go to the park. While we were at the park, they asked me the same question about my leaving for Tehran. I give them the same answer I gave my mom. I wanted to keep my story straight and not mix anything up. If everyone had the same information, that would make everything very safe.

I waited impatiently for the next night and when the time finally arrived, I went to a florist I knew and he made up a beautiful bouquet of five red roses and one white. It came out very nicely. I went to the place we agreed to meet for our date. When I arrived, she was already there, so I walked up to her table, kissed her and give her the bouquet. She stood up, hugged and kissed me saying, "This is the most beautiful thing I have ever gotten. Thank you, Chubby!" We spent a wonderful evening celebrating and then we went to our separate homes.

On Thursday night, my nephews came to my parents' house; we had a great time and like before, we read poems from Rumi, Hafez and some newer writers. They spent the night at our house and we stayed up until three in the morning with our discussions. They stayed with us until Saturday and left shortly after lunch. Later that afternoon, I went to see Mahsa. When I knocked at the door, Mama opened the door to let me in. She informed me that Mahsa was upstairs taking a nap and I suggested that we let her be. Mama protested, "She will be mad if I don't wake her up." I reassured her that it would be O.K. "I will tell her that I wouldn't let you wake her up." We went into the kitchen and she brought me coffee and apple pie. I had just finished my pie and was smoking a cigarette and suddenly, there she was! She was standing in the kitchen as if she had magically appeared, I stood up, walked over to her, took her in my arms and said "Good afternoon honey bunch." She said "Hi Chubby." and looked over at Mama, "Why you didn't call me?" I spoke up, "I told her not to wake you. I wanted you to rest for a while." I pulled out a chair for her at the table, gave her a cigarette and Mama brought her coffee. We sat close side by side, holding hands. She then turned to me and asked, "Monday or Tuesday?" Surprised, I said 'What's the good news? I am ready for it."

CHAPTER 5

Summer in Tehran, 1975

I stayed there until six then went home. I went to my mom saying, "I will be leaving Monday, Tuesday or Wednesday." I added, "We will be going to Esfahan first, then to Tehran." She didn't have any objections with that. The next day, Mahsa called, saying, "I couldn't get a ticket until Wednesday. "O.K." I said "That's fine." She then added "Come here for lunch tomorrow." I answered "Then see you tomorrow alligator." "Don't let me bite you!" she warned. I laughed, "I will love that bite and will be waiting for it!"

I met her the next day for lunch and Mama made my favorite Iranian dish for me and it was absolutely wonderful. After lunch we had tea and then went upstairs. We got into the bed and started tickling each other and playing games; suddenly Mahsa bit me! "Ouch!" I yelped, "What did you do that for?" She smiled wickedly, "I warned you that I would bite you." "My God!" I exclaimed, "You are really something." After our rough housing, we held each other, kissing and talking until the time came for me to leave. I headed over to my sister's and visited with her family for a couple of hours, then went home.

The days passed agonizingly slow until Wednesday. The night before, I was packing my stuff and my father asked to speak to me before dinner. He brought up the topic of the family name again saying, "My son, sometimes we get involved with something that seems wonderful at the beginning, but we don't see that there can be fire with this wonderful thing. That fire can burn you so deeply that the pain is unbearable. Just be careful not to get burned." He added, "That's all I had to tell you." We ate dinner and had tea without another word on the subject. I said good-night to my parents and went back to my room and finished getting ready for tomorrow. On Wednesday afternoon I say good-bye to my father and my mom. They both saw me off saying, "God be with you and bless you!" As I left the house, I realized that I was going to the airport. Normally I would go to Tehran by bus but this year was different.

Y. JOSEPHSON

Tehran – Summer, 1975

I waited for Mahsa and we went into the terminal together. She went up to the counter and returned shortly with our boarding passes. As she handed one to me, I noticed that we were seated in first class. I smiled, but didn't say anything. We boarded the aircraft, I felt nervous and excited. This was my first time first class flight! When the plane lifted off the runway, I felt a thrill. The flight was fun and we both enjoyed ourselves. We landed in Tehran and went to the baggage area to claim our luggage. She had two bags and I only had one. We got a porter to help us with our bags, hailed a cab and we headed over to Mahsa's place.

The cab pulled up to a beautiful building, a door man opened the car door, saying to Mahsa "Welcome home." She paid the cab and we went upstairs with the door man behind us carrying our bags. I tipped him and he left. When we were finally alone, Mahsa turned to me and said "Welcome to your home. This is for us only and nobody else." I stood for a moment letting her words sink into me and a strong feeling of love and contentment came over me. 'Is this really *our* home?' I kept asking myself over and over. Yes, it was ours and ours alone and that is what I felt deep in my heart and nothing would change that.

Mahsa went through the place like a whirlwind, turning on the gas and electricity, while I took our stuff to the master bedroom. The place was gorgeous; a penthouse and very tastefully decorated. We started unpacking, Mahsa put her things away, I opened my bag and put some of my things in the closet and left the rest in the bag to take to my sister's house. After everything was put away, we went to the kitchen and Mahsa asked me if I would like some coffee and I said sure. She made us some very good coffee. When it was ready, we went out to the balcony and took in the magnificent view. Beneath us lay the eastern section of Tehran and Mount Damavand in the background. It was so beautiful! After our second cup of that outstanding coffee, we went back inside and rested on a sofa; I lay with my head in her lap. We talked a while as Mahsa played with my hair, and she mentioned that we would have to go food shopping tomorrow. We switched positions and she rested her beautiful head on my lap and asked me what I would like for dinner. Without thinking, we both said, "Pizza!" Laughing, she got up and called down to the front desk to order the pizza. "No bell peppers." I added.

In less than twenty minutes, our pizza arrived and we both start devouring it; eating like a couple of pigs. After stuffing ourselves with pizza, we put the leftovers in the refrigerator. I made tea and we went outside again to enjoy our tea and smoke. After an hour or so, we both started to feel really tired, so we went back inside and got ready for bed. I turned off all the lights and made sure that the stove was off and headed back into the bedroom. When I stepped into that bedroom, I stopped suddenly - oh my God! I saw the most beautiful angel sitting on our bed. My God she was so gorgeous! I went in and took my clothes off and she asked me to leave off the T-shirt too, I obeyed because I knew that she preferred me to sleep with her shirtless. As I climbed into bed, my heart started pounding, I could hear the blood rushing in my ears and I felt myself turning red hot. As I turned to her, I notice that the same thing is happening to her too.

I asked if I could give her a massage, she asked me to get some lotion and use that. Before I started, she put down some towels on the bed. I applied some lotion to her back and gave her a good rubdown, paying special attention to the tight areas. I massaged her magnificent body from neck to toe and when she turned over, I massaged the front too. She then suggested that I lie down and let her give me a massage in return. I must admit; she worked me over pretty well, back and front. The room got so hot and although the air conditioner was on, it didn't seem to make a difference. The room got hotter and hotter. Maybe it was because Mahsa poured extra lotion on herself and me and began a body-to-body massage.

Oh God! I nearly lost my mind. I experienced feelings that were completely beyond my imagination.

As we started making love, we felt free; here we didn't have to worry about anyone hearing us make a sound and maybe that's why it felt so different. Little by little room became hotter than an oven. We got so hot, but didn't care. Together we soared higher and higher and went to a place we had never been before. That night we became one body, one mind and there was no way to tell where I ended and she began. We reached orgasm together in such absolutely perfect harmony. I almost forgot to tell you that in the middle of making love, our sweat and that lotion mixed together and made our bodies so slippery that we held onto each other for dear life to keep from slipping away from each other. I think that was what made it so much more exciting. After more than an hour, we collapsed into each other's arms, completely exhausted. Then she sweetly rested her face against my chest and I placed my head on her shoulder as always. We fell blissfully to sleep together as one unit holding each other fast. Everyone should be able to curl up with their love and go to sleep like that.

We awoke around eleven. Mahsa got up first, took a shower and then she woke me saying, "Wake up Chubby, it is so late!" I opened my eyes and looked at her lovely face as she kissed me, "Good morning

Chubby. Did you have nice sleep?" While I took a shower, she made breakfast. I shaved and put on some of that eau de cologne she bought for me. I put on a robe and went to the kitchen. I kissed her and said "Good morning my sweetie." Mahsa kissed me back and said "Good morning my lovely Chubby you are so nice today!" Laughing, I said "Thanks to you." I made tea and we sat down for breakfast. It was good despite the few supplies we had, but that coffee was amazing.

After breakfast, I brought the tea out to the balcony so we could enjoy it with our morning cigarettes. We took in the scenery below us for more than an hour, at which point, I got up and called my mom to let her know that I arrived safely in Esfahan. I had a nice chat with them. After I finished my phone call, Mahsa called out from the kitchen and asked me if I would like a second glass of tea. "Yes" I answered "Thank you" She brought the glass to me in the living room and as I began to sit on a chair, she moved it back a bit; smiling asked me "Can I share that tea with you?" I was uncertain, but said 'Sure." She sat on my lap and we finished the tea. Then she turned me "Can you make love to me now right here?" I felt myself blushing, "Right now? In here?" "Yes please!" she replied quietly. "It is one of my dreams; to be with you in here, in this house." I held her close and kissed her, saying "Are you absolutely sure?" Her answer was "Yes."

She straddled me and opened my robe, saying "Bear with me, because I have never tried this and neither have you. Please just be with me and let's make something beautiful out of this. All I could say was "O.K." Mahsa pulled off her robe and started to make love to me in that chair. My goodness! That felt so good! She was so romantic and beautiful from head to toe. Everywhere I looked, all I could see was her. Then suddenly, she squeezed me so damned hard and pushed herself onto me — oh yes that was it! She held me so hard that I felt like I couldn't breathe. After we had finished, I tried to move but couldn't. There was a stabbing pain in my ribs. Concerned, Mahsa asked me what happened; I said that I didn't know. She helped me to bed and got out a different lotion – a very smelly lotion. She massaged it into my ribs, wrapped me in a bandage, and continued to massage me again for at least an hour. After she had finished, I felt so much better and could move again.

I went back into the living room with her and we lay together on the sofa with my head in her lap. It felt so good to lie down and rest my aching back. Mahsa stroked my head and neck and after a little while, I fell asleep. I awoke to her shaking me, saying "Chubby, wake up! It is my turn now!" We switched positions and it was my turn to give her a head massage. Unlike me, Mahsa didn't go to sleep but later admitted that she tried so hard to stay awake, that she got dizzy.

Later that afternoon, Mahsa asked me what I might like for lunch. I shrugged, saying "I don't know something light." "O.K.", she thought about it and said, "I know where we can go and after that we have to go shopping for food and other things." I agreed with her plan.

As we got ready to leave, Mahsa called downstairs and asked them to bring the car out. We put on jeans and T-shirts and went downstairs, where the car was waiting. We went to a very nice place that was like a fancy diner and had lunch there. Then we went to a local market for food and bought meats, chicken, milk juice, different kinds of vegetables and the other staples. After the shopping was done, we went for a walk in the park then headed for home.

When we got home, I started preparing dinner; a green celery stew with meat and rice. Whenever I make this dish, I like to add herbs like mint and parsley. I let the stew cook as slowly as possible so the meat stays nice and tender. Once the stew is almost ready, then I make the rice.

It was about ten o'clock when the dinner we made together was ready. Mahsa set the table for two and I made tea for after dinner. I put the food on the table and we sat down to eat. During the entire meal, Mahsa never once looked away from me, nor I from her. This was a first for us both of us and it made the dinner quite magical. Together after dinner, we washed the dishes, dried them and put them back in their places. When we were finished, we took our tea out to the balcony and sat enjoying the evening, the tea, our cigarettes and just being alone together.

This was my first day in our house and it seems very funny how quickly time passes when you are with your true love. Time doesn't even matter when you are enjoying doing the littlest things together like cooking dinner or washing dishes. It is truly a beautiful feeling to have!

We got into bed and started talking when Mahsa asked me how I felt about the house and being here with her. I could only answer her honestly, "I have such a nice feeling here. I feel like I have always been here; that is how comfortable I am. It is far better than my own house." She replied, "Because this is your own house not your folk's home. Again she said the words as if to make them sink into me, "Yes this house is *our* house. My father bought me this house for me right after this place was built. Now this is *our* house and I think my father would be proud to have son-in-law like you." Then she hugged and kissed me, saying, "If there is anything you don't like in here, you can remove it. If you think we need something, just say so and we will go get it together?" I felt so overcome by emotion and said, "Thank you for your kindness. Everything here so nice and very good quality, I really love everything and wouldn't change a thing!" She turn to a nightstand on her left and handed me a set of keys to the house. One was for the main entrance and the other was for the house. Then she kissed me, saying "I love so much Chubby! Everything I have is yours. I kissed her back and hugged her hard, "The only thing I need is your heart, your eyes and your mind. And I think I already have those and that's worth everything to me." Mahsa kissed me again "You have all of that my sweet Chubby!" She was holding me so tight and kissing me when she started to cry. Surprised, I asked her "Why are you crying?" She wiped her eyes and sniffed, "Did you know that you are the first person I have ever met who doesn't want anything except what you just said?" I then added, "It's because I don't need anything except you, that's all I want. You are priceless! What more could I possibly ask for?"

Mahsa's only answer to that was to kiss me all over. She moved to sit on my stomach, grabbed me by my shoulders and pulled me upright to make love. She was so hot that she could burn anyone who got too close. Oh yes she burned me inside and out, until I too was full of fire and we burned together. Oh that was such fantastic lovemaking! We didn't know whether we were on the bed or on the floor - what a night that was! When we finally came to our senses, we indeed found ourselves on the bare floor and that was really something.

We lay together exhausted on the cool floor, unable to move. Eventually we got up and went back to bed again. We held each other and as always, she put her face on my chest and I laid my head on her shoulder and deep sleep soon followed.

We got up the next morning and while having breakfast, Mahsa turned to me, "Yousef, what a night that was last night! Both of us went crazy." and I said, "Yes you made me crazy, but it was fantastic wasn't it?" She agreed, "Yes it was."

After breakfast we took our tea out to the balcony to relax and enjoy our cigarettes. Around one, we took showers and went out. Mahsa wanted to stop at the mall and buy some things for herself. From time to time, she would ask my opinion about some of the things she was interested in and I give her my advice. After a while, she turned to me and asked, "Are you getting bored with this?" I shook my head, saying "No this is fun for me." She added, "We have one more place for just a couple of things; but I promise it won't take too long." I reassured her, "I am fine, finish you're shopping. I'm enjoying myself." We stopped at another place outside the mall and I noticed there were some men's clothing shops as well; so I occupied myself browsing through those while Mahsa did her shopping elsewhere.

When she was finished with her shopping, we stopped by one of the shops I was in earlier, and she asked me if I had seen anything I liked. I told her yes that I saw a couple of nice things, but I don't need anything. Mahsa was surprised, "You mean to say that you are not interested in buying anything?" I answered, "That's right. Yes, I would love some new things, but not right now. If I needed anything, believe me, I would let you know." "Promise?" "I promise you!" and we left. When we got to the car, she asked "What do you want for dinner?" Shrugging, I replied, "What do you recommend?" "We can choose from Chinese, or go to Chattanooga, Sorrento or Hilton. What's your pick?" After some thought, we decided to go to Chattanooga; we had a wonderful dinner there and got home around eleven o'clock.

After we got home and took everything up, Mahsa said, "Let's open everything I bought today, one by one!" and that was pretty exciting. She mostly bought cosmetics, but she had a little surprise for me too; she handed me a bag and said "This is yours and I don't want you to say anything because I love them." I just watched her as she opened everything she bought for herself and when she was finished, she looked at me and asked, "Why haven't you opened yours?" I said "I will, I am just trying to guess what's inside." Laughing, she said "You are not going to be able to guess, just open it!"

Inside were four matched sets of underwear and T-shirts. I didn't understand, "Why these?" "Because," Mahsa told me, "I really hate the ones you have. You can leave them here, so when you come, please wear them for me. That's all I ask." I kissed her, saying "Thank you, these are very nice, but I have to keep them here because if my family finds out about them, I will have a problem. But I love them." I got up and changed into a set and put on my robe. I lay down next to her and took the robe off, saying "Look this is what you bought for me!" "Yes, baby!" she hugged me "That is it and please don't put robe back on, just stay like this for tonight." What else could I do, but obey the wishes of my love, just for that night?

She went to change and put away all the things she bought, while I went to the kitchen to make tea. When she came out in her robe, tea was ready and I served it out on the balcony. We loved sitting out there, drinking and smoking; enjoying the night air.

This would be the last night of three beautiful days we spent together, because tomorrow I was expected at my sister's house. While we lay in bed together, I reminded Mahsa about that and she said "Don't worry, we will be together forever. This distance is nothing." She held me tight, kissed me and kept saying over and over, "I love you more than anything in the world." I wrapped my arms around her and told her "I am your Chubby and you are my Honey Bunch and nobody can ever change that!"

We started making love, and together we went to a new place neither of us had been before, but we got there together. We soared so high that no other person had ever been before and what we saw, no one has ever seen before. First we got so hot that we could feel the insides of our bones. The heat radiated out of us like summer heat coming up from the asphalt. Then we became weightless and floated upwards into the atmosphere and went ever higher. We came to a point that everything around us dissolved and we were surrounded by a blinding white light. It was if we were placed upon a snow white goose down mattress and suddenly some unknown force pushed us toward each other. It seemed that we were making love in the middle of nowhere or in a vacuum of time and space. The bright white light that surrounded us squeezed us tighter and tighter until we dissolved into each other and became one body and we burned together with a fire hotter than the sun itself. At one point, we opened our eyes and saw each other bathed in fiery red light. This was no dream! It was a shared experience and we felt it together. Mahsa and I had no way to express ourselves with words as they would be meaningless, so when we finally landed in ecstasy, we curled up together and fell asleep without speaking a word.

 When morning woke us, we kissed each other, washed up and made breakfast. As Mahsa prepared the food, I put the water on to boil for tea and set the table. I put out milk for her and orange juice for myself and toasted the bread. I put out butter and cheese as Mahsa brought out the breakfast. As we ate, I asked her how she felt about last night. Quietly, she replied, "This is not the time or the place to talk about that. We will talk, but not now." So I let the matter be.

We finished our breakfast without any further talk, but from time to time, our eyes met and we would smile at each other. Mahsa asked if I would bring the tea out to the balcony. She met me outside with her eyes saying a million things. I asked her again, "Do you want to talk about it now?" She nodded, "Yes, but let me have my tea and a smoke, then we can talk." After the first cigarette she began, "What was that last night? What did you do and where did you take me?" I lit a second cigarette, "I was going to ask you that same question! Where did we go, how did this happen? I do not know the answer, but this time was different than any other when we made love. Was it not?" Mahsa exhaled smoke into the air, "Yes it was so very different. I loved it, but I was also scared to death. Weren't you?" I smiled at her, "I loved every moment, but I wasn't scared. I knew that I was with you."

She moved to sit next to me and kissed me, saying, "I could feel the power but I didn't want to believe in it. But it is true that such power between two people can exist, isn't it?" I hugged her, "Yes my sweetie, my honey bunch it is true." Mahsa started to cry, "Do you think we are blessed?" "Yes." I said, "I think we are so deeply in love, aren't we? So the power of love itself blessed us and I think we should be very happy and proud." She kissed me again and said "I have always been proud of our love. What about you?" "Yes, I am very proud of our love, mostly because it was out of our hands from the very beginning."

We went back inside, took showers and got dressed. I washed the dishes and put them away while Mahsa got ready. She called the valet for the car and we went out. We weren't sure where to go, so after driving around for a while, we stopped at the North Side Park and got out.

Holding hands, we walked into the park and climbed

a set of stairs to a high point. We sat down to rest on a bench under a tree, enjoying this time we had together. We sat and talked about anything and everything, the people we knew and so many other things. Around three o'clock, Mahsa asked me, "Are you hungry?" I answered, "No, I am not very hungry now." She smiled then said "But you would like some very good coffee, wouldn't you?" Laughing, I replied, "Sure! How could I pass up an offer for good coffee?" She stood up, "Let's walk; it's not too far from here." She led the way to the coffee shop, which was not far at all. As soon as we walked in, the man working there recognized her and came out from behind the counter and said "Hi my dear, long times no see! Welcome back. What brings you here?" Mahsa returned the greeting and told him that everything is the same as always. She then asked him to bring two coffees and a roast beef sandwich cut in half, so we could share. He came back after fifteen minutes and brought us the coffee and sandwich. After we had finished, Mahsa asked if she could get a half pound each of Italian and French. "By the way do you have my favorite tea also?" He told us "I have the coffee, but not the tea. I get it for you, put them all together and it will be ready for tomorrow." She said "That's fine, thank you. I'll take the coffee with me now." He gave us the coffee and Mahsa told him "Change my order to a full pound for the tea." She paid for everything and said, "Either he or I will come to pick up the tea." The shop keeper said, "That's fine, is will be ready by late afternoon tomorrow." We said bye to him and left. We got back to the car and Masha said "I should drop you off at your sister's before it gets too late." We went home so I could pick up my stuff and she dropped me off by an alley near to where my sister lived. As I got ready to leave, I said to her, "See you later, alligator!" Mahsa answered, "Watch out that I don't bite you!" and then left.

From her diary:

Note: There are times when I will add some passages from Mahsa's personal diary.

I dropped him off at his sister's house and went to visit one of my friends who lived nearby. She is a good friend but can sometimes talk too much, which is why I hadn't brought him to meet her yet. I stayed the night there because she wouldn't let me go. We talked about everything and suddenly she asked me, "What did you do to yourself? Did you have surgery or use some new skin care product?" I said, "No, why you asking these question?" She replied, "Because you look totally different from the last time we saw you, especially your face. You are looking much younger!" Then her husband asked me "Is there anyone in your life?" I told them not really. Yes I had to lie, I didn't have a choice. I spent a very nice night with them and left early the next morning. I went about my business and for three days I was so busy that I couldn't call Yousef. I didn't want him to see me because I was dead tired every day. I miss him so much! God knows how much I miss him. I can still smell his scent on the pillows. I love him so much more than anything in the whole world. I finally called him the on the fourth day and in no time, he was at the house right next to me.

I was in Hell for those four days and as soon as she called, I got a cab and went to our house. When I got there she was laying on the sofa, so tired. When I came in, I said "Hi Honey Bunch!" And she jumped up and ran to me, hugged me, kissed me and inhaled my scent and I found myself doing the same to her. We missed each other so much and really didn't know how or exactly when we got so hooked on each other; but that was the truth, we missed each other a million times over.

I went to the kitchen to put the kettle on to make tea and when it was ready, I took it outside to the balcony. Mahsa came over to me and kissed me, saying, "My angel what would I ever do without you, my sweetheart?" We sat outside enjoying our tea and smoking as we just enjoyed being together again. She rested her head on my shoulder. We then went inside to lay down on the sofa next together and cuddled until after nine. At that time, Mahsa asked, "What would you like for dinner?" I asked in return, "When did you have lunch?" She had to think about it, "Around one." "Well," I said "you must be very hungry!" Mahsa shrugged, "Sort of." I added, "You know that I like just about everything, so what would you like?" Thinking again, Mahsa said, "Either Chinese or a Subway sandwich. I decided, "Chinese is good, but no bell peppers!" So she called downstairs and ordered Chinese. We were starved by the time they delivered the food about a half hour later. When we finished eating, there was nothing left. After cleaning up, I made tea and brought it to her. We drink the tea and smoke the last cigarette of the day. By eleven o'clock we were ready for bed.

As we settled in, I took off my T-shirt out and climbed in beside her. She took off her robe and lay there almost naked as was I. we held each other close, but she was too tired for making love, instead, we found a way to have a good time that does not necessarily involve having sex. We had wonderful night just holding each other and exploring each other's bodies; we did everything possible except have sex which was a new experience for us and we found it very enjoyable. When we both were satisfied, we curled up together and went to sleep in our usual fashion.

The next morning we got up around ten, washed up and went to the kitchen. Mahsa started to make eggs and I got to work on the table and made tea. I put out milk for her and orange juice for me and we enjoyed our first breakfast together after four days. We took our tea out to the balcony to take in the morning air and have a smoke. We spent a beautiful, quiet day together until around nine when she gave me ride back to my sister's.

Life went on like this for at least two weeks. We were able to see each other every other day and that was great for us. There were some nights that I stayed with her while other times, I would come home and we would spend the entire day together.

One afternoon as we were enjoying our time together, Mahsa turned to me and asked, "How would you like come up north with me for three or four days?" Thinking hard, I answered, "It's not going to be as easy as with my parents in Shiraz, but yes, I would love to go with you. Just let me work on it. I can make it happen, but I need a little time." She reassured me, "I am sure you will find a way. But please try to do it as soon as possible." "O.K. I will."

I wracked my brain for a plan and finally one day I approached my sister. "I will be going up north for three or four days with some friends." She asked me "When are you going?" I said, "We are still making the plans, I will let you know tomorrow." When I saw Mahsa later that day, I told her the good news. "It is done, when do you think we can go?" She looked so happy. "How about the day after tomorrow?" I agreed "That will be perfect." We spent the day together and when I got home later that evening, I informed my sister that we would be leaving the day after tomorrow. The next night I went back to our house as we wanted to leave early the next morning.

CHAPTER 6

A Trip North

Early the next morning we headed north. When we passed the mountains, the roads became flat and winding. Mahsa stopped at the side of the road and asked me if I might like to drive for a while. I was a little uncertain, but said, "Sure, but you think it will be O.K? I am not an experienced driver." She encouraged me "You will be. All you need to do is practice!" She got out and we switched. After about 10 minutes, I felt a little more comfortable at driving. Mahsa too could tell that I was capable of controlling the car and she put her head on my shoulder, saying, "Do you know how long I have waited for this moment?" I said, "No, how long?" "Since we first started going out together; I have always wanted you to drive. Now it's happening, I got my wish!" She leaned over, kissed me on the cheek and put her head back down on my shoulder. We talked until we got to close to town when she said "You should let me drive the rest of the way." I pulled the car over to the side road so we could switch again. She drove through the town and a few more miles when we arrived at a house. Mahsa pulled up to the gate, beeped the horn, the gate opened so we could drive in.

When we drove up to the house and got out, our hosts came outside to greet us. Mahsa made the introductions and we walked over to the porch and sat down. Someone asked me what I would like to drink and I said "Tea would be very good for now." Tea was brought out and everyone sat around talking. A lady named Susan approached Mahsa with a hundred questions, "So, tell me all about him!" Mahsa said, "Let's wait until we have some drinks, then I will tell you everything, I promise!" Ali, Susan's husband, asked us when we would like to have some lunch. We agreed that one-thirty, two o'clock would be perfect. He went inside and informed the maid to have lunch prepared for that time.

Lunch was served around two, followed by more tea. Afterward, it seemed that Mahsa could barely keep her eyes open. Susan noticed right away and said, "You both must be very tired. Let me show you where you will be staying." She took us to the guest house and we said "Thank you and we will see you later." What a guest house it was! It was so cozy and beautifully decorated. Our bags were there waiting for us, so we unpacked our stuff and put them away. I undressed down to just my underwear and Mahsa did the same. She was really tired and fell asleep as soon as her head hit the pillow. I wasn't so tired and contented myself by watching her sleep for a while until I eventually drifted off as well.

We got up around 6 and went back to the porch. The maid brought us tea and some sweets, which we found to be very refreshing. Susan came out and Ali just behind her and the maid brought them tea as well. As we sat enjoying our tea and snacks, Ali asked us what we would like to drink. I threw a cautious look at Mahsa and she caught my eye and signaled that it would be O.K. We gave Ali our drink requests and he went back inside to fix them. When he returned with our drinks, there was also some chips and dip. As we moved to stronger refreshments, Susan nudged Mahsa smiling, "A promise is a promise. Now tell me all about it. I want to know everything!"

Mahsa sighed and said, "There is really not that much to tell." Susan frowned and pressed on, "What you mean? C'mon, you have a lot to say!" So Mahsa started by explaining how Meetra and Assa one night went to the Hafez memorial, and met Yousef there while he was reading a book. "Yousef is an old friend of Assa's, so Meetra invited him to her party, but it was very hard for him to accept. Assa kept telling him 'You have to come!' so he did." Mahsa went on, "He didn't know much about parties, because he wasn't allowed to go to any. So Yousef showed up at our house dressed to the nines, in a full suit complete with black tie and he was sitting on the sofa on the left hand side - you know the one?" Susan nodded yes. Mahsa continued and I could feel my face getting a little warm at that point, "That night I decided to wear one of my white dresses and when I started to come down the stairs; I really don't remember whether it was on the first or second stair from the top, I saw him sitting there by himself." Everyone sat in rapt attention. "Suddenly, it seemed like some invisible force pushed me toward him and when I walked over to him, he stood up and kissed my hand. Then Mama came up and we ordered Turkish coffee but I asked her to bring it outside to the balcony and we went out to drink the coffee and talk in private. Suddenly he placed his hand on top of my hand, like this." She showed them by putting her hand over mine. "That is when I lost all my control and I grabbed his face and kissed him full on the lips and then he kissed me back. After that first kiss, our hearts were racing. And you should have seen Yousef's face; before that kiss it was so red." She looked at me and laughed, "Well, it was much redder than it is now! Afterwards, we went for a walk and I asked him to stay the night, he did and that's about it."

Susan asked breathlessly, "Then what?" But Mahsa didn't say anything else. Then Susan exclaimed, "Oh my God! You finally did it! Son of a gun, you did the one thing you always wanted. You finally found your love!" Mahsa beamed and said "Yes, I finally found him and I am not going to lose him." Then Mahsa's face darkened, "But things didn't stay that perfect for too long." Susan was surprised, "What happened?" Sighing, Mahsa continued, "One day, Assa went out and suddenly returned home. He was so angry and for one full hour he was yelling and calling Yousef all kinds of names, using horrible language. Finally he forced me to call Yousef and have him come to the house. I called him and he came right away. As soon as Yousef walked through the door, Assa slapped him hard across the face then start calling him all those awful names again. Assa just went on and on and said some other shit too. But Yousef didn't say anything until Assa started repeating himself. Then Yousef spoke up and said, 'Let us talk about this.' But Assa kept going on and on. Suddenly Yousef got mad and raised his voice, telling Assa to shut up. That's when Assa fell silent and Yousef started speaking very calmly, explaining to Assa everything that had happened between him and me. That is when Meetra stepped in to defend Yousef, telling Assa to 'wake up, grow up and be a man' and so on. Since then Assa has calmed down and is civil. So, thankfully the problem is solved, but Assa does not want to see Yousef in the house at all." "My goodness!" Susan exclaimed, "You guys have had some very hard times, didn't you?" Mahsa shrugged saying, "It wasn't all that bad. I thought it would be much worse." To relieve the tension, Ali brought us a second round of drinks, telling us that we needed another one for sure. Mahsa and Susan went off the side still talking together and I was talking to Ali when the maid came out and asked him what time he wanted to start making Kebabs. Ali looked at everyone for a consensus; we all agreed around nine or nine-thirty.

Ali made kebabs which all of us enjoyed with bread, followed by tea. After our meal, he then asked, "Would you like to go down to the beach?" We responded with a resounding 'Yes!' The beach at night was so beautiful and quiet. We walked along the shore for a while and sat listening to the waves, talking. It was getting late — around midnight, so we headed back to the house. Mahsa and I said good night to them and went over to the guest house. We got ready for bed and curled up together as always; holding each other, Mahsa put her head on my chest and I put my head on her shoulder.

The next morning, Mahsa shook me awake saying, "Sweetie, my Chubby, wake up! They are outside waiting for us." As I got out of bed, I discovered that I had blisters on my feet from walking on the sand last night. Oh how they hurt! Mahsa got some ointment to put on my feet and wrapped them in bandages. "Don't worry." she said as I limped around, "Just come out in your pajamas and robe, it will be O.K."

When we finally came out, two beautiful children came running up to Mahsa, jumping around calling, "Auntie, auntie!" Mahsa scooped them up in her arms and kissed them. The youngest one was a girl who clung to her side and stayed there the whole time.

We sat down to breakfast and tea and Ali asked me, "Are you O.K.?" I gave a brave answer "I am O.K." He laughed, "Then let's go out somewhere that doesn't involve any walking." I readily agreed. As we piled into his late-model GMC Blazer, we had to work out the seating arrangements. Both of the kids wanted to sit next to Mahsa. So how was that possible? First, I went in, then one kid, then Mahsa followed by the other kid. Problem solved and everybody was happy. Ali drove toward the mountains; and we went up and up until we finally reached a little village. It was so beautiful and picturesque and we could see the ocean from that height. Everybody got out so we could look around and stretch our legs. We went from shop to shop admiring the handmade goods. Each of us bought something special to take back with us. After we had visited most of the shops, Ali asked, "Are you guys hungry yet?" I asked, "What time is it?" "It's almost three o'clock." We went to a cute little cottage where Ali said has very good fish. We ordered several kinds of barbecued fish, each one flavored with different spices. The food was fantastic! The fish was very fresh and the even bread was wonderful.

After lunch we headed back home, but this time, Ali took a different route. As we descended back down the mountain, we passed other villages, although they were not nearly as scenic as the one we just left. We arrived home around six-thirty and Susan advised Mahsa that we should go to the guest house and relax for a while because we were invited to a party that evening. Susan said that the party was for Mahsa. Mahsa asked Susan about the dress code. She said that evening dress would be fine, but nothing too fancy.

We went to our room, took our clothes off and lay down on the bed, holding each other. Mahsa said, "I am sorry about today that I couldn't be with you for the ride. Those kids love me so much and I love them too, I just couldn't say no to them." I smiled, "Don't be, it was very nice for me to see you with them. I loved it." We lay, holding each other for about an hour and then it was time to get ready for the party. Mahsa got up and took a shower. I went in after she was done and shaved. As I waited for her to finish with her hair and makeup, I asked, "What you going to wear?" She went to the closet and took out a shimmering silver dress. Oh that dress was gorgeous on her! Then I asked her "What should I wear?" She said, "That dark suit you brought will do nicely." As we finished getting ready, Mahsa fixed my hair. With some water and her expertise, it came out very nicely. I put some cologne on and she did the same. Just before we went out, I turned to her and said, "Let down your hair." "But why?" "Just trust me, it will look gorgeous." She did. We got to the house as Susan and Ali came out. As soon as Susan saw Mahsa she gasped, "Oh my God! You finally decided to do that with your hair. Now I know that you are really in love!" Mahsa blushed, "Then why you didn't tell me that before?" Susan laughed, "I did tell you once and you told me 'I like it this way!' so I didn't say anything after that."

Together we left for the party. I kept praying to myself that everything would be O.K. that night and it was. The hostess greeted us at the door and hugged Mahsa saying, "My God, don't you look pretty! Have you become younger too?" Mahsa thanked her and we chose a nice cozy corner to sit. As soon as we sat down, drinks were brought to us. I started with something light while Mahsa said, "I want to get drunk tonight!" Surprised, I asked, "Are you sure?" Her answer was still yes.

The party was getting lively as the music song by song slowly began to change to something more danceable. It moved from jazz into rock 'n' roll to pop then to tango. Mahsa and I danced the tango two or three times that night. I kept trying to tell her, "You know that I don't know how to tango." Laughing, she told me, "Don't worry, you will know it after tonight. Remember what I told you; just watch me and follow my moves. It will be O.K. Try not to worry so much." So we danced and danced and I think I finally passed the test. We sat down to rest at our table and watched the other guests, while Susan tried to tell me who was who. Both she and Mahsa were enjoying their drinks and playing cards. I asked when dinner would be served and Mahsa guessed in about half an hour. As dinner was announced, Mahsa turned to me and said, "This is your dinner, go." "No!" I said, "Not without you." She shook her head, "I have to finish this, and then I will come." Stubbornly I replied, "Then I will wait here until you finish." And there I waited patiently until finally she was done. Mahsa took my hand and said "Let's go." and we went to the dining room. Oh my God! What a fantastic dinner I couldn't decide what to eat. I started by taking a little bit of different things and took my place at the table. I was joined by Mahsa, then Ali and Susan. After dinner the DJ played some different music and everybody was talking to each other. The hostess came over to us and sat with us for moment and then went off to visit with the others. We stayed and enjoyed ourselves until one o'clock and then went home.

We went to our room and she flopped down on the

bed still in her dress. I took my clothes off, came back out and she was still lying there. I asked, "Are you O.K.?" Her muffled answer was "Yes, but have you ever undressed a woman before?" I replied, "I know what I have to do." I started by taking her boots off, she was like a rag doll. Then I pulled her upright, unzipped the dress and tugged it off. Mahsa tried in vain to remove her bra, but failed miserably. So, I unhooked it for her and we snuggled under the covers. First she put her face on my chest but after a few minutes she turned over with her back to me and asked me to hold her tight. That's exactly what I did and we both fell asleep in no time.

Suddenly, I heard Mahsa's voice, "Yousef honey, my Chubby. Don't you want to wake up? It is almost noon!" I slowly opened my eyes and she gave me a good long kiss and said to me again, "Time to get up, everybody else is already out." So I got up, washed up and we went out. They had nice hot coffee waiting for me and that was exactly what I needed. Mahsa had one also as we ate breakfast followed by tea. Ali asked us if we would like to go to beach again and everybody; especially the kids gave a resounding "Yesssss!" So it was decided. Susan packed some small sandwiches, soda and fruit in a cooler and each of us put on bathing suits under our clothes, piled into Ali's truck and headed to the shore. When we got there, I asked, "Is there any place less crowded?" Smiling, Susan said, "Yes, Ali knows a place and we went there.

As we were settling down on blankets on the beach, I

suddenly noticed that Mahsa was wearing very loose-fitting dress. Later, when we were alone, I asked her, "Why are you wearing such a loose dress? Is there something you're not telling me?" She frowned at me, "Oh shut up!" So I began teasing her, when she finally said, "Give it up! It's nothing, believe me." "O.K." I became serious, "I was just teasing you." Mahsa looked at me trying to hold an angry expression and said, "Now because you did that, you will be the last person to know. How do you like that?" Laughing, I said, "Fine we'll see about that."

Everybody stripped down to their bathing suits and ran into the water. We had great fun chasing the kids and splashing around. When we came back to the blankets, everyone would rub virgin olive oil on their skin. The bottle was passed to me and Mahsa asked if I would rub the oil on her. Then she told me to turn around so she could put some on me. I hesitated, "What for?" She answered me as though speaking to a child, "I have to put the oil on you, so you won't get sunburned, crazy!" I complained, like a child, "I hate the smell!" "Oh shut up and turn around!" she snapped and I obeyed. But I really loved it when she spoke to me like that.

We lay in the warm sand as the kids played together. Finally I got up and went over to the kids and joined them for a while. We chased each other and built sand castles. I got tired and went back to where Mahsa was lounging. The day passed pleasantly with intervals of swimming, applying more olive oil and resting. After a time, Mahsa said, "I am going to play with the kids."

I called after her "O.K. have fun!" Later in the afternoon, Susan brought out the food, giving each of us a soda, fruit and sandwich. We ate and went back to our routine of fun for a while longer. When we decided that we had enough of the sun, sea and air, we headed home, where everybody went to their rooms to shower and met back on the porch.

As soon as all of us got there Ali brought drinks and asked us what time we would like to eat. I joked, "If we wait until six-thirty, then we can eat lunch and dinner together!" Everyone laughed and agreed. So we enjoyed our drinks while the maid prepared dinner. The kids came out, freshly scrubbed and red cheeked from the beach. They flocked to Mahsa's side until after dinner. The maid had excellent timing; she made a wonderful dinner and put it on the table by seven o'clock. After dinner, we had tea and then it was bed time for the kids and they went reluctantly to their rooms.

We stayed for a while and just talked. Mahsa and Susan regaled us with stories of growing up and going to school together. I learned a lot hat night! I found out that they both were at the head of their class, but they were heads of a gang also and they captained the school soccer team. So while the stories were very educational for me, I finally realized why we understood each other so well. It seemed that Mahsa and I were fashioned the same way and perhaps that is why it felt like we shared the same soul. By midnight, we could barely keep our eyes open, so we said good-night to Susan and Ali and went to our room. We were so tired we dropped out clothes and went straight to bed. As always, she put her face on my chest and I put my head on her shoulder and we slept.

Suddenly I felt something; I thought I was dreaming, when Mahsa kissed me saying, "This is supposed to be our honeymoon and here you are sleeping!" Quickly, I realized that I wasn't dreaming. This was very real. I opened my eyes to find Mahsa making love to me. She lowered her beautiful head and kissed me again, smiled and said, "Good morning Chubby!" I didn't know what to say and it all felt so good that I couldn't say anything. I reached up and massaged her breasts, grabbed her hand and kissed it. She was something that morning, believe me! She was an angel that day. As we made love, we would sometimes kiss passionately, other times she would massage my chest and then she would wrap her legs around my back, but not too tightly in the beginning. Then she would pull me upright and hold me so tight and twine her legs around my back again. She would lock her legs together with her heels and squeeze me so hard, put her head on my shoulder and rub my back hard and deep. I could feel her nails digging into my back, but it felt so good, that I didn't bother to say anything. We held each other like that for a long time. At some point, she turned to her side and resumed kissing me again. She rested her face on my chest and kissed it. Laying there, my senses returned and I felt a searing pain on my back. I ask Mahsa to take a look and see what was the matter with my back. To my amazement, she burst out laughing and exclaimed,

"My God!" Worried, I asked her "What is it?" Gaining her composure, she replied, "I am very sorry, Chubby, but the cat scratched your back! Don't move." she ordered, "I'll be right back." She went out and come back in no time with some cream which she rubbed on my back and then wrapped it with bandages. She kissed me, looking a little guilty, saying, "You will be better tomorrow. Sorry baby!" She added, "Thank you my love, my Chubby and sorry again from the cat." I kissed her and said "You're both welcome, you and the cat."

We settled back into bed and wrapped our arms around each other for an early nap and got up two hours later. We took showers and she applied a new bandage to my back. We pulled on our jeans and T-shirts and went to join the others for breakfast. They welcomed us with cups of hot coffee and then breakfast was served. Around eleven we got ready to leave, said good-by to our friends, kissed the kids and started our way back home.

On the way back I shared with the driving. We stopped at a cookie shop along the way and bought ten boxes. It might sound like a lot of cookies, but each box only held four cookies. They were the best cookies in Iran! Mahsa took over driving the rest of the way. Back in Tehran, we got home around seven. After freshening up and changing clothes, I put kettle on for tea. In our usual custom, I brought it out to the balcony. Mahsa followed me out and we had tea and smoked. We talked about the trip and the fun we had. She said, "Thank you for coming with me." I smiled at her, "You're welcome and I have to thank you for taking me with you. I had such a wonderful time and your friends are very nice people." Mahsa agreed, "Yes they are." We had been outside for quite some time and realized that it was already nine thirty. We were starved, so she called out for pizza. When it arrived a half hour later, we devoured the whole thing! Mahsa exclaimed, "This is the first time ever, that we finished one whole pizza." I agreed, "We were pretty hungry." We finished our dinner with some more tea. By eleven, Mahsa told me that she was so tired and we should go to bed. She went to wash up while I turned off the stove and the lights. I washed up and went to bed. As always I took off my T-shirt and she wasn't wearing anything either. We lay there holding each other and after a while, she turned her back to me. I put my left hand under her head and my right arm around her chest and we fell asleep quickly.

Mahsa woke me the next morning. She took a shower while I made tea. Suddenly she called me from the bathroom. When I came in, she said, "Come on in and take shower with me!" But I replied, "I don't feel like a shower right now." "Oh, just shut up and get in here!" She demanded. What choice did I have, but to obey? When I stepped in with her, Mahsa pouted, "What's wrong? Don't you want to take a shower with me?" "No, it's not like that." I said, "I just didn't feel like a shower right now." Mahsa disagreed, "But it is good for you." and promptly started lathering me up in soap from head to toe. She scrubbed my back as I washed my hair. Then she got out and I rinsed myself off and got out as well. Pulling on my robe, I went back to the kitchen to check on the tea. Mahsa came out to the kitchen and made breakfast. After breakfast and tea, we went to the bedroom to get dressed and I got ready to go. I packed up my things and took five boxes of cookies: three for my sister and two for my cousin. Before leaving, we held each other, saying nothing for more than ten minutes. We wanted to feel each other one last time before I left. Mahsa said softly, "Let's go, it's getting late my love. I am going to miss you but we will see each other in a couple of days." Then she gave me a hug and kissed me so beautifully that I shall never forget that kiss. I still can feel that kiss after all these years. She gave me a ride to my sister's house and said "I am going to see my friend and will stay there tonight, then tomorrow I going to fix the problems we had." she added, "See you later alligator." and I replied, "See you later Honey Bunch." then she left.

That night without her was a disaster! I missed her so much that I wished I could fly. I would fly to see her even if it was only from outside looking in. But I couldn't fly; I had to stay at my sister's and try to sleep.

Three days passed and still Mahsa hadn't called me. By the fourth day, she called, but she sounded awful! Worried, I told her "I am coming right over!" Mahsa replied, "You don't need to rush I am O.K. There is nothing wrong with me." But there was no changing my mind, "I am coming over anyway!" I got there as quickly as I could. I found her lying on the sofa and looking absolutely exhausted. I sat next to her and gave a good long massage to her head, neck and shoulders. It seemed to revive her a little. I then went to the kitchen and made tea and took it out to the balcony. We sat drinking tea and I lit two cigarettes one for her and one for myself. Mahsa rested her head on my shoulder and smoked her cigarette. I leaned over to kiss her neck and she kissed me back, saying, "I missed you so much." I told her "I know, I missed you too baby." We spent the evening just enjoying each other's company. Around ten, Mahsa turned to me and said, "I am going over to my friend's tonight. I can give you a ride to your sister's on the way." Before dropping me off, she told me "The next three or four days, I will be very busy. But I will call you and try to see you." Disappointed, I said, "O.K. but please don't kill yourself! If there is anything I can do to help you, please let me do it!" Mahsa smiled, "O.K. Chubby baby, I will." and she left for her friend's house and I was alone.

Each day I thought that I might be lucky and hear from her. But that didn't happen. Finally, on the fifth day she called just as I was finishing lunch. I said to myself as I picked up the phone, 'Here you go, it's her!' But I couldn't talk to her right then, so I told her, "I will have to call you back." I went out with an excuse to buy cigarettes, but first thing was to call her. She asked if I would come over. I said "Sure, as soon as I take a shower, I will be right there." I took the quickest shower in history and ran over to the house. I found her again, dead tired. As I held her, her body felt limp and lifeless. I went to the refrigerator and saw that we had some wine. I poured her a glass and she drank it down very fast and her body seemed to regain its strength a bit. I fixed some tea and she seemed much better. As we sat, she told me all about the past four days. She was quite upset and said, "Do you know that everybody wants to chide me! They all must think I am stupid or something. They don't even know I am an architect and a damned good one! And I know what needs to be changed and what doesn't. I get so mad, these bastards make me crazy!" She raged on, so I let her vent while I held and kissed her. After she had calmed down a little, I picked up the phone and called a guy I knew, but he wasn't in town. I then called the guy who built my brother's house. When he picked up the phone, I told him who I was and asked him if he could do the type of work that Mahsa needed. He said, "Sure, I can't see why not." He added "I can come to the site tomorrow to look at it and then I can say for certain when I can start working on it and what my price will be." I thanked him and confirmed the appointment for the next day between eleven thirty or noon. I then told Mahsa about the man who will look at the project and take care of it. I said, "Didn't I tell you to let me know if you need help?" She shook her head, saying, "I didn't know that you would have everything in your pocket." She walked over to me and gave me a huge kiss, and added, "You are such an angel! You cannot imagine how much I love you!"

We spent the whole afternoon together and then around nine, Mahsa asked, "Are you hungry?" I said "No, how about you?" "Not really." She said, "I am still full from a big lunch." So I made fresh tea and brought it outside. We stayed out there talking and enjoying the evening until midnight then we turned in.

Mahsa started by gently massaging my chest, but then she climbed on top of me and started to get wild. Leaning over me, she said savagely, "You are mine tonight!" She got wilder and wilder making love to me. There was no rest for me that entire night. We made the craziest, wildest love ever. After a while, I lost my own self-control and got pretty wild too. There were times that I held onto her for dear life and other times that I would bite her shoulder. Mahsa took no notice of that as she was too immersed in her own passion. But after we were done, and lying on our sides, panting like animals; she checked my back and found nothing. "But it hurts!" I complained. Mahsa checked again and said "There is really nothing, just a couple of nail marks on your skin." I offered to check her as well, but she shook it off, saying "I am fine." I pressed her, "Let me look." I was relieved to find that her back was O.K., but the shoulder was a mess! One area was an angry looking purple that was punctuated by my teeth marks. I felt so bad and leaned over to kiss it. "Ouch!" She flinched and asked me what it was. I smiled and told her, "It's nothing really. I only bit you a little." She went to the bathroom to look at it; came running back out and jumped on me. "You bit the tiger did you?" I couldn't help myself from looking smug and said, "Well?" Pretending to be furious, she threatened, "I will bite you now!" She clamped her perfect white teeth down on my lips, "Nobody bites this wild black cat without getting bit right back!" We rolled around on the bed laughing.

For the rest of that night, we lay close together, happy and contented. We caressed and kissed each other's war wounds until exhaustion overtook us.

We woke up around nine and took showers. After breakfast and a morning smoke, we got ready to go out. She drove to another house she owned. Along the way, Mahsa informed me that she has a German shepherd, a big one and his name is Booboo. I grinned at the name, "BOOBOO?" "Yes." She continued, "As soon as we get in the house, stay close to me. Booboo will come over and smell you. I will give you a cookie and you will give it to him, he really likes them." After that, he will be your best friend and he won't bother you." I said, "That is fine." We got to the house and I did as Mahsa instructed. Booboo took the cookies from my hand one by one and when they were gone, he put his head on my feet and gave a kind of half growl, half whine as he looked up at me with begging eyes. When that failed to produce more cookies, he got up and walked away. Mahsa asked the gardener to tie Booboo up. The construction guy kept his appointment and got there around noon. He and Mahsa went through the house as she told him everything that needed fixing. When he came out, I walked up to him, saying, "She is my dear friend. If you can find a way to give her a good price, you would be doing us a great favor." He said "I will be sure to do my best." He went back to talking with Mahsa, they agreed on a price and he wrote up a contract which all three of us signed. The guy then

BE HIDDEN LOVE

told her "I will have two guys come out tomorrow and get started. All of this should be finished in about ten days." Mahsa gave him some money and he left. She turned to me, amazed and said, "This is almost too good to be true!" We said bye to the gardener and to Booboo and left as well.

It was lunchtime, so we stopped for hamburgers, fries and Cokes. After lunch she drove to my sister's house and dropped me off in front of an alley by the house. I got out and said, "I will be back it about an hour." Mahsa replied, "Then I will come back in about an hour." We kissed and parted ways. When I got in, my sister asked me about my friend and I said "Oh, he is O.K." I went to my room to shave and change clothes. I waited until the time came; said bye to my sister and said "I will be back later." I went back to the spot where we were supposed to meet and she arrived shortly. I got in and we went home. Once we were home, we could relax, so we both put robes on. Mahsa made coffee, and as our custom, took out to the balcony. We leaned against each other, savoring that delicious coffee and a smoke. It was so beautiful outside and we loved just sitting out there taking in the views and enjoying each other's company. It was almost sunset when Mahsa turned to me and said, "Let's go in and do something different in this beautiful sunset. I couldn't help but agree. She took my hand and led me straight to the bedroom. There was a small window from which we could watch the sunset from the bed. Mahsa walked over to the bed, her eyes never leaving mine. My God! Those sea-green eyes were so beautiful in that sunset light; I was hypnotized. I approached the bed, slowly, as though I were being pulled by gravity. I shed my robe and let it fall to the floor, while she did the same. I sat on the bed and her lips met mine. It felt as though we were glowing in the light of the setting son, but that we were also glowing from the inside outward. We slowly blended into one body and one soul. I could feel her inside of me as much as I could feel myself inside of her. It was so beautiful to be as one. Mahsa and I wrapped ourselves tightly in each other's arms and legs, until it felt like we had become a complete and perfect circle of flesh and spirit. Together we reached the highest peaks of ecstasy and even after we descended again, we noticed that the sheets and pillows had formed a circle around us.

We sat in the middle of our circle for a little while, basking in the afterglow of our love. I got up and brought more coffee that we both could share in bed. That coffee gave us a really good buzz. No drag could match that feeling! We cuddled for a little while longer than I dragged myself out of that glorious bed and took a shower. I had to go back to my sister's and Mahsa knew that all too well. I couldn't get away with staying two nights in a row. When I came out, I went to her and she held me, kissing me again and again. She then spoke, "I have never ever made love at sunset, until now." This was such a special feeling for me because this experience was something new to us both and only we could own it together.

Around nine or nine-thirty, as I started to get dressed, Mahsa said sadly, "You are leaving me alone again."

Her words nearly broke my heart. I ran over to her, grabbed her and kissed her, stroking her hair; I said softly, "The best place for me is to be with you. Don't you know that?" She tried a brave smile. "I know my love, my Chubby. Neither of us has much of a choice in the matter." She offered to give me a ride, but I said, "No I can get a cab. Don't worry; I know how to get home from here." Mahsa called down to the front desk to call for a cab. I held her so tightly and kissed her from bottom of my heart. She let me out, saying, "Go my love, my heart and my love goes with you. God bless you." I went down and found the cab waiting to take me to my sister's house.

As promised, the house was finished in ten days. Mahsa and I stopped by to watch them finish the job and she had to pay the balance. The house was transformed by the fantastic job they had done for her and she was so happy with what she saw. As Mahsa wrote out the check, she added extra to the balance for him to give to the guys. When he saw the amount, he was surprised and asked, "What is this for?" She replied, "That is a bonus for the guys. They did such a good job!" She thanked him and he left.

After he left, the gardener let Booboo out. He came running out and started jumping all over Mahsa to get her to play with him. She beckoned for me to come over. I walked slowly over to her and the dog Booboo had no problem playing with me instead. Mahsa then called Booboo to the car, he jumped right in and we went for a ride. She told me that Booboo likes a drive from time to time. We looked at him in the back seat and laughed. Booboo certainly enjoyed the ride today. We drove around for about an hour and then we headed back to the house to drop off Booboo. Mahsa gave the gardener a long list of things that needed to be done and he promised that he would have them done in a few days.

Days passed quickly and we would see each other every other day. Many times we would do different things and have a wonderful time together. But we would mostly stay at the house. A month went by and one day Mahsa asked me to come over. When I got there, she told me she has to go back to Shiraz. I was concerned, "Is everything O.K.?" "Yes." she assured me. "Everything is fine, but I have to go. I promise to call you every other day."

My face fell along with my mood as I asked, "When are you leaving." She just looked at me, sadly. I got upset, "No, this is not fair!" She took me in her arms and held me saying, "Baby what is fair in this world, do you know?" I didn't know what to say to her I just held her so tightly against myself and we both started crying as we kissed. Our lips were wet from tears. Those tears were salty and bitter to the taste. We both cried uncontrollably and kissed each other for a while. After we regained our composure, Mahsa tenderly wiped my face with napkins and said, "Oh my baby, my sweet Chubby, it won't take that long. I will be back in no time." I swallowed hard, "O.K. Honey Bunch, O.K. But my loneliness will begin again." and she told me, "We will be lonely together as a couple, but as a couple." She made coffee and brought two mugs outside. We sat in silence, drinking coffee as I smoked one cigarette after another. Mahsa smoked as well, but not as much as I did.

Breaking the silence, I asked, "What time is your flight?" "Midnight." "Well." I said, "We have almost five hours. We should at least enjoy this time." She hugged and kissed me saying, "I love how well you understand me! I love you my sweet Chubby. Nobody else has someone like you. I have my very own Chubby!" But then Mahsa turned serious and told me stop smoking that much. "It is not good for you. Please do it for me." I opened my mouth to protest, but she cut me off. "No 'ifs', 'ands' or 'buts'. Stop it!" What choice did I have but to cut down on my smoking? She went back to the kitchen and brought more coffee. As we sat there, I took her hand and kissed her. Mahsa grabbed my hand; pulled me to my feet and practically dragged me to the bedroom. We jumped on each other, like two crazy people and made the most wonderful love ever. Breathless and blissful, we held each other close. Mahsa got up and asked, "Can you help me pack?" "Sure." I said, "But it is hard for me to pack your stuff, but I guess we don't have a choice do we?" Sadly, Mahsa replied, "You are right, we don't have a choice." So I helped her finish packing and then she asked me to leave before her. I felt as though my heart weighed a thousand pounds and each step toward the cab was unbearable. The ride back to my sister's felt like an eternity.

When I got in, I headed straight for bed. I took half a Valium and tried to sleep, but my dreams were filled with her, our relationship and us. It was like a movie that played back scenes of our times together on and on through my head. I got up around noon, washed up and had my morning tea. By then, it was time for lunch. I didn't have much of an appetite, but forced myself to eat something because if I didn't, my sister would ask too many questions and I wasn't in the mood to talk to anyone. After lunch, I got dressed and got out of the house. I really didn't know where to go or what to do, so I said to myself 'let's go see a movie'. I was hoping that would take my mind off her, but it didn't work. From there I decided to visit my auntie and cousins. Her son and I were very close, but I couldn't bring myself tell him about my love. When I got there he was home and once we started talking, my mind shifted its focus on his stuff, which was a relief. I ended up staying there for almost two days.

Mahsa kept her word, and called me as often as she could; whether it was every other day or every three or four days. Each time we talked long enough to really feel connected with each other. There were times that I couldn't talk in the house and I would have to go outside to a payphone and call her back. It was much more expensive but well worth it for our privacy. Two weeks went by and at that time, two of my brothers came home from the U.S. The atmosphere got a little lighter; especially in the late afternoon, after five. They would come over to our cousin's house and stay until after midnight, laughing, joking and telling stories.

My brothers' presence was very good for me, but still I

BE HIDDEN LOVE

felt so alone and there was nothing I could do about it. One night we were all together when Mahsa called. One of my cousins picked up the phone and she handed it to me, saying, "A lady wants to talk to you." I knew it is her! I took the phone, but couldn't say much to her. Mahsa got the hint and said "I think you cannot talk right now." I asked her wait a couple of minutes. I put down that phone and went upstairs to pick up the other phone so I could talk to her in private. I told her about everything that was going on and my brothers' return home and she was happy for me. She said "That is great, at least you are not alone all the time." We talked a while longer then she kissed me and said, "See you later alligator." I replied, "See you my Honey Bunch!" I hung up the phone and went back downstairs to join the others.

When returned my two brothers and another cousin started making fun of me. My older brother teased me, saying, "In all those months we weren't here, something happed!" I didn't say anything and he added, "Wait a minute! You've got a girlfriend?" He pressed further, "Who is she? What does she look like?" They all started in and went on and on and on. Another cousin stepped in on my defense, saying, "Hey guys leave him alone! At least he's got a girlfriend!" She took me into the kitchen and asked, "Is she really your girlfriend or just a friend?" I was defensive, "What's the difference?" But she didn't buy my vague answer. "Sorry but I heard the last few minutes of your conversation. And what I heard is not just for a 'friend'. You son of a gun! You're in love with her aren't you?" I didn't say anything but my face betrayed me. I said, "Let it be until later. I will tell you everything when the time is right." She just looked at me, "Is that a promise?" I nodded, "It's a promise."

That night I stayed with my cousins and chose to sleep in a room we called 'the small room'. That room has lot of history, for a while it was a play room, but everyone in my family believed that it was haunted. Anybody who knew the history of that room wouldn't stay in it for very long, especially at night in the dark.

But that night I decided to stay in that room. I figured my ghosts could keep the room's ghost company. I turned the light off and got into bed and fell asleep. Suddenly, in the middle of the night, I heard Mahsa's voice so loud and clear; it was as if she was right next to me. I really wasn't sure if I was awake or if I was dreaming. I asked her "What are you doing here? You are supposed to be in Shiraz, aren't you?" She answered, "Yes, I am. But tonight when I talked with you and you told me everything that was going on, I just wanted to make sure you are O.K. Now I know you are O.K." She kissed me and then she wasn't there anymore. I thought about that room and its spooky history and I got little scared. But then I said to myself, 'If the ghost is that beautiful, I am not afraid of it anymore!' With that last thought, I went back to bed and slept undisturbed until morning.

Three weeks crawled by and I stayed mostly with my aunt or other cousins. Each time Mahsa and I talked to each other she would tell me "I'm sorry baby. I didn't know that things would take this much time. Please bear with me. I will be there very soon." First a month passed and we were well into the second month; I had an opportunity to go back to Shiraz for four days with one of my cousins. He was one of my best friends. I called her and told her that I was planning to come to Shiraz myself for a visit and she was breathless with excitement, "I would love to see you!" Is it possible? Yes, please come my love! I want to see you as soon as possible!"

My cousin and I made our plans and got bus tickets for next day. We got on the bus, and it was supposed to have air-conditioning, but it wasn't working. The weather was so hot and we were miserable on that bus. So at the first stop, we got a small cooler and filled it with some ice, fruit and soda. The bus started up again; my cousin and I had such fun all the way to Shiraz. Neither of us will ever forget that bus ride! We arrived at Shiraz in the early morning. My cousin went to his house and I went to see my parents. When I arrived, they were surprised to see me. My mom asked me "Is anything wrong?" "No" I reassured her, "My cousin was coming and he asked me to come with him. It is only for four days." My mom hugged me and said "Welcome home!" I went to my father and he said, "Welcome back, my son."

I was very tired because we didn't sleep on the bus at all. I went to my room and slept until my mom woke me for lunch. After lunch and a quick glass of tea, I went to my room and called Mahsa. She picked up the phone and first thing she asked was, "Are you here?"

"Yes I am." We talked for a few minutes and arranged a time and place to meet. Before hanging up, we said to each other at the same time "See you." I stayed up in my room, took a shower and got ready. I said 'bye' to my mom and left. I stopped at the florist for roses, the same arrangement as before – five red and one white. I then went to our appointed meeting place to wait for her. When she arrived, she parked the car, got out and ran to me. I ran to meet her; we caught each other and kissed. Smiling, I give her the flowers. She kissed me again and we got lost in each other's eyes for a moment; no words needed to be spoken. We went to a coffee shop and just gazed at each other without saying a word, until someone came for our order. There we sat silently with our eyes locked until our coffee was brought out. Mahsa spoke first, "What did you do to me?" I was confused, "What do you mean?" She leaned in close to me, "You know what I mean!" I returned, "You did it to me as well." Yes we missed each other so badly and that one month felt like more than a year and we realized that both of us suffered the same way.

After we spent some time catching up, Mahsa said, "Before you plan anything else, meet me tomorrow at Alam Square around six. I pick you up and we will go to that hotel. Can you arrange that?" I said, "Sure I can. I will be in Alam square tomorrow at six. Is that O.K.?" Mahsa beamed, her entire face lit up, "It is more than O.K! I love you Chubby and I missed you so much I know you can imagine." I smiled back at her, "Yes my sweetie, I can." We stayed in that coffee shop for almost four hours and it was time to go, so we walked to the car and she asked me where she could drop me off. I told her that I was going to my sister's. She pulled up to the street where my sister lived; we kissed and said to each other again at the same time, "See you later, alligator."

When I arrived at my sister's, everybody was surprised to see me back in Shiraz so soon. I told them about my adventures with my cousin then took my two older nephews over to my parent's house for the night. We had a very good time together. I told them that tomorrow night I would be out of town and would be back the next day sometime in the afternoon. I invited them to stay in my room until I returned. The three of us spent the night talking and reading poems from the classics to the contemporary. We went on until two-thirty in morning and had so much fun together.

We got up late the next morning and went down after washing up and said good morning to my mom. She put our breakfast on one big tray which we took back up to my room. After breakfast and tea, we went to see my father and read some books for him. He spoke to us about philosophy for a long time and we enjoyed that a great deal. At times, I felt that his messages were directed at me and I learned a lot from them. As my father continued to speak, he didn't address me directly, but I knew what he was referring to because of the last conversation we had together. I knew he was right about the things he was saying, but I couldn't say anything that might reveal my secrets and I just couldn't do that. He knew that I was in love,

I was sure of that but he never ever confronted me about it directly.

We had lunch and tea then my nephews and I went back up to my room and hung out there until four-thirty, then I started getting ready to go. My younger nephew seemed surprised and said, "You are really leaving?" "Yes." I said, "I told you so, last night." "But I thought you were joking with us." I replied, "No I wasn't joking." I got dressed and took my time as we talked. By five, I was ready to go. I say bye to my nephews and my mom, telling her that I would not coming home that night, but would be back the next day. She protested, "Why are you leaving? They are here." I looked at my mom, but remained firm, "I told them that I would not home tonight and they are O.K." Then I said, "Bye, I will see you tomorrow. My mom replied, "God be with you and bless you." I left the house and hurried to the meeting place and she arrived ten minutes later.

I got in the car and Mahsa sped out of Shiraz as fast as she could. After we left Shiraz behind, she slowed down and started to tell me a little about the problems she was having. She had originally promised to tell me everything back in Tehran. I let her talk for a while before saying, "Good, but you know that if I can be of any help to you, will you please let me know?" She nodded, "For sure if I need the help I will come to you first. You know that, do you?" "Yes I know." We talked until we got to our destination; I didn't know that it was possible to get there as fast as we did. Maybe it was because Mahsa drove so fast. Mahsa went in and got the room key and handed the car keys to the valet. When we got to our room, Mahsa immediately called for room service and also ordered other things for us as we didn't have any bags with us. Everything was delivered in about ten minutes. I tipped him and he left. We undressed and put on the robes that were brought. After we were comfortable, we took the coffee and sweets and sat by a window to take in the view.

Suddenly, like the flick of a switch, we became crazed! We stripped each other naked, barely made it to the bed and jumped on each other. It was almost animal-like the way we kissed, smelled each other and rubbed our bodies together. We made love like we hadn't seen each other for almost a year. But four weeks was way too long for us to be apart anyway, Oh, that love making felt so good. I could feel it all through my bones and running through my blood and I knew that Mahsa could feel it too. This time was different than any other time; we felt the loneliness flow through and out of us. It was amazing. After we reached the peak of ecstasy, we were so sweaty, so we just held each other tightly for a while and catch our breath. Mahsa shifted position so she could rest her face on my chest. As we both relaxed blissfully, I held her in my arms as if I held the most priceless thing in the whole world.

Mahsa raised her gorgeous head to look deep into

my eyes and asked, "Where were we?" Then she started kissing me again, got back on top of me, saying, "Here we are!" At that point, we started making love again. Oh, God as my witness, she drove me crazy; but it felt so good! I didn't know at that point if I was crazy or sane, because our lovemaking was a combination of both. She took me with her to the highest reaches of heaven. It's hard to describe, but when you are there with your love, you know it. Afterwards, she brought me back down very slowly, as if we were snowflakes drifting gently down to earth. She squeezed me in her arms so hard and tight I couldn't move an inch and then slowly released her grip. She covered my chest with a million kisses and I held her like it was our first time.

Making love is a great way to work up an appetite, and we were starved! After getting dressed, we went downstairs for dinner. Looking over the menu, Mahsa asked me, "Shall we try some seafood like oysters and mussels?" I didn't want to say no to her because she knew those foods better than I. Uncertain, I replied, "O.K. Are they good?" Surprised, she asked, "Haven't you had any of this before?" "No." She called the waiter back and asked to change the way the seafood would be prepared. She turned back to me, "You will like it this way."

The waiter brought wine, appetizers with hot bread and butter and chips with two kinds of dip. He filled up her glass, then mine and put the bottle on the floor in the bucket at her request. We raised our wineglasses to toast each other and started with the chips and dip. Suddenly all the feelings we shared upstairs came rushing back to us. My God! I was ready to leave the table and take her back to our room.

Our food arrived almost forty minutes later, but it was worth it. It looked and smelled wonderful. It was awkward for me as I didn't know how to eat what was in front of me, but Mahsa was so clever, she knew I needed help. She fixed oysters and mussels, two by two and put them on my plate, so I started on those. The food was delicious, especially the way she fixed it by mixing in some salsa. I called the waiter over and asked that he send a bottle of the same wine up our room with bucket of ice. He asked if there was anything else we might like for the room and I said, "No thank you that will be all." The waiter bustled away to take care of my request. Mahsa beamed at me, "My goodness I was thinking the same thing but you did it first. I am proud of myself to have you!" She added, "Sometimes I think that you don't know yourself that well, but I also happen to think that I know you better than you know yourself." After that amazing dinner, we took a nice slow walk for about a half an hour to enjoy the evening, then we went back up to our room.

Once in the room, we changed back into robes. The wine was waiting there already nicely chilled. Mahsa settled onto the bed and asked if I would open the wine. I uncorked the bottle and filled our glasses and we drank to each other. I put the cork back in the bottle and the bottle back on ice and joined Mahsa in bed.

She turned to me and looked deep into my eyes, saying "My goodness, there is something about your eyes I cannot get enough of! What is it?" I replied, "I don't know, but your eyes have something as well. I can't take my eyes away from them." I added, "I think it might be something that comes from our hearts, and that's why we can't stop staring into each other's eyes. "Yes." Mahsa agreed, "It is from our hearts." She said.

Mahsa started by placing little kisses all over me, then began to play with my ears which she know was the best way to turn me on in no time. She massaged my ears with her lips, which she knew her lips would drive me crazy and get me horny. She kept teasing me until I couldn't take it anymore. I grabbed her and pulled her to me. I was so hot and horny as she wrapped her arms and legs around me. Very slowly she locked her feet behind my back and massaged my spine with soles of her feet; that slow, rhythmic up and down stroking drove me even more crazy. She made me so high I didn't ever want to come down, but that is the nature of everything both emotional and physical — what goes up must come down eventually with no ands ifs or buts. But now was our time to enjoy the heights of rapture then to come back down to earth. We lay close together in complete contentment; until just before falling asleep, we curled up in our usual fashion holding each other.

We got up around nine-thirty the next morning and enjoyed some more snuggling before getting up and taking showers. Breakfast was served buffet style and what a breakfast it was. There was such an assortment of food; we didn't know where to start. Together we got a little bit of this and some more of that and sat in the salon where they brought us coffee, orange juice and Mahsa ordered milk.

After that sumptuous breakfast, we went back to the room and Mahsa gathered our robes and toiletries into a small bag. I went outside as she paid for the room. She came out as the car was brought out front and we headed back to Shiraz.

On the way back I thanked her, "That was really the best. I had such a wonderful time." I added, "Thank you; I don't know what to say." Mahsa replied, "First, you're welcome and second, shut up! You know everything I own is yours. You just don't get it! I don't know how many times I have to tell you this, but still you say that." I looked hurt, and she smiled at me, "Oh come on!" She kissed me and added, "You are sorry for that nonsense you just said, right?" And I was.

CHAPTER 7

The Bus Trip

We arrived in Shiraz around one and Mahsa dropped me as close as she could get to the red line that was my parent's house. We kissed each other and she asked, "When will you be going back to Tehran?" I sighed, "The day after tomorrow." She looked so sad, "We must see each other one more time, but I have a lot of things for tomorrow. I try to see you even if it just for an hour." I kissed her and we said together, "See you later alligator." She left and I got a cab for the rest of the way home.

When I returned home, my nephews were still there; I said 'Hi' to everybody and my mom asked, "Did you have lunch?" "Yes mom." I answered, "I had lunch already." I went up to my room and both of them followed me up. The eldest watched me carefully, but didn't say anything. I still don't know to this day if he knew where I went. For the rest of the day, we spent our time together and enjoyed ourselves. We stayed up until two, talking about everything. I got up around nine and my nephews got up two hours later. The reason why I got up earlier was that I was waiting for her call. But I waited to have breakfast with my nephews.

Later that afternoon, my nephews told me that they had to go somewhere together. I didn't ask anything about it because I learned not to ask those kinds of questions. When they left the house, I went to my room to check if Mahsa had called, but I wasn't that lucky, she didn't call at all that day.

The next day I woke up around the same time, washed up and had breakfast. I decided to stay in that day and spend it with my father. We talked about Rumi for a couple of hours. After lunch, I went to my room and called her, nobody picked up, so I called another number. Mama answered the phone I said, "Hi Mama." She returned with a cheerful, "Hi there, 'lovey' boy. Where are you? I said, "I am at my parent's, but only until five. Please tell Mahsa to call me in Tehran if she cannot reach me by four." Mama replied, "Sure, but I have hardly seen her these past two days." "O.k." I said, "When you see her, tell her to call me in Tehran." I wasn't lucky enough to hear her voice that day. My cousin and I we left Shiraz at five and we really had so much fun on that return trip. We laughed all the way from Shiraz to Tehran because of all the things that happened on that bus!

I wasn't in a good mood because I knew that I wasn't going to see Mahsa again for quite a while. I met my cousin at five that afternoon at the bus depot parking lot. As I walked up, I saw my cousin standing there with a grin from ear to ear and he had a bunch of stuff with him. He saw my long face and started teasing me, saying, "What happened? Did you lose your oil cargo?" I answered, "I am not in good mood and don't want talk about it." We put our stuff in the storage area under the bus and waited until the driver let us in. For the return trip we were able to upgrade our tickets for first-class seating on the bus, so it was quite different from the one we took to Shiraz. The seats were wider and more comfortable. My cousin had two medium-sized brown bags. One contained dried watermelon seeds and the other had pumpkin seeds. I had two packs of Winston Reds cigarettes which we could share. This was the mid-seventies, a time when everyone could smoke on the bus or anywhere else for that matter. Anything and everything was possible in Iran and I guess all around the world as well.

The driver started the bus about half hour late and by that time; there were only three or four seats open. As soon as we sat down, we looked around to see who was who among the passengers. We spotted some funny guys in the back of the bus and we started cracking jokes about them, laughing and enjoying the seeds and smokes.

The trip between Shiraz and Tehran by bus is about fourteen hours and required two bus drivers trading shifts. About two hours into our trip, we had just passed Seines and came upon an accident that involved two other busses. The driver stopped and about a half an hour later, two women and one man who were going to Tehran came aboard our bus from one of those involved in the accident. That's when our fun really started! One woman had broken her right hand and had it in a makeshift sling around her neck. As soon as she got on our bus, she started nagging and complaining that she wanted to sit next to the driver and watch him drive.

Here is where I have to explain that our buses in Iran are not like buses in the U.S. Ours had two seats next to the driver, one was for the relief driver and the other for the guy who worked on the bus as a conductor and he was also responsible for cleaning the bus and toilettes and replenishing supplies. There was an intercom system that we could use to talk to the driver and the other staff members if anything was needed.

So, there was this woman who wanted to sit right next to the driver to make sure he didn't get into an accident. At first, she wasn't allowed to sit there, but she kept screaming from her seat in the middle of the bus, "Please no drive so fast! No pass that car! Make sure you no sleep driving!" She kept on and on and on and on, disturbing all the other passengers. Finally, as an attempt to shut her up, the attendant brought her up to the front, to sit in his seat next to the driver. As soon as she sat down, she started in again with more complaining and then started a conversation with other woman who was still sitting in middle of bus. From time to time they would shout back and forth advising each other on the situation. We couldn't help but laugh and make fun of those two women. They had such funny clothing and accents, it was like they had just come down from the mountains and this was their first time on a bus. They spoke with a rough language; which made it even funnier for us teen-aged boys. It was like listening to the 'Beverly Hillbillies' characters. My God, we had such a fun time. Oh and about my mood, I think God really sent those two redneck ladies to help get me out of that bad mood and turn me into a happy laughing guy. Yes God can do anything He wishes.

My cousin and I were sitting in second row of that bus, so we could see and hear every single thing and laughed all the way back to Tehran. Sometimes I would make comment that would start her screaming again. I would say something like, "Oh come on Mr. Driver if we keep going like this, we won't get to Tehran for another two days!" or I would say to her, "Don't worry so much, I'm sure that you will go to heaven." That would cause her to scream ever louder, "I no want to die! I no want to die!" At that point the driver turned his face toward me to say, "Let it be please!" When he did so, she became even more frantic, shrieking, "Look at road! Look at road! We will get to accident again!" So my cousin and I held our stomachs laughing, eating those seeds and from time to time, I would throw some of the shells at her.

About halfway through our trip, seven hours or so, the bus stopped for a dinner break. It was great to leave the bus and that screaming woman behind to stretch our legs. My cousin said, "I am so hungry, I could eat as much as you!" I turned to him and scoffed, "No you can't!" So we made a bet. We got into the restaurant and ordered food; kebabs with rice and started eating. The bet was that the loser would have to pay the entire food bill for us both. This is how it went: I was already on my second order when he finished his first. My cousin started his second when I got my third. But my poor cousin could not finish his second order. After I had polished off the rest of my third order, I looked at his unfinished plate and sneered, "Little baby, that's why I am a Chubby and you are not. Pay up!" He paid the whole bill and we took pictures of my winning third food order. We did eat like couple of hungry pigs that night.

After that bit of fun, we had to get back to that bus. As we approached it, we saw an argument taking place in front of the bus. As it turned out, it was caused by the other woman as she wanted to set in that first row close to her friend. But the seat she wanted already belonged to a gentleman and he didn't wasn't about to give it up to her to sit in the middle of the bus. He shouted angrily, "I got this ticket two weeks ago and I will not give it up for anything." Finally another guy stepped forward and gave up his seat, partly because the driver refunded his money. He moved back to her seat in the middle of the bus. For us, the fun doubled as we watched the ensuing argument. We certainly weren't going to move, neither of us wanted to miss any of that fun for a million dollars.

After the dinner break was over, the drivers changed shifts. The new driver was a funny, gangster-type guy and he put some new music in the tape deck. Some people asked him to put some old pop 'Drivers' songs which he gladly did. We thought that was the best and really enjoyed the tunes, but unfortunately, there were some people on board with their families, so they protested that the driver should change the music. They said, "We have kids with us and those are not good songs for them to hear and it is too loud." Those people kept complaining about the music until driver changed the tape and turned the volume down. Everyone settled down after that except those two women; they drove everybody crazy with their loud complaining and weird dialect. Everyone that is, except us, because we had fun at everyone's expense. Believe it or not, we laughed the entire trip of 450 miles! By the time we got to Tehran our stomachs hurt so much from all that laughing. We didn't even go to sleep during that trip. How could we risk going to sleep and missing all that fun? We carried on until the bus let us off in Tehran and we kept laughing all the way through breakfast.

Back in Tehran, we went to my cousin's house because he had a lot of cool stuff for that time. When we got there, we called another cousin to come over and join us. The three of us had a great time that night. We raided the refrigerator for dinner and made cold cut sandwiches.

Time crawled for me over the next three weeks. When Mahsa called me to say she was coming to Tehran the day after next, how happy I was! She warned me not to meet her at the airport because Assa would be there. I wisely took her advice even though I was dying to see her. At least I knew that she would be near and that we could at least see each other every few days. That was fantastic news for me.

She called me around nine in the evening while I was at my cousin's house and we talked for almost half an hour. She asked, "What are you doing tomorrow?" I said hopefully, "Nothing except to see you ASAP!" She laughed, saying, "Then your wish is granted! Meet me tomorrow between three and three-thirty." I kissed her over the phone and said, "Thank you baby!" Everybody started in on teasing me again, but I was so happy that I couldn't be bothered by it. My big brother was making jokes, "You see how Yousef ignores us? It's like we didn't say anything or that we are not here at all!" Then he called over to me, "Hey, lover boy, where are you? Are you here at all?" Smiling, I answered, 'Yes I am here, but I don't have anything to say. So keep going and tease me all you want. It's good for me!"

That comment changed the tone of their voices; everyone started asking me all kinds of questions: is she pretty, is she tall, is she good, on and on and on.

I gave them no details, just yes or no answers. Suddenly my cousin got up and thumped my big brother on his head, saying, "Just look at Yousef, he is the youngest of us, but we have to learn from him." He came over to me and gave me a huge bear hug and continued, "He is really my only cousin!"

He turned to me and asked, "Where is she?" I replied, "She is at home, but one day soon, all of you will get to meet her and see for yourself."

The day finally arrived. I bought my usual bouquet of flowers for her and went to the house. I asked the doorman, "Has the Madame arrived yet?" He answered, "Yes she got here five minutes ago." I said "Thank you" and went up.

I knocked on the door and when she opened it, threw her arms around me. She pushed the door closed with her foot. I handed her the flowers and she asked, "What this is for?" I simply said, "This is from my heart to your heart." She put the flowers down, started kissing me and half dragged me to bedroom.

I really don't remember how we got undressed; it might have won a record for how fast it was. In the next moment, we had flung ourselves onto the bed and were making rough, hard and crazy love. I never saw her like this before. We were like two wild animals, but we took each other so high and made each other so hot and crazy. It was overwhelming and amazing! It was almost too much for me and yet I couldn't get enough. I will never ever forget that afternoon of wild lovemaking. Then as she always did, Mahsa tenderly laid her face on my chest and kissed me left and right. We took a short nap and when we awoke, we were refreshed, happy and full of energy. We put on our robes and she made coffee for me. Then we took our coffee and went out to the balcony. We sat drinking the coffee and smoking together as she rested her head on my shoulder. We didn't need to speak, we just enjoyed the feelings we shared for that time.

We stayed out on the balcony until somewhere around eight. Suddenly, Mahsa looked at her watch and said, "I have to go!" She kissed me, saying, "I'm sorry, chubby." I said, "Don't be." We went to bedroom and got ready to go. As we left the house, she asked me, "Where are you going?" I replied, "To my cousin's." She dropped me off at my cousin's house and left.

When I got in, a cousin came up to me, "Go put some perfume on or wash up." "Why?" "Because" she said, "You still have her smell on you." "Shit is that right?" "Yes! Go now, before somebody catches on!" I ran upstairs and put some cologne on and came back down. But there was nothing I could do about my face. My lips were swollen from her passionate kisses. That alone said everything about me. But no one said anything to me directly, except for some small comments here and there.

Two days went by and finally Mahsa called late in the evening. She asked me to meet her the next day around one. I said, "Fine, I will be there." That next day, I got to the house before her, went to kitchen to have tea ready when she got in.

As soon as she saw me she said, "Thank God you are here!" Her face looked tired as were her eyes. I told her to go relax on the balcony I brought the tea out. We sat on the loveseat and I asked her what was going on. She said one word, "Assa" I was immediately concerned, "What is wrong with Assa?" "Nothing he is O.K. He has his mind set on whatever he wants to do." I offered, "Let me know what's going on and maybe I can be helpful." She began her story, "Before we met, Assa was telling me that he wants to go to London. I tried to change his mind, but he really wants to go. I took him to see a lawyer in Shiraz and he told us our options." Mahsa continued, "First option: Assa must serve in the army for two years then he is free to leave. Second option: Assa must first finish school here, pass the exams then he can go. The third option: He would have to change his status and surrender his Iranian citizenship. They will give him an Exit Visa in order for him to leave, but he might not be allowed to return. And the fourth option is that he can go to England as an exchange student for two terms and might be able to extend his stay." She sighed, "Those are our options." I brought fresh tea and suggest, "Let me call a friend's father who is a lawyer and see what he says." Mahsa agreed, "O.K. Go ahead and do that." I called him and he told me the exact same thing, but he added, "I would advise working on last option. It is the best one." I thanked him and hung up. I lit a cigarette for Mahsa and told her what my friend's father had told me. As I lit one for myself, I said, "I think my big brother can help us in this matter. He really loves a person wants to study especially if that person is very good student." Then I became firm, "But first I have to know if Assa would want me to get involved. And if I do get involved, he has to do exactly what I tell him. He must know that." I added, "You know that I have to have his permission first."

Mahsa went inside to make a phone call and after ten or fifteen minutes she came back and said to me, "You got it. I just finished talking to Assa and he asked if you were with me. I told him no. He said, 'tell Yousef O.K. I will do everything he says. Just get me out of here.' Then he said 'I think Yousef would like very much to get rid of me.'" Mahsa continued, "I told Assa that you are not like that and that he should know better than anyone. So Assa said 'Just tell him to do it please ASAP!'"

BE HIDDEN LOVE

I lit another cigarette and said, "I am doing this for Assa because I love him and want him to be happy." Then I became very serious and asked, "Is he involved with any rebel groups or any political organizations?" Mahsa was shocked, "Oh come on! No! You know him!" I stood my ground, "I was only double checking. I needed to be sure, but yes, I do know him very well; maybe even better than you sometimes."

We stayed out on the balcony until about six-thirty. Then Mahsa turned to me, saying, "I am so sorry, but I have to go." She kissed me and added, "I hope you understand." "Yes" I replied, "I understand. Let's go my Sweetie Bunch. Can you give me a ride to my cousin's?" She laughed, joking, "No, you can walk there, can't you?" "Okay" I stood up, pretending to be hurt, "In that case - see you." Mahsa grabbed me, hugged me tightly and kissed me again and again, saying, "It would be my pleasure to give you a ride my Chubby love!"

She dropped me off at my cousin's house and left. I went in to find everybody out on the balcony, drinking. I said 'hi' and got a drink as well. I sat talking for a while and then went down to the yard for a smoke. My brother came after me and he asked me if I wanted to talk or if there was anything he could do. This was my golden opportunity! So I told him all about Assa wanting to go to London. My brother then asked me the exact same thing I asked Masha; was Assa involved with any groups or secret activities. I assured my brother that I knew this guy for a long time; and the only thing Assa was after were girls and parties. My brother said, "In that case let me talk to some people and we will find the best course of action for him. Tell him not to worry, everything will be O.K."

Sadly, I had to wait for Mahsa to call me. For three agonizing days, I waited. I was at my cousin's as usual, when around seven, she called. My cousin called me to the phone, "It's her." I went upstairs so I could talk to her in private. We set a time to see each other the next day. When I was done, I went back downstairs and everyone started in on me again, making fun of me. I took it all in stride, happy in the knowledge that tomorrow I would see her! I stayed until late then went back to my sister's. The next day after breakfast I took a shower, left the house and headed over to *our* house to meet her. When I arrived, I found her in the garage with her car. I went up but didn't go inside, instead I waited for her and we went in together.

Mahsa made coffee for me and what a delicious coffee it was. We went out to the balcony and made ourselves comfortable. I reported to her everything my brother told me and said, "Now we just have to wait and see what's going to happen." I reassured her, "He will find the best way for Assa, don't worry about that."

We held each other, drank our coffee and enjoyed our time together. After while she said, "I am little tired. Let's go lay on the bed." We took off our clothes and lay down on the bed. Mahsa kissed me and stroked my face and neck and I rubbed her shoulders.

Then she shifted and turned her back to me and asked if I would hold her. I held her so close and so tightly that it seemed that our bodies would stick together and become one. That feeling was so wonderful and comforting. We both had a nap and didn't wake up around five. We put our robes on and I went to the kitchen to make tea as she relaxed outside. There we sat as she rested her head on my shoulder and I massaged it until after six-thirty. We got ready to go. She dropped me off and left.

Over the next two weeks we saw each other regularly. One night my brother took me aside and gave me some good news, "I looked into Assa's case." He said, "Yes he appears to be very good and also happens to be one of the top ten students in school. They have agreed to send him to London for one term, but he has to put some money aside just in case there might be some unforeseen problems." He added, "Assa has to get an I-20 form, which is for exchange students from one of these three places. Then your friend must take the I-20 to the administration office and ask for 'Mr. X'. Tell Assa to say that I sent him. He knows all about Assa's situation, but the process will still take some time as they have to coordinate with the school in London too. After all that is completed, 'Mr. X' will give him a paper in order for him to apply for a passport."

I waited for Mahsa to call so I could give her the good news. I didn't have the phone number for the other house, so I waited and waited until she called two days later. When we spoke, I said, "I have to see you ASAP!" She agreed, "Meet me this afternoon after two." I met her at the house and pulled her outside so we could talk privately, lit two cigarettes and told her everything my brother said. As quick as a cat she jumped on me and kissed me all over my face saying, "I told you that you are an angel!" I laughed, "I am not, you are! It's because of you that I do these things. So that means that you are the angel."

Then she said, "Let's go out and celebrate the good news!" We went to Chattanooga and we ordered coffee and cream cheese pie. We sat for some time, enjoying the coffee and pie, laughing until she had to go. Mahsa gave me a ride back to my cousin's home, but she detoured to the parkway and pulled into a viewing area. We sat on the ground and gazed at the late afternoon sky that formed a backdrop for the city beneath it. It was a fantastic sight. We hung out there for half an hour and then she drop me off and left.

I went to my cousin's home as usual and everybody was there having fun. I went outside to smoke and my brother came out and we talked about the plan for Assa. He said, "Everything is O.K. But if Assa can get the I-20 to me as soon as possible, I could push it through even faster." I assured my brother that I would tell Assa to act quickly. After our discussion, we went back inside and joined the others.

The last time I saw Mahsa, I was sure to get her number to the other house. I called her first in the morning and told her and she said that she would speak to Assa right away. "I have already started things on my end too." She added, "I called a friend in London last night to see about making arrangements for Assa when he gets there. As soon as I hear back about that, I will give the form to Assa to fill out." Then I asked when I could see her again. Mahsa assured me that we would see each other within the next couple of days. We kissed each other over the phone and hung up. I spent the rest of the day just hanging around my sister's house. The next day I went to my cousin's and stayed until late. There was always fun to be had at my cousin's and it helped to take my mind off things for a little while. The next day around noon, Mahsa called and the first words out of her mouth were, "I got it!" "What have you got?" I asked. She sounded so excited, "I got the I-20." "That's great!" I told her, "Can you come and pick me up?" "Yes sir!" She said, "How about in half an hour, our usual place?" We went over to my brother's office; I went up and gave him the I-20. He asked if I could stay I shook my head, "Sorry, no. I have to go." I said 'bye' and went down to Mahsa.

As we left, she said, "I would love to have kebab and rice for lunch." That sounded good to me, so we stopped at the one of the best kebab places in town and got two orders to take home with us. We ate lunch, cleaned up and put the leftovers in the refrigerator. Then we went in to lie down for a nap. By the time, I came into the bedroom, Mahsa was already asleep, still in her clothes. I crept in bed so as not to disturb her and wrapped my arms around her. She was so deeply asleep that she didn't even notice. I'm not sure how long we slept, but Mahsa awoke and shook me. She told me that she would have to go soon because she and Assa had to go to a party that evening. She washed up and put on some makeup then asked me, "Are you coming?" I grumbled, "Yes I am coming! What do you think?" Mahsa laughed, "My goodness, you ask too many questions. Let's go!" She dropped me off at my cousin's and left. I didn't see her for the next two days. On third day she called me, so I went to see her. When I got there, I could see that she was tired; we had a glass of tea then went in for a nap. When we awoke, she asked, "Would you like to stay tonight?" "Sure!" I said, delighted, "I would love to." At that, Mahsa asked me, "Come back to bed, I missed you so much." How could I argue with that? So back to bed I went. We stayed in bed, lazed and cuddled until almost nine-thirty, when Mahsa got up, called in a dinner order and made some coffee. After about half an hour the food arrived, she set the table and we had a nice meal together. We took our coffee out to the balcony to enjoy the evening; then we went back to bed.

As we were getting comfortable, I said, "I have more good news." Mahsa was surprised, "What is it?" I continued, "I found a place just for us. We will be sharing it with my other brother, but it will be fine. It will be ready within next two or three weeks." She suddenly sat upright and threw her arms around me saying, "That is such good news! When did you find out?" "The same day I found out about Assa's paperwork." I answered, "But his news was so important that I totally forgot to tell you about this." She hugged me so hard and said "No wonder I love you so much! My son's good news was more important to you than your own." She kissed me saying, "I love you my Chubby. You are the best Chubby in the world!"

Mahsa lay back down on the bed again and I held her close. I whispered to her, "I want to make love with you tonight." She replied, "I am all yours, do whatever you wish." I started by kissing her neck, then her shoulders and moved down to her breasts. I kept going down the length of her magnificent body, leaving a trail of kisses all the way to her feet. Yes, I covered every inch of her with kisses before beginning to make love to her. I carried her with me to great heights of ecstasy. We were hot and sweaty but neither of us cared or wanted to stop. We drifted farther and farther away from the everyday world, away from our cares and worries. We got so intoxicated with each other that we couldn't let go. After our pleasures were fully spent, we held each other tightly and drifted off to sleep. What a beautiful night that was.

Mahsa awoke before I did the next morning. She began waking me slowly and deliciously. As soon as I opened my eyes, she gave me a big kiss, saying, "Thank you for the beautiful night you gave me. I will never forget it. Last night was so good I still can feel you."

She went to the kitchen and started making breakfast, while I got out of bed and washed up. When I joined her in the kitchen, she had already made coffee and was preparing omelets. I put water on for tea and I toasted some bread. It was so nice that we made breakfast together. I soon noticed that we didn't have milk or juice, so I went down to a small market and bought some. When I came back in, Mahsa asked, "Where did you go?" Then she saw the items I had brought and kissed me, saying, "Yes, I have a man in the house now."

In the middle of breakfast, Mahsa gave me one of those looks. I felt uneasy, so I asked, "What do you want to tell me?" She sighed, "You do realize that I have to go get Assa in Shiraz. It's because I am worried that he might have messed up everything." She added, "You know he is a master of disaster!" I nodded in agreement, "I know, when you will leave?" Mahsa looked sad, "Tomorrow." She said quietly. I was dismayed, "That soon?" "It's better that I get there as soon as possible; so I can make sure that everything doesn't get screwed up." Then I asked, "How long are you going to stay?" "At most ten days." Mahsa tried to reassure me, "I will be back very soon." I resigned to the truth, "We don't have any choice do we?" I asked. She answered, "I don't think so. But it's what I have to do." We finished our breakfast in silence. We then took our tea out to the balcony and sat smoking cigarettes. We remained on the balcony sharing the love seat and watched the day go by. From time to time we would rest our heads on each other lap and enjoy our time together until six. It was time to go; we took showers and she gave me a ride to my cousin's place. We kissed each other and I said, "See you later alligator. Mahsa replied, "Don't let me bite you!" She left for Shiraz next day.

She called me nearly every day and when she didn't, I called her. Time passed quickly until one day she called me she saying, "I am back!" I couldn't believe it! I asked, "Are you serious? Are you really here?" Mahsa said, "Yes, with Assa and he wants to see you, but only if you can meet us at the airport." I said, "That's fine, no problem. When is he leaving?" "On Thursday at ten in the morning. Can you be there to see him off?" "It's fine." I promised, "I will be there for sure. I want to see him too and say bye to him. No matter what, he is still my friend." Mahsa agreed, "Yes he is."

On Thursday morning I arrived at the airport a little earlier then when Mahsa told me. I went up to the bar area and ordered a coffee with a double shot of liquor. I figured that it would help me remain calm in case anything should happen.

After I finished the coffee I checked my watch, I still had time; I paid my tab and very slowly headed down to meet them. I saw them from the top of the escalator. I took a deep breath and thought to myself, 'Here goes...' I walked up and said 'Hi' to them. Assa thanked me and my brother for helping him. I said, "You're welcome, don't mention it. But one thing my brother asked me to tell you, 'Please don't get into any trouble. Go enjoy your new school and hassle the girls as much as you want.'" Assa laughed and said, "You are the same son of a bitch I have always known!" I replied, "And you are the same son of a gun that I know." Than we hugged each other and he whispered in my ear, "Please take care of my mom for me. I know how much you love her but do this favor for me." I replied, "Don't worry, Assa, I will do that for you and for myself as well." Assa muttered, "You son of a bitch!" He hugged me again and kissed me, saying "Good-bye!" and headed to the boarding area. I couldn't go but Mahsa went with him, took him to the duty-free shop and bought some stuff for him. Then he went to find his gate and she wasn't allowed to go any further, so she came back to where I was waiting. She put her head on my shoulder and started to cry. I didn't stop her because she needed to let it all out. I just held her and stroked her hair, telling her, "My shoulder is yours for as long as you need it. I am here for you." Mahsa kissed me and said, "I know my Chubby, I know. Thank you."

We waited until the plane took off; Assa was gone. Mahsa turned to me and said, "I need a drink." I nodded and took her up to the bar and ordered a not-too-strong drink which she drank down faster than was normal for her. We sat there in silence for about ten minutes. At that point, she asked, "Have you had breakfast yet?" I realized that I was starving, "No, I haven't." Mahsa replied, "Neither have I." So we headed to other side of the bar that had a restaurant and asked if they were still serving breakfast. They told us yes, but only for another half an hour. After we had finished eating, I asked Mahsa if she was okay to drive. She gave me a dark look and snapped, "I can break your nose too!" I surrendered, "You can definitely still drive."

When we got home, Mahsa immediately changed into her robe. She then asked if I would like some coffee and I answered that I would love some. She brought two steaming mugs, hers with milk and mine was black, out to the balcony. We sat on the sofa and she rested her head on my shoulder. Suddenly she began to cry again. I held her tightly and stroked her hair. I held her mug for her and suggested that she drink some and that it would help her feel better. Mahsa took a sip, but still she continued to weep softly. After a few minutes, she regained her composure and said, "I am O.K. these are happy tears! I am happy for Assa, but I miss him already." All I could do was just hold her and say, "I understand."

As we finished our coffee, Mahsa yawned, saying, "I am so tired! I am going to take a nap; do you want to join me?" I smiled at her, "I would love to. I'll be there in a little while." She went to bedroom to lie down and I went to kitchen, turned off the stove and cleaned up. Then I went in, changed into my robe and I joined her in bed. As soon as she felt me near her, she turned her back to me and we snuggled so tightly that it felt like we might stick together. That nap lasted for almost three hours.

We got up from that most refreshing nap; I went to the kitchen and put water to boil for tea and Mahsa went out to the balcony. When the tea was ready, I brought it outside. She asked me for cigarette. I went to the living room and found a pack. We sat drinking our tea and smoking, Mahsa rested her head on my shoulder and fretted, "I am worried about Assa, he hasn't called yet. Surely he must have arrived by now." I asked, "Does he have this phone number?" She nodded, "Yes, he does..." she didn't get finish what she was saying when the telephone rang. She jumped up and ran to pick up the phone. I could hear the excitement in her voice. Yes! That was him. They talked for a while then she hung up. I felt her relief, "Was that him?" Mahsa was giddy, "Yes he just got to the hotel and is going to the school to check in and see if he can get into a dormitory or if he has to rent a place with some other guys." She paused to catch her breath, "He said he will call me as soon as he finds out about the housing situation, but he's not sure when that will be. This is so stressful!" I told her, "I keep telling you not to worry! Everything is going to be O.K. These things have a way of working themselves out." I held her and kissed her gently. This was a time when she wasn't the strong, determined Mahsa I knew. She felt so small and fragile in my arms, like a newborn baby. I held her to my heart and she buried her face in my shoulder and started crying again. I took her face in my hands and kissed her. Trying to comfort her, I said, "You have to be happy he is there and that he got what he wanted." She sniffled, "Yes, I am very happy for Assa. But this is the first time he has been so far away from me and I am not used to this." I kissed her again and then told her what Assa said to me in the airport. She look at me, her eyes wide, "Are you serious?" I continued, "Have I ever lied to you?" Mahsa threw her arms around me, kissed me, took a deep breath and said, "I do feel so much better! I love you my Chubby, I love you more than ever."

Mahsa asked me if I would like more coffee. I said, "Absolutely, how can I pass up your delicious coffee?" She went into the kitchen and made the coffee and brought it outside. We sat down on the love seat very close to each other and I draped my arm around her shoulder. From time to time our eyes would meet and we were locked into each other's gaze. After what seemed like an eternity, Mahsa put her coffee down, took my face in her hands and kissed me just like that first night and that first magical kiss I got from her.

She took my hand and I squeezed her shoulder. Mahsa broke the silence, "Thank you for holding me and just being here for me." I replied, "You're most welcome, anytime. But do you know what you did?" She was confused, "No, what did I do?" I told her, "The way you kissed me just now was exactly like our first kiss that night we met, out on the balcony." Mahsa beamed at me, "That's because I have the exact same feelings now as I did that night. But the only differences are that you and I are here together alone, that time you held my arm and this time you are holding me by my shoulder. Yes I have those same feelings now and that kiss was the same and still has the same meaning it did that night."

I held her hand and kissed it. I said in earnest, "I hope that I am still the same guy for you as I was that night." She kissed me again and replied, "No you are not that person any longer." Now I was confused, "Who am I to you now?" She continued, "That night I met you, I fell in love with you, but now you are my love, my life, my time, my soul, my body, my mind and my heart. Yes you are not just my love anymore my Chubby."

My eyes were full of tears, a couple rolled down my face and dropped on her hand. Mahsa held my face and kissed me again, saying, "All those things I just told you are true. You are not just my love anymore my sweet Chubby." I sniffed loudly, hugged her tightly and kissed her again and again. I felt like I could never kiss her enough. I said, "If I compare myself to you, I am nothing." "No." Mahsa argued, "You are all those things to me and more. Much, much more."

She then asked, "Do you want to stay tonight?" I

said, "Yes my Honey Bunch. Where else would I want to be? I am here which means I am you and you are me and my home is here." Mahsa cut me off suddenly, saying, "Can we talk about this later? Now I want to order dinner. What would you like to eat? Without thinking twice, I said, "Chinese would be good. But tell them to make it extra spicy." Mahsa's laughter rang out, "I almost forgot that you like it hot." Grinning I said, "Yes I love hot and spicy and I got a double order of it too!" "Oh shut up!" She snapped and she went inside to order our dinner.

The food arrived within a half hour and as we were eating, she asked, "Is it hot enough for you?" I shrugged, "its O.K." Mahsa shook her head, amazed, "My goodness, you want it hotter than this?" I grinned at her again and said, "Oh yes, I would love to have it hotter." After we had finished dinner and cleaned up the balcony and the kitchen, we headed to the bedroom and got ready for bed.

Climbing in next to Mahsa, I continued, "You do know that I meant it when I said that I love the hot and that I got it?" It was her turn to grin, "You are not exactly mild either." She added, "Let's try together to be as one." I told her, "It's not that easy, it needs a lot of work, but we can start tonight.

Why not?" She whispered to me, "I would love to be you and would love for you to be me." "Okay." I said, "We will do that, but it might need some time."

I sat up in bed and she sat in front of me and I said, "Let's start at the very beginning. This step you can start now and we will practice it until we are ready for the next step." Mahsa was so excited, she could barely contain herself, "I am ready to go, let's do this."

I held her and said, "By now you know how much I love you and nothing is better than for me to be with you. Tonight we will try something very important. Tonight we will make love without sex. We will experience ecstasy through body heat and body energy. We will get what we want without engaging physically, but it will still be very active." Then I asked, "Are you ready?" She said, "Let's try it."

Oh my God! That night was most beautiful night I have ever experienced with her. It was completely new to both of us. I had studied the philosophy before and that was only advantage I had in trying this exercise. After we finished making such love that we both were brimming with each other's heat and energy. We were soaked with sweat. We were blissfully exhausted and at that point, Mahsa turned her back against me and I held her very tightly to myself and we fell into a deep sleep.

The next morning, as usual, Mahsa got up before me and took great pleasure in waking me. Her face was glowing and she looked so happy. We both found ourselves full of energy, which had everything to do with our experience last night. After washing up, we went to kitchen for breakfast. We also felt ravenous and ate so much that day, another side effect of great intimacy. We were lounging out on the balcony as usual with our tea and cigarettes; Mahsa turned to me and exclaimed, "What did you do to me? I never eat that much for breakfast!" I just smiled at her knowingly, but didn't say anything until we went back inside. Then I explained it all to her, "What we did last night opened one of the doors to the other side and that energy you are experiencing is from that opening, which is also why we have such appetites." Mahsa was intrigued, "Have you had this experience before?" I answered her honestly, "No, not ever. But I studied it for a long time. It is like a long journey, we will get there in time. We have to be patient. This is not something that happens in just one night. We must continue the exercises in order to continue to the next level."

CHAPTER 8

Meetra

Two days went by and by the third day I was really going I stayed the afternoon until she gave me a ride to my cousin's house and she went to visit her friend. We got to see each other almost every day for about a week. One day, I stopped by and Mahsa didn't seem her usual happy self. Concerned, I asked her what matter was. "You are not here today!" I said. She put her face against my shoulder and sighed, "Meetra called me this morning and she wants me to come back to Shiraz right away. I tried so hard to find out what was wrong with her but she wouldn't tell me. She just kept begging me to come to Shiraz even just for a week. I am so worried for her!" She blurted, "I spoke to Mama and she doesn't seem know anything either. So after we talked, I called the travel agency to try and get a ticket for me to go today. There was nothing available, but I got one for tomorrow afternoon." She took a deep breath. "That's why I am not happy; I am worried sick about Meetra because she is too independent to call me for little things. I hope nothing is wrong. I am so very worried!"

I stayed with her that night. I knew that I couldn't leave her alone. When we got into bed, she turned to me and said, "Tonight is one of those nights that I really need you." I reassured her, "I am here for you baby." She sighed, "I know but I need your support and your energy." I replied, "It would be my pleasure to give you as much as I have." She rested her face on my chest for a little while then turned her back against me. I wrapped my arms around her so tightly that I was sure that we would be stuck together and we went to sleep like that.

The next morning when we awoke, Mahsa felt much better, I, however, was exhausted. I did not want to move from the bed but I didn't say anything about it to her. I had to show her that I am strong, the last thing she needed was to worry about me. But I think she knew that I was tired. She hugged and kissed me, saying, "Thank you for last night." I answered, "I didn't really do anything, but you're welcome."

We ate breakfast and had our tea and morning cigarettes. I helped her pack a bag. She called for a cab and we went down. I asked, "Do you want me to come with you to the airport?" She said, "No because I am just going to say 'See you later' and I mean it." I won't stay much more than one week. You can wait, can't you?" What choice did I have? I reassured her, "I will wait until whenever. Just take care of Meetra. I wish I could be there for her. Please say 'Hi' and give her a kiss for me if you don't mind. She hugged and kissed me, saying, "I will definitely do that on your behalf." We took the cab together until we got to the parkway, where I got out. I said, "See you later alligator." Mahsa shot back, "Again don't let me bite you!" Laughing, I closed the cab door and she was gone. I caught another cab to the end of the parkway and I had to get out, I wanted to stretch my legs and just think. Along the way I had to stop several times to sit down and think over and over about all the things I have to deal with.

I walked the rest of the way to my cousin's house to kill some time Again the loneliness began to settle over me. Whenever she was away from me it was like there was nobody else around me that I could relate to. I was thrust into a lonely world where no one else but her could enter. I would become so lonely but knew deep inside that we didn't have any choice. She had to go and take care of her family. Neither of us knew how to solve this problem, but I promised myself that we will find the solution sooner or later.

Some night's I went to my cousin's to hang out with other guys. And Mahsa would call me every day or every other day and I was so happy to at least speak to her. Two weeks passed and the place we were waiting for finally came through. I called her the next day from our place and told her to guess where I was calling from. Mahsa howled with delight, "Nooooo!!!! You are calling from our new place, aren't you?!" I was so happy to hear her excitement, "Yeeeesssssss! That is exactly where I am calling from!" She started shouting and kissing me over the phone. She promised me that she would be back in Tehran very soon and for me not to worry." We talked for half an hour then we kissed each other, said 'See you' and hung up. I wouldn't have missed that conversation for a million dollars. My knees were shaking and I sank down on the floor and fantasized about the day when she would arrive here and all the things we were going to do together.

Time passed very slowly and painfully for me when Mahsa was away. I couldn't do anything about it; I just had to be strong and wait until she gets back. In the meantime, school was starting. Now I had two problems: I am without her and now I had to go to school which was also a mess. During one of our conversations we had at our house, she gave me good news, she announced, "My chubby, we will be in Tehran very soon!" I asked, "How soon?" "Next week." She said, "We arrive on Thursday." We talked for a little while longer and hung up. I couldn't believe it! They are coming home! I couldn't contain myself. It felt like my insides were going to pop out from all the excitement. Little by little I came down from my euphoria and told myself 'Yes they are coming home next week.' Then I opened one of my books and started to study.

The rest of that week passed agonizingly slow. Slower than you can possibly imagine, but the days did pass. Thursday was here; the promised day had finally arrived! Mahsa and Meetra would be arriving sometime after two, so on Thursday around noon during school lunch break I went to principal's office and I told him that I have a one o'clock dentist appointment and I need permission to go. He knew me and my family; he looked at me carefully and asked, "Are you sure? You are new in this town you have to be very careful." I knew that I had to reassure him, "I know thank you for your concern but I really do have a dentist appointment. I have to be there by one o'clock." The principal checked his watch, nodded then wrote the permit for me to get out of school which I did as fast as I could.

Once I got out of school, I stopped at a hamburger shop one block down and ordered a burger and a refreshing yogurt drink served with mint, called (doogh). After lunch, I caught a cab and headed to airport to await their arrival.

I got there too early so I had to wait; I went upstairs to the bar and ordered a double. This would help me pass the time as I watched the arrivals board for updates. After I finished my drink, I still had ten minutes to spare until their arrival; so I went back downstairs and waited outside the baggage claim area. Those ten minutes crawled by slower than ever. After what seemed an eternity, they finally arrived. I saw them get off the shuttle bus and they headed to the baggage claim where I was waiting.

As soon as Mahsa saw me, she started running and I ran to meet her; she jumped into my arms. I spun her around as she kicked her feet in the air. We didn't care at that time who was around to see us as we kissed each other until I heard the sound of someone coughing, saw a hand waving and a voice saying, "Mom, mom!" Then we came back to reality. I set Mahsa down on her feet and turned to Meetra, saying, "I am so sorry, Meetra, I didn't see you." I gave her a hug, kissed her and said, "Welcome to Tehran!" Meetra frowned at Mahsa, "Mommy you are not a teen anymore, don't do that!" I cut in and asked, "Where are we going?" Mahsa told me to the house, I got a ticket for the airport taxi service and called for the girls to come out. They got into the cab as the driver secured the bags to the top of the car and put the last two in the trunk then we headed home.

We got to Mahsa's place and everybody got out. As the driver went to take the suitcases out, I told him to wait until the women got inside. Meetra was uncomfortable with the area and wanted to go inside right away, she asked Mahsa to take her up to the penthouse. Mahsa agreed and said, "I thought you might like it here and you can relax, but it's okay, let's go and then we went to our peathouse." I turned back to the cab driver and instructed him to drop off the bags. I went up to join Mahsa and Meetra. Mahsa asked Meetra, "What would like for lunch?" Meetra said, "Chinese would be good." Mahsa called in the order and asked them to make it extra, extra hot.

The doormen brought up the four suitcases up and left them next to the door; I tipped them and they left. Regarding the suitcases I asked, "Ladies who's is who's?" Mahsa came into the room, "What are you talking about?" I pointed to the collection of suitcases and asked again, "Which suitcases belong to whom?" She laughed, saying, "Poor Chubby, these two are mine and those belong to Meetra."

Mahsa suggested that I show the bedrooms to Meetra and let her pick the one she liked best. I showed her the two extra rooms that she could choose; one was next to our bedroom and the second was on the other side of the living room. When Meetra picked the second room, I suggested, "But the first one is bigger." She agreed, but held firm with her decision, "This one will have more privacy and will be quieter." She grinned and both of us laughed.

I was about to bring her things into her room for her, but she waved me out of the way saying, "I can do this myself." I scolded her gently, "I am the boss here." Meetra relented, and then thanked me. As she unpacked, I asked her if she wanted wooden, plastic or metal hangers. She smiled and said, "I'll take plastic, please." I took out the wooden hangers and replaced them with some good plastic ones from other room and gave them to her.

After finishing with Meetra's luggage, I took Mahsa's suitcases to our room, opened one and started putting her clothes on hangers in the closet. Then I arranged them in the order I knew Mahsa liked best. Mahsa was in the kitchen making coffee and the food arrived. She called me to come for lunch. I called back, "I will be there in a few minutes, just let me finish this first." After I had finished with that suitcase, I went to the kitchen, where she had the food ready. It was so good and hot. Mahsa asked me, "Is it hot enough for you?" "Yes!" I said, "It is very good, I love it."

After lunch she brought out some very good, freshly made Italian coffee, which we took outside to the balcony. I brought out an extra chair that unfortunately took up the rest of the balcony. Meetra and Mahsa took the love seat and I sat on the chair. After coffee, Meetra stood up and told us that she was a little tired and was going to her room to lie down. I said, "Any time you need help with unpacking, I will be happy to help." "O.K." She said, "Thank you!" Meetra went to her room and we also retired to our room. Mahsa opened her other bag, started putting things on hangers and joked, "O.K. now that you have started rearranging my closet, are you going to finish?" I saluted her, grinning, "Yesss Ma'm!" She handed me the hangers so I could put them away, then I arranged her shoes too.

Mahsa then took a closer look at me and observed something, "Hammm, let me see. How long do you plan to be in those clothes?! Are you going somewhere? I stopped short, "No, I am staying here." Crossing her arms, she ordered, "Then go and change out of those clothes! Every time I see you, I have the feeling that you want to leave." Without a word, I changed into my robe. When I came out, Mahsa wrapped her arms around me, saying, "Yes, this is the way it's supposed to be." We cleared off the bed and lay down for a rest.

As we relaxed, Mahsa started kissing me and said, "Do you know how much I missed you? Because I think I know how much you missed me." That fact became quite obvious as she continued massaging my chest, neck and head. Suddenly she turned into a tiger and jumped on me; and began to bite my shoulder, but I loved it! Then she raked her nails lightly across my chest leaving faint red lines. It became a delicious confusion of pain and pleasure that melted into one incredible sensation. All I could do was lie there as her ever-so-willing victim as she had her way with me. She moved her hands down the length of my body and continued down until she reached my feet and proceeded to give me a very nice foot rub.

After that she made her way back up my body and stopped by planting a kiss on my lips. Then she grabbed me by my shoulders, pulled me upright and sat on me as we started to make the most amazing love. Maybe it is difficult for you to believe me that every single time that Mahsa and I made love together, it was a different experience. This time we both got so wild that we ended up leaving scratch marks all over each other's back. But Mahsa did more damage to me because her fingernails left bloody puncture wounds on my skin, but I didn't notice them until afterward. After reaching our climax, we could barely move, because we were sticking to each other as though we had been glued together. It was too much effort to move from that blissful state, so and we fell asleep just like that.

We woke up around seven-thirty that evening, showered; Mahsa went to the kitchen to make coffee and tea while I straightened up in the living room. A short while later, Meetra emerged from her room, came into the living room and sat on the sofa. Mahsa brought out the coffee and sat next to her daughter and I made myself comfortable in the easy chair, enjoying my tea, Mahsa and I both lit cigarettes.

Meetra turned to her mother, "I am so sorry about

yesterday, Mommy when I said you were acting like a teen because everybody was looking at you two. I was just upset when I call for you three times, but you weren't listening. That was when I grabbed your hand again. I am so sorry." Mahsa hugged her and said, "No my baby, don't be sorry. You did the right thing. I *APOLOGIZE FOR GETTING SO CARRIED AWAY.*" They stood up and hugged each other tightly and Mahsa said to me, "You know chubby, Meetra, here, is my safe deposit box, she keeps everything safe for me and knows everything about me. And I try my best to do the same for her."

We went out to balcony for some fresh air and just talked for a good hour. Mahsa then asked us, "Where do you want to go for dinner?" Meetra thought about it for a little while and said, "Somewhere nice, but different from what is in Shiraz." Mahsa and I looked at each other and said at the same time, "Chattanooga!" We knew Meetra would like it there because they had live music. We got there by nine-thirty and were told that we would have to wait about ten to fifteen minutes. At least it was a beautiful night as we stood outside. Mahsa and I lit cigarettes and this time Meetra asked if she could have one too. I looked at Mahsa, who nodded; I gave her one and lit it for her. By the time we finished our cigarettes, they called us for our table. Mahsa ordered white wine on ice and appetizers. Meetra then picked out three different entrees that we could all share.

We enjoyed the appetizers as we waited for our main course. By time our meals arrived, the first bottle of wine was finished, so Mahsa ordered another. This was brought out with our food. The food and wine were fantastic and we had no trouble finishing the second bottle. After dinner I informed Meetra that they have wonderful ice cream, so we each ordered three scoops of different flavors to sample: coffee, apricot and strawberry. The three of us enjoyed the ice cream so much that we ordered six more scoops; two of each flavor. Full of food and wine, we sat back to enjoy our cigarettes, Meetra too. As I called for them to bring the bill, Mahsa passed me her wallet under the table. I hesitated because I knew how much money I had on me. However, when the waiter brought the bill and laid it in front of me, I was shocked to discover that it is so much more than I had with me. Sadly, I opened her wallet, paid the bill and the tip. As we pushed away from the table, two waiters rushed over and moved our chairs back and thanked us for dining with them. I asked their names and promised that we would return soon.

As we walked out to the car, I asked Mahsa, "Are

you okay to drive?" She turned to me sharply, "Are you kidding me?" I was firm, "No I am just asking." Mahsa laughed, "Don't worry Chubby; I won't kill you just yet. It is still the beginning of the road." Then we went home.

When we got home Meetra turned to me, "I had such a nice night, thank you for dinner." She added, "Plus you are so wonderful, Mommy is right to love you that much, because you are good guy." She finished by saying "Good night." I returned, "You're welcome anytime. It was my pleasure." At that point we all went to our rooms and turned in. Mahsa washed up and fell into bed without her robe. I did the same, only taking off my T-shirt and climbed in beside her.

That night was such a special night for us. I said to her in the dark, "Honey Bunch, this is the first night after thirty-three and half days that we have been apart. It is so good to have you back and we are in our own home." Mahsa wrapped her arms around me and said, "You don't know what I went through all of those days we were apart. Maybe tomorrow, I will let you read my dairy. Then you know how I got through it." I kissed her, saying, "The past is past and I thank God that both of you are here with me." Mahsa squeezed me tightly and added, "I missed you so badly I want to squeeze you and bite you sometimes. I just want to hit you so badly and those all come from bottom of my heart."

As she sat on me, I whispered to her, "Tonight will be totally different than any other time. I want you to hold me and take me inside of you. I want you to make hard love to me." I felt like I was losing my breath, "I really need that feeling - to be one with you as we have never felt before. I want it much stronger and more powerful than ever we been together." She started kissing and squeezing me so hard so that I would know that she really meant it. We made love with all of our feeling; and I could feel our love rushing through my blood and deep into the marrow of my bones. We made love nonstop for almost two hours and we both got so lost in each other's pleasure that the passage of time didn't matter much. That night became one of the hottest nights we had up to that point. Then after that we held each other like we each had found something absolutely priceless and went to sleep that way. Our feelings of bliss took us into a beautiful sleep until morning. When we woke up, we were still holding each other in the same way as last night.

We got up and took showers. Mahsa went to the kitchen to make coffee and I put the water on for tea. I set the breakfast table for three this time just as Meetra came out of her room. She was always such a cheerful girl. "Goooooood morning guys!" She announced as she went over to her mother. "Mommy can you make scrambled eggs?" Mahsa smiled, "Sure, why not baby." Then mimicking Meetra for fun, she called out to me, "And what do yoooou want Chubby?" I couldn't help but laugh at those two, "I think I'd like to have the same thing." Mahsa said, "Fine. Scrambled and scrambled." I toasted some bread, put juice on the table and said to Mahsa, "I'm sorry Honey Bunch but we don't have any milk. I can go get some if you want it." But Mahsa said, "No, I will drink juice too. But remember when we go shopping that we need buy all the things we don't have. You might want to start a list before we forget."

After breakfast we went out to the balcony to have our tea and cigarettes. I then asked Meetra, "How do you feel being here with us?" She didn't say anything first but after a few minutes she said carefully, "Well, at first when you two got together, I had very mixed feelings. On one hand you are much younger than my mom and it's almost like you could be her eldest son and I didn't have a good feeling about it. But on the other hand, she is my mom and she has suffered too much for too long and I saw the love in her eyes after that first night. I could never take that away from her because I am girl and I know that I will have those feelings someday, so I understand her love." Taking a deep breath, Meetra continued, "Day after day I see Mom get better, happier and her face gets younger and younger looking. After seeing all that, I always was proud of myself because I was responsible for inviting you to my party. I still don't know way I did that, but I remember when I looked into your eyes for the first time, I saw something that compelled me to ask you to come. Now I know that it must be destiny and nothing else." Meetra looked a little embarrassed as she looked over at me and added; "Now I feel fantastic! I see you two together so much in love. It's just great!" Mahsa leaned over and took her daughter in her arms and kissed her, saying, "No wonder she is my safe deposit box and my life."

Meetra then said to me, "You are the best thing that has happened to us in a long time. And I am so happy about that." I got up to get the teapot to refill everyone's tea and then took it back to the kitchen. That also gave me a little bit of time to wipe the tears from my eyes. Meetra's words really touched me. We sat in silence drinking tea and smoking. This time I give Meetra one too and three of us enjoyed our cigarettes and talked about making plans for the future.

Later that afternoon, the three of us went to City Park and the mall. Meetra bought some items for herself, while Mahsa and I only window shopped. At nine, we stopped for dinner then headed home. By the time we got home, we were tired, especially Meetra. She said "Good night." and went to her room and we went to our room too.

That night Mahsa and I went to bed early as she set her alarm for seven. We wrapped ourselves in each other's arms and held each other tight until morning. The alarm rang dutifully at seven and I was not in a hurry to get out of bed. Mahsa took me to school and promised, "I will pick you up after school."

After lunch, Mahsa and I went to my brother's house. When we got there, she paused and asked, "Is this the house?" I said, "Yes. Let me show you around." As she looked around the place, she said, "It's nice and clean inside, but outside isn't so great." I replied, "Yes, I know. It is what it is because my brother is not home much, only one day a week. Actually he got this place more for me than himself because he often goes to our brother's for that day."

After some thought, Mahsa said, "Then we should be thankful and keep it the way it is, nice and clean." She turned to me, "You now have to start taking responsibility for what is yours. This place is simple, but at least it's clean and it's yours." I tried to speak, "Yes but..." Mahsa cut me off, continuing, "No ifs, ands or buts! That's the way it is." I knew better than to argue as we walked into a traditional style living room. There two twin-sized mattresses on the floor that each had a very big soft pillow leaning against the wall. We sat on one mattress and lay on the other.

We started kissing and making out. It was a fantasy of mine; to make love with her in my house. But she stopped me short, saying, "Yes, this place is yours as much as your brother's. Does he know that you were going to bring me here?" I felt shame creeping over me as I answered her, "No, he doesn't know." Mahsa became stern, "You have to tell him! At the very least you can tell him that you have a girlfriend and that you want to bring her here." I argued weakly, "He knows that I have a girlfriend and I might bring you here." Mahsa shook her beautiful head in flat refusal, "Your girlfriend doesn't feel comfortable to make love here." Sadly, I had to forget about that fantasy of mine for the time being.

We went back to her place to find that Meetra wasn't home yet. We decided to wait for her before having dinner. When she got home, Mahsa asked, "Meetra, did you have dinner?" Meetra shrugged, "Not really, I had something earlier this afternoon." Mahsa decided to call for pizza. I turned to Meetra and said, "Sorry I didn't see you this morning when Mahsa dropped me off at school." Meetra rolled her eyes and glanced over at her mom, "Here you go again!" Then she turned to me and explained, "Mom would take us to school every day and she would pick us up too every day. When we got to university, we begged her to stop because it just wasn't cool anymore. She did stop eventually, little by little. Now she's doing it to you. But for you it might be better to refer to it as the 'office'. Isn't that better Yousef? Ha!" I didn't quite know what to say to that!

We got our pizza and washed it down with soda; that was a real treat for us. After dinner we had tea; the three of us sat out on the balcony and talked for a while. Meetra then said "Good night." and went to her room. Mahsa and I lingered outside a little longer and smoked one last cigarette, then we went retired to our bedroom.

As we lay in bed, I couldn't help feeling that Mahsa was upset about something, but I wasn't sure what it was. I whispered to her, "Sweetie, what is the matter? If there's something wrong, I want to know what it is. I feel like I did something." At first she said, "It is nothing." But I insisted on knowing, so then she told me what I did wrong.

Mahsa took me in her arms, kissed me and gently explained, "Chubby, the way you took me to the house and tried to make love to me wasn't right. I know you were excited to show me your house and you wanted to make love there. Believe me, I love the place. But the way you did it was wrong. You are so bright and you are always aware of my feelings; and for that I love you Chubby. I love you very much!" Shamefully, I confessed, "I really didn't notice anything was wrong until we got home, and then I felt like I couldn't feel you anymore. It was if you cut me off; especially when you were so quiet after we got home." I let out a long breath, "I thought to myself, there is something wrong and I am sure it's because I did something. I didn't want to say anything until we were alone. I thank you for letting me know what I did." Mahsa squeezed me tightly to herself and said, "My Chubby love, how I can be mad at you when I love you so much?" I had to tell you what you did wrong so you won't do that again. Remember, I love you no matter what."

We hugged each other and she kissed me again and again. We just lay together enjoying this intimate time together. When we could no longer keep our eyes open, we smiled and kiss each other. She turned back against me and I slid my hand under her neck and wrapped my other arm around her chest and we stuck to each other as one body and feel to sleep.

That awful alarm clock rang at seven; I dragged myself out of bed and took a shower while Mahsa made coffee. When I got to the kitchen, she asked, "Are you coming back here tonight or will you go to other house? I thought about it and said, "It is best that I go there tonight. There are a lot of things to take care of." She said, "Fine." and went to the bedroom to put on her jeans and T-shirt. When she came back out, she handed me a notebook, saying, "Please guard this with your life or better yet, my life. Be sure to only read about the trip to Shiraz. I think I can trust you to do that." I took it and I knew that was her diary. I promised keep it safe.

She gave me a ride to school and said before dropping me off, "See you alligator!" To that, I replied, "See you and don't let me bite you!" She laughed and drove off. I went off to school; after classes I went to the burger shop for lunch and then headed home. When I got home, I stripped down to my shorts and t-shirt, flopped down on the mattress and opened her diary, finding the section when she returned to Shiraz.

From Mahsa's diary: 'Going Back to Shiraz'

'...When Yousef got out of the cab, it felt like something got up from deep inside of me and left. But I didn't have any choice. I had to go back to Shiraz to see what was wrong with Meetra. I got to airport and boarded the plane; I couldn't help but notice that the seat next to me was empty. As we prepared for takeoff, I could feel him, like he was next to me, holding my hand just like the first time because he was afraid. I kept thinking about how I am stuck between two loves - Him and Meetra and there is no easy way for me to leave either of them alone. When I got home, Mama greeted me at the door and took my suitcase. I went up to my room to change and came back down. She had made me some good Turkish coffee which was exactly what I really needed. Then Mama told me that Yousef had called asking for me. She said he was home and worried about you. I finished my coffee then called him. He sounded so down, his voice was sad and I knew why. So I told him that I would call him every day and that I would be back as soon as possible. We talked for about half an hour. Mama brought me some lunch but I couldn't eat much. To make her happy, I ate some then said that I was going to take a nap.

I got up so late that afternoon and went downstairs to the kitchen. I said hi to Mama and she smiled at me and said, "Hi baby, are you O.K.?" I shrugged, "I am O.K. But what is wrong with Meetra? She didn't tell me much, only that she is little tried. Is that it?" Mama shook her head. I said, "I didn't buy that either. Maybe she doesn't know or she doesn't want to tell me." Mama brought me a cup of tea and I lit a cigarette when Meetra came in. She ran up to me and hugged me so tight, saying, "I missed you so much!" I said, "I missed you too baby! How is everything?" She looked at me, "Everything is O.K. There is nothing to worry about." We sat down and talked all the way through dinner. Around eleven, she told me that she was a little tired. Meetra kissed me good-night and went to her room. After all that, I still couldn't get anything out of her. My God she is just like me!

I went to my room, took two sleeping pills and climbed into bed. I fell asleep in on time. When I got up the next morning, I felt much better. I went down to the kitchen and said good morning to Mama. She is always so worried about me. She said, "Hi baby, you look much better this morning. Did you have a good sleep last night?" "Yes." I said, "Thanks to the pills, I was dead tired, but I feel good now." Mama then brought me a glass of milk and some coffee and started making breakfast. Meetra came in and sat down next to me and rested her head on my shoulder; something she had never done before. I just thought that it was because she missed me. Mama brought her juice and breakfast and sat down *with us. After breakfast, I lit a cigarette. That was when Meetra again put her head on my shoulder and started to cry. I held her and tried to comfort her, "I am here baby! What is wrong?" This time, she told me everything. I got so upset and although I didn't mean to, I shouted at her, "Meetra! Why you didn't call me about this?" I told Mama to bring the phone to me right away.*

I start calling every doctor I knew for appointments as soon as possible. One was able to see us that afternoon. I hugged Meetra again and tried to reassure her, "It's probably nothing my baby. Everything is going to be O.K. Try not to worry." Only God knew what I was thinking inside and how I felt; I was so afraid. I took her to the appointment that afternoon and the lady doctor examined her very carefully and then wrote down what tests Meetra would need to have done. The doctor told me, "Try not to worry, but if it is what I think Meetra will need to have surgery. It might be a tricky procedure, but her prognosis is good."

When we got home, I called a friend who was also a doctor to make appointment with her as well. I wanted a second opinion, plain and simple. After I explained the results of our previous appointment, she snapped, "Just shut up and bring her over here right now!" As soon as we got there, she took Meetra inside for an examination and then performed all the tests that were needed. She took me aside and said, "The doctor you saw earlier is excellent, but it is always best to get a second opinion and even a third to be hundred percent sure." She informed us that all the test results should be ready the next day. "I will push to get them as quickly as I can." She promised.

It was already eight o'clock by the time we got home again and Meetra was exhausted. Mama brought out dinner and immediately after, Meetra excused herself and went to her room to rest. I thought about calling Yousef, but was not in any condition to talk because he would know that something was wrong and I didn't want him to start worrying as well. But I missed him so much and really wanted him here with me now, but knew that wasn't possible. Around eleven, I went to my room and lit one last cigarette I thought how he would always light my cigarettes for me. I finished my smoke and laid down on his side of the bed, I caught his scent on the pillow. I wrapped my arms around the pillow and inhaled, thinking that if he was here he could help me or at least be here for me. So that night I slept with his pillow right next to my heart.

I got up early the next morning, had breakfast and called my friend to see when the test results would be ready; she told me to check back around noon. I had a smoke, then went up and got dressed. I had to get out of the house; I just couldn't sit at home and wait around. I got to her office at noon and the results were ready. I paid *the bill, thanked my friend and went in to wait for the specialist. I waited for over half an hour, barely being able to keep myself calm. Finally, she called me in and asked if I had the paperwork, which I handed to her. She looked over the results for a long time before she spoke, "It looks like your daughter has a small growth on one of her ovaries, I don't think it is serious, but it will need to be removed. Unfortunately, the procedure is a bit invasive and she will need some time to recover, but in the end, she should be okay." The specialist continued, "I am going to schedule the operation, but in the meantime, I am going to prescribe some antibiotics for her to start on right away." We talked for a while longer as I wanted to make sure I was perfectly clear on all the details.*

I arrived home around two-thirty, and found Meetra in the kitchen eating lunch I sat down and told her everything and she seemed to relax a little. Mama brought me a glass of juice, followed by some lunch, which I couldn't really eat much of because I was so tired. After pushing away my food, Mama brought me some hot tea, which was exactly what I needed. I lit a cigarette and Mama frowned at me, saying, "Baby you smoke too much. You must stop now!" I was too tired to argue with her, so I just nodded and said "O.K. Mama I will." At that point, both Meetra and I went to our rooms for a nap.

It was well after sunset when I went downstairs. Meetra

had come down with her guitar. We went out on the balcony and Mama brought me some coffee and she sat down as well. Meetra played and sang a couple songs for us. She turned to Mama and asked if she could have a coffee as well. Mama jumped up and got Meetra a cup and fresh cups for me and herself. We drank coffee while Meetra continued to play. It was wonderful to see her in such a good mood tonight and I was so happy for her! Yes my dear diary, who can I tell these things to, except you? Oh my dear, it is getting so late and I am exhausted, but I needed to tell you everything from today, because you are the only one I have here with me. Good night my dear, I love you and will talk to you next time.

Time passed so slowly for me in two aspects, on one side, Meetra's next doctor's appointment was next week and another one after that. I couldn't really do much or go anywhere because of Meetra's situation. I knew that there was no way I could get back to Tehran now. On the other hand, I missed Yousef so much and I knew that he must be lonely too. I felt so badly that he really doesn't have anybody to talk to and I don't know if he has anything to put his thoughts into, like you dear diary.

Yes, my dear diary, Meetra's next doctor's appointment is tomorrow. We need to see what the second doctor will say. As you know, I didn't go out that much last week.

Yes my dear, the only times I was really O.K. was when I spoke with Yousef. We try to talk to each other every day or at least every other day for about a half hour. My dear diary, he is a lot like you; he is the only one I can really talk to and if I need to cry, he always gives his support no matter how far away he is. Yousef is the only one who has ever been able to know what I am feeling, it's like he can sense everything going on just from the tone of my voice. I don't know how he does that. He is also the only one who can give me the energy to fight my problems. Yes my dear, you are the only one I can tell these things.

We went to see the doctor and I give him all the paperwork. He examined Meetra very carefully for more than forty-five minutes. When he was finished, he advised that we go ahead with the surgery as soon as possible, like tomorrow. "I can clear my schedule for the procedure myself." I hesitated and said, "But we still have to wait for the third doctor to see her." He shrugged and said, "That is completely up to you, but from what I see, the sooner she has the procedure, the better." I didn't know what to say, so I told him that we would think about it and let him know as soon as possible. When we got home, I could tell that Meetra was feeling very down. I tried to reassure her by saying, "Please don't worry; I don't think it is as bad as he said. Please, try to relax, come and have some dinner. You need to eat something." We sat down for dinner and ate in silence. After dinner,

Meetra excused herself and went up to her room. I let her be for a while and after I smoked a cigarette, I went up her room and knocked softly. When I opened the door, I found her lying on the bed, quietly crying. I took my sobbing daughter in my arms, rocking her like a baby. Kissing her, I said, "Oh my poor baby, I know that this is scary, but everything will be O.K. I promise you." Meetra put her arms around my neck, buried her head in my shoulder, and cried even harder, "I don't want to die mommy!" That was when I lost it. I couldn't control myself any longer and I started crying too as we held each other. All I could say over and over, promising not only her, but myself as well, "My daughter, you not going to die and this is my promise!" I stayed with her until she fell asleep and then I went into my room to you, my dear diary. Now we have to wait for the next doctor's appointment. Just the stress of all this alone is sure to kill myself and Meetra both.

Yes dear diary now is time for the last doctor. I hope he has good news for us. I have to go now and will talk to you later.

The third doctor looked at all the previous examinations and test results first, and then examined her very carefully. His findings were similar to those of the first doctor we saw. "It's not that serious, but I recommend one more scan. I want to see if there is a difference in these three weeks." He added, "Continue taking those pills for now." I called my friend from the office to find out about the scan. She suggested that we stop by her office that day. After our discussion on all the tests, she recommended that we schedule the scan for Saturday. We got home and Meetra seemed to be in much better spirits. We decided to stay home for the rest of the day. Yes my dear, I talked to Yousef earlier this afternoon, before I took a nap. He sent me energy, spirit and power to fight all these things. We talked for more than an hour because I really needed to hear his voice.

Friday we stayed home and tried to enjoy ourselves. For lunch Mama made barbeque in the back yard, for the three of us. It was a beautiful day to be outside and we had such a good time. Bright and early on Saturday morning I called the doctor's office, but nobody was there yet. I ate some breakfast and took Meetra for the scan. When it was ready, my friend gave it to me and we went to see the third doctor. We waited almost two hours before he saw us. He compared the new scan to the earlier on and discovered that the size of the growth had increased slightly. He advised us to act very soon to reduce further complications. I thanked him and went back to the first doctor who was my friend who told me the same thing. We headed home and by the time we arrived, I was so thirsty, I begged Mama to give me some ice water. That is what Yousef would always ask for when he would arrive. Then I called the travel agency for two tickets to Tehran. The next available flight was on

Thursday. I got them without any hesitation. Then I called Yousef and told him that we were coming to Tehran. My dear diary, I wish you could have heard his voice; it was so full of love and happiness!

My dear diary, I am writing to you on board the airplane and we are getting ready to leave. I am very sure he will be there waiting for us. I am so very excited to see him and see what going to happen next; I do not know what, but I am very sure will be amazing. I hope talk to you later...'

After I read those entries, I closed the notebook and read no further as I had promised her. I started to cry until my sobs became louder and louder. I wailed like a lost frightened child; I couldn't help myself. (I also have to mention, how I cried again as I did on that day, while I was typing this part and from time to time, I had to stop typing because I couldn't see through my tears. Yet all those feelings came rushing back to me even after thirty-four years. I find that amazing.) Suddenly the phone rang; it took me some time to regain my composure before I could answer it. After about four rings, I was able pick up. It was my sister, who was very upset with me. "Where the Hell has you been?" She demanded, "We have been calling and even came to your place. But nobody was home." I took a deep breath and said, "I have been busy, but

I will stop by there tonight." Her temper cooled a little and she only said, "Then come early." "O.K." I replied meekly, "I will see you in a little while." She let out an exasperated sigh and hung up.

Despite the confrontation with my sister, my mind immediately went back to Mahsa as I reflected on all that she had been through. My tears started again and it took me little while longer to be O.K. I then picked up the phone and called her. As soon as I heard her sweet voice I lost control of myself all over again and started sobbing aloud. Again I struggled to get a hold of myself and was finally able to speak. My voice was still shaking as I said, "Oh my sweetie! I am so sorry that I couldn't be with you when you really needed me!" She sent kisses to me over the phone and asked, "Did you read everything like I asked?" I sniffled, "Yes my dear, my sweetheart. I read it as soon as I came home and just finished. My goodness what you have gone through and again I am truly sorry I couldn't be there for you. But what I don't understand is why you didn't tell me anything? Please know that I am 100% yours." Mahsa smiled at me over the phone and said, "I know my Chubby. I know you are with me. You don't need to tell me."

Mahsa asked me where I was and I told her that I

was at home; she asked if I wanted her to pick me up and bring me back to her place. Sadly, I told her no, "I would love to, but my sister is so mad at me because I haven't been around for the last three days and I didn't call." I sighed, "I have to go there tonight." She then suggested, "I can pick you up at our usual place across from the burger shop, tomorrow around one-thirty. I brightened up at the thought of seeing her, "O.K!" I then asked about Meetra and she updated me, "Today we went to see another doctor, one who my friend from Shiraz recommended; he scheduled the surgery for next week because we have to do this as soon as possible. Everything is in order. I asked, "How is she doing? Is she okay with the plan and is she getting enough rest?" Mahsa thanked me and said, "Yes, Meetra is O.K." We talked for more than half an hour, then we kissed each other and hung up.

I headed over to my sister's, joined them for dinner and stayed for about three or four hours. All the while, she kept trying to get information out of me, anything that would give her a clue about what I have been up to. I kept the conversation light without giving away anything important. I couldn't tell her that I had a girlfriend. If she found out, she would definitely want to know who she was and to meet her. Then everything Mahsa and I had kept secret for so long would be lost. So I had to lie because I didn't have any other choice

I got home around eleven, took my clothes off and lay down on the one mattress that Mahsa and I had made out on a couple of days ago. I thought back on the comment she made about this mattress, "It feels like goose down..." and I smiled at the thought because that's what it really did feel like. I was in the middle of my lovely fantasy, when suddenly, the phone rang. I jumped at the sound and picked up. It was her! Mahsa sang out, "Hiiii Chubby!" I sang back, "Hiiii Honey Bunch!" She then asked, "Where are you?" I shrugged, "I am home." Mahsa retorted, "I know that, you retard! I mean where you are in the house?" I laughed, "Oh, I am lying on that mattress you said feels like goose down; I see what you mean." In turn, I asked, "Where are you?" She replied wickedly, "In our bedroom and I still smell you here - lucky me." We talked about today, the things she and Meetra did and where they went. All of a sudden, Mahsa's tone changed, "Why are still you awake at this hour anyway? You know you have school tomorrow don't you?" I groaned, "Yes, don't worry; I will wake up in time for school." Her parental tone continued, "Okay then, good night, stay in bed and go to sleep right away, I will give you a wake-up call tomorrow." She kissed me and hung up. I thought she was kidding, but at seven o'clock in the morning, I found out she wasn't. The phone rang and woke me up; we talked for a few minutes until she was sure that was I awake then she said, "See you later alligator!"

I went to school or as Meetra said 'my office' and when classes let out at one-thirty, I hurried to our meeting place and met her there. She then suggested that we have something for lunch. I motioned to the burger joint across the street, "They have good food, would you want that?" She shrugged, "Sure, let's try it and see." I went over and I when I got in, the place was packed. I ordered two burgers, one order of fries, one (Doogh) yogurt drink and a Coke. I paid the bill and was given an order number. After several minutes, they called my number and give me everything on a plastic tray. I took it over to the car and Mahsa had already made space for everything. We shared our drinks and the fries and Mahsa agreed that it was a good lunch. I returned the tray to the burger and when I returned, she asked, "Where do you want to go from here?" "I'm not sure." I replied, "Just somewhere nice and quiet please."

She headed down some side streets, but I drifted off to sleep. I heard her voice followed by a kiss, "Wake up Chubby, we are here." I opened my eyes and apologized, "I'm sorry I fell asleep, I guess I was tired." She gave me a sweet smile, "Don't be sorry, it is okay. Now you are fresh so you can fully enjoy this." I took a look around and the place was bursting with flowers and other plants. My sweet God! What a beautiful place she had brought me to. It was so perfectly beautiful; I couldn't imagine Heaven being anything like this. I opened the trunk and took out a big picnic blanket and laid it on the ground in a small clearing that was surrounded by flowers. We sat down on the blanket and Mahsa rested her head on my shoulder. I then asked if she might like to lay her head in my lap, so that way I could look at her. She made herself comfortable as I stroked her wavy auburn hair and massaged her head and neck. From time to time I bent down to kiss her, savoring the sweetness of her lips. I lay down next to her, we held each other close and kissed. After a while, we broke the silence and started talking. Mahsa asked me about yesterday and how I felt after I finished reading her diary. My emotions came flooding back as I told her all about it. She squeezed me again and said, "We did not make a mistake! Did we? I shook my head, "No, we didn't. We are like twin souls and that's a perfect way to be."

I held her close to my heart. "I really missed you last night when I went to sleep. I fell asleep with your voice in my ear and then woke up to the sound of your voice. It felt so good to go to sleep feeling your love and to be awakened by it too. What could be better than that?"

We spent the rest of that glorious afternoon in the midst of nature's beauty and then headed home. But as soon as we got in, Meetra came running out, looking upset. She glared at her mother, "I thought you were just supposed to pick him up. But you were gone all these hours, what happened to you guys?" I offered an explanation, "My sweetie, it was completely my fault, not hers. I will tell you later." I hated to see Meetra upset, with all that she was going through. I asked her, "When did you get home?" She frowned, "Almost two hours ago. When you didn't show up, I got very worried for you two. I guess I was wrong, but………….." Her voice trailed off.

I then asked, "Meetra, would you like some hot tea?" She brightened a little, "I would love some." I went to the kitchen and put water on to boil, then went to change my clothes. Mahsa caught up with me in the bedroom and playfully punched my arm, "You son of a gun! You didn't ask me if I wanted any tea!" I grinned at her, "I already know what you like but O.K. from now on I will be sure to ask you too. Will that be O.K.?" She hissed at me, "Yesss my Chubby, that would be very good."

I made tea and brought it to the living room. The three of us sat down for tea and cigarettes. I give a cigarette to Meetra and we started talking about all kinds of different things. Then Mahsa asked, "What are we going to have for dinner tonight?" I suggested, "One day we will have to go shopping for food so I can make dinner for you sometime." Both women looked delighted at that idea and Mahsa said, "O.K. the first chance we get, we will definitely go to the store and buy whatever you need. But what do you guys want for tonight?" Meetra suggested something nice and light. I agreed, "Good idea, how about that Italian sandwich shop?" Mahsa found the number and ordered three different kinds of sandwiches for us to share.

The sandwiches arrived a half hour later, and we cut each one in half and relished the different combinations. After dinner, we had tea. It was almost eleven, when Meetra said good night and went to her room. Mahsa and I lingered a little while longer, then headed to our room, washed up and went to bed.

As soon as we both had gotten comfortable, Mahsa wrapped her arms around me, gave me a kiss and said, "Chubby, I won't be able see you for the next two or three days because I have to take Meetra for

BE HIDDEN LOVE

some final tests and other things doctor has requested. I will see you as soon as we finish all this." My spirits sank, but I kissed her, saying, "Don't rush this on my account, take your time with her. I will call you in the evening. Please don't worry about me, I am here for you and anything I can do, you know that you can count on me." She snuggled against me, "Yes I know that. Thank you and I will let you know if I need any kind of help. But that's not the reason, if you can or you can't It's just that I really don't know how much you can really handle yet." I squeezed her tight and said, "This is called love and trust. I love you so much my Honey Bunch. My capacity for handling things might be very limited, but I know a lot of people who might be helpful. And through them, my dear, my capacity is unknown."

As we held each other, it just didn't seem powerful enough. We both needed something much stronger. Slowly and tenderly, we began making love, but we still felt like we needed something more. Collectively we threw our passions together and made love not only as one body, but one soul as well. This got us so hot and we soared out of this world! I cannot fully explain how we felt, so I definitely leave it to your imagination.

Yes, that is how we got what we both were craving

for. Our bodies were so very hot that we burned together as a single flame. We were also both sweating like hell, but we couldn't stop until we exploded into each other in a firestorm of ecstasy. We lay together basking in the afterglow in a tangle of arms, legs and torsos, just holding each other for a while longer. Then Mahsa rolled to her side and rested her face on my chest and with an arm flung around my shoulder. I slid my arm under her shoulder and with my other hand I gave her a nice little massage on her back. We sweetly fell asleep like that until at seven o'clock, that damned alarm clock rang out. Mahsa awoke first as always and proceeded to wake me with a light massage with those beautiful hands. From far away in my dreams, I heard her sweet voice calling me, "Chubby, Chubby…." When that didn't work, she then kissed me awake. What a wonderful way to wake up and give me energy for the whole day.

I finally got out of bed, took a shower and she greeted me with coffee, I hope you know how it feels when your love cares about you that much. We had our coffee together and then she gave me a ride to school. On the way, she kept stopping the car so we could kiss some more. This went on and on, until she ordered me to get out of the car, "You are going to be late!" But I didn't care if I was a few minutes late, but Mahsa cared.

BE HIDDEN LOVE

After school, I went to my sister's for lunch and she was so happy to see me. She is a little like my mom as she helped raise me when I was little.

I hung out at her house until about seven, then headed home to study the lessons they taught us that day. Around eleven, I called Mahsa and was surprised at how fast she picked up the phone. I don't know how long we spent talking to each other but before too long, we kissed each other and as always, said to each other, 'See you later alligator.' She warned, "Don't let me bite you!" and hung up. I closed my books and lay on that mattress and tried to feel her through the dark. The next thing I remembered was the simultaneous ringing of the alarm clock and the phone. Mahsa asked, "Are you awake?" Rubbing my eyes, I answered, "Yes, I'm awake." She talked to me for a few minutes to make sure that I was indeed awake and out of bed.

After school, I went back home and laid on the mattress for a nap. When I awoke, I flipped open my books to study. I mainly concentrated on the subjects I liked best and left the others for another time, when perhaps I would be in a better mood for them. The week passed quickly and Mahsa and I talked by phone until Thursday when she told me that she would pick me up from school. I left a note for my brother, telling him that I would not be coming home that night and that I would see him the next day. Then I headed off to school. When Mahsa picked me up that afternoon, I asked her if we could go back to that beautiful place even just for an hour. She nodded, "Sure, but we can't stay long, we have to get home because Meetra is there waiting for us." I said, "Fine, even just a little time here will be enough for me." We stayed for less than an hour, but that was enough to lift my mood and I could just relax. We headed home and she drove really fast to get home as soon as we could. But as soon as we got in, Meetra was waiting and upset, "You were just supposed to pick him up!" She pouted, "What happened now?" I patiently explained that it was my fault again, that I had to stop somewhere and take care of something last minute. Meetra continued to sulk, "I'm sorry." I said again. Then she asked, "Do you guys have any plans for tonight?" Mahsa and I looked at each other, "No not really." Meetra was surprised, "What do you mean you don't have plans? It's Friday, you 'lovey' guys must have plans for a Friday night! Well, if you don't, then I made plans for all of us. Now go and make yourselves ready for a really good party." She looked radiant in her excitement. "I am going to take you two to a very nice place tonight. And don't bother to ask where, it's a surprise." I just looked helplessly at Mahsa, who said, "Meetra, you probably didn't know that this 'kiddy' doesn't like surprises." She jerked her head in my direction. Meetra looked so disappointed, "No, but if I tell you, would you still be surprised?" I walked up to Mahsa and put my hand on her arm, "Let it be. If she wants to surprise us, then it's all good. I hope we all have fun there.

We took showers; Mahsa fixed my hair and then started on her own. As she put on her makeup, I told her that I was going to make some tea and that she should have tea before putting on her dress and she agreed. As I went out to the kitchen, I called Meetra and told her as well that I would be making tea.

I brought the tea out to the balcony and lit a cigarette. Shortly after, mother and daughter joined me. As we settled down for tea, I looked up and noticed Mahsa. M y sweet Jesus! She had become a totally different person with that makeup. She also looked so much younger maybe twenty-six or seven tops. I tapped Meetra on the shoulder, "Did you see your mother?" Meetra didn't answer me, but she turned to look at Mahsa then said very loudly the exact same words I had just thought, "My sweet Jesus! Mommy, what did you do?" Mahsa looked at little embarrassed, "Nothing, just a little makeup." Meetra laughed, "Oh mom, you look beautiful!" Then she threw a playful glance at me and added, "Can you do something about him? I think he too might need a touch of makeup just for tonight!" and they laughed together. I couldn't help but feeling a natural blush rushing to my cheeks.

We finished our tea; Meetra went to her room to change and we did the same. Mahsa instructed me to wear a black suit with the fine silk yellow and red tie that she bought for me; I also put on the cologne. I was ready, so I left the room to get out of her way while she finished getting ready. I went back to the living room, had more tea and smoked a cigarette until Mahsa was done.

My Holy God! Mahsa was absolutely gorgeous; she took my breath away. I never saw her dressed up like this before. She was wearing this amazing slinky and long black dress that sported a daring neckline and an open back. She wore a gorgeous necklace with matching earrings that looked something like one of those glamorous actresses would wear to the Oscars. Mahsa could hold her own among those beautiful actresses.

I just stood there, struck speechless when Meetra emerged from her room. Oh my Lord! She too looked so beautiful that night. And when the two women stood together, Meetra was a little shorter and thinner than Mahsa. But standing side by side in this fashion, you would not think them to be mother and daughter, but instead, older and younger sisters! All I could do was just stare at these two beauties, dumbfounded with my eyes wide open - not blinking at all.

Then Mahsa called to me "Hey, Chubby! Where are you?" I snapped back to reality, "I am here, but I don't know what to say about you two! The only thing I can say is that you both are absolutely beautiful." Mahsa beamed at me, "Thank you. I could see it in your eyes; you didn't need to say anything my sweet Chubby."

Mahsa motioned for me to with her, "Just let me put something on your face. Don't worry, no one will even notice." When we rejoined Meetra in the living room, she was pleased with what Mahsa had done to me. I was transformed into a more mature, dashing looking version of myself. I asked if they would like another cup of tea. Both said yes so I brought them more tea. We finished our tea and smoked cigarettes, and as the ladies got ready to leave, I turned off the stove and we headed out.

We paraded down to the lobby and because we were so well dressed, it caused a bit of a stir. As we got into the car, I suggested that Meetra sit in the front because she knew where we were going. Meetra directed Mahsa on where to go; turn right, now left, okay, now turn right and another left. From the back seat, I asked, "Where are we going? We are almost in the mountains!" Meetra shushed me, "We are very close to their home." Finally Meetra said triumphantly, "This is it, turn right here." Mahsa turned onto the driveway which was not even paved and it took us four minutes to get to the building. We were relieved to discover that they had valet parking. Once inside, Meetra found her friend; they hugged each other as Meetra said, "Happy birthday!" As Meetra introduced us to her friend, a guy came up and hugged her. Meetra looked delighted, "Happy birthday!" she told him. Catching our confused glances, she introduced him as well, saying that he and the girl were twins. She then took us to their folks. As soon as they saw Meetra they greeted her warmly with hugs and kisses. Meetra motioned at us with a delicate gesture of he hand, "This is my mom, Mahsa and my stepfather, Yousef." I was shocked and just stood there, utterly speechless. Mahsa poked me in the back and I quickly recovered my wits. I shook hands with them, saying, "It's nice to meet you and thank you for inviting us." We were then showed into the main party room where other guests were seated at small cocktail tables. The three of us went in and found a table.

As we took our seats, Mahsa hissed at Meetra, "What the hell did you do that for?" Do you know that Yousef damned near passed out before I hit him on the back? He just stood there in shock, while the family was waiting to shake his hand!" You should really tell us about these things before you say anything to anyone." Now Meetra was exasperated, "Well, what did you want me to say? That he's your boyfriend? I thought that stepfather sounded much better." She then looked at me and said, "Don't you agree? You are that aren't you?"

The tension broke and the three of us burst out laughing. Catching my breath, I told Meetra, "I am delighted and would feel honored to be your stepfather." I jerked my head at Mahsa, "That's if she will let me." Mahsa rolled her eyes and exclaimed, "Oh, shuuut up!"

Meetra's girlfriend came to our table and asked, "Why are you sitting here by yourselves? Please let me show you around. She walked us to the ballroom and pointed out the bar and then politely excused herself to attend to other guest. We made a beeline for the bar. Meetra and Mahsa ordered white wine while I ordered a double Scotch. We went back to our table and I made sure to drink my

Scotch very slowly, but I needed to warm up especially after the bomb Meetra just dropped on me. Oh it tasted so good and I really needed that drink! I noticed that Mahsa did too by the way her hand shook slightly. After about twenty minutes, I asked Mahsa if she would like to dance. She playfully snubbed me saying, "I am sorry, but I am waiting for my husband. Thank you, but no thanks." I could feel the heat returning to my face, but I decided to play her game. I leaned over and whispered in her ear, "Hey there, Honey Bunch, would you like dance?" At that she beamed at me and said, "I would love to!" I took her hand, kissed it and led her out onto the dance floor. As we moved together, I asked her, "So how is the married life, is it good?" She replied sweetly, "It is wonderful and couldn't be any better than this!" I kissed her between dances and she wrapped her arms around me and kissed me back so wonderfully. We danced three songs. We then went back to our table where Meetra was sitting by herself. I asked her, "Why aren't you dancing?" She shrugged, "I don't really know anybody here." Then Mahsa said, "Yousef why don't you dance with Meetra?" I held out my hand to her, but Meetra hesitated, "Not this song, I will let you know when it is my song. Besides, you owe me a dance from my birthday don't you? I agreed, "Yes my dear, I do owe you a dance."

After about ten minutes, the music changed and Meetra jumped up and said, "This is my song! Let's go!" She practically pulled me on the dance floor. I went with her, but suddenly this awful feeling washed over me, I couldn't explain it. So I shook it off and we started dancing to a rock 'n' roll tune that I believed to be an Elvis song. Meetra and I danced a couple more songs until I had to stop; "It is too hot! Let's take a break." She looked a little disappointed, but I promised her hat I would come back for some more. We left the ballroom and I went to the bar to get a glass of ice water to help me cool down. I went back to our table and Meetra smiled at me, saying, "Thank you for the dance." I smiled back at her, "You're welcome, any time." From across the room, she saw her friend and went over to join her. Mahsa leaned over to me, "I am so proud of you tonight. I am really proud!" I looked at her, "Why, what happened?" "I watched you two dancing together. You did very well. But it was also the way you danced with her that amazed me. You danced like two close friends, or." She paused for effect, "More like father and daughter." I shook my head and laughed, the heat coming back to my face again. "You son of a gun! Do you want to see my feelings for her?" Now I paused, uncertain, "What *did* you see?" It was Mahsa's turn to laugh, "I saw such love and tenderness. The exact feelings a father and daughter share. Seeing that makes me so much prouder than ever. And I do love you to death my Chubby love!" She kissed me and repeated herself so it would sink into my thick head, "I love you, Chubby. You just don't know how much."

Meetra rejoined us and we sat talking to each other, when a man came out and opened a set of very big doors and announced, "Everybody please come in, dinner is served." We filed into the banquet hall along with the other guests. Oh my God! What a table stood before us; almost eighteen to twenty feet long and there was every kind of food imaginable on it. French, Italian, American, Iranian, not to mention foods I have never seen before. I had never seen a table setting like that before. Next to me, I heard Mahsa exhale in amazement, "This is too much! I've never seen a table that large with so much food ever for this kind of party." She added, "Yousef, be sure to get some of that white meat of the turkey, you will really like it." Each of us loaded our plates with whatever we wanted then we went back to our table and sat down to enjoy the feast, while two waiters crisscrossed the room, serving drinks.

As we ate, Meetra explained that this was the twins' twenty-first birthday and that's why the party was so elaborate. I said, "I see; it's no wonder then." And kept eating.

Later that evening, the twins cut into an enormous two-level cake that looked very much like a wedding cake. The cake was served by the wait staff with coffee. I whispered in Mahsa ear, "No coffee can ever be as good as what you and Mama make!" She smiled and whispered back, "That's so sweet of you, but this coffee is good too." I shook my head, "It is good, but it is not as good as yours, no way."

Mahsa, Meetra and I found ourselves partied out around one-thirty. We said good night to the twins and their folks and headed home. We were tired, especially poor Meetra; you could see it on her face. She went straight to her room as soon as we got in. Mahsa and I went to our room too and got ready for bed.

As we lay in bed, Mahsa propped herself on one elbow to gaze at me. There was some light from outside that gave the room a soft, romantic look and was bright enough that we could see each other. My eyes met hers. We lost ourselves in each other's eyes and moments ticked by like years as we lay without moving or speaking. Mahsa broke the spell by reaching out to touch my shoulder, and pulled me toward her. We squeezed each other tightly and it felt so good. I kissed her tenderly and that's when she said, "I would like us to make love the traditional way - face to face, eye to eye. Her wish was my command. We started slowly, tantalizing each other with kisses and caresses, moving up and down each other's bodies, loving every inch of each other. Passion built steadily like a bonfire until we could no longer resist the heat. We burned together until passion's embers were completely spent. We lay together as sleep overtook us, when she turned to lie against me and I held her close until morning.

I awoke to the sound of her sweet voice, "Hiiii honey! You must get up and do your stuff." We snuggled together and made out as if we both were a couple of teenagers, hugging and kissing. Okay, I am still a teenager, but I seemed to bring out the teenager in Mahsa! She lounged in bed and I couldn't help but notice that she was still tired. So I decided that I would spoil her that morning and let her sleep in. I took a shower and headed to the kitchen to make breakfast. I checked a cookbook for some ideas. I found a recipe for Eggs Benedict, but had to improvise with whatever we had and used toast instead English Muffins.

When everything was ready, I made some fancy designs on the plates and set the table. The

BE HIDDEN LOVE

delicious smell drew everybody out of their rooms and to the breakfast table, where I served them. After breakfast we took our tea to the living room to drink and smoke. After breakfast, or more like brunch, Meetra went back to her room; I cleaned up and left the house around five.

When I got back to my place, my second eldest brother was home. We said hi to each other and talked for a few minutes. He said, "Yousef, I'm sorry that I couldn't see you at all this week, but I promise we will be able to spend some time together next week." He then asked me about school and my classes and if there were any problems with the apartment. I updated him about all those things. He gave me some money for the week and left after a half hour. I couldn't help but feel a little lonely again. I called Mahsa later that night and we talked for more than an hour. That helped me feel a little bit better.

The next morning, I was awakened by her phone call. She playfully scolded me, "My God, are you still asleep? Get up, get up! It is so late, it is seven-thirty already. I thought you would already be gone." I tried not to be grumpy and said, "I am up, really. Thank you for waking me, I must have forgotten to set the alarm clock last night." She continued, "Hurry up and I'll talk to you later." I kissed her and hung up, and then I washed up and kind of hurried to school.

Days passed and we just talked by phone, until one day after school, there she was, across the street from the burger shop. I went over to her car and asked her if she would like a burger. Mahsa shook her head no saying, "Just get in please." As I got in, I asked, "What's wrong?" "Tomorrow is the day." Mahsa announced, "I have to take Meetra to the hospital and I want you to come home with me now." I replied, "Then let's go, what are you waiting for?" And we took off.

When we got home, Meetra was lying on the sofa and as soon as we got in, she tried to get up. I went over to her saying, "Please, try to relax. It is just me." Meetra looked shamefaced and apologized, "I'm sorry, Yousef." and lay back on the sofa. I told her, "Please don't be sorry." We went to our room and I put on my pajamas and robe; Mahsa also changed into her robe.

I went to the kitchen and to make tea which I brought to the living room, where Mahsa and Meetra were sitting. I pulled out my cigarettes and I lit one after another and I passed them to the ladies. It was too quiet and tense, so I decided to lighten the mood with some jokes and it wasn't long until I had them both laughing. Mahsa then asked if I would bring them more tea. To that I leapt to my feet, made a bow, saying, "Yeees, but you have to promise me to keep having a good time!" Mahsa laughed, "If you bring the tea, we will be sure to have more fun."

We did have a lot of fun that night. Mahsa then told us a couple of jokes as well. I then winked at her and asked if she might like to tell some 'different' jokes. She looked at me in mock horror, saying, "No it's not proper to say such things!" But Meetra and I insisted and begged to hear them. Finally Mahsa gave in and said, "O.K. just for you two!" She told us a couple raunchy ones when Meetra suddenly exclaimed, "Mommy! Those jokes are so old! I heard them back in high school." Mahsa threw up her hands in surrender. "I guess you kids have all kinds of new jokes now." Meetra replied smugly, "Yes, we do!" and wouldn't say anything more.

The three of us did have a wonderful time and I like to think that it helped Meetra to get her mind of everything that was going to happen the next morning. It was getting late and Meetra said 'goodnight' to us and I promised her that I would be there for her before she goes in for her surgery. She smiled and said, "Thank you." and went to her room. She was supposed to be in bed by ten so she could rest. She was also not allowed to eat anything after four. Mahsa then asked what I wanted to eat. I suggested something light, "Let's see what we have in the refrigerator." I took a look and found some bologna, so I made some sandwiches and that was our dinner. After we cleaned up the kitchen, we went to our room, washed up and went to bed. That night we held each other tightly until morning. As I went off to school, I promised Mahsa that I would be there before Meetra went in for the operation.

I took a cab to school, but what was school for me today? I wasn't there mentally, as all I could think about was poor Meetra going in for her surgery. I spent the day going through the motions until finally escaping for lunch an hour early and got to the hospital as fast as I could.

When I got there, they were in the hallway and Meetra was already on the gurney. I held her hand and said, "We are both here, try not to worry about anything. It will be fine, trust me." All the while, Mahsa was holding my other hand, squeezing it tightly and I knew that I had to take care of her too. The hospital staff arrived and took Meetra inside the operating room. Mahsa and I went to the waiting area, and sat down to wait. Those benches were so uncomfortable! Mahsa rested her head on my shoulder and asked me to pray for Meetra and I promised that I would. We all pray for our loved ones and it does not matter what language you use; what matters most is that the prayers come from your heart. You turn inward and pray and that is exactly what I did.

As we sat in the waiting area, Mahsa buried her face in my shoulder and cried softly. I tried to comfort her saying, "My dear, do not cry, it's not going to do any good for you or her. Try what I just told you to do, but please do not cry." Easier said than done. She kept her head on my shoulder all throughout our long wait. We saw the doctor emerge from the operating room; we hurried toward him. At first he regarded me and then asked Mahsa, "Who is he?" Without hesitation, she said, "He is my husband and Meetra's stepfather." The doctor then told us that the surgery went well and not to worry. "The tumor was not cancerous, our tests proved that." Then he said, "They will take her up to the recovery room and maybe in fifteen minutes, you can see her. But she is not going to be 'with it'. It will take at least an hour before she will be fully awake." He shook our hands and said, "Good luck to you." We waited by the door for them to bring her out. When they did, the doctor was right, she wasn't awake yet, but

Mahsa took her hand and caressed her face, then had to let her go as they took her to recovery. I suggested that we go downstairs to have some coffee, but she refused to move. I gently reminded her that we couldn't do anything now but wait until she woke up. "Let's go then we'll come right back." Mahsa finally agreed. We went down to the cafeteria and had sandwiches and coffee. We ate quickly without tasting our food and went back up to recovery, but Meetra wasn't wake yet. We looked at her lying there lifeless from outside until the nurse called us in. We sat next to her bed; Mahsa took her hand and talked to her. I held Meetra's other hand and told her, "You see? I promised that everything would be fine. You are going to be okay!" As Meetra came to, she smiled at us, but couldn't talk much. She managed a whisper, "I am so sleepy, you guys should go home and I will see you guys tomorrow." That was when Mahsa was satisfied that her little girl would be okay and asked me to take her home. We both kissed Meetra and she went back to sleep. Mahsa had a million questions for the nurse who said, "She did very well in the surgery. The medication that we have been giving her is working. We will take her to her room later. But you both should go home and rest." She smiled at Mahsa's worried face, "The worst is over. Come back tomorrow and she will be much better." I put my arm around

Mahsa to lead her to the exit, but she resisted. I said, "You shouldn't stay, please let me take you home." She wanted so badly to stay but they wouldn't let her and I felt terrible that I was forcing her to come with me. I finally got her to leave and we went home.

As soon as we got home she went to change, but she was still crying, and tried to cover it up as soon as I came into the room. I didn't say anything as I changed into my robe. When I came back out, I saw her sitting on the sofa, still crying. She motioned for me to sit with her. I wrapped my arms around her and kissed her saying, "Crying isn't going to solve any problems." I then started to give her a neck and back massage, she was so tense. Gently, I pulled her shoulders toward me; Mahsa took my hint and laid her head in my lap so I could give her a thorough head massage. She slowly drifted off to sleep but I kept stroking her hair until I was sure that she was deeply asleep. This left me in a situation, I couldn't move without disturbing her, so I smoked a cigarette.

I just sat there smoking and watching her as she slept like a baby. Mahsa looked so peaceful as the worries fell away from her lovely face. I didn't move a muscle; I didn't need to, everything I needed was right there. After about an hour, she opened her eyes, reached up and took hold of my neck, bringing my head down so that my lips met hers. She gave me one of those incredible, unforgettable kisses. Then she asked, "Have you been sitting here all this time?" I smiled and shrugged, "Well I didn't need anything because everything I want has been in my lap. Why would I ever move?" Mahsa sat up, hugged me and kissed me again as we gazed deep into each other's eyes. We didn't need to say anything to each other because we could communicate with our eyes much better than with our lips.

Like a bubble bursting, the spell was broken and we came back to reality. Mahsa got up, rinsed her face and browed some coffee. Filling up the mugs, she suggested that we go out on the balcony. We sat in silence with our coffee and cigarettes. It was such a peaceful evening, Mahsa rested her head on my shoulder and we just enjoyed each other's company.

I was the one to finally break the silence, asking Mahsa, "What do you want for dinner?" Mahsa seemed indifferent, "Whatever you make or order will be fine with me." I looked at her, "No, really what would you like right now?" She just shook her head and said, "Nothing really, just being here with you is enough for me right now." She shut me down with that, so I didn't say anything more. I just continued holding her and stroking her hair as we sat and smoked the occasional cigarette together until late. Mahsa lifted her head from my shoulder and asked, "What time is it?" I checked my watch, "It is past eleven." Mahsa stood up and stretched then asked, "Would you like some scrambled eggs?" She added, "I feel like having scrambled eggs." I replied, "That will be nice. Yes, thank you." She went into the kitchen and I followed her. I offered to help, but she said, "No let me do it Chubby. I love doing this." Instead, I put some bread in the toaster asked, "Do you want tea?" She said, "None for me, but if you want it you can make some for yourself. I thought about it, but changed my mind saying, "No I don't need it either. We ate our egg dinner. Then I washed the dishes and went to the bedroom. By the time I came in, Mahsa was already in bed. I washed up and got in beside her. I put my arms around her, she asked me to hold her closer. As we snuggled, she said again, "I am still cold, please hold me tighter." I held her to me so tightly as she buried her face in my chest and quickly fell asleep. I don't remember much after that, falling asleep myself.

Both of us were awakened by the alarm clock. I got up and took a shower and as usual, Mahsa made coffee. After getting ready, I came to the kitchen for my coffee and a morning smoke. When Mahsa offered me a ride to school, I refused, saying, "You must go to see Meetra right away. I can take a cab." I went to school, but much like the previous day, my mind wasn't with it at all. I left quickly after the last class and stopped at the burger shop because I was starving. I got my usual burger and doogh, but ate quickly so I could grab a cab and head over to the hospital. I went up after I was asked a lot of questions about who I was. When I finally got to Meetra's room, I announced my arrival, "Good afternoon guys!" Mahsa was surprised to see me and asked, "How did you get in?" I winked and replied, "The same way you and Meetra now introduce me to people. I told them that I am her stepfather and they let me in."

Dear Reader: Now I will explain where all of these references to husband and stepfather are coming from. A week after Mahsa and I first met, you will remember that we didn't have any contact for almost a week after that fateful night. When we met again in Táchira we did something very important that I didn't tell you then because it was done in complete secrecy. Now that both Mahsa and Meetra have started referring to me as husband and stepfather, it is important that you know exactly what happened in Táchira. Yes, it after that night in Táchira, that Mahsa and I decided to get married, for ourselves. In Islam, you don't need necessarily be a member of the clergy, or a so-called license for a wedding ceremony. It can be done by yourselves and only requires you to read a specific paragraph out of the Qur'an to each other as soon as you both agree to be each other's spouse. This is a marriage between your two souls and recognized by God. You write down your vows to each other on paper and have four witnesses sign it. Nobody can do anything to stop it, but it is not legally binding until it is registered. Mahsa and I however didn't register our marriage because of the millions of reasons that will become clearer throughout this book. That's why at this point; Mahsa has started calling me husband and Meetra referring to me as her stepfather.

Both women laughed, saying, "You son of a gun, you are doing it now as well!" I gave Meetra a fake frown, "You started it!" And we laughed together. I looked over at Mahsa and yes she was okay now. She returned to being the same old Mahsa and I was very happy for her. I was happy for all of us because we were going to get our lives back to normal again. I asked Mahsa, "Have you eaten anything yet?" She said no. I then ordered her to go and get something to eat. As soon as she left the room Meetra confided in me, "Please take her home. She has been here since eight this morning. I know she hasn't eaten anything and she is tired. I know that you are the only one who can do something with her." I promised Meetra that I would take care of her mother.

Twenty minutes later, Mahsa returned and we stayed for a while longer. Then I suggested to Mahsa that we should go. She said, "It's okay, Yousef, you go and I will be home later." But I stood firm, keeping my promise to Meetra, "No we have to go together. You can spend another half an hour, but Meetra needs to rest and you are tired too." I waited patiently until finally, I was able to get Mahsa out of there and home.

As soon as we got home, she took off her shoes and dumped herself on the bed and was asleep in no time. I changed clothes quietly so as not to disturb her, went to the kitchen and made tea. With my nice big glass of tea, I headed for the balcony to smoke. I just sat, alone with my thoughts and admired the view of the mountains. I didn't pay attention to how the time flew by. It wasn't until Mahsa called for me from the bedroom, that I noticed how late it was. Hearing her voice, I went to the bedroom. Mahsa was still in bed, awake and rubbing her eyes. "How long I was out?" she asked sleepily. I looked at my watch and said, "Close to two hours." She sat bolt upright, "You're shitting me!" "No." I said, "You were out for two hours, which means you really needed it." I lay down next to her and kissed her, saying, "When I asked you to do something for me and not be too stubborn. I suggested to you that we should go home. But you thought you could just keep going. I saw it in your eyes that you couldn't go much further." I continued, "You always keep your word, even if it means taking on more than you can handle. I know how much you wanted to stay and push yourself." Mahsa sighed, "You are right, we are so alike; we both are stubborn and maybe that's one of the reasons we understand each other so well. Believe me, nobody else could drag me out of there and take me home, except you. Thank you for doing that." I replied, "You're welcome, don't mention it."

Then she kissed me back and held me tight, saying, "I know God sent you to me and me to you. The only thing I really don't understand is I didn't do anything that great for Him to deserve this." I replied, "It's the same for me too. I was never that good of a person, so I don't know why either. But one thing I am sure of is that we are His children. He always wants what's best for us. But sometimes we don't know what is good or bad for us."

We locked eyes for a moment and Mahsa added, "Whatever this is, we have to be thankful to God for it." I agreed, "I think we are grateful without knowing it." She looked confused, "How is possible that we are thanking God without knowing that we're doing it?" I answered, "It is as simple as this; you love me and I love you. There is no question about that and by thinking about each other all the time that kind of thinking is like praying, which gets offered up to God. Our love by itself is a symbol of God's love." I smiled at her, "So you see, every minute we are thanking God and praying to Him, we are also with Him without knowing it. And as He said, 'We are his children and we share his soul.'"

She squeezed me tighter than ever, kissed me deeper than before and whispered, "How is it possible that you can say these things like you are a fully grown adult? It's hard to remember that you are just barely nineteen years old. I want to know how you do it." She sighed, "I really don't know what to do with you!" I suggested that it might be better that we think about dinner instead, because I was so hungry and knew that she must be hungry too.

Mahsa frowned at my sudden change of topic, "This is what I mean! We were in the middle of an important conversation, when suddenly you are hungry; just like a little kid!" I pouted at her playfully, "Well isn't it fun for me to be both?" She messed my hair and told me to shut up, then she got up.

We went to the living room and she asked me if I was really hungry or just a little hungry. She suggested that if I was a little hungry that I could make some tea and a cheese sandwich. I replied, "Okay, Honey Bunch, I will make tea and cheese sandwiches for us both. That will be fine for me."

We went into the kitchen and I put the water on for tea and she brought out the cheese and bread. She cut tomatoes and cucumber with fresh basil then put those around the cheese and took the plate to the living room. I brewed the tea and toasted the bread and took them to the living room.

For a simple meal, it was delicious. After dinner, we went outside on the balcony with our tea and a pack of cigarettes. As we sat, we noticed that it was a little chilly, so I went inside and got a blanket. I put it around her shoulders and snuggled close to her. Together we took in the peace and quiet; the sky was filled with the diamond twinkling of stars and the moon sailed high as if to meet them. The lights from the street and nearby houses shone pale in comparison to those of the heavens. But together they created an atmosphere of such tranquility that was made even more perfect by the gentle breeze singing in the trees. Mahsa and I sat in complete silence enjoying the natural beauty of the world around us. Nothing mattered in that moment. Our problems and worries melted away by the light of the moon and stars.

After some time had passed, Mahsa shivered, "I am going inside, it is too cold for me. Are you coming in too?" I wasn't cold and it would have made me happy to sit outside all night, "Yes, I'm coming, but I like this breeze. She said, "You can stay then, if you like." "No" I said, "I would much rather be with you." She went to the kitchen to turn everything off for the night. As she turned to go to the bedroom, I said, "Wait, there is something I want to do." I walked over to her, kissed her then picked her up and tried to carry her to bedroom. Laughing, she said, "Yousef, what you doing? I am too heavy!" I replied bravely, "Not heavier than love!" Trying not to struggle, I carried her to the bedroom and laid her on the bed. She then asked, "Would you let me change my clothes?" I answered, "Why we can do that right here can't we?" She tried not to giggle, "Sure we can."

I turned off the light off and the moon peeked in through the window and cast a silver light over the bed as we started undressing each other. We sat opposite each other caressing, kissing and

BE HIDDEN LOVE

breathing in each other's scent. Mahsa pushed me on my back; started kissing my chest and covered my body with hers. As we made love that night she took me to valley overflowing with poppies and other wildflowers. We were making love among those flowers and their smell drove me crazy, this was much better than any opium on earth. That valley was so hot and beautiful, I didn't want to leave but eventually she brought me back to the bedroom where she lay on top of me as we both tried to catch our breath.

After our brief rest, Mahsa started to kiss my neck then moved to lick my ears. She knew that was the most sensitive area where I loved to be touched. In no time, she turned me on again and we started all over for the second time. I held onto her for dear life as we turned and twisted this way and that. When I finally got the upper hand and pulled her beneath me. Oh my God, we got so hot and wild we didn't know what we were doing anymore. We lost all our senses until she wrapped her legs around me and locked her feet behind my back and squeezed me. We climaxed together as she became a wild animal with her cries of passion. As we lay basking in our love, my shoulder started hurting so badly. I asked her, "What did you do to my back?" She replied, "Nothing." I persisted, "But it hurts so badly!" Then she said, "Okay, let me look at it."

She turned on the light next to the bed and looked at my back. Suddenly she exclaimed, "Oh myyy God! I must have been out of my mind." Then she said accusingly, "This is your fault entirely. You drove me crazy. Fearing the worst, I asked to her please tell me what it was.

Mahsa tenderly kissed my shoulder and reassured me, "It's not that bad. I am so sorry, but my nails broke through your skin." I didn't want her feeling guilty, "It's O.K. it doesn't hurt really anymore. Besides, anything from you is very sweet and worth the pain." Mahsa ordered me to shut up and stay put, as she searched the bathroom and brought out what looked like a first aid kit. She applied some ointment to my wound and wrapped it up with a bandage. As she washed her hands, I heard her say, "My God!" I asked, "What is it?" After a few minutes, she came back out and said, "I'm sorry baby, but I had you blood under my nails." She shook her head, "No wonder I called you Chubby, your skin is so sensitive." I gave her a wounded look, "It helps that your nails are so strong too."

Mahsa turned off the light and climbed back into bed. She held me and have me a kiss, saying, "You wanted that two-in-a-row, didn't you?" I cut her off, "Ah, excuse me! I wanted the three-in-a-row.

Not two!" Running her hands through my hair to mess it up, she grumbled, "Oh shuuut up!" As we lay in each other's arms, she asked, "Is it hurting now." Although it hurt like hell, I dismissed it saying, "Only a little, but it's nothing. I will be fine, don't worry."

Still holding each other, we drifted off to sleep. When the alarm rang, I held her to me, "Please don't move. I really don't need coffee or anything else. I can take care of these things myself. Just stay here and rest." I took a shower and got dressed. Before leaving, I told her, "You know what? If you promise to be good girl and get some rest, I let you stay with Meetra tonight." Mahsa just looked at me, "What you talking about?" I was firm, "Just go back to sleep. If you want, you can pick me up and we will go to hospital together. Then around six or seven, I will go home and you stay with her tonight." Like a rabbit, she jumped out of bed and kissed me, saying, "You are the best crazy son of a gun I know!" I smiled, "Thank you very much, now go back to bed and let me go." She kissed me good-bye and went back to bed, telling me, "Go, go, you are going to be late. I said, "See you later wildcat." Mahsa grinned at me wickedly, "See you later my hunt."

I headed to school (my office) and just spent the

day waiting for it to end, so I could get out and wait for her. She picked me up and we stopped for burgers then went to the hospital.

We found Meetra sitting on the bed, talking with one of the nurses. When she saw us, the nurse left; Mahsa gave her daughter a big hug and I kissed her. We asked how she was feeling. Meetra assured us that everything was fine, "The doctor told me that I can go home in the next couple of days." I said, "Wow, what good news this is! It is fantastic that you're going home very soon." Mahsa beamed with delight and Meetra looked so excited. I kept my promised and stayed a little past six then I told Meetra, "Your mom got some much needed rest, so I agreed to let her stay with you tonight. How would you like that?" Meetra was ecstatic, "Oh this is great! I would love to have her stay. But I worry that sometimes she gets too tired, like last night." I said, "I would love to stay too, but I have to go. You know – the 'family'." Meetra smirked and said, "I know and don't worry about mom, everything will be okay." I kissed her, saying, "I will see you later." I went over to Mahsa who hugged me and joked; "Now you are going to be the one who doesn't want to leave?" I looked sheepishly at the floor, she smiled and said, "You go baby. Go have a good time with your brother." She had to throw in the last line, "I'll see you later alligator." I waved, "See you later sweetie." and left.

It was so funny when I got home because my brother and I got home almost at the same time. I found him trying to unlock the door. As he fumbled with his keys, I had mine out already and let us in. He took a shower, then we went to our cousin's, But my brother was tired, so he left around nine-thirty and I stayed there with bunch of other guys including my eldest brother. I got home around mid-night, undressed and flopped down on that mattress. Before falling asleep, I had the feeling that she was right next to me.

I woke up late the next morning to find that my brother wasn't home, which meant that he didn't come home last night. I washed up and fixed some eggs and toast, but most importantly, I had to have my tea first. As I ate breakfast, I called the hospital to talk with Mahsa. I told her that I was eating breakfast all alone. "Poor baby!" she said, "Don't worry, I will fix you a nice breakfast and we will eat together. Oooh my Chubby is alone. I missed you so much last night." Mahsa then gave the phone to Meetra and I told her, "I will stop by this afternoon, but I don't know what time." "Okay." she said, "See you later." and we hung up.

My brother got home by mid-afternoon, took a shower then said, "I have to go. Do you need anything?" I said no. then he give me some money for the week, grabbed his stuff and left. After he left, I took a shower went over to the hospital. When I arrived, Mahsa looked up, "I didn't think you could get here this soon." I shrugged, "You know my situation, I never know what my plan is ahead of time." She agreed, "Yes, I know that by now." We hung out with Meetra until eight-thirty, then we said 'bye' to her and went home.

Along the way, we stopped at a fast food shop and bought two sandwiches, an order of fries and two Cokes to take home. As soon as we got home we changed into our robes and sat down for dinner. We both were pretty hungry and the sandwiches were delicious. After we had finished, I made tea which we had in the living room. I opened the balcony door for some fresh air and so we could smoke. I asked her what happened there today. Mahsa said that because of the holiday, there was nothing major. Only one doctor came to check on Meetra and he said that everything looks very good and that she is healing quickly. She and I talked a lot and it seems like we got much closer than before. She told me a lot of things too, so that was very good. I then asked Mahsa where she slept last night. With a guilty look on her face she said, "At first I tried to sleep in the chair, but they brought me very small bed, which was much better. Then they just took it away in the morning." Mahsa and I sat drinking tea, smoking and catching up on the day's events. Around eleven, we got ready for bed.

She was pretty tired so I asked her if she would like a massage. She loved the idea, "Yes, but only a massage." I understood, "O.K." I slowly removed her robe as she stretched out on her stomach before me. I started on her neck, gently working out the kinks and slowly moved all the way down to her feet, working on them as well. She then turned over and this time I started from her toes, moving up to her chest and then her neck again. I finished with a long time spent on her head. I noticed that she was already asleep. So I climbed in next to her very slowly, wrapped my arms around her and went to sleep too.

We woke up to the ringing of the alarm as usual. Again, I wouldn't let Mahsa get up. I kissed her and said, "My dear, please stay in bed. You are too tired, just rest." I took a shower and got ready to go. I leaned over her lounging in bed, gave her a hug and a kiss, saying, "See you later alligator." "See you honey." She murmured sleepily as I left for school.

After school I called Mahsa at home, but nobody was there. I then called the hospital and Meetra picked up. We talked for a little while and I asked how she was feeling. Then I asked, "Is your mom there?" "Yes she is." she said, "Do you want to talk to her?" then Meetra paused and said, "How stupid I am! Of course you want to talk to her!" Laughing at herself, Meetra added, "See you." and handed Mahsa the phone. I said, "Hi sweetie!" and asked, "What time did you get up and get to the hospital?" She said, "I got up around eleven and got here at noon. Are you coming over?" I replied, "Sure I will be there around four." We said bye and hung up.

Then I called my sister and asked her if I could come for lunch. She was delighted and said, "We are having eggplant stew." To that I said, "I will definitely be there. See you soon." I caught a cab and got there just in time. Lunch was very good. I stayed there, catching up on family news until quarter to four. I then told her, "I'm sorry, but I have to go." Disappointed, she said, "Aw, why so soon?" I felt bad, but said, "I have to visit a friend who is in the hospital." "Oh." then she asked, "Will you be coming back for dinner?" I said, "No, I won't be back until late tonight. Thanks for lunch and I'll see you later." I got a cab and went to the hospital.

BE HIDDEN LOVE

I said hi to Meetra and kissed Mahsa who frowned at me and said, "You said you would be here at four." I raised my hands in resignation and said, "Well what time is it now - what four-twenty?" Checking her watch, she said, "Yes." I patiently explained, "I have to cover my tracks as you know. I went to my sister's for lunch because I knew that I must stop by and see her. If I don't, she would call everywhere, looking for me. And I mean to avoid having that kind of trouble again. I always have to be very careful." Mahsa sighed and hugged me, saying, "My poor Chubby, he has to work undercover for me." I added, "It is for me too."

We hung out for a while talking and cracking jokes, but these were not as bad as the other time. Around nine Mahsa and I got ready to go and I asked Meetra, "Do you know when you will be coming home?" She answered, "Sometime tomorrow afternoon but probably not until later." "What good news! Why didn't you guys tell me earlier?" Meetra looked sheepish and said, "Sorry, well now you know." Mahsa kissed her, saying, "Good night, see you tomorrow baby." I kissed her and said, "See you tomorrow." Meetra said, "Bye you guys." and we left.

When we got out to the street, Mahsa turned to me, "Let's go eat somewhere." We decided on one of the best pizza shops in the north part of town near the university. After dinner, we headed home. At home, Mahsa thanked me with a huge hug, then she went off to change her clothes and I went to the kitchen to fix some tea. She came out wearing her silk robe, the one I liked the most and asked me, "Aren't you going to change?" I answered, "Yes, I will, I just wanted to put some water on for tea." I changed into my robe and brought the tea out to the living room. Mahsa lit two cigarettes, one for me and one for herself as we sat enjoying our tea. That first smoke was so good, that we both reached for a second one. Yes, it was chain smoking, but we both felt like we needed the extra. As I sat there, something was bothering me, so I asked, "What were you thanking me for when we got in? I don't get it." She kissed me and said, "I was thanking you because your intentions are always so pure, like crystal clear water. I was thanking you for being with me through all these hard days. You support Meetra and me one hundred percent. It means so much to us and that's why I thanked you." We sat up talking about Meetra and all the other things in our lives. By eleven-thirty we were exhausted, so we went to bed.

In bed, we lay holding each other close, sharing our body heat and energy. We locked ourselves in each other's arms and fell asleep. That hated alarm clock woke us up promptly at seven and I went about my usual routine. Mahsa made me coffee and I was surprised, "You didn't have to get up just to make me coffee." She just smiled and said, "You deserve it; just give me a kiss in return for luck with Meetra today." We had our coffee together and before I left, I gave her the biggest kiss from bottom of my heart. Thoroughly delighted, she sighed, "Yeees that's the one I wanted. Thank you Chubby." "You're welcome, for you any time." Even after all these years, I can still feel and taste that kiss.

I went to school, but spent the day watching the clock just waiting for the damned day to finish. I was out of there like a shot at the sound of the bell. I grabbed a cab and told the driver that I needed to stop at two places first then to the hospital. The guy just looked at me and said, "It will cost you." I said, "Don't worry about it." Then he asked, "Where do you want to go first?" I asked him if he knew of a good florist in the area. He answered, "Yes let me take you, it is not too far." True to his word, the florist was a very nice one. I ordered ten red roses and two large white. I then asked the florist to add some fresh greens and baby's breath and arrange two separate bouquets. He made two very lovely arrangements for me. Then I asked him about vases and he showed me his selection. I picked out two that I thought were the nicest and he put my bouquets in vases and wrapped them up. I paid him and got into the waiting cab. The next stop I told him to stop at was Mahsa's place. I went inside to ask the doorman if he could take the two bouquets up to our unit and leave them in the living room. He said that he would take care of it, so I gave him some money and hopped back into the cab. I got to the hospital and went up to Meetra's room. She was all ready to go but Mahsa wasn't there. I asked Meetra where she was and Meetra said that she went down to pay the hospital bill. Mahsa returned a few minutes later and I greeted her at the door with a bow, "Good after noon Madam, what can I do for you?" Mahsa laughed, "Well, to start, you can give me a hug and a kiss. That's exactly what you can do for me!" So of course I had to do what she requested. Meetra sat on the bed, laughing, "You both are crazy, really crazy. But it's so sweet, I love you both!"

We had to wait for the doctor to come and sign Meetra's release form. When he finally arrived, he gave Mahsa the form, which she took with the paid invoice to the counter. The nurse brought a wheelchair and we took Meetra down while Mahsa went to bring the car to the front. I opened the front door for Meetra as the nurse helped her into the car. Mahsa thanked her and give her some money.

I sat in the back and as we headed home, Meetra said to me, "I'm sorry that I stole your place." I smiled her, "Please don't worry at all that, because it's your place too." I put my hand on her shoulder and added, "Welcome back sweetie!" Meetra turned her head toward me and just for a moment, she looked exactly like a younger version of her mother as she said, "Thank you very much."

Those words Meetra said to me had a million meanings and each one was worth a million dollars.

We got home and Mahsa pulled the car up to the front entrance and gave the keys to the doorman to park it. Everyone in the lobby welcomed Meetra back. We went up and as soon as we stepped in, there they were. The doorman had placed the vase where it could be seen immediately. Meetra asked Mahsa, "Who brought those flowers?" Mahsa replied, "Who do you think would do something like that?" Meetra turned to me with tears in her eyes, "Thank you again!" I was touched by her tears, "Don't mention it. It's the very least I could do for you."

CHAPTER 9

Our Daily Lives

Mahsa helped Meetra to her room. When she came back out, she walked up to me, threw her arms around me, saying, "You dummy! I love so much that you are sentimental, but I do not know what to do with it." She rewarded me with one of those special kisses, the kind that you could get lost forever in. I told her that one set is Meetra's and the other was for her, "I hope that we will always be happy together as a family." This time, Mahsa had tears in her eyes, "We will for sure."

She took a vase to Meetra's room and I could hear Meetra ask, "What does the color combination mean?" Mahsa laughed, "You will have to ask that sentimental guy in the other room. I really don't know." When she came out again, I winked at her and said, "You call me sentimental now, but what else are you going to call me in the future?" Mahsa flashed me her wicked smile, "You will always be my Chubby. You might be a crazy one, but I love you just the same!" She paused, "Thanks a million for the flowers you got for us both. It was really sweet of you to do that." Then she asked me when did I have time to do all those things; I told her that my secret weapon was a very good cab driver.

Mahsa went to change into her robe; then fixed us some coffee. She gave me a sidelong look and asked, "Why are you standing there, why you don't go and change? Unless you want to go." I said, "No I am staying." "You had better." she retorted, "There is no way in Hell I am letting you go tonight anyway. Go and change your clothes and put your robe on. Let yourself relax. We are home aren't we?" "Yes dear." I dutifully changed into my robe and came back out to the living room.

Mahsa asked Meetra if she would like some coffee and she could either have it in her room or join us in the living room. Meetra said, "I will come out to the living room, don't worry I can come by myself."

Mahsa brought out the coffee; she and Meetra made themselves comfortable on the couch and I sat in the easy chair. She had brewed an Italian coffee and it was fabulous. But I must admit that having it with a cigarette made the whole experience complete.

As we enjoyed our coffee, Mahsa asked Meetra what she might like for dinner. Meetra considered her options, "I have to have something light tonight." Mahsa suggested that Italian sandwiches can be light enough and Meetra agreed. Mahsa called the Italian place and ordered three sandwiches; she didn't need to ask us what we wanted, she already knew what we liked. We each had a second cup of coffee as we waited for the food to arrive. We were in the middle of a conversation when the bell rang; our food and sodas had arrived.

After dinner, Meetra excused herself and went to her room to rest. Mahsa and I stayed little while longer in the living room; finishing our sodas and smoking a couple more cigarettes before turning in.

We got into bed and Mahsa hugged me tight, saying, "I wouldn't have missed tonight for anything, because tonight was a very special night for me. I was curious, "Why?" She said, "Tonight all those problems are behind me, I have my two loves with me together tonight. That's why tonight is so important to me." She kissed me and added, "I will never ever forget what you did for Meetra and me today. It meant so much to me. Yes my Chubby, it wasn't just flowers or the way you had them arranged that was important. It was that you thought of Meetra as well. You are everything to me and I don't know what I would ever do without your beautiful sentiment."

I kissed her and said, "I am what I am, but it was you who made me this way." She fell silent for a while and then I felt that she had started crying. I rubbed her shoulder and asked, "What's the matter?" "It is you!" Mahsa sniffed, "You drive me nuts, the way you talk, the way you transmit feelings to me and the way you just seem to understand everything about me; it's all really too much for." She drew a shaky breath, "I am not as strong as you think…" I cut her off, "That's the problem, you don't realize just how strong you are! Look deep inside of yourself because it's obvious that you've never been there." Mahsa opened her mouth to protest, but I held up my hand to stop her. "One day we will go there together and I will show you. Yes I will show you to yourself so then you will see how much influence you have on me." I added, "And when we do that, you will be able to see deep inside me and how much I influence you. You will see, we both will see."

As quick as a cat, she got on top of me and held my shoulders and softly hit my chest saying, "Stop it, stop saying these things!" She leaned forward to plant numerous kisses on my chest. I wrapped my arms around and said, "I love you so much, more than anyone can imagine. Only God knows how much I really love you."

She moved up to my lips, bit then gently and moved over to nibble on my ear. That turned me on like a switch; I grabbed her and pulled her to me as we began to make love. It felt exactly the like the first night we were together. We got so high, higher than any drug could ever take us. After reaching our climax, Mahsa laid on top of me and fell asleep and I soon followed.

When we awoke the next morning I announced, "I am not going to school today. I want to stay with you guys." Mahsa got mad, "Oh no, you have to go. That is the only thing what I want from you and if you love me as much as you said so last night, then you will go to school for me." My face fell as she continued, "I know you hate it, but you will do it for me, won't you?" I felt sabotaged; she put me in a very bad position. On one hand I really, really didn't want to go, but on other hand I loved her so much that I couldn't let her down and she knew that! Resigned to my fate, I kissed her and got ready to go. It was a tough decision for me, but I made up my mind. Just before I left, Mahsa motioned me toward her and rewarded my decision with one of those kisses saying sweetly, "See you alligator. And please know that I love you the same as you love me."

That day I paid close attention to the teachers for a change and to my surprise, learned a lot. After classes let out, I hailed a cab and went to my place for a quick change of clothes, then headed over to my sister's for an hour. Afterward I went to our home, and as soon as I stepped through the door, Mahsa teased me, "I told you to go to school but you didn't have to stay late. Oh, you went home. Ha!" Smiling, I said, "Yes, I stopped at my place quick then went to my sister's for a little while. Now I am here." She then asked, "Did you have lunch?" "No." I said, "I waited to have it with you." I sat down as she brought out a salad she made. I was so hungry and it was so good, that I ate all of it. Mahsa looked at me in amazement. "You were hungry, weren't you?" I nodded, "Yes, I guess I was. Thank you that was so delicious." We finished our lunch with some of her fine coffee.

As we drank our coffee, Mahsa asked me how school was. I said, "It wasn't too bad today. I really listened to the teachers and I felt like I learned a lot of good things. But you should get the credit, not me." Mahsa's brow furrowed, "What do you mean, what should I get credit for?" I explained, "I only went to school today because of you. While I was there, I told myself 'She wants you to listen and learn not just come and go.' So you see, that's why you get the credit for all I've learned today."

Mahsa shook her head and said, "You will kill me with those words, but I know you really mean it, so thank you very much for listening to me. I am very proud of you Chubby." Then I asked about Meetra was doing and she said, "Meetra is okay. But she needs a lot of rest." I agreed, "Yes, I'm sure she does; rest, vitamins and good, rich food." I had an idea, "How about I fix us dinner tonight, what do you think?" "I think that is a fantastic idea." Mahsa replied, "We will look forward to that." She took my hand, "But first you need a nap, lets go lie down together." We went to bed holding each other tightly and had a not-so-short nap that lasted nearly two hours.

After our nap, we got up. I went to the living room and Mahsa knocked on Meetra's door and asked, "Are you going to stay in there all day? Won't you come join us out here for coffee?" Meetra said, "I will come out to the living room too." Mahsa then made coffee as Meetra came out to join us; we said hi to each other and I asked her how she was doing. Meetra shrugged, I am okay for the most part, but I don't have any energy." I said, "You will get it back little by little. Tonight I am going to fix us a good dinner and you will get some energy from that for sure." She smiled and said, "Thank you, Yousef. You are a true friend." "Oh don't mention it." I said, "It's not any trouble for me to do this for you."

Mahsa brought out the coffee and sat next to Meetra and we had such fun that afternoon. I got up, opened the refrigerator and pulled out celery, mint and parsley then got some meat from the freezer to thaw. After I had gotten my ingredients together, I rejoined them in the living room.

When the meat had thawed, I went back into the kitchen to start cooking. I decided to make a savory stew with rice; I put the stew on to simmer and prepared the rice. Both needed time to cook, so all we had to do was wait. I went back to the living room and about hour and a half later delicious smells started drifting from the kitchen. Dinner was ready and we were ready to eat.

Mahsa set the table and helped me serve the food. The stew came out very well; Meetra and Mahsa both seemed to enjoy it. After a most delightful mean, we cleaned up, put the leftovers in the fridge and we went back to the living room for tea. The three of us hung out enjoying our company until late. Meetra yawned, said good night and went to her room. Mahsa and I were ready for bed too. As we snuggled together in bed, Mahsa kissed me and said that my dinner was fantastic; then turned her back against me as I wrapped my arms around her. I got up the next morning to the alarm, took a shower and went off to school. After school, I stopped at the market to buy some stuff to make dinner and brought them back to our house.

So our lives together were like that of a happy family and I enjoyed it to the fullest; although I couldn't stay with them every night, I managed to stay nearly four nights a week. This went on like this for weeks until one day Mahsa told me, "Meetra wants to go back to Shiraz and I have to go with her." Her eyes searched mine, "I hope you understand." What could I say? "Yes, I understand that you have to go, it's important that Meetra is happy."

Three and a half weeks later, Mahsa informed me when they were planning to leave Tehran. That day was tomorrow! I stayed with them that night and we had a wonderful time together. The next morning I told Mahsa today that I would not go to school. She became upset with me, "You have to go! I promise that I will come back as soon as I can and will call you every day or at least every other day." Meetra came out of her room to say goodbye. I kissed her and said, "I hope you have a nice trip baby." As I headed for the door, which was the hardest part, Mahsa pushed me out with one hand and pulled me back in with the other saying, "Go my Chubby, you're going to be late." She had tears in her eyes, "Go my sweetie go." But she still pushed and pulled at me. This was very difficult for me to handle as I was pushed and pulled inside as well. Finally she shoved me out the door with both hands saying, "You have to go my sweet Chubby go, go!" She nearly closed, but left if open just a tiny crack so she could watch me leave. Defeated, I put my head down and walked away. I didn't go to school because I just couldn't sit there miserable all day. I was considering my options when I remembered what Mahsa told me the night before. "Please don't drink at all next week, because I can tell that your throat is not good and if you drink it will only get worse."

So instead of going to school I bought a small bottle of vodka and went home. I just sat there like a zombie until around noon when I poured myself two or three shots right in a row. That warmed me up and I called her house in Shiraz to see if they had arrived. Mama answered the phone and told me that they were not home yet. "Where are you? I can have her give you a call when she gets in." I told her that I was home, said bye and hang up. I don't remember how much time had passed when she called; we talked for a half an hour. Before we hung up, Mahsa asked, "What's wrong with your voice? You don't sound good." I answered, "It's nothing, I am okay."

I then fell asleep and didn't wake up until late in the afternoon. My throat felt horrible and I could barely talk. I got dressed and went to see my sister because she knew all those old herbal remedies. As soon as I got there, she began to scold me like a small child, "What did you do to yourself?" But as she was yelling at me, she put me to bed and made some cough syrup. As soon as I drank it, I began to feel much better but still couldn't talk. She made an appointment to see the doctor the very next day. He was one of my cousins from my father's side. He examined my throat and asked, "What did you have to drink?" I told him that I didn't drink. "Bullshit!" he snorted, "Just tell me what you drank and what you've been doing, then I can give you a prescription. I told him about the vodka and he gave me a strong antibiotic and some other pills. We thanked him and as we turned to leave, he pulled me aside and slid me a note, "Don't go to school for two or three days. Give them this note and do not drink anything! Do you understand?" I felt my face redden, "Yes I got it." On the way home, my sister started in on me, "Yousef, why are you doing these things? Why are you drinking? Please don't do it!" I had to pacify her somehow saying "O.K. I will not do it anymore, I promise."

We got back to her house and she sent me straight to bed again. Around noon the school principal called looking for me; my sister informed him that I was sick and that I would be out of school for a few days, but would bring in the doctor's note. She mentioned the name of the doctor (because they knew each other). The principal extended his wishes for my speedy recovery and agreed that I should stay home for two or three days.

Later that afternoon she went to pick up her son from school. When the coast was clear, I could call Mahsa. Thank God she was home and picked up the phone. I croaked, "Hi sweetie!" She started in on me, "It's only been two days since I left you - two days. What did you do to yourself?" I felt like a little kid again, "I did nothing, it's only my throat. I went to the doctor this morning, he gave me some pills and now I am O.K. don't worry." I added, "I am at my sister's and will stay here tonight and then I'll go home tomorrow. I will call you from there."

I wanted to go back home the next day, my sister tried hard to change my mind, but I refused. My voice was much better and I felt fine. I got home and called Mahsa. This time Mama picked up the phone, but for some reason I thought I dialed the wrong number and was about to hang up when Mama called for Mahsa to pick up. "Hi sweetie!" Mahsa hesitated, "Yousef, is that you?" I apologized, "Yes it's me. I'm sorry I dialed the wrong number." She said "Oh don't worry about it, it isn't that important. How are you? Are you feeling better?" I smiled at her motherly concern, "I feel much better now that I hear your voice and that I am home." "That's fantastic!" She said, "Your voice sounds much better. I told you to be careful." I changed the topic, "How about Meetra, how is she?" I could hear Mahsa smile over the phone, "Meetra is very good. Mama takes very good care of her and she is doing much better and getting stronger every day." We continued to talk for close to an hour. Then she said goodbye, "You must some rest and remember to study. Try not to miss any more classes okay?" I replied dutifully, "O.K. I will try." "What does that mean? 'You will try'" Her voice took on a hard tone, "Now you listen carefully, you have to go to school!" We argued about school and talked a little bit more and then we finally hung up.

I was feeling back to my old self after three or four days, when my oldest nephew, the son of my other sister arrived and kindly got me out of my funk. We grew up together although he was almost two years younger than me. He helped fill some of the gaps in my schedule after school. We would sit and chat about the old days, although that sounds pretty funny coming from a couple of teenagers. His father wants to send him to a state university, but he didn't want to go, he had his own things he wanted to do. It was good to have his company and he took my mind off my own misery for a little while.

During this time, my brother had just finished the first part of his program that required him to serve in the army. He had some time before starting the second part. He didn't want to talk about it with me and would often wait until after I went to bed to talk with my other brother and nephew. I didn't know what it was about and I didn't try to find out either. Between my nephew and my brother, there was more going on than I wanted to deal with. My nephew stayed a little over two months and my brother's program allowed him two weeks out of Tehran and one week in.

As the weeks passed, I became thirstier than ever to see her. A month had gone by and although we spoke every day or every other day, it was not enough for me. She kept promising that she would be back soon and I patiently told her to take her time with Meetra; she needed her more. Five weeks, six, seven then eight weeks crawled by and I felt like my Hell would never end. My nephew was finally able to get an I-20 from LSU in Baton Rouge, Louisiana. We had other relatives there, so it was a little easier for him to get what he needed. We were happy for him but he wasn't very excited to go.

Some days after my nephew left for the States, Mahsa called me; I could tell that something was up, her voice was exceptionally cheerful. She announced, "I have news!" I wasn't in the mood for more promises, so I cut her short, demanding, "When is your ticket for?" She burst out laughing, "I don't have it yet, maybe by Thursday afternoon or Friday." I changed my tone and said "That is great! I love you all the more with this good news." We talked for a little while then hung up.

Two days later, Mahsa called me to say that she would be arriving on Friday around noon and gave me the flight number. I wrote everything down, word for word as I didn't want to miss anything. As I waited for Friday to arrive, I went to the house and scrubbed the place until it was spotless. I then bought some jasmine scented air freshener and spray it everywhere to get rid of the musty smell.

It was finally Friday! I got up early, took a shower and put on some of the cologne she liked. I picked up some roses in the usual arrangement, five red and one white then headed to the airport to meet her. Of course in my nervousness, I got there early, so I went up to the bar and had a coffee. That helped steady my nerves. I waited just outside of baggage claim area. I spotted her getting off the shuttle. I sunk around the back of the baggage claim so that I was able to come up behind her and said, "Excuse me, Miss, can I help you?" She turned around and when she saw me, her face lit up as she jumped into my arms. She kissed me and asked, "How the hell did you come in without me seeing you?" Grinning, I gave her the roses answered smugly, "Money honey." I suggested that she sit and let me find the suitcase. But Mahsa wouldn't have it, saying,

"I want to be with you." We went over to where they were bringing out the luggage. We found her suitcases and I pointed them out for the attendant to retrieve. He brought them over and placed them on a cart. I hailed an airport cab and the attendant placed the suitcases in the trunk. I gave him a good tip for taking care of us and for letting me sneak into baggage claim. We got into the cab and stuck to each other like glue until we got home. The doormen came, got her stuff out of the cab and brought them up for us. Finally we were home together, alone.

She placed the roses in a vase on the coffee table then jumped on me again, kissing me over and over. I picked her up, carried her to the bedroom and laid her down on the bed. I don't know how those clothes came off, but they flew in all directions. I also don't remember how long we spent just looking, kissing and caressing each other before starting to make love. What love making that was! We melted into each other until we were inside each other's bones, blood, organs and skin. We couldn't let go, which was just as well because we were stuck together side by side. There we lay without making a sound; we just gazed into each other's eyes. It was Mahsa who eventually broke the silence and whispered, "Hi Chubby." I whispered back, "Hi Honey Bunch my sweetheart, welcome home." To that, she replied, "It's so nice to be home."

We fell asleep and had such a wonderful nap. Later that afternoon, when we woke up, we both were full of energy.

She kissed me and suggested, "Let's take a shower together." I paused, "Are you sure?" "Yes Chubby." She prodded, "Come on, hurry up, let's go!" That shower was probably the most fun I have ever had that involved soap and water.

As she fixed her hair, I reached for my robe. She said, "Aren't you going to get dressed?" "What for?" I asked. Mahsa said, "Let's go out tonight and celebrate." Again I asked, "Are you sure?" "Yes!" She exclaimed, "Now get dressed, and hurry." I got dressed and put on some cologne and said, "I am ready." Mahsa called over her shoulder, "Well good for you, but you will have to wait until I am ready. We ladies need little more time than you guys, you know."

When Mahsa was ready, we went out; but it was too early for dinner. "Now what?" I asked. Mahsa suggested, "Let's go someplace where they have a bar and restaurant." I didn't have a clue, so I said, "I'll leave that to you. You would know better than me on such things." She thought about our options, "Why don't we try the Intercontinental Hotel? They have very good food." It was decided, we went there. First, we reserved a table for dinner then we went over to the bar for drinks and a snack.

It was a great place and there were a surprising number of people chatting away at the bar, probably like us, waiting for their dinner reservations. Mahsa and I made ourselves comfortable with our drinks and talked. I asked her about her trip to Shiraz. She confided, "It wasn't as easy as it might sound." She took a sip of her drink, "When we get back home I will have you read about it. Or you could read it for us both." I knew that I wouldn't be able to get anything more from her about that subject, so I asked about Meetra, "How is she doing?" Mahsa looked relieved, "She is doing very well. Thank God. She is pretty much back to normal. She is very good."

It was finally time for dinner. We settled our bar tab and headed into the dining room.

We brought our drinks as the hostess seated us. She informed us of that evening's specials and said, "Your waiter be with you in a moment." As we waited, our conversation continued as Mahsa said sadly, "My sweet Chubby, I wish my trip was as simple as other people's trips; but it's all written in my note book so you will see for yourself what I am talking about."

Our waiter gave us two menus: one for drinks and another for food. We knew exactly what we wanted to drink; Mahsa ordered the usual bottle of her favorite wine. Then we decided to try the steak which was supposed to be an unusual style. The wine was brought followed by some chips and dip. But the food would take them much longer.

Fortunately we had our wine, chips and conversation to

occupy us as we waited. Mahsa then asked, "So tell me about you. How you did manage? I shrugged and said, "You already know much of my news." I filled her in on the rest, then I added, "When you told me that you were coming back, I was counting the hours and minutes right down to when I was at the airport. She asked, "When did you get to the airport?" I casually waved my hand, "Oh, about an hour and a half before your arrival. It's where I had my morning coffee." She took my hand and gazed into my eyes for a moment. Hypnotized, I gazed back. A million words passed silently between us during those moments. We didn't need to say anything else after that because we knew everything we want to know with that look.

The food was brought out and as we ate, we moved our talk to lighter topics for a bit. Meeting my eyes over her fork, Mahsa winked at me conspiratorially, "As soon as we get home, we spend some time with my other secret friend — my diary. We will look at the part where you left the house…" I suddenly cut her off, spluttering, "What you meant to say was *kick* me out of the house as you might remember!" Mahsa gave me a wounded look, "I'm sorry my Chubby. I didn't have any other choice, you will see."

The food was so good that we cleaned every last morsel from out plates. Mahsa then ordered some Italian gelato which we shared. At that point, we were stuffed full, we paid the bill and left. We drove around a little bit, enjoying the evening before heading home.

As we stepped in and turned on the lights, Mahsa sniffed the air and asked, "Have you been here before today?" I tried to look innocent, "Why?" She traced a finger along the coffee table, "Thank you very much, Yousef. But you didn't have to do all of this; we could have called a cleaner." I said, "I did it because you told me that this is our house and I wanted to be clean it for when you get back." She hugged and kissed me saying, "You are right, yes this is our house but I didn't want you spending your time and energy cleaning it. That's all. Please don't get upset with me." I laughed, Of course not, because I know you better than this. This is too small a matter to get upset over."

Mahsa draped her arm around my shoulder and lead me to the bed room. We got undressed, I climbed into bed and she went to the closet and came out with a notebook and got in next to me. She asked me to read it, but I shook my head, "No, You should read it aloud. That will be much better because then I can feel what you are saying and you be better as expressing the right emotion from your own writing." Making herself comfortable, she started form the time when I tried to leave the house.

From her diary:

'...Yousef was in the door as I pushed him out with one hand

and pulled him back in with the other. I finally got a grip on myself and pushed him fully out telling him, "You must go my Chubby, go to school for me." Then I closed the door slowly and saw him as put his head down and went to the elevator. I closed the door fully and pressed my back against it and started crying. Meetra asked, "Why didn't you let him come with us to the airport?" "Because!" I said "I know him too well; he couldn't just stand there as we left. This way might be hard for us both, but it is much better for the long run." She put her arms around me and took me to my room. We sat on the bed and this time, it was I who put my head on her shoulder and just cried. I told her, "I feel really guilty because of the look in his eyes said a million things and each of those things had a million feelings attached. What could I do? I couldn't do anything and he knew it."

Meetra gave me so much support and helped me pack my stuff. She then went to her room and packed up her suitcase as well. We got to the airport and boarded the aircraft. Meetra and I sat next to each other, and when the plane took off, I told her about how Yousef didn't like the feeling of takeoff. The flight was uneventful and we landed in Shiraz and got home. Mama told me that Yousef had called to see if you guys had arrived yet. He said that he is home. When I called, he didn't sound good, his voice was all scratchy sounding, but of course he wouldn't tell me anything. I took our suitcases up and couldn't help but think of him. I told myself 'If he was here there would be no way that he would let us even touches those suitcases'. Yes, it's a fact, I feel so much more secure with him around. When he is around I feel good to have a man around me again who supports me. I really miss him already.

Meetra and I went to our rooms to settle in and after a little while, Mama called us for lunch. After lunch I went back up to my room and got into bed for a nap. Mama woke me up; it was so late already. I went downstairs but I kept feeling like there is something missing inside me. Actually, that feeling is quite correct, because half of me is not here. I had to remind myself over and over that's the way it is, you cannot do anything about it. The only thing you can do is to be optimistic about the future and that's the only way you are going to cope during the time you are here.

That night I took two sleeping pills so I could get to sleep. I didn't get up until around eleven. I went downstairs to the kitchen. Mama came out from her room and we said hi to each other. She asked, "Did you have good sleep last night my baby?" I said, "Yes, thanks to sleeping pills." Mama doesn't like it when I use them, "Those are not good for you baby. You should know that." I really didn't want to argue with her so I agreed, "I know, but I didn't have any choice last night. But tonight I will try not to use any. O.K. Mama? You shouldn't worry so much." To change the subject, I asked, "Did Meetra wake up yet?" "Yes she got up around nine and I made sure that she had a good breakfast." Mama continued, "She told me that she was going to school to see her teachers about catching up on her classes. She promised me that she would be back soon. She did not want to stay too long."

(Mahsa paused in her reading and asked, "You probably don't want me to read all of this, do you?" I replied, "Let me have it all!" But I have to be somewhat selective in this book because if I were to tell you every single thing, this book would be over a thousand pages long.

Mahsa continued reading.)

Meetra came home for lunch but was exhausted. Mama gave her a mixture of juice and vitamins. She sat down next to me to finish her drink. I was concerned at how run down she was, "Why did you go to school today?" Meetra looked a little guilty, "I just wanted to see my friends and see what's going on. That's all I did, but got so tired." I decided to call my friend the doctor to see if she could give us an appointment for the next day. She said, "I'm sorry, but I'm pretty booked up tomorrow. If you don't mind coming in much later, I can fit you in after the last patient. I was so grateful to her, "That will not be a problem. I want you to see her and check if anything might be wrong. Thank you and we will see you tomorrow."

Later that afternoon Yousef called me; he sounded terrible. I was relieved when he told me he had already seen a doctor and that he was staying with his sister until tomorrow. I was beside myself; it was very hard on me to have a loved one sick close by and another sick loved one far away. I asked God, "Please can help me? Please do something, I cannot take it anymore!" After I finished speaking with Yousef, Mama asked, "What is wrong, is he okay?" I was close to tears, "Mama everything got messed up.

I just don't know anymore." Now Mama is worried, "Oh my baby you were always so strong, what happened to you?" Thanks Mama, that didn't help. "I really don't know Mama, the only thing I know is that I have to grin and bear it until everything gets back to normal again." Yes my dear diary these things I am writing you will stay between you and me always. You are the only one except Yousef who can dry my tears. I see your pages that bear the stain of my tears. And you will hold them forever.

That night I had to rely on the sleeping pills again, but only took one; I was able to finally get to sleep but not that fast as the night before. Later that day, I took Meetra to the doctor, who examined her thoroughly and prescribed some pills and two liquid injections. On the way home, we picked up the prescriptions. Meetra started with the pills today and tomorrow I have to bring her in for the injection.

The days passed, and I talked to Yousef almost every day. I thank God he isn't alone right now. His nephew is visiting for a time. Although I am taking care of Meetra the way I am supposed to, my heart flies back to Tehran to see him. I really miss him so much and these days are moving for me too slowly. I never thought that time would drag like this. I am ready to lose my mind.

So Yousef and I talk as often as we can, sometimes over an hour. I get my energy and strength from him so I can do what I have to do. The good news is that every day Meetra gets better and stronger; she has gained almost eight pounds and she is not happy about that at all. I tell her 'Baby you are fine, don't worry about the weight. If it's that important to you, you can lose it after you are completely recovered. Don't worry about that now.'

It's now been a month since Meetra and I got back to Shiraz. Every time we talk, Yousef reminds me how many weeks, days and hours it's been and he keeps saying that if I need any help to please tell him. That maybe he can assist in some way. I think about that every day and wish that there was something I could do. Finally, one day I called him to say that I am coming back. But he wouldn't let me finish, it was like he read my mind because he asked me when I was arriving. I told him that it would be either of these two days. I wanted the next couple of days past like seconds, so I could fly and be with him again. Finally the day is tomorrow....'

I hope this excerpt from her diary will help you, dear reader to understand that she and I were going through the same things, feeling the same emotions and the same stresses of family obligations. I hope that one day I will start writing again and tell you about all the outside currents that were affecting our lives.

Mahsa finished reading the passage from the last two months in Shiraz. At that point, she said, Okay, enough is enough for tonight." I took her in my arms, kissed her and said, "I am sorry I became your second problem. But it seems that all of this is now out of my hands. I guess we should just let it go and see where it goes." She hugged me tight, kissed my chest and started to play with my ears. Mahsa could be such a vixen; she knew that I would get hot and horny whenever she played with my ears. I know she did it on purpose. I turned her on her side and we started making love. She continued playing with my ears and running her fingers through my hair; those two things drove me nuts and she continued until we both climaxed. I didn't notice then that she pulled my hair until afterward when I rubbed my tender scalp. But I didn't say anything to her about it, I just accepted the hazards of loving Mahsa.

The alarm woke us up as usual and she got up to make coffee, I didn't say no because I really missed her coffee! I took a shower, got ready and joined her in the kitchen. She didn't just make coffee, breakfast too. As we ate, she said, "Oh don't worry I will get you to school on time." At that point, I was beside myself and burst out laughing. Mahsa stared at me in surprise, "What is the matter with you?" Catching my breath, I explained, "It is just so funny, that you do all these things for me, including making sure that I get to school. I've never worried about that in my entire life." Mahsa laughed too, "Well, now that you have me in your life; things are different, aren't they?" I could tell that she was serious while she joked, "Yes Ma'am!" I replied going back to my breakfast.

After breakfast Mahsa changed quickly into a t-shirt and jeans and dropped me off at school. Before leaving, I told

BE HIDDEN LOVE

her that I would be going back to my place after school. She said, "I will call you and pick you up at your house but I will call you first."

The day passed quickly and when I got home later, she called me and swung by to pick me up. I told her that we would have to wait until my nephew gets home. Her eyebrows raised, "Your nephew?" "Yes." I said, "He is only seven or eight years old, but he is a good kid." We waited in the living room until he rang the bell. I let him in, introduced him to Mahsa, and said, "Can you guys wait outside while I change. I'll be out in a minute." When I went outside, Mahsa and my nephew were nowhere in sight. I looked around and finally spotted them coming out from a shop. I asked, "Where did you go?" Mahsa gave me a conspiratorial wink; I just found out that my new boyfriend loves ice cream so we went to get some. Oh and I bought some for you too." We went to my sister's place, but Mahsa parked a safe distance away. As I helped my nephew out of the car, he invited Mahsa to the house. She gave him a little hug and said, "Thank you, my sweetheart, not today but maybe next time." I walked him to the house and told my sister, "I will see you later." then ran back to the car; she drove away quickly.

We spent the afternoon driving around until we decided to stop at a beautiful park just north of town and stayed there for about three hours. After we had gotten tired of walking, we went back to the car and Mahsa asked,

"Where would you like to go for dinner?" I suggested a place, "If you are not too picky, there is a place that makes an amazing chicken kebab. But it's nothing fancy." Mahsa shrugged, "I don't care what the place looks like, as long as they have good chicken, let's go there." I gave her directions on where to go, "It's on that street just before the parkway." She said, "Oh I know the place you are talking about. "Yes, that's it." I said, "Have you been there?" "No." She said, "But I've heard about it and always wanted to go, but never had anyone to come with me." I understood what Mahsa was saying, this was an area where a woman could not go without a man to accompany her. I smiled at her and said, "Then you will have your chance tonight and you can see for yourself."

She parked the car, we went in and they seated us on the second floor. We knew exactly what we wanted so I wasted no time and ordered two chicken Kebabs, some yogurt with chopped garlic and two sodas. I also requested some vodka which they brought in those small carafes that they put olive oil in. There was the equivalent of about four shots of vodka; Mahsa looked at me curiously. I winked at her and said, "Trust me on this." Then we waited in great anticipation for our food to arrive.

As we started eating I poured a shot of vodka for her and said, "Here, drink this; it will bring out the taste of the chicken." Mahsa opened her mouth to protest, but I stopped her short, "Just try it." She downed the shot; I passed her some of the garlic yogurt to have with the chicken and I did the same. Halfway through our meal, we had the second shot with yogurt then more chicken. We finished the whole thing; there not a crumb left as we finished our soda. Looking at the empty plates, Mahsa shook her head, "This is the first time ever that I eaten at a restaurant and finished everything. But this time, I couldn't control myself especially after the way you suggested. I couldn't get enough and didn't want to stop until everything was gone." She grinned at me slyly, "It's kind of like how you eat." I smiled, "You did very well. But can you drive after all that vodka?" She shot me a dangerous look, "Are you kidding me? Yes, I'm pretty sure I can still drive after those little drinks." We called for the bill and I reached for my wallet and said, "I am going to pay tonight. At least I can afford this." Mahsa smiled and said, "Whatever you wish."

When we got home I tried yet again to carry her into the bedroom, but she was quicker and jumped into my arms. Luckily I caught her, swept her down the hall and laid her on the bed. She kissed me all the way to the bedroom and as we lay on the bed together, she kissed me again and said, "That was most wonderful night I have ever had. Thank you for everything!" I bowed my head, "It was my pleasure. I am available anytime, anywhere and anything for you." She smiled up at me, "I know you mean it, my Chubby we have each other and I think we need each other because we are soul mates."

She got up to change into a gorgeous nightgown with a silky see through robe. I washed up and got into bed next to her. I caressed her shoulders and asked, "Will you be reading the rest for me tonight?" "Yes." She answered, "The notebook is right here. But don't think that I will finish it tonight. You are dead wrong; we still have a long way to go."

She made herself comfortable and began to read. I rested my head against her and could feel her heart beat; rising and falling with her breath. It registered her emotions as she read and I was able to feel them through her. After about an hour, she asked, "Is this enough for now?" For me it wasn't enough, but I just asked, "Please just finish that day." She shifted, "You don't want to miss anything, do you?" Innocently I replied, "How can I resist?" After she finished reading the last entry, she turned off the light and we lay face to face. We played with each other's hair and neck. After a while she turned her back against me. I slid my arm, underneath her neck, cradling it and held her close. I planted a kiss on her shoulder and she kissed my hand in return. I kept kissing her until I felt her completely relax; I knew that she had fallen to sleep. I stopped kissing her only because I didn't want to wake her up and sleep came for me in a short while. Seven arrived and we got up. I begged her not to get up but she wouldn't listen to me. I took a shower, got ready and went to the kitchen where she had coffee waiting for me. I scolded her lightly, "I asked you not to get up." She gave me a look that I couldn't be upset with, "No I didn't want you to go without at least some coffee. We had our coffee and as she made ready to give me a ride, I put my foot down and said, "No! I will take myself, you stay home and relax." We kissed each other goodbye and she said, "I will call you in the afternoon I waved, "Okay, that will be perfect." Then I left for school.

I actually had a good day in school, but I still waited anxiously to finish so I could leave. I stopped by my sister's for lunch then went home. I got in around four-thirty but had no way of knowing whether Mahsa had called. I called her house, but there was no answer. I thought to myself, 'she is not home, so I can just wait here'. I opened my books to study for a while; and about a half an hour later, she called and said, "I called earlier, but you weren't home." "Yes" I told her, I went to my sister's for lunch." "That's I thought." She replied. I said, "I called the house about half an hour ago and nobody was home." "I am not home yet." Mahsa informed me, "I will be by to pick you up in forty-five minutes." "Okay" I said, "I will be ready."

I continued to study until she arrived and let herself in; I had given her a set of keys. When she walked in and saw me surrounded by my school books, she beamed at me, "That's my Chubby!" I got up to give her a kiss and went to other room to put my clothes on. Casually I mentioned that one night we have to stay here together. She reminded me, "Did you ever tell your brother about me?" I looked down, "No but he told me that if I wanted to bring my girlfriend here, it would be no problem at all." Then she said, "Well, okay, we can stay here one night. We shall see."

We got home and Mahsa headed straight to the kitchen to make us coffee. We both changed into our robes; when I came out she was walking into the living room with two steaming mugs. We made ourselves comfortable on the sofa with our coffee and I lit our cigarettes. We shared what happened that day for me in school and her at work. I brought out more coffee for refills and we talked some more. I then asked, "What do you want for dinner?" Mahsa shrugged and said, "I will leave it up to you." I went back into the kitchen, looked in the refrigerator and checked the freezer; I found chicken and some vegetables. I took the chicken out to thaw. I went back to where she sat and said that I would be making dinner and if we had any rice. She replied, "I don't think so but let me come and look." She checked the kitchen but didn't find any. I said, "It's okay, we will have our meal with bread." I paused, "We do have some bread, don't we?" Curious about my talents in the kitchen, Mahsa kept me company. I pulled out a large pot to boil the chicken until it was about half-cooked. I chopped up the vegetables and put them in with the chicken to boil. I put everything together in a fry pan as I sliced some tomatoes and added some broth then left it to simmer for a while.

BE HIDDEN LOVE

While I was cooking, Mahsa checked the coffee and said, "This coffee is no longer fresh, do you want any more or would you like your tea instead?" I called back, "Whatever you like is okay with me." "All right" she said, "I'll make some more coffee that will be just enough for two more cups and then we make tea for after dinner." I liked her thinking, "Beautiful, I like the idea, so be it." So she made coffee and we went back to the living room while dinner simmered on the stove, it was starting to smell delicious. Mahsa turned on the stereo and put on some jazz by Louis Armstrong; that was such great music from that time period.

We sat listening to the music, drinking our coffee and smoking. I periodically went to check on the food, which was coming along very nicely. I would then take my seat again right next to her, listening to the music. After a while, Mahsa turned to me and asked, "What happened to dinner?" I said, "Dinner is ready for anytime you want to eat." "Well then" She stood up, "Let's eat!" She set the table and as I lifted the lid, I saw that a little more juice was needed, so I added a little more chicken broth. Mahsa toasted some bread and suggested that I bring the food out in the pan, I joked, "Are you sure you want to feel like you're in the country again?" As we ate my chicken vegetable dish, Mahsa asked, "What did you put in this food? It is so delicious!" I shrugged saying, "Nothing special, you were right here with me. I didn't do anything unusual; just spices, saffron, some butter…" I paused for effect, "Oh, and also a little bit of love!" She kissed me and said, "I love you: dummy, 'lovey' Chubby!"

After dinner I fixed the tea and we went back into the living room with our tea and cigarettes. Time flies when you're having fun; we look at the time only to be surprised that it was already past eleven. And we still had to clean up the dinner mess. After we finished our chores, I poured a second glass of tea, which she suggested that we take to the bedroom. We both got ready for bed, made ourselves comfortable with our tea and she looked sidelong at me, saying, "I believe that now you want me to read the rest." Excited like a little kid, I said, "Oh for sure! What fool would want to miss this?"

She found her place where we left off the previous night. I held her like before and again it felt like that the story was full of ups and downs. After about an hour, Mahsa stopped reading, she didn't want to finish it all in one shot. I tried to persuade her to finish, but she refused, "No way, not tonight. Maybe tomorrow, but not tonight." We held each other close and started to get hot. Oh yes we made such love together; but without any sex. We both felt the same as any other time when we did have sex together. I will leave it up to your imagination, dear reader.

As promised, Mahsa did finish the last part of her diary the following night. Hearing her experiences allowed me to have a much better understanding of who she was and how much she suffered whenever we were apart. Life was sweet for us as days passed. This went on until one night when I was at Mahsa's place and it was still early, about seven when decided to call my sister. Oh she was so mad at me because I hadn't shown up there for four days and never called to check in with her either. I kept apologizing, "I am so sorry, I completely lost track of the days!" (Which was the truth?) "I will be right over." That was when she informed me, "Everybody will be here tomorrow night and you be better be here immediately after school because I need you very much to come and help." I knew I couldn't argue, so I said, "Yes, I will definitely be there after school." We said bye to each other and hung up.

Red faced, I turned to Mahsa for support, when suddenly she said, "It's not fair that you are spending so much time with me and have forgotten all about your sister. She must love you very much to get that angry." Mortified, I asked her how she knew. She smiled wickedly, "She was yelling so loudly I could hear everything she said. Now what are we going to do about that? Do you understand?" Sheepishly I said, "Yes I understand." Then I stopped short, "What do you mean that I will take care of that from now on?" Mahsa explained, "I won't see you tomorrow night, isn't that right?" I swallowed hard, "Yes I will go straight to my sister's right after school. But I will call you!" She said, "I want every detail of tomorrow night. Can you do that for me or should I stop by?" I was a little thrown off by that, "Whatever you wish. You can do that." She shook her head, "No, I only need the details of what goes on that night. I would love to know what is what in your family."

That night when we went to bed, Mahsa asked me to tell her about my sister in Tehran. Taking a deep breath, I started, "She isn't just my sister, she is like my second mom because she raised me and took care of me ever since I was born. She is so sweet, but is the type of person who worries too much. Especially when it comes to me." I smiled at the memories that came flooding back to me, "I remember when I found out that she was leaving home, I got sick for almost two months. We were always close and she took care of me, so I didn't know what I was going to do without her. She told me 'I will come back to visit. Don't worry, Yousef.' She said, 'I am not going too far away and can come here in the blink of an eye. I promise.' She really cared about me and I always thought she was the only one who really loved me unconditionally. And that was true. She always put me first even when she had a child of her own." Tears filled my eyes, "So that's why she gets so upset with me and she is right to do so. And you are right too, I have to spend time with her too and I will do better." I lost control and hid my face in her shoulder and just sobbed loudly. Mahsa gently stroked my hair and my face and tried to soothe me. Wiping my face, I said, "Now I have two people who really love me, for me and not for anything else and I love them too the same way."

She hugged me tight and said, "I do love you unconditionally; you're my Chubby love. You are my life and I guess she feels the same way. You are still her baby brother." She smiled, "Now I understand why she got so mad at you and I agree with her. She has every right to be mad at you."

As she held me tight and kissed me, she sighed, "Myyy God we are so much alike. We have so much in common, that it's no wonder that we have gotten so close." She wiped my tears and said softly, "Don't cry baby, I am here and you know how much I love you. We will make it, I promise." Then she began to give me a massage me in the way I loved most, and we made the most wonderful love; it offered me the release of tension that I really needed. That night she knew what to do to bring me out of that bad mood and as she held me that night, I fell asleep like a baby.

We woke up the next day and carried on our usual routines. As we drank our morning coffee together, Mahsa asked me to wait, "Let me take a quick shower and we will go together." I agreed because I knew she would be going that way anyway. She dropped me off saying, "I will see you tomorrow Chubby. Have a good one and tell anyone who you think is safe that I said hi.

After school, I went home first to change then headed over to my sister's for lunch. Then I took a little nap until my sister called me with a list of things to do before the party. "Yousef, go to the market and buy these things. Be sure to come back fast, we are late." I said, "But they always come late anyway, don't worry." She literally pushed me out the door, saying "Just go and come right back. And please don't waste time stopping and talking so much just go and come back fast." I went and picked up the supplies quickly and came right back without any adventures.

Little by little people started arriving and I found out that the party that night was for the birthday of someone, but I didn't know who.

Everybody was so happy: singing, playing and dancing. But in their midst, I was alone; I was there with them physically but not mentally. Finally I couldn't stand it anymore; around ten-thirty, I picked up the phone, took it into a bathroom and called her. When she picked up the phone, I said "Good evening Sweetie! Did I wake you up?" She smiled over the phone, "No, I just lying in bed." I said, "I just called you to say how much I miss you and that I love you so much." Mahsa then asked, "How many people are there?" "Oh, about thirty." "Your poor sister! She had to cook for all those people?" I shrugged, "Yes but she had little help this time." We talked for a little while until she said, "You should go, go Chubby, go and I will see you tomorrow." and then hung up. I returned the phone to its usual place and went back into the living room to rejoin the others. My brother and a cousin started in on teasing me and asked, "Where is Ms. Doctor?" My sister turned sharply toward them, "What?" she demanded. The room got quiet as my brother spoke up, "Yousef has a girlfriend and she is a doctor." My sister looked at me hard and said, "So that was her the other day, the one my son was trying to invite in the house. Why you didn't tell me?" Thinking quickly, I assured my sister, "Those guys are just teasing me. There's nothing going on believe me." I repeated myself, "There's nothing going on." Turning so they could hear me, I said, "Yes I *do* have a friend, but she is just a friend that's all." I took a seat as if there was nothing more to be said on the matter. But inside, I was shaking. I wanted to kill my brother and cousin for squealing on me.

As the party guests left one by one; my other brother was one of the last to leave when he came up to me and said, "Yousef, you didn't tell us that you have a girlfriend." Quick as a cat, my sister got between us, scolding my brother, "Stop teasing him so much! It's none of your business whether he has one or not."

I spent the night at my sister's and the next morning I went home to pick up my books and went to school. After the classes let out, I headed to the intersection by the burger shop and waited for her. She picked me up and we drove to the north part of town when I asked, "Where are you going?" She replied, "There is this great place to have lunch." It was an Italian sandwich shop and true to her word, the food was great.

As we waited for our food, Mahsa asked, "When is your birthday?" Surprised, I asked, "Why do you want to know?" She laughed, "I just want to know. I promise there won't be any parties or surprises. I would just like to buy you something nice, like some cologne. That's all." So I told her when my birthday is, and while we carried on with that little argument, the food and sodas arrived. We ate and talked and at that point I asked her, "When do you want to come to your house for a night?" Mahsa smiled and promised me, "Very soon, it will be a night on a very special occasion. Then I will come. Don't worry; it's my house too right?"

Days passed and I made sure to visit my sister more often for lunch which made her happy. One afternoon, I was home and Mahsa was supposed to call me. But I didn't hear from her until about six. She asked, "Are you home?" "Yes I am home." "Good." she told me, I am coming over in about half an hour. Do you what anything?" I didn't have to think too hard about that as I answered, "No I don't need anything. The only thing I want is you here with me, that's it."

CHAPTER 10

For The Love of Rumi

Mahsa took forty five minutes to get to the house. She rang the bell and I opened the door. She stepped in and presented me with a bottle of very good wine. She made herself comfortable in the living room as I hunted around for two wine glasses and an opener. I opened the bottle with a beautiful little 'pop' and filled up both glasses. Then I asked her to wait for a moment while I got the room. She waited with a delighted look on her face while I lit some candles, turned off all the lights and sat next to her. We raised our glasses to toast our love and friendship.

When I refilled our glasses, we toasted our love and our trust. In the middle of this, I had an idea and asked if she would like me to read some poems for her. She asked, "Poems by whom?" "Rumi and Hafez" "Oh yes." She said,

Y. JOSEPHSON

"I would love to hear them in your voice." I grabbed a book of Rumi off a nearby shelf and began to read:

You are my king of kings; you are my Lord and my God.

You are my belief inside my soul and my heart.

If you blow on me I will rise and be alive again.

What's one life worth, when you are my hundreds of lives?

Without you my life is poison - not life.

You are my soul and you are my life.

The poison from you will be anti-poison in my body.

You will be my sweet (happiness) and sugar (good time).

You are my garden, green land and my haven.

You are my straight pine (pure love) and smiling flower (joy).

You are also my God and my beautiful Angel.

You are not just a big diamond; you are the source of that diamond.

I will be quiet because you have to tell me who you are.

Because in speech you will be my cause.

(Translated by: Yousef)Divan Shams Tabriz #3365

BE HIDDEN LOVE

As I read, Mahsa rested her head on my shoulder. When I fell silent, she softly asked, "Why did you stop?" I replied, "Because I wanted to look at you and celebrate a toast to you and to your love for me. I kissed her and added, "Rumi speaks from my heart too." Then I asked her to wait as I was not finished yet. I start reading again:

O lovers, lovers, this day you and we are fallen into a whirlpool: who knows how to swim?

Though the world torrent should overflow and every wave become like a dromedary, why shall the waterfowl worry? It is the bird of the air that should be anxious.

Our faces are lit up with gratitude, schooled as we are in wave and sea, inasmuch as ocean and flood are life increasing to the fish.

Elder, hand us a towel; water, let us plunge into you;

Moses son of Imran, come, smite the water of the sea with your staff!

This wind concocts in every head a different passion; let my passion be for yonder cupbearer, and you may have all the rest! (Translated by: A.J. Arberry)

This is not the whole poem because I don't want you, Dear Reader, to get bored. But if you really like this poetry, you can get a book of Rumi and read the whole thing.

Mahsa was holding me as if I was going somewhere and she didn't want to be left behind. She begged me to read more and this time I opened a Hafez book and read some of his work to her. If I can find a good translation of the Hafez poem I read for her, I will share it with you later; on this I promise.

After I finished reading the Hafez poem, Mahsa grabbed my face and gave me one of those kisses I will always love. Then pointed out how two candles leaned into to each other and melted onto a third between them and made something of a mirror image in 3D. She then said, "That one is me and the other one is you and we made something that looks like us but is not us. Overwhelmed, she buried her face in my shoulder and started crying. I asked her, "Why the tears?" And all she could say was, "Because."

Poor Mahsa had gotten so emotional. After she regained her composure, we checked the time and it was almost ten. I asked, "Are you hungry?" She sniffed, "Yes but I cannot drive." Then I asked, "Can you walk?" "If you help me, then yes I can walk."

Holding Mahsa's arm, I told her about a Mexican restaurant I knew of just down the hill; about a ten minute walk. Straightening herself, she said "Then let's go." We walked to the restaurant in silence arm in arm.

BE HIDDEN LOVE

As we looked over the menu; I knew exactly what I wanted. I said, "I want the special house combo, it's my favorite!" After looking the menu over carefully, Mahsa decided to order the same, and added a margarita. The waiter brought out chips and salsa and an enormous margarita for Mahsa. We munched on those until our food was brought to us. We ate our food and shared the margarita. When the waiter dropped off the bill, I was going to pay, but she wouldn't let me. It was already eleven when we stumbled home. The temperature had dropped and it was cold, but we both were a little drunk so we didn't feel the cold that much. That uphill walk helped warm us up anyway. As we walked, Mahsa held my hand in both of hers and asked me to explain the Rumi poem I read for her earlier. I explained the many layers of meaning to that specific poem. If we look at it from a Gnostic perspective the poem would have one meaning as opposed to a literal meaning which would also be valid from Rumi's standpoint.

When we got home, I relit the candles and made some tea. I took a seat next to her as she opened the Rumi book, selected a poem and gave it to me to read. I read that poem to her and as before she rested her head on my shoulder. When I finished, she sat a little while considering the words, then said, "I think I understand a little better. Can you open it up a little more for me?" I then asked, "What was it exactly that you understood about the poem?" She explained what she had gotten from it and it was a good start. I went over the poem again line by line, explaining the meaning of each one for her. When I was done, I got up to refill our glasses with more tea. We talked some more, finished our tea and decided that it was time for bed; it was quite late. Mahsa looked around and asked, "Where should I sleep?" I brought out the other mattress and placed it next to mine and got out some blankets and a comforter; we both washed up and went to bed.

We made ourselves comfortable in our makeshift beds and I said, "I am so sorry that I don't have anything else to give you except my long shirt." "It's fine." She said "There's nothing wrong with it. Don't worry, it's very comfortable."

As I lay next to her, I could feel the heat radiating from her body and felt her heart beating wildly. She turned to me and kissed me deeply. It was the kind of hot, romantic kiss that you could get lost in forever. That kiss turned me on too, this was the night we made love right there on the floor, it was an exciting and romantic experience for both of us.

Mahsa and I got so hot and out of control; we just couldn't stop or get enough of each other. I think those poems acted like an aphrodisiac, as our love making became part of the poetry we read earlier that evening. We wanted to experience for ourselves how it felt to be truly free from the land, its laws or any other limitations. We wanted to free our souls to feel our love the way, Rumi had described in his art.

We went beyond the limits of ecstasy and exploded into each other, much the same way a star might supernova. We embraced each other as though our bodies would dissolve into a singular mass of energy and love. It was through sheer exhaustion and the physical limitations of our bodies that caused us to finally relax. Basking in each other's afterglow, Mahsa asked, "What happened? Why couldn't we go any further?" I replied, "Oh my sweet Honey Bunch, it is not so important of how far we go, but our journey along the way. We have to learn the proper technique and that's not easy, plus we cannot expect to make the trip in just one shot, but we can get there with time and patience." Then we wrapped our arms tightly around each other and went to sleep.

The next morning was business as usual; we were up at 7 and I got ready for school. Mahsa asked me if I would like to have breakfast out this morning, I said, "Sure, why not? I'd love to." We went to a coffee shop on the way to school and had a good breakfast. We didn't realize how hungry we were until the food arrived and we devoured everything on our plates. Then she dropped me off at school, saying, "See you, I want to be you."

Dear Reader,

Here is the poem by Hafez I promised you a few pages

ago. I couldn't find any translation I liked, so I made one myself. I hope you enjoy it and may it have as much meaning for you as it did for Mahsa and me. Be a lover and love as love loves.

My beloved is love; she showed me the door of heaven, then she showed me the road to get to heaven's door, Oh my beloved is like a saki who brings the red wine and moves within a circle and then comes to me; my beloved is the soul and gives me one too.

The blood drops from my heart because, when finally the wind blows the silent air and blows through your long black wavy hair; it breaks the base of that perfumed Babel and that I cannot bear.

How I can rest and be secure in my beloved? Is it love's heart? When every second we heard the sound of the bell and that sound means that we have to be ready to move out again.

If your old dear master tells you to drop the red wine on your clean prayer rug, staining it - do that! Because he knows the customs of that place better than anybody else.

How do people who relax on the beach know! How we went through the heavy terrifying lonely ocean waves when the tornados were around us in that truly lightless night.

In the end everything I did from selfishness for my beloved shall love become open to the public, then how I can hold my love in secret, when they talk about it; make a place and gathering for my love.

Oh Hafez! If you wanted to be with your beloved, then love shall never ever forget you have your love inside your heart. And when you are lucky to see your love, stay with it and forget about this life - just throw it away.

Translated by: Yousef   (first poem from the book)

From that point on, I spent more time with my sister in the afternoons. Sometimes I would wait for my little nephew to take him home after school and would stay for a couple of hours then I would return to my other house.

My schedule was like this: three or four nights a week, I stayed with Mahsa and two or three nights she stayed with me. This lasted for the two weeks my brother wasn't in town but when he was in town, we would have to change the program. I would head to her house straight from school and stay until six or seven and sometimes push it until nine. On such nights, Mahsa sometimes asked me to read poems to her which I was delighted to do. After I would finish, I explained my interpretations. But it was never quite like the first night I read for her.

This went on until my birthday; when my sister decided to plan a family gathering for a weekend night because then my other brother could be there too. So I was free for my actual birthday and Mahsa offered to take me out for dinner. I said, "I'd love to, but on one condition; I never go to school on my birthday - no way!" Laughing, she agreed with me.

The special night arrived and Mahsa requested that I wear a tie. She took me to a place I had always wanted to go; one of the hottest nightclubs in Tehran. But it had a lot restrictions and I couldn't just go by myself. Many of the nicer nightclubs in Iran at the time never allowed entry to singles alone; they always must be accompanied by a date. This night, I was with her and getting inside was extra special. This place was mostly known for its live music and tonight was no exception; there was a particularly good Iranian singer onstage. Excited, I asked Mahsa if she knew about the night's entertainment. She beamed at me with a dazzling smile, "Oh yes that's why I brought you here!"

We were led to very cozy table in a secluded corner; it was quieter there, but offered a vantage point that we could see everything. I thought to myself, 'She must have had to reserve this table several nights ago!' Which was true, because when I asked her about it later and she told me yes? So as soon as we were seated, a waiter handed us each two menus. Mahsa didn't even bother look at them as she promptly ordered a bottle of champagne and was very specific about the name. She also requested some caviar with crackers. When the waiter brought us the champagne, Mahsa checked the bottle and told him that it wasn't cold enough. "Please bring a colder bottle and an ice bucket." He quickly returned with another bottle which she approved. The waiter then opened the champagne with all the formality a good bottle of champagne should have; presenting the cork to Mahsa, then pouring a small amount for her to sample. Upon her approval, he finished pouring her glass and turned to me, filling mine and then covered the opened bottle with a cloth and deposited it in the ice bucket. Mahsa lifted her glass and I copied her. She said, "I offer this toast to you as we celebrate your first birthday together." I then toasted to her love. We feasted like royalty on the caviar, which Mahsa made very tasty with some butter and lime on crackers.

We finished our first glass and I filled our glasses just as the singer returned to the stage to sing one of his best songs. He sang in both Farsi and English which we thought was great. Mahsa motioned for our waiter and we order our main course, but she requested that the food be ready in an hour. The waiter took our order and left.

We set our drinks down and went to dance; first one, then a second; when the singer is on cue, began a very slow, romantic song. As we moved along the dance floor, Mahsa asked, "Do you want to keep dancing?" Holding her close, I said, "Of course I want to stay, this is my favorite dance." There were only four couples on the dance floor and we lingered in each other's arms until the last note faded away. Mahsa brushed a stray strand of hair from her face, saying, "I am little tired, how about you?" I agreed. She said, "But why you didn't say so?" Shrugging, "I will never complain of being tired, not while I am with you - no way!" Smiling at her, I added, "I couldn't bring myself to ask to go back to our seats because I was enjoying myself. What else could I want?"

We returned to our table and sat down, I refilled our glasses and we drank to our love and to a good New Year for us both. We finished the first bottle and asked the waiter to bring a second, which was much nicer than the first. He opened it and filled our glasses. We were just about to enjoy our first sip, when the singer began one of our all-time favorite Italian songs from the early sixties. Mahsa grabbed my hand and practically dragged me onto dance floor, saying, "Follow my lead!" The song was a little long, but we didn't feel hunger or thirst, we just danced. Breathless, we stumbled back to our table just in time for the food to arrive. As plates of filet mignon and wood-fired barbecued chicken kebab were set before us, I refilled our glasses and we shared that sumptuous meal together.

After dinner we hit the dance floor again and had a lot of fun. As the old saying goes, 'Time flies when you're having fun.' And before we knew it; it was two-thirty and Mahsa was asking me if I would like to stay or if I wanted to go home? I looked at her and cocked my eyebrow as if to say, "What do you think?" She grinned, "Well, it's going to be like this until four-thirty or five." I laughed and said, "I would much rather go home and be with you." Mahsa called for the check and we went home.

As soon as we got home, Mahsa headed straight for the bedroom to change. I went to pour a pitcher of cold water which I brought to the bedroom with two glasses, and then I went in to change. When I came back out, I saw a box, beautifully wrapped on my pillow. I just stood there looking at it. Mahsa came over to the bed where I was standing and asked, "Don't you want to open it?" Looking up at her, I said, "Yes but first I want to see if I can guess what is inside." I picked up the box and shook it to see if that would offer me any clues as to what was inside, but no such luck. I gave in to curiosity and started to open it very slowly. When I pulled the gift wrap away, I discovered a beautiful box, which I opened to discover a gorgeous cologne bottle. I uncapped the bottle and put some on. My sweet Jesus what an exquisite smell it had! I had never smelled anything like it before; it was something that was totally new to me. I turned to her, "What is the name of this cologne?" She pointed out the name on the bottle and pronounced it for me; the cologne was from Hermes of Paris. Slyly Mahsa confessed that she had always loved that scent, so I put on a little more and placed the bottle on the nightstand next to her beauty products.

I climbed back into bed when Mahsa held up her hand, "Did you forget something?" Confused, I looked around and couldn't think of anything; then suddenly I looked down at myself. Oh yes, I did forget one important thing - my T-shirt. I shrugged it off and now I was ready for bed.

Mahsa held and kissed me, saying, "Yousef this is your night, my night, our night." She added, "I am totally yours!" First I kissed her and thanked her for such a perfect night and added, "This is my first birthday with us together and I hope we have many more of each other's birthday to celebrate together." I looked at her in the dim light, "Yes this is your night, my night, our night but I am totally yours as well."

Then she got up and went into the bathroom. It was that point that I noticed that she had put another flat sheet over the fitted sheet and I couldn't figure out why. Mahsa came out with a small bottle then I knew why she put the flat sheet down. She said to me to turn on my stomach which I did; she poured some of the cool lotion on my skin and gave me a massage from neck to feet. I turned over and she massaged the entire length of my body. When she finished, she put some lotion on herself and a little more on me and began to give me body-to-body massage.

We made love for a long time, slow and sensuous. The lotion she put on our bodies totally drove me nuts; we couldn't hold onto each other so we crashed against each other like waves making hard passionate love to the shore. She took me further beyond any imagination. She gave herself to me like never before, and she had me utterly and completely. I was totally under her control and wanted nothing other than her pleasure. I was like the moths that buzz around a fire; burning with her flame and smoldering in ecstasy. The place she took me so willingly and lovingly made love her much, much more from that night on. I don't know how she did it but she did.

After we had come back down to earth and reality, Mahsa gave me one of those kisses, the kind that I die for every day. She whispered in my ear, "Happy birthday my Chubby, my sweetheart." She hugged me tight and kissed me again.

That was most beautiful gift I had ever gotten from anyone. With such a gift, I was like clay in her hands and she could do anything to me after that night.

But all she did was giving me more love and kindness.

We fell asleep holding each other tightly and didn't get up until around noon. I opened my eyes at her kiss as she said, "Wake up Birthday Boy! Happy birthday!" When she kissed me again that got me up and out of bed.

After I washed up and joined her in the kitchen, Mahsa said, "All you need to do is fix some tea if you want. I am making breakfast for you today." I made tea and just sat there, watching her bustle around the kitchen on my behalf.

She made a wonderful breakfast complete with Italian coffee. After finishing our meal, I helped her clean up the kitchen and then we went out to the living room with our tea to relax and smoke. As we sat on the sofa, I asked if she could open the sofa to make more room. Mahsa pushed a pillow aside, following her lead; I removed the rest of the pillows. She looked me curiously and asked, "What are you doing?" I said, "I am making more room on the sofa." Confused, she said, "Why?" I flashed her a wicked smile, "So I can make love with you out here." Mahsa's cheeks colored, "Are you kidding me?" She searched my eyes to see if I was joking, "Oh my God, you are *not* kidding me!" I took her in my arms and we made such beautiful, tender love. Afterward, I rested my face on her breasts as she stroked my hair. We laid there in perfect bliss until she looked at the clock and said, "Chubby, it is three-thirty. You have to go! Quick, take a shower and get to your sister's. You have to get up my love my Chubby."

I got up reluctantly and gazed sadly into her eyes, I really did not want to leave. Mahsa smiled at me sweetly, "I love you and yes, I am going to miss you. But go, take a shower and go, you will be late and you know how I feel about being late. Go my Chubby, my sweetheart go." I took a shower and got dressed. I came out, all ready to go; I kissed her saying, "I am going to miss you so much. I will call you." Mahsa wrapped her arms around me as we walked to the door and kissed me saying, "I hope you have a wonderful time. I will be with you in spirit. Just try to be happy."

I went back to my place and changed clothes again; I also put on some of that amazing cologne Mahsa had given me, and then headed over to my sister's. I was lucky because when I got there a little after five, nobody was there yet. Guests started arriving around seven. By eight-thirty, or nine, the party was fully underway with just about everyone there, having fun. I was okay, but I missed Mahsa so much that by ten I broke down and called her; we talked for a few minutes then she said, "You should go back to your party. But don't forget I need details, okay?" I said O.K. and we hung up.

I went back to living room to join the others when my brother asked me, "Where is your friend Ms. Doctor?" "Shut up!" I hissed at him, "Don't mess it up like the other time or sister will get mad." But my brother pressed me, "Will we ever meet her or not?" I answered quickly, "In time yes you will meet her. Now let it be!"

To her credit, my sister outdid herself with the wonderful dinner she made for everyone. This night was for family only and one of the younger ones started singing and dancing and they helped make it a fun night for everybody. Then after dinner they brought out a cake with a single candle. Tea was served with the cake and everybody sat around talking and having fun together. By twelve-thirty, people started leaving and last ones as always were my brothers and my eldest brother's family, I spent the night at my sister's and went home the next day around noon. My brother was home and gave me some money for my birthday. Then he took a shower and told me that he would not be coming home that night. What else could I want from God! I sat alone in the house and looked over all the things I had gotten for my birthday; my eldest brother also gave me some money and I got small gifts from others. All in all, I had a fantastic birthday.

Forty minutes later, I called Mahsa. When she picked up, I said "Hello Honey Bunch!" She squealed in delight, "Hi Chubby, where are you?" "I am home. I just called to see if you were home." I was hopeful, "I can run over there." "Yes" she said, "I am home and I am so looking forward to seeing you!" I kissed her and said, "I'll be there in a few minutes!" She laughed and said, "Okay, then I will see you later. I hung up the phone, took a quick shower and ran over to our house.

When I got there and opened the door, she was lying on the sofa. She got up, gave me a hug and a kiss and asked, "Do you want coffee?" "Yes" I answered, "But let me make it." "That's okay" she called from the kitchen, "I already made it for you. She emerged from the kitchen with two mugs of coffee. We sat down on the sofa and I lit two cigarettes. Then she asked about the party last night, saying, "Tell me everything. I want to know all about it."

I regaled her of everything that happened that night and who gave me what. "I must confess" I told her, "The most exciting and lovely gifts I got was from you the night before. I will never ever forget them because it was our first birthday together and it meant so much to me." She hugged me and gave me one of those lovely kisses saying, "That was nothing, everything I have is yours. My heart is yours as yours is mine I didn't give you anything yet. You will have to wait for it until right time." Her eyes sparkled, she was so beautiful. "You will see my real gift in good time." She kissed me again and again. Leaning into her, I asked playfully, "Now where were we that last time?" Mahsa caught that naughty twinkle in my eye and retorted, "Yousef, shut up and finish your coffee!"

Mahsa got up and went to the bedroom; I finished my coffee and lit another cigarette. Moments later, she came out wearing a jogging suit and said, "Let's get the hell out of here." She went to kitchen to turn off the coffee maker then we went out. I didn't know where we were going, She drove to the west side of town and we left Tehran altogether. Mahsa then headed north, past the dam. She continued until we found the shore and saw boats. Mahsa parked the car and we went to check things out.

We went over to the boat rental area and picked one. We boarded the boat and the guy motored away from the docks. I asked him, "Where do you plan to take us?" The skipper shrugged, "Just around the lake and that's about it." I told him that we wanted to go out to the river that followed the road. He said, "That's fine, but it will be more expensive." Mahsa stepped in saying, "Don't worry about the money, please take us there." "Yes Ma'm." the boatman answered. He took us around the lake and out to the river. He followed the river for a while and then turned to a side waterway. At that point, the boatman turned off the motor and rowed the boat with oars.

The channel was narrow and quiet; overgrown with weeds and rushes, while the air was filled with birdsong. It was so beautiful and peaceful. As we drifted among the greenery, we held each other so close and kissed, fully enjoying the serenity of the place. Those moments were so romantic even though the weather was chilly; we kept warm with our shared body heat so that we didn't even notice the cold. Locked in our embrace and lost in each other's gaze, we didn't speak. Nothing needed to be said out loud as we could feel what the other was thinking. We let ourselves dissolve into the natural world around us as we became one person, which was a million times better than talking. We could feel each other's heartbeat, temperature and the flowing blood inside of each other veins. It was one of the most precious moments that we have been waiting for. We spent two or three hours drifting and enjoying ourselves and the beauty that surrounded us. In truth, we lost all track of time; until the colors of sunset lit the skies and boatman informed us that we have to go back. Boats were not allowed to be on the lake after dark. He hurried back to the docks as fast as he could. Mahsa handed the skipper some money and he hesitated, saying, "Ma'am it's not going to be that much!" Mahsa told him to keep the rest. Grateful, the boatman gave us his name and said, "Anytime you need a boat, I am at your service." We thanked him for giving us such a nice ride. We got back to the car just in time to catch a glorious sunset. It was the perfect end to a very romantic day.

After the sun had set we headed back to Tehran. I sat right next to her as she drove with my arm around her. She took her time and drove at a leisurely pace, even on the freeway until we got into town. On our way home, we stopped at an Italian shop and bought two sandwiches and a bottle of wine. Mahsa parked the car, shut off the engine and turned to me. She took my face in both hands and kissed me full on the lips; time froze for those minutes and when she finally released me, she said, "You drove me crazy all the way home! I so badly wanted to pull the car over and kiss you. But it had to wait, until now." She sighed happily, "I love you so much, Chubby, you cannot imagine how much," We grabbed the food and wine and headed upstairs.

As soon as we got in, we both went to the bedroom and got out of those cloths and put our robes on. We were both starving, so we set the table and down for dinner. After dinner, we turned on the TV, but the state run programs did not keep our interest, so we listened to some music instead until around ten. We could barely keep our eyes open; all that fresh air had worn us out, especially Mahsa. We wrapped our arms around each other and quickly fell asleep. I got up first in the morning and begged her not to move because I knew she was so tired. I took a shower and just before I left for school and kissed her saying, "I'll see you later this afternoon."

Important note:

I think it is best for you, my dear readers, to know that while I have been typing this manuscript, I would become so emotional from all these memories coming back to me that I would break down in tears. I would have to stop sometimes even for a few days to regain control over my emotions. Then there would be times that I was so happy to remember minute by minute all those special times. But the times that I would get so sad of what I lost and what I am still missing are the hardest to deal with. Although I felt that sometimes writing this story would kill me; I thought you should know about my process to bring you this story. Writing this has been one of the most difficult things I have ever done and will most likely do in my life.

After school I went straight to our house and when I opened the door, Mahsa was relaxing on the sofa drinking coffee, smoking a cigarette and listening to music. When she heard me come in, she greeted me with a hug and asked if I would like some coffee. I could never pass on her amazing coffee. She brought me a mug and I joined her in the living room and lit a cigarette. Then she asked me if I had lunch yet, and I said, "No, how about you?" She shook her head, "No and I didn't have breakfast either." At that Mahsa decided to call in an order to our favorite Italian restaurant for two foot-long sandwiches. When the food arrived, we enjoyed them with some of the wine left over from the previous night. Mahsa and I had a very nice lunch together.

After lunch we curled up together on the sofa and listened to music. Mahsa then confessed to me that she didn't feel good and that she felt really tired. So we just laid there in each other's arms and relaxed to the sounds of the music. I think we both drifted off to asleep for a couple of hours. When we awoke, Mahsa got up and made fresh coffee. When it was ready, I filled up our mugs and lit our cigarettes, when she asked me if I could read some more poetry to her. Of course I was happy to do so; I found a book of Rumi, which I knew was what she really wanted to hear. I gave her the book to pick one for me.

I began reading as she held my hand; when I finished, I started to explain the meanings of the poem. Halfway through my explanation, Mahsa grabbed my face and kissed me hard saying "Oh thank you Chubby!" I have never been thanked that way for reading Rumi before, but the feeling that I got from her was like no other. I didn't say anything and continued my explanation, and after I finished, I took both her hands in mine and we looked deep into each other's eyes. We understood each other very well and didn't need to say anything out loud. The timing for this magical moment could not have been more perfect! The sun was just about to set and the sky was filled with brilliant orange which painted the clouds deep red along the horizon.

I don't know how long we sat eyes locked to one another; time froze and it seemed that the universe itself held its breath. All I remember is the spell broke, like a bubble bursting as Mahsa suddenly caught a glimpse of my watch and whispered, "I'm sorry Chubby, but I think it is time to go." I looked at my watch too, it was after seven and she was right as usual. We held each other so tightly that I can still almost feel it. Then we kissed and I said sadly, "I'll see you later alligator and she quipped back, "Just don't let me bite you. See you - I want to be you."

I went home, but nobody was there. I made a couple of phone calls and found out everybody was at my cousin's, so I went there to join them. I spent the evening surrounded with family but still felt so alone. My brother and I went home together just before midnight. I went to school the next day and headed over to Mahsa's.

As soon as I got in, I noticed that everything was exactly the same as last night; dishes were unwashed and right where we left them. I found Mahsa in bed; but when she looked at me, I could tell that something was wrong. "What is wrong?" She groaned, "I feel awful! All my bones hurt and I think I have a fever too." She warned me not to get too close to her because she was afraid that I would get sick too. I asked, "Do you have anything for the cold?" "Yes" she motioned, "Look in there and bring me that medicine chest." She found couple of things and I went and got her some water and she took some pills. I let her rest and went back to the kitchen and checked the freezer; we had one piece of chicken left. I took it out to thaw and then looked in the refrigerator and found some vegetables; so I started preparing a nice chicken soup for

325

Y. JOSEPHSON

her. I put everything in a large pot on the stove to simmer then went and sat next to her.

I reached out to hold her hand but she pushed me away, saying, "Don't get close to me or you're going to get sick too." Despite her protests, I held her hand anyway and tried to think of anything else I could do for her. I suggested that I give her a deep muscle massage that would help take away the chills and aches. Mahsa finally agreed and I gave her a very deep penetrating massage. From time to time I went to check on the soup see how it was coming along.

After a couple of hours, the soup was ready. I made it very spicy. I spooned some into a bowl and brought it to her on a tray. I helped her to sit upright then gave her the tray. She lifted to spoon for her first sip and I told her, "Be careful, it is hot!" She took the first spoonful then sputter, "It is very hot! Why did you make it that hot?" "Because" I said, "It's good for the cold!" When she finished the whole bowl, I asked her if she wanted anymore, but she said, "No that's enough hot for now." and she settled back under the covers again. I put another heavy blanket on her and let her rest.

After about ten or fifteen minutes, she started sweating; I wiped her face with tissues and finally she fell asleep. I just sat there and look at her red face, but knew that I couldn't do anything more. I went out to the living room for a smoke and got myself a bowl of soup; Mahsa was right, it was very hot!

Mahsa got up around sunset and was surprised to find me there. I said, "Yes, I stayed, where else do I have to go? I have to stay with you tonight to make sure that you are okay; no ands, ifs or buts." Mahsa shook her head, protesting, "But you risk messing everything up if you don't go see your sister tonight!" "No" I reassured her, "I will call and let my brother know that I won't be home tonight." I continued, "I did call several times but nobody was at our house; then I called my sister and told her if he calls for me to let him know I am at a friend's house tonight. I talked with my sister for a few minutes and she is okay with it." She looked doubtful and said, "You know that you are crazy." To that I replied, "It's because you made me that way."

With that matter settled, Mahsa then asked me to turn on the stereo so at least we could listen to some music. As I joined her on the couch, she pushed me away again. Now it was my turn to protest, "Oh come on, I am far enough away from you; don't be such a bad girl! I am fine, don't worry about it."

Around eight-thirty, I heated up the soup again and brought her a bowl. Mahsa asked me if it was the same soup as before. I said, "Yes and there is enough for tomorrow too. She smiled at me and said, "Yousef, you are such a good chef to think for two days ahead." We talked while she ate her soup and after she was done, she took some more medicine. A half an hour later, she started to get a little dizzy. I asked her to relax and to go back to bed; to comfort her, I gave her a little ear and face massage. She fell asleep like a baby. I stayed with her for a little while then went to living room. I got a cup of tea for myself, went back to the living room and lit a cigarette. As I sat there; I couldn't help myself, tears started running down my face as I recalled how much fun we had on that sofa just a couple of days earlier. Now she is sick and I felt very much alone. I finished my tea and got a cup of soup then I went to bed and lay down next to her. Mahsa was sound asleep and didn't even move when I crept in next to her; I couldn't help myself I kissed her on the chin and rested my arm under her neck and quickly fell asleep. The next morning, I got up first; shortly after, Mahsa stretched and yawned and got up too, I innocently asked, "Would you want me to stay here with you today?" Mahsa was adamant and snapped, "No you go to school!" I knew I couldn't win this argument, "Okay, but please stay in bed and rest." Then I asked if she needed anything. She told me what she wanted and I got them for her and went off to school.

After school, I stopped at a nearby pharmacy and asked the doctor what might be wrong with her. He gave me some cough syrup and two kinds of pills, but warned me, saying, "If she doesn't feel better within a couple of days, you had better take her to the doctor."

When I got home, Mahsa was still in bed but awake. I sat down next to her and tried to give her a kiss, but she pushed me away again. I gave her the bag, and she looked at me and asked, "What is this?" I replied with a smile and said, "Look inside and you will see." She looked delighted at what she found and blew me a kiss saying, "Thank you Chubby. I love you so much! You are and angel." I blew a kiss back at her, went to the kitchen to heat up the soup and brought two steaming cups; one for her and one for myself. After we finished the soup, Mahsa asked, "When do I have to take these?" I explained to her that she needed to take them every six hours and she replied, "I will start them tonight at six o'clock."

I stayed with her until eight, when she told me firmly, "Yousef, you have to go. Go home don't you mess this up." I hesitated, reluctant to leave, "Are you sure you will be okay?" Mahsa reassured me that yes she was okay, "Please just go, I can take care of myself, don't worry you just do your thing." I kissed her hand and went back to my place.

When I got in, I was thrilled that my brother wasn't home yet. I changed into shorts and a t-shirt and made some tea. My brother came home, so I made some tea for him as well. We caught up on the last few days and I asked him if he spoke to our sister. He said no and asked why so I told him about last night. He shrugged and said, "It is okay, as long as we know where you are. We hung out for about an hour; then he took a shower and got ready to go out again. Before he left, he said, "I'll see you later." After he was gone, I called Mahsa see how she was doing. She told me that she felt much better but was still in bed. I told her that it was probably best for her to stay there and get more rest and she agreed. I also said that I was going to my sister's for dinner. She asked, "Now what am I supposed to do?" then she laughed and added, "Go Chubby, have a lot of fun, baby and say hi for me!" Her laughter made me miss her even more, but what could I do? All I could say was that I would certainly do my best.

I stayed at my sister's until midnight then headed home. I went to bed and waited for sleep to come; what a night and what a sleep. The hours passed and every thought was all about her. The next day I dragged myself to school and went over to her place in the afternoon, but she wasn't home. As I waited, not sure what to do next, when suddenly Mahsa came bustling in; her hands were full of bags. I ran to greet her and took some bags from her and we put them on the counter. She turned to me with a huge smile, gave me a hug and said, "I missed you so much baby!" I looked her up and down, saying, "Where have you been? When I found you weren't home, do you know how many things crossed my mind?" I gave her a kiss and added, "I missed you too Honey Bunch."

She looked deep into my eyes and sighed, "My poor baby. I'm sorry; I just went over to the other house to grab my backgammon set and the projector. I had to take care of something over there anyway." She kissed me again and said, "I'm sorry baby, I didn't know that you would get here so early." She handed me the backgammon, saying, "Now go set it up, I will challenge you to a game. And you should know that I am a good player!" Then she went into the bedroom to change.

In the middle of our game, Mahsa announced, "By the way, you have been invited to a charity party in the near future. It's just after the New Year, I think. So you can be ready for it." I was concerned, "Are you sure this will be okay? Will you be there too?" I had a million questions. She reassured me, "Yes, everything will be fine. We will arrive separately; I only used your first name, so now you are Mr. Yousef. How do you like that?" Mahsa looked very pleased with herself, "Do you like it?" I shrugged and said, "Yes, I think so. Thank you. At least I am only Yousef.

We continued on with our game. Mahsa was right, she was much better than I was as she kicked my butt. After she claimed her backgammon victory, we went out for an early dinner. Then she gave me a ride home. She called me when she got home, because she knew that I would worry if she didn't call. We talked for a few minutes then kissed each other good night and hung up. I made myself comfortable and opened up my school books and began to study. Around eight, my brother got home and when he saw me studying, he looked so happy. But I could tell by the look in his eyes that he was surprised too. What he didn't know was that I was studying not so much myself, but because Mahsa asked me to.

Days passed and it seemed that everything was back to normal. One day, I stopped by Mahsa's place and knocked on the door. Mahsa opened the door and said, "Thank God you came! Do you want some coffee? I just made some." A chill crept up my spine, but I shrugged it off and said, "Sure." but I didn't like the way she sounded; something wasn't right. My fears were confirmed when she brought the coffee and I looked into her eyes and could tell that she wasn't really there. I couldn't stand it anymore; I asked her what was wrong. For quite a long time, she didn't say anything, so I asked again and she blurted out, "Meetra called today and I have to go back to Shiraz. I don't know what I will be facing when I get there!" I braced myself for the worst and asked, "When are you going?" She looked at me in utter despair, "The day after tomorrow." Then she crumpled into my arms. I held her tightly and tried to comfort her, "It is probably nothing. Try not to think about anything bad!" She rested her head on my shoulder and I could feel something wet against my neck. I turned my head toward her, and discovered her crying. I hugged her tighter, kissed her and wiped the tears from her face, I gazed into her eyes, those ocean blue eyes that had suddenly become so red. I kissed those eyes and burst out laughing. Mahsa jumped, startled at the sound and demanded, "What is so funny about this?" Chuckling, I answered, "It's your beautiful eyes; they are so bloodshot. She started to get upset with me and snapped, "And you think this is funny?" I shook my head, "No, of course not! It's just the way I saw it that was funny - I never saw the ocean get so bloody." As soon as she heard that she couldn't control herself and she too started laughing loudly, throwing her head back, saying, "You are absolutely crazy to see such things at this time!"

She grabbed my face, kissed me hard and said, "I love you Chubby. You know how to make a difficult time a little more easy on me. Yes sweetie my blue eyes got all bloodshot because they won't be seeing you for a while. But you should see my heart, it is much worse off than my eyes. Maybe it's a good thing we cannot see that." I hugged her tightly and said, "Then you know that my heart is as bloody as yours don't you?" Mahsa sighed and said, "I know Chubby. Both our hearts are torn apart together in this matter. But what can we do?" We held each other and cried together for most of the afternoon. Later that evening, we went out for an early dinner, and then she dropped me off at my house and went home. When I got in, nobody was home. I made tea and changed my clothes. I had poured a glass of tea for myself and just sat down when the phone rang. I picked it up and it was Mahsa calling to let me that she had gotten home all right. We talked for a little while, then kissed and hung up.

I sighed and opened my school books to study because I was behind on several lessons and knew I had to catch up on them. I didn't have any other choice. My brother got home very late to find me still awake and studying. We talked for a little bit and I told him I would not be coming home tomorrow night; that I would be staying with a friend to study. He asked me to leave a note reminding him tomorrow. I nodded and promised that I would do that.

When I got home from school the next day, I was sure to leave my brother a note reminding him that I was staying with a friend tonight and that I would see him the following day. I put it on the mirror, where he was sure to find it. Then I picked up my nephew from school and brought him to my sister's house and stayed with them for about a half an hour then I went to her penthouse - my real home.

When I knocked on the door; Mahsa quickly opened it, grabbed me and pulled me inside. "Where have you been?" She demanded, "What took you so long to get here?" Then her expression softened as she kissed me saying, "I missed you so much. Today is last day and I want every moment I can with you."

I hugged her and kissed her back, saying, "I miss you already, my Honey Bunch." I took a seat on the sofa in the living room as Mahsa went to the kitchen and brought out two cups of coffee. She had made my favorite, the Italian blend, a little strong, just the way I liked. I lit our cigarettes and we took a moment to savor them. We looked intently at each other, saying nothing. There were no words to say, just to get lost in a loved one's gaze that alone is worth a million words. Yes we didn't need to talk anymore.

I will never forget that day; the time we spent together was so amazing! I asked her if she would like me to cook dinner rather than going out. Mahsa had a better idea, she asked, "I love to watch you cook. Would you be so kind as to show me how to cook?" I looked at her in surprise. She continued, "Mama always promised that she would show me someday, but we never got around to it." I got some chicken out of the freezer to thaw. While we waited, she refilled our mugs and we went back to living room.

After half an hour, we went back to the kitchen. As Mahsa watched, I put the chicken in the pot with some water, chopped onion and some spices. I put the pot on a high flame so the water would boil, and then brought it down to a medium flame to simmer. We went back to the living room while the chicken cooked.

Periodically we went into the kitchen to check on the chicken, I showed her how to make the rice. Dinner was ready by seven and it smelled wonderful. We had prepared the stew and rice. Fifteen minutes before serving I added some salt and lime juice to the stew, explaining that these would bring out the taste of the chicken. Mahsa set the dinner table as I placed the rice on a large plate. I included the hard rice from the bottom of the pot, which was always my favorite. I ladled the stew into a big bowl and brought everything out to the table. Somehow the meal tasted so much better that evening with Mahsa's help. After dinner she suggested that we go for a walk.

We walked for more than three hours. We each had a cup of tea to start us off. It was a beautiful evening and we went wherever our feet took us. We walked, talked and smoked. Mahsa and I went through quite a few cigarettes that evening. At one point, Mahsa suggested that we sit for a little while on a bench. But after short time I said, "It's too cold to sit here, let's go home." Mahsa looked at me teasingly, "Are you cold?" Saving face, I quickly said, "No I am not cold! How could I possibly be cold when I am with you?" I hoped she didn't see me shivering, I added, "But it is easy to get cold because the temperature is below zero." We had just finished our last cigarette, I coaxed her, "C'mon, let's go home." Giving in, Mahsa said, "O.K. Chubby O.K."

When we got in, I went to the bathroom and caught sight of my red face in the mirror. I called Mahsa into the bathroom. I asked her to touch my face and when she did, she said, "I can't believe how cold your face is!" I told her to check herself in the mirror and she was amazed when she saw her own red face. "I didn't realize how cold it was out there!" she exclaimed. "Yes" I told her, "It's a good thing that we are both okay and didn't get frostbite!"

We changed into our warm and comfy robes, washed up and went to bed. Lying close together in the dark, I whispered, "Tonight I need something to remember you for all the time you are away." Mahsa whispered back, "What do you mean? What is this 'something' you need?" I said "You know, you are leaving and I will be all alone. I need something very strong and powerful to hold me until I see you again." Mahsa tried reassuring me, "I am not going anywhere so far away. It is just Shiraz." I shook my head, "It doesn't matter for me whether you go to Shiraz or London. It is all the same to me. I cannot be with you no matter where you are going."

We looked at each other in the dim light; Mahsa took my face in her hands and asked, "What could I do with you that I haven't done before Chubby? What would be something stronger than anything else I have given you?" We lay in silence as we lost ourselves in each other's eyes once more. Mahsa took my face in her hands again, but this time, it felt completely different and gave me one of those kisses that burned my insides from my lips all the way down to my toes; it turned me on like the flick of a light switch.

I heated up quickly as I started kissing her, gently nibbling her neck and her ears. I let my lips travel down the length of her body to her toes. That night, she took me to some magical place beyond imagination and I have never been back there since that night. That night we were like two love birds that roamed outside of their cage. But one must go back into the cage while the other must fly away. I remember that night especially because I felt it so deeply and I am very sure she remembers that night too. I know this because in her notes she mentioned that night two or three times, so she must have been moved by that night as much as I was. I will remember that night for rest of my life.

I said this because I remember every single inch of her body from our lovemaking that night. I wish I could tell you more about that night but I promised her that everything that happened on that special night was only for us. My hand tightens at the memory and doesn't allow me to tell you anything more than what I already written. Other than we felt asleep after such beautiful lovemaking curled together with our bodies entwined.

The next morning, Mahsa was up before me, had already taken a shower and was in the kitchen making coffee. Before I opened my eyes, I could smell the delicious aroma of coffee and could hear her calling me to wake up. I did hear her but I was waiting for her to come back to bed and kiss me. The one thing I truly wanted from that morning was to get up with her kiss. Finally after several times she called me, Mahsa came in to see what was wrong. As soon as she came to me, I grabbed her and pulled her to me. That's when she knew this spoiled guy wanted his kiss and she was so generous. She kissed me unbelievably; happy with that, I got up and took a shower then went to the kitchen.

When I got to the kitchen I asked her, "How many eggs would you like this morning?" She asked, "How many eggs do you have?" Again I asked, "How many do you want?" She asked in return, "How many do you have?" But this time I told her, "It doesn't matter how many you want, does it?" She gave me a wicked look, "Two" "Good" I quipped, "I think I'll have two too." Mahsa threw me a sidelong glance and smirked, "Good for you, keep it that way!" I made the eggs and put two on her plate and two on my own. I handed her the plate saying,

"Firm, sunny-side up." Mahsa sampled the yolk and nodded, "Perfectly done!" I gazed at her trying to figure out if she was actually pleased or just being sarcastic. In mid-bite, she looked over at me and we burst out laughing at each other and continued eating.

After breakfast, Mahsa suggested, "Why don't we take our tea to the bedroom and relax on the bed?" We lit cigarettes and lounged for a while. We began massaging each other from head to toe, which quickly turned into making morning love.

This time she let me completely take charge; I did all of the things I knew she would enjoy. My instincts were right, I took her up and up and I went up with her. When we finished we both lay there breathless for several minutes; then she kissed me with one of those kisses that took my breath away again. After recovering, I said, "I will keep this one with me until we see each other again."

We got up and took a shower together; Mahsa got out faster than I did. She dried her hair as I got some of her things together for her and she said, "I am not going to take everything." She showed me which ones she wanted to take in one suitcase. I pulled out her dresses for her to place the way she liked them in the suitcase. After that came the shoes, I put each shoe in separate bags and handed them to her. Suddenly Mahsa stopped, looked at me and asked, "How did you know which ones I had in mind? How do you do it?" She came over to me and kissed me saying, "I love you Chubby! You don't have any idea how much you mean to me. You are priceless." Tears started streaming down her face and I broke down too. Wiping her eyes and sniffing, she turned back to the suitcase and finishing packing, but she didn't say another word until we finished. I took the suitcase and put it next to the door.

We had more tea and cigarettes. Then Mahsa called the front desk for a cab and to have somebody come up and take her suitcase down. We went through the house, turning off everything from gas to electric and went down to the lobby. The cab was waiting for us; we got in and left for the airport.

At the airport, Mahsa checked her bag and got her boarding pass. We had some time, so we went up to the bar, Mahsa ordered a glass of wine and I got a double scotch. She just looked at me, "A double?" I answered, "You are leaving; don't you think I could use a double?" She smiled sadly, took my hand and said nothing. The bartender brought our drinks and we saluted each other. We sat there until they announced her flight, then we went down to the gate. We hugged each other, both of us crying but I was sobbing loudly. Mahsa tried to quiet me saying, "Hush Yousef, people are looking at us!" I said, "Who cares? Let them look!" It was time and Mahsa had to leave me standing there, tears running down my face.

Y. JOSEPHSON

After I lost sight of her, I sat down on the corner like an orphaned child. Yes I sure felt like an orphan that time. One poor guy came to me and asked if there was anything he could do for me. I was too miserable to really listen to him, "No thanks, this is a personal problem, everything is fine." He tried to continue giving me advice. Finally I snapped at him, "I just need to be alone!" and that poor guy said "Sorry!" and left. Now I was upset with myself after the way I treated that poor fellow.

After her flight took off I caught a cab and went back to my place. I crawled into bed with my clothes on. I wanted to just sleep until she came back to me. The ringing phone got me up; I picked up and it was her letting me know that she had just gotten home, and wanted to know what I was doing. I said, "Nothing I got home and fell asleep in my clothes. We talked for about ten minutes when she kissed me and hung up. That's when my loneliness took over.

After our conversation, I grabbed my books and started to study; mostly because I didn't have anything to do anyway. On other hand, I had promised her that I would study, especially the subjects I wasn't so good in. The days dragged and we talked to each other every other day and sometimes every day, if I was lucky. As the first week went by, I couldn't help but hope that Mahsa would return the following week. But I wasn't that lucky to get her so soon. The second, third and fourth weeks passed and although we talked by phone, there was no evidence when she would return. On the fifth week, Mahsa called to say, "I am sending a ticket for you to come to Shiraz. I just need a date." I stammered, "But..." she cut me off saying, "Yousef, don't argue with me just tell me the date and the time!" All I could tell her was, "I will have to let you know by tomorrow." I had to clear the way through my family before I could do anything.

That night I asked my sister when she planned to go to Shiraz. When she told me the date, I said, "I am planning on going at this time." My sister looked at me curiously and said, "But that's too early for us. And what about school?" I thought fast and said, "I already cleared it with the school and that week school is not supposed to be very busy." My mind was made up for the date to leave. Now I only had to coordinate with Mahsa for the ticket and I called her as soon as I got home. We set the date, but the time wasn't so good for me. Mahsa advised me to go to the airline ticket office the next day to pick up my ticket. Now everything was set!

Y. JOSEPHSON

CHAPTER 11

A New Year

The day before I left for Shiraz, I visited my aunt to wish them a happy new year and to also say bye. This was the Persian New Year which takes place on the spring equinox. My cousin took me aside and said, "You said that you are leaving the day after tomorrow." I replied, "Yes, I know but tomorrow I will be very busy. I will see you in Shiraz." I left and went home. At this point, my second brother was working of the town for two weeks and he would join us and be with my other brother and me in Shiraz later on. That night I packed my suitcase and got ready for the next day. I never thought that I would ever go to Shiraz so happy, but because of her, it happened. And to top it off, I flew there in first class.

I arrived in Shiraz and picked up my suitcase from

baggage claim. As I stepped outside to get a cab, there she was waiting for me. She had sneaked past the taxi stand to pick me up; I have never been so happy to see someone in my life. I threw my suitcase in the trunk and jumped in her car. Mahsa sped out of the airport, past the Circle and Rose Restaurant, until she pulled off the road and stopped the car. She grabbed me by my shirt collar and started kissing me all over my face. Of course I did the same to her. I pushed my seat flat and she did the same; we lay there holding, kissing and touching each other for a while. Mahsa beamed at me and said, "Welcome back to Shiraz!" She wisely drove the car the rest of the way home using the back roads so nobody would see us together.

Mahsa knocked on the door and Meetra opened it for us. As soon as she saw me, she threw her arms around me, welcoming me back to Shiraz with a big hug. We went into the kitchen, where Mama was waiting. She too hugged me and welcomed me home. We sat down at the small breakfast table across of each other as Meetra brought out a bottle of champagne freshly chilled from the refrigerator. As Meetra struggled to pull the cork, Mahsa offered her assistance, but Meetra waved her away, "Yes Mom I know how to do this." With another determined tug, the cork came out with a lovely pop. Meetra served us very elegantly and we raised our glasses to love, health, and being together forever. Our glasses made a lovely clink, and we drank.

Mama was busy preparing a late breakfast for us, but it was more like a feast. I asked Mama to join us but she refused, saying that she would join us for pie later, which she did. After breakfast, or brunch, Meetra excused herself and went upstairs to change because she had a date. As she got ready to go, she said to me, "Bye 'Lovey, see you later!"

Mahsa and I took our tea outside to sit and enjoy the fresh air; then took a leisurely walk through the side and back yards. My God I never before paid any attention to the changing of the seasons, especially that magical time of early spring in Shiraz. Everyone would say that early to mid-spring in Shiraz is like heaven in Iran, but I never believed them. But this year, it was completely different for me. I experienced it deep in my bones and through my blood. I finally understood what springtime meant to others. When I told Mahsa, she laughed and said, "Don't be such a sentimental 'lovey'! Shiraz has always been like this..." Startled at her reaction, I cut her short, "Do you mean this year and last year are the same for you?" She caught my eye and said, "No dummy, of course it's different, a million times different. Yes Chubby, I know what you mean; this year is completely different thanks to you." I interrupted her again, "No, thanks to our love that made this spring like this."

I explained to Mahsa that I always used to avoid this time of year ever since I started having a feeling that I was missing something. Maybe it was because I was always alone; or maybe that I was in the middle of a big family where everyone else had things going on around me. I always felt that nobody could help me. Mahsa put her arms around me and kissed me, saying, "The past is passed, I am here now and we are here for each other. Try not to worry any more than you need to. Our lives are changing for the better. I promise you that much!"

As we walked, I felt more alive than ever! My holy God, everywhere I looked, I could see new life emerging and that included us. I held Mahsa close to my heart and I could smell her hair and her body; which drove me absolutely crazy. We just stood there amidst all the new life springing around us, kissing. We were in the middle of the back yard, which was private and nobody could see us. Mahsa was wearing a see-through silk shirt and a little jacket over it when she picked me up at the airport. But here at home, she wore the shirt alone. I held her close to me and caressed her neck, when suddenly it seemed that the temperature around us changed. I pulled off my T-shirt and opened her shirt so I could feel her body heat because my body felt so cold and that was the only thing could help me. She held me tightly as we rested our heads on each other's shoulders. We could feel our heartbeat and breathe almost as if we were one body. Then as quick as a cat, she jumped on me and locked her legs around my waist as I buried my head in her breasts.

We enjoyed ourselves in the garden for almost three hours and then decided it was time to head back to the house. Our timing was perfect because lunch was ready. After lunch, we took our tea to our bedroom.

From the side window in the bedroom, we could feel the warmth of the spring sun and from the other window, we could feel and smell the beauty of spring breeze and between those senses our love was absorbing and growing and we were blissfully in the middle of it all.

Mahsa pulled open the sliding door to the balcony I was right, the spring air felt and smelled wonderful! We sat together on the chair and gazed at each other for a moment. Mahsa asked me, "Do you have any cigarettes?" I took out two and lit them. She inhaled deeply, like she hadn't smoked for a long time and blew out the smoke very slowly. To my surprise, I noticed that I was doing the exact same thing and I didn't know why. After a little while, we went back into the bedroom and lay down together on the bed. I told Mahsa all about my loneliness during those five weeks that we were apart and she confided in me the same; nothing was exciting about her life. The bed was so comfortable and the atmosphere was so soothing that I drifted off to sleep and later on Mahsa teased me saying that I slept like a baby for almost an hour. When I woke up, Mahsa wasn't there, but when she heard me, she came back to me.

It was around six-thirty and we went downstairs to the kitchen for some delicious Italian coffee. Around that time Meetra got back from her date and joined us. Mahsa told her, "Go get your backgammon set, Yousef's a player!" Then she stole a look at me and said, "Meetra is for real. You just watch yourself; she will crush you in no time." Smiling, I said, "We'll see."

Meetra went to her room changed and brought the game down with her. We played the Iranian way, which means whoever first gets a five-pip lead to the other side wins the game. Our game took a long time, when finally Meetra and I were tied four by four. So we agreed that whoever won this hand would be the winner. We played and played and Meetra won by one point. But she argued that it wasn't fair and that we should call it a tie. So as soon as she said that, Mahsa burst out laughing and Meetra asked her, "There is nothing funny, why you laughing?" Sighing, Mahsa told Meetra that I had told her the exact the same thing. Meetra grinned at me and said, "That is so funny."

Mahsa took my place and challenged her daughter, "Let's play for real this time. I will show him who the master really is." They played very hard and the game was more like a competition. They played the last set, Mahsa lost by a very close margin but not as close as I did previously. Mahsa looked at her daughter in disbelief, "You really did win! How is this possible?" I was amused by the game and told Mahsa, "It's unbelievable, but true; Meetra really did win. And there is nothing you can do about it." Mahsa pouted, "You might be right, but it's not fair." Meetra stood up and hugged her mother saying, "I love you mommy, but that's the way it is. I have become a very good player haven't I?" Mahsa frowned at Meetra, pretending to be angry and said, Yes dear, you are a good player, but you had a little bit of luck. Don't forget that."

So we declared Meetra the grand winner when Mama came out and asked, "Don't you guys want dinner? Do you know what time it is?" Mahsa looked up in surprise, "Why, what time is it Mama?" She said, "It's almost ten! Shall I set the table and bring dinner out here, or do you want to play more?" Mahsa looked over at me and I said "No the game is finished. Thank you Mama, it's so nice to have you here to think about us. We forgot all about dinner." Mama laughed saying, "Thank God you have come to the house again, Yousef. Now we have more happy times."

Mama started clearing the table then set it. I tried to help but Mama shooed me away. She brought out dinner for us; oh my God what a dinner she made. Sizzling Porterhouse steaks bathed in mushroom wine sauce. It was so delicious and Meetra topped off the entire meal by serving us a very expensive Khohlar Shiraz.

BE HIDDEN LOVE

We enjoyed that dinner a great deal and it came as a surprise to me that I couldn't finish my steak because it was so big and had too many side dishes with it. Of course the ladies didn't finish theirs either, but I am naturally a big eater, but it was probably best that I didn't finish it.

After dinner Mama brought us freshly made, hot apple pie and coffee. We felt so full after such a feast. Meetra excused herself, saying good-night and went to her room. Mahsa and I went to our room and got ready for bed. She changed into her lovely silk nightgown and robe and I wore my silk robe as well. As we cuddled together, Mahsa said, "It's so unfair that we only have one day and night together after five weeks apart. I answered, "I absolutely agree, one day is not enough. But who said we only have one day?" She looked at me, confused, "What do you mean by that? I smiled back at her, "I agree, one day isn't enough, so I arranged to have a second day for us." Mahsa couldn't believe what she heard and made me repeat it. After that, she kissed me hard saying, "That's my Chubby! With you nothing is impossible." I explained to her what I did and added, "I am supposed to leave Tehran tomorrow night, so we can have the extra day for ourselves."

Mahsa switched off the light on her side and said, "Welcome to my heart." and began kissing me all over my face. My, oh my, what night we shared after such a long wait. She was absolutely gorgeous; she gave strength, self-confidence and hopes back to me that night and filled me with energy. We made beautiful, tender love for hours and enjoyed every second of it.

After we came down from the heavenly place we went together, I asked her to turn on the light for me; she asked me, "Why, what do you need it for?" I said, "I need to read something to you." She turned the light on as I went to the closet, dug out a piece of paper and came back to bed.

She rested her head on my shoulder as I read some poems to her, one after another. When I had finished, Mahsa asked me, "Who were those poems from?" I replied simply, "From a lover to his beloved." She sat bolt upright, gazed at me in amazement, "Do you mean to say that you wrote those poems for me?" Smiling, I said, "Something like that." She asked me to read them again, but this time more slowly. I did as she asked, and she just sat there, absolutely quiet, listening very carefully to every single word.

After a few moments of utter silence, Mahsa said quietly, "Please give it to me." I handed the paper to her and she kissed it, placing it over her heart saying, "This is the perfect place for it. May I keep it?" Nodding, I replied, "Yes it's yours but I want to rewrite it more nicely for you." She kissed the paper again and gave it back to me,

BE HIDDEN LOVE

"When can I have it back? I want to take it to a frame shop and have it framed to keep it with me always. I can hang it someplace in here, so I can look at it every time I am in the room." I promised her that I would rewrite it as soon as I could. As soon as I could get back that feeling I had when I wrote it.

Again she rested her head on my shoulder and kissed my neck as I held her to my chest right next to my heart. We could have stayed like that for an eternity, but I started feeling very sleepy, so I asked her to turn off the light. We curled up together and fell asleep very quickly.

Suddenly I felt very hot, and when I opened my eyes, I saw a vision that could only be from heaven. Mahsa was sitting on top of me and massaging my chest and shoulders; she was strong, beautiful and hot. Her face was like a model for a beauty salon and her wavy hair looked so lovely. The silhouette of her shoulders looked as though she had worked out for a long time and all the rest of the curves of her body were dangerously sexy. I could go on and on, but instead I'll leave the rest to your imagination.

She held me by my shoulders and pulled me toward herself as we started making love. Just imagine the most beautiful woman of your dreams right here in your arms. When I looked at her she was red hot and red like lava flowing from a mountain and I was the flat land below her waiting to be enveloped by the hot fiery substance. Together we climbed to the summit of that raging volcano, until our passion erupted like an explosion and we soared through the air down from heaven like hot ash. As we floated down from being so wild she caught me and we drifted gently back down to earth. Afterwards, Mahsa leaned over me and gave me a long, tender kiss and said, "Thank you for your love and the poems you wrote for me." Then she wrapped me in her arms and I don't remember anything else until ten-thirty the next morning when we awoke just in time for breakfast.

I slowly became aware of Mahsa's voice as she called me from the bathroom for me to wake up, but I didn't say anything. She eventually came out and sat next to me and massaged my head and ears saying, "Chubby, it's past ten-thirty, wake up! We have to go. Wake up!" She then rubbed my shoulders and kissed me twice. I slowly opened my eyes and gave her a big smile, "Good morning sweetie." Mahsa replied, "Goooooood morning to you too Sleeping Beauty! It's getting late, get up and take shower." She pulled at me, "Come down for breakfast, we have to go. Come on, hurry up we don't have too much of time, please hurry!" I got up, kissed her then went in to take a shower and then I hurried downstairs to join Mahsa. She had already started by the time I got there. We ate breakfast quickly; then went up to get dressed and we hurried out the door.

BE HIDDEN LOVE

Mahsa drove to a place just outside of town; I asked, "Where are we?" She explained, "This was my father's garden and some friends are coming over for lunch." We pulled and she honked the horn a couple of time so that the gardener could open the gate to let us in. She asked him if they had shown up yet and he replied, "Nobody is here yet." She said, "We are going to go down and have a look around. When they arrive, tell them to come and join us." The gardener nodded, "Yes Ma'm".

The garden was so beautiful! I turned to Mahsa, "This is really the first time in my adult life that I have experienced spring like this." I shook my head, "It is all because of you that I feel and see the beauty of this time of year. I missed it for all those years." I took a deep breath, "What are the flowers that I smell, or is it you?" Mahsa smiled at me and nodded, "Yes, honey this year is different for me too; I can feel it as well." She took my hand as we walked, "This is not because of me, it is because of our relationship - our love for each other that we feel like this." She paused to listen to a bird's song, "Spring always been like this; just because I missed it or you missed it doesn't mean that spring didn't appear every year. No it takes place every year, but thanks to our love, honey, we can see it now."

We wrapped ourselves in each other's embrace and kissed. From time to time, wondrous scents of cherry, almond, apple, apricot, peaches and countless others would waft over us. We stopped beneath an enormous walnut tree and I held her close to my heart as she twined her hands around my neck; we could not stop kissing each other. From a distance we heard the sounds of voices calling out for Mahsa. She shouted back, "We are over here!" We shouted back and forth until they found us. It was Mary, Mo and Ali! We shook hands and hugged, "Happy New Year! Happy New Year!"

Mo turned to Mahsa, "Do you mind if I borrow Yousef for a minute?" She said, "Not at all." Mo motioned for me to follow him, "Yousef, come to the car with me." before we left, he asked Mahsa, "Where do you want to stay?" Mahsa shrugged and said, "It's up to you guys. Do you want to go inside or stay out? This place is very good because we have a lot of sun, but I will leave it totally up to you guys." Mo thought for a moment and then said, "Well, if we're going to do it here, we should get started, it's late already." We went up to his truck with Mary and Mahsa right behind us. We unloaded his truck and everybody helped bring the stuff inside.

We brought everything back to the garden area. Mary and Mahsa put down the blankets and sleeping bags. Mo and Ali opened a cooler that was stuffed with food. They had brought fish, fillet minions and a lot of other tasty treats. Ali lit the charcoal and got everything ready to grill fish and fillet minions, we had our choice of either kebab or barbecue.

BE HIDDEN LOVE

We all decided to have a barbecue and it came out so delicious. Why is it that food cooked outside always tastes so much better? Everybody was so full, we couldn't move; so we relaxed for a while. I got up after a little while and made tea for everyone. They asked me how things were in Tehran and if I liked it there. I shrugged and explained, "Tehran different from what it was before. I do love it there more than Shiraz, but my situation changed now." I nodded toward Mahsa and continued, "Wherever she is, will be my favorite place."

Mo laughed, "Yousef is such an honest guy, I like that! Ali, you should learn from him; this is the way to love somebody!" Mary jumped into the conversation, "And Mo has to learn too!" Mahsa added, "I think all of us can learn from Yousef. He is really honest; I know that firsthand as we shared life together in past eleven months I know what I am talking about."

After that the conversation turned to different topics including the personal lives of all the others. We remained outside until around four-thirty when Mahsa invited us all in the house, so we packed up and moved our merry gathering indoors.

When we got to our place, Meetra wasn't home, but arrived shortly after we did. She turned on the stereo and put a tape in. That tape was very good, I loved the singer.

Everybody decided to stay for dinner and Mama made a very nice one for us. Like two schoolgirls giggling, Mary and Mahsa jointly chose a tape. When music started, Mahsa grabbed my hand and pulled me up for a dance. Before I knew what was going on, everyone else was up and dancing with us. We kept it up for about an hour until everybody was tired and out of breath, Mahsa called Mama to see if dinner was ready.

Mama had already set the table and was laying out the meal, so everybody sat down to eat except me. Mahsa asked me, "Why aren't you coming for dinner?" I told her "I will be right there." I stood off to the side watching them; they were here because of me, nothing else. That was very important to me because I had never experienced anything like this before and I was very happy for it. So I just stood there for a moment and took it all in.

Mahsa came to see what was wrong with me and that was another thing that made it so nice for me; she grabbed my hand and brought me to the table, saying, "Poor Yousef, he's still too shy!" and everybody laughed including me.

Mama had made a fantastic dinner, like always, as I started heaping food on my plate, Mama suddenly appeared at my side; she had brought me the really crunchy rice from the bottom of the pan, saying, "I saved this especially for you!" I smiled up at her and thanked her for being so thoughtful; then I added some savory bean stew to it. Ali pointed, "Look, Mama even brought him special food; she must like him a lot. Is it not true Mama?" Mama looked over at Ali and replied, "Yousef, is a sweetheart."

Mahsa nodded and smiled, agreeing with Mama as I bowed my head back at her in thanks. After dinner, Mama brought out freshly made hot apple pie with Italian coffee. Mo leaned back and patted his stomach, "What a nice dinner! I wish Yousef would come back every month so we can have this more often!" Mahsa frowned at Mo playfully, "What's matter with you? We did this the last time, don't you remember, you nutty guy?"

We spent the evening sitting around cracking jokes and poking fun at each other; most often I was on the receiving end of their good humor. But I just sat there, smiling and gave it right back to them. Around midnight, our merry party was breaking up as Mary, Mo and Ali got ready to leave. We said our good-byes and I promised them that I would return as soon as I could. So now, it was Meetra, Mahsa and me; we talked and told more jokes until one in the morning. Meetra then got up, said good-night and went to her room. Mahsa and I said good-night to Mama and went to our room.

After we had washed and up snuggled up together in bed, Mahsa asked, "Do you have any more poems you could read for me?" I said, "I'm sorry, but no not yet." Mahsa persisted, "Then can you read those again for me?" How could I refuse? "Sure." I told her, "Why not? I would love to read them to you. I enjoy it."

I went to the closet and dug out the poems and read each of them to her twice as I had done last night. When I was done, I noticed tears in those ocean blue eyes. I took her in my arms as she placed her head on my shoulder. Softly she said, "I love you more than anything in this world." I knew deep in my heart that she was telling the truth.

As I held Mahsa tightly to me, I kissed her shoulder, neck, ear and made my way to her beautiful lips. She had totally surrendered herself to me that night. We didn't speak; there was no need to say anything to each other because we could feel. And feeling is so much better than symbolic words. We fell asleep, holding each other and the next thing I remember was the next morning, Mahsa massaging and kissing me to wake up. I got up that morning with her lips on mine as she said, "Good morning my poet!" to that I answered, "Good morning my Juliet!"

We went down to kitchen and said good morning to Mama who was bustling around the kitchen. "Good morning my children, sit down and I will bring you breakfast. After breakfast, Mahsa and I went outside to the back yard to take in more of the early spring; together, we could not get enough. I thought back on my dark, cold years alone and I felt like a man who was just released from prison. We discovered that some of the almond trees already had green almonds ready to eat, so we took some. I have to add here that green almonds are so tasty, especially sprinkled with a little salt. Later in spring, we get green plums and sour green apples. All of these are usually ready within the first month of spring. Then the Persian markets overflow with delectable fruits.

We picked some green almonds and sour apples. Mahsa suggested that we go to other side, to the next lot that belonged to her and her brother left to them to share by their late father. Our trip rewarded us with larger almond and apple trees that were laden with fruit. We picked as much as we could carry and went back to the house. Mama washed them for us and we took some outside to enjoy on the balcony.

Mahsa and I both knew that this was the last full day we could be together. So we wanted to enjoy ourselves as much as we could. Around two-thirty, Mama called us in for lunch. Afterward, we went up to bedroom and Mama brought us sweet tea, which was very good after all the fruit we had. We luxuriated with our tea out on the second floor balcony.

As we sat, Mahsa had a faraway look in her eyes as she mused, "I missed a lot of spring times in this house even when I was married and was raising the kids. Yes I missed a lot you know Yousef, I was too busy with my company and taking care of the house. I didn't have time to feel anything and it got worse when my husband passed away; I had even more stuff to worry and think about. But since I met you, my life has turned upside down; I feel totally changed and I can't help but think that it was truly our destiny to meet each other." She continued, "Yousef, you know I love my kids so much, but I owe them big for bringing us together. Because if Assa hadn't known you, then Meetra wouldn't have invited you, and we never would have met, we wouldn't be together right now." She took my hand, "You know we used to live in two different worlds; I couldn't imagine being in the world you come from. And you would never be allowed into the world I live because of your family restrictions. Do you see what I mean by destiny?"

I kept silent as Mahsa went on, "I don't know why I am telling you all these things. Nobody can believe how I talk to you; a nineteen year old guy. But they don't know you the way I know you. Ali, Mo and Mary for example, they now understand who you are and when I tell them what we talk about, how long, they are no longer surprised. Yes my sweetie, we might be from two different worlds; both in age and society, but we understand each other perfectly and that makes us different from any other couple. Do you understand what I am telling you? I know you understand so let's let it be."

I hugged her and said "I understood perfectly. We are two of a kind and we are also twin souls, which is why we are together. That's why we understand each other and most importantly we can feel each other can't we?" Mahsa nodded, "Yes we can and I feel the same way I have never felt like this with anybody else; not even my late husband or my brother. The only one who was close to me like this was my father. Yes, he and I understood each other two hundred percent!"

Mahsa hugged me back and kissed me saying, "Now you know where you stand with me and where you are in my heart. I love you more than anything in the world and I need you as much as you need me! Please believe it Chubby we need each other, there are no ands, ifs or buts."

We decided to go back inside and lie down on bed; face up, holding each other's hands without any conversation. Our minds and feelings made up for the lack of words.

It was Mahsa who broke the silence, "How do you feel?" I replied, "I feel fantastic! How about you?" She sighed, "Me too." We turned on our sides to face each other. I stroked her face with the back of my hand and said, "Can you explain to me what the difference is between saying 'love you so much' and 'I love you to death'?"

She wound her arms around my neck and after taking a deep breath said, "Yes my Chubby, I love you to death and as matter a fact I know you love me the same way. You want to know what the difference is then I will tell you. Yes, my love when I say 'I love you to death' it means that I love you no matter if I am alive or dead. If I am alive, I am in love with you, but if I die, I would take that love with me to heaven or wherever and wait for you until you join me. Death cannot separate two lovers from each other. On the other hand, when you say 'I love you very much', you give that love the limitation of lasting only as long you are alive. It means that I am in love with you now, but when I die, I am gone and our love would stop at death. It could possibly go further, but not necessarily. Yes, my sweetie this, is the difference between the two.

I looked deep into her eyes,; they were a little red with the ocean blue in the middle surrounded by red veins. I gently wiped her eyes with my hand and kissed each one. Mahsa sniffed sadly, "This is the last night we have together." I frowned, "Says who? We will just have to have a good time together. And we don't just have the night. Remember to count the day too!" She leaned over and gave me such a hot kiss; one that burned the inside of my mouth all the way down to my toes. It took my breath away. Gulping air, I said, "I am in love with you and love you to death. I have no other explanation for the burning except that."

I told her, "One day when the time is right, we should tell each other, our life history all from our childhood to just before me met." I continued, "Because I think we can find other reasons for our closeness. I am very sure we can possibly find it in other places of our lives. Do you agree?" Mahsa nodded yes, "I agree with you and one day we will do that."

Around seven Meetra called to us from downstairs, we got up and Mahsa went down first and after a few moments, she called me to go down as well.

Meetra was in kitchen and she hugged me saying, "Where have you guys been?" Mahsa and I looked at each other, feeling a little guilty, "Just upstairs talking." Mahsa said. "My God!" Meetra teased, "How much could you possibly have to say to each other? I was getting so bored. Come on, let's play a game!" I knew that Meetra was challenging me, so I said, "Okay, let's play! And this time I will win."

Meetra and I played for over an hour and we were caught in a tie. Then Mahsa and Meetra played almost the same length of time but neither of them could win either. So we put the game away and sat down to talk. We talked about all kinds of things, and I mentioned old Shiraz and how small it was. Suddenly Meetra burst out laughing and said "My God he says that like he is fifty or sixty years old! How do you do that?" I was confused, "Like what." Meetra explained, "It's the way you talk, like somehow you are much older than you really are. How is that?" I smiled, "Well, I'm not sure; I have always been like this. Maybe I got it from my father he is very good speaker." Mahsa seconded me on that, saying, "Yes it's true, his father is one of the best speakers we have in Shiraz."

Meetra said in a sober tone, "I don't know what it is, but I do know that it's not fair. He and I are the same age but anytime he speaks, I become nothing! I feel like I am so much younger than him and that's not fair is it!" Mahsa and I just looked at her in surprise; we didn't know what to say.

The mood lightened later that night and we had a lot of fun together; sometimes Mama would come out from the kitchen to join us too. By ten, Mama announced that dinner was ready and started bringing out the food. This time all of us helped her, no matter how much she protested. Tonight's dinner was sea bass; it smelled and looked so good, we could not wait to taste it. The meal did not leave us disappointed, it was fabulous!

After we finished dinner, Mama brought us pie and coffee and we enjoyed every bite. A little while later Meetra said good night and went up to her room. Mahsa and I were far from tired, so we went outside for a walk through the side yard. We came back in an hour later, said good night to Mama and went up to our room to get ready for bed.

Laying there in the dark, Mahsa whispered to me, "This is it; our last night together and tomorrow you have to go." There was such sadness in her voice. I tried to comfort her, "Yes, I will be going but my heart will stay behind with you. I know we want to be together in both body and mind, but I will see you from time to time. I cannot promise all the time, but I will definitely come here as often as I can. You know that I will not miss an opportunity to see you. Be sure of that."

She held me close and kissed me, saying "That's enough for me for now." I kissed her back and said, "But it's not enough for me! I want to be with you as often as I want." Mahsa tried to sound reasonable, "But you know that's not going to be possible. We always have to think about what is doable. Yes, you know that's what we have to do."

Mahsa and I had such a wonderful night together; we stayed awake almost all night, alternating between talking and making love. We both wanted me to stay another night, after New Year. But that was going to be very difficult. I knew that my family was expecting me back as well. I wanted nothing more than to come back and stay there for another night - just one more night. I promised her that we would have to see.

I asked her to set the alarm for nine and we held each other like we would never let go. We fell asleep for what seemed a very short time, when that alarm went off. Reluctantly I got up, showered and got dressed. I brought my suitcase downstairs with Mahsa right next to me the whole time. She called for a cab to take me to my parent's home. As we waited for the cab, she grabbed my shirt color and give me such a kiss that I would never forget. Sadly, I said, "See you later alligator." And as always her reply, "Don't let me bite you!" She kissed me again and again until the cab arrived; I left my heart's home went to the home that I always felt like running from.

When I arrived, my Mom and Father showered me with their unconditional love. Yes I knew my parents loved me, although it was not the same as what I got from my love. They both hugged me and my Mom kissed me several times; she had never really done that before. Secretly I had to be sure that I was in the right place. The funny thing that struck me as my parents fussed over me was this; I felt different from before. I didn't hate the house anymore and everything was really nice. I went to my room where everything was left untouched, even my messy desk still was the same as I had left it. I was amazed.

I unpacked my suitcase, changed into something a little more comfortable and then joined my father for breakfast. As we ate, we talked about all different things and I found that we had a very pleasant time together. I then called my nephews to say hi and let them know that I was home. A short while later, they showed up at the house and a different type of fun began. I think my folks were happy to see some action in the house again.

Each afternoon, my nephew and I visited different places throughout Shiraz; there were the tombs of Hafez and Sadee and some beautiful flower gardens to walk through. One day while we were visiting the tomb of Sadee, something amazing happened! Can you guess what? We ran into Mahsa there; she came over to us and said hello, then asked about my father in a very formal manner. She said to me, "Please give my regards to your father, until I come over for the New Year. After she had left, my nephew asked, "Who is she?" I shrugged and said, "She must be one of my father's followers." I left it at that and there was no more discussion over the beautiful mystery woman. I have to admit that Mahsa knew we were there because I told her; but I didn't have any idea that she planned to show up. I found out later that she did want to see my nephew.

In the meantime, we talked every day but I couldn't get away to see her before New Year because I was constantly surrounded by family. As New Year approached, more and more family arrived. My eldest brother got home two days before New Year, my second brother later that evening and my sister arrived in Shiraz the following day. As you can imagine, I couldn't turn my head without catching a family member's eye, so there was no way I could see her, but we talked sometimes twice a day. Mahsa understood my situation and told me "Just take it easy and be careful not to get caught sneaking phone calls."

It was finally the night before New Year and everybody was happy because this was the first time in six years all of us were together again for New Year. I wasn't that excited because I couldn't be with the one person I loved most on this special night. I had so many mixed feelings rolling around inside me; on one hand I was happy to have my family around me, but on the other hand, Mahsa is my family too and we couldn't be together. Those mixed feelings were killing me, leaving a dull ache in my heart. Perhaps you know what I mean, but I had to deal with it because I didn't have much of a choice. And that was that.

Note: *Iranian New Year:*

The Iranian New Year, called Nowruz is not like the Western celebration that takes place at midnight on the last day of December. Our New Year begins on the first day of spring. We would sometimes wait all day for the precise moment for the sun to reach a certain point in the sky that would signal the exact moment that spring would arrive.

That year the moment of New Year was just before noon and my other sisters and their children had arrived at our house just in time for the celebration. There was a huge crowd of people around, but I was missing the most important one - Mahsa. Exactly at New Year, everybody started cheering and kissing and wishing each other 'Happy New Year'! I had snuck away, grabbed the phone and called her to say Happy New Year. We kissed each other and that's all we could do for the time. After we finished talking, I left my room and went to my father's room to say Happy New Year to everybody.

Amidst everything going on, my older brother caught my arm and asked, "How is Ms. Doctor? Is she okay?" I gave him a blank look and asked, "What you talking about?" He flashed me a grin and said, "I saw you sneak away to your room with the phone. We usually don't call anybody right on the spot in the middle of New Year unless it's someone we love very much. But that's exactly what you did and that was a mistake." He turned serious. "Someone else could have noticed. But you did what you are supposed to do, good boy!"

That entire day was a mess for me, it was too crowded and too noisy, but I couldn't escape it; I just had to wait until the right moment. I found my opportunity the next afternoon. I left the house and went straight to my love the only love I needed and wanted. I knocked on the door and Meetra opened it.

As soon as Meetra opened the door she shouted, "He's here!" Mahsa flew down the stairs so fast that I got worried that she might fall and break her neck. I ran to meet her halfway and we practically fell into each other's arms on the stairs.

I carried her down and kissed her, saying "Happy New Year!" Mahsa kissed me back and replied, "Happy New Year to you my Chubby!" I then hugged Meetra and Mama and wished them Happy New Year as well. We all went into the kitchen and Mama brought out pie and coffee and we sat there, chatting. I told them about everything that happened the day before; minute by minute accounts of my whole family coming together when Meetra interrupted suddenly, laughing, "You should be a reporter because the way you're describing everything that happened, it's exactly like we are there with you. It's amazing!"

After half an hour, Mahsa and I went outside to the backyard and we walked among all those beautiful trees. She couldn't stop squeezing and kissing me, saying over and over, "I missed you, I missed you." I cupped my hands around her face and kissed her saying "I missed you too baby. Happy New Year to you." We spend a long time in the garden and when we finally came back in, Meetra came down from her room and complained to Mahsa, "It's not fair that you took him out for so long! I know you guys missed each other, but we missed him too." Mahsa nodded at her daughter, "I'm sorry, baby, you are right."

I stayed there for the entire afternoon until Mahsa became concerned and said, "You should go soon, I don't want you to get caught." Meetra was disappointed, "Mommy, why are you kicking him out of the house? What's wrong with you?" Mahsa tried to explain, "Yousef has to be very careful when he comes here. You don't know the kind of situation he has to go through. It's much safer this way. But you do know that he can come here as often as you like. How about that?" Still disappointed, Meetra seemed to understand.

I kissed them good-bye, then Mahsa asked me, "Before I call the cab, where are you going? Are you going home?" I answered, "I'm going to the place I always go." She smiled, "Oh you want to go to your aunt's, right?" Surprised, I asked, "How did you know that?" She grinned, "Are you kidding me?" I smiled back at her then she kissed me and said "You really are something! Now go, go."

Y. JOSEPHSON

After leaving Mahsa's place, I headed over to my aunt's and waited there until my eldest nephew got home. We hung around her house for a little while and then went to my parent's home; everybody was still there. Everyone asked me, "Where you have been?" I said "I went to see a friend then went to auntie's house to wait for my nephew so we could come here." He and I then went to my room. I have to admit that it is very annoying when everybody in your family wants to know everything you do. I think it happens mostly if you happen to be the youngest. I wonder if they think that perhaps the youngest doesn't know anything and that everything must be discussed in full. I refused to do that and it made everybody mad at me and maybe that was one of the reasons that they were always on my case.

A week after New Year, I stopped by in the morning and joined Mahsa and Meetra for breakfast. As the day wore on, I really didn't want to go home for lunch and thank God there weren't cell phone at that time; I called home and one of my nieces picked up. I told her to tell grandma that I wouldn't be coming home for lunch. I knew that my mother would want to know where I was and I didn't feel like having to come up with a story right then. So I stayed for lunch as well. Mahsa gave me a concerned look, "Are you sure that was enough of an explanation?" I shrugged, "Mahsa you don't know them; nothing is enough for them. That was more than enough." She shook her head and said, "You are so bad."

BE HIDDEN LOVE

After lunch we went up to our room; we kissed and caressed each other, then I dropped her on the bed and started to give her a massage. She groaned with delight, "You've never done it like this before, but I love it!" I kept going and slowly pulled her clothes off. I couldn't help but hurry through that part, but felt like she didn't mind.

As we started to get hot; Mahsa sat up to undress me. As she removed every piece of clothing, it was very sensuous and so sexy!

We spent the better part of the afternoon making love; and it was very different from before and we enjoyed it. Once we had finished, Mahsa kissed me and massaged my chest until we fell asleep for a short time. After we had awakened, feeling completely refreshed, I got up to take shower but Mahsa raced in, turned the water on and kept calling me to join her. What was I to do? Of course I joined her and we had a fun time in the shower too.

I stayed in Shiraz ten days following the New Year and the return trip consisted of me, my brother's driver, my sister, her kids and my brother's wife's aunt. We piled into the car and left Shiraz early in the morning and got to Tehran by ten that evening.

A week later, Mahsa called to announce, "I am coming to Tehran!" I tried to hide my excitement, "Oh, it's about time you finally decided to come back. I am looking forward to it." "Oh, shut up!" I laughed, "Oooooooookay, so when is my princess coming to Tehran?" Mahsa replied, "Your princess has a ticket for such and such a day at such and such an hour." I said "I will be there to meet you." "No!" she warned, "Don't meet me, unless you want to meet my brother as well. I don't think you really want to do that." I was disappointed, but Mahsa continued, "I will see you the next day at three-thirty at home." I brightened, "I will see you there baby, and don't be late!" Mahsa scoffed, "When have I ever been late! Don't be such an ass!"

That important day happened to be a school day. I dutifully went to school and once out, I went to catch a cab. I checked my watch and discovered that it was only two o'clock. I had plenty of time, so I stopped at the hamburger shop, got a burger and then caught a cab and went over to our place.

I went up and made sure that Mahsa was not there yet. I opened the sliding door that lead out to the balcony to let some fresh air circulate through the place. I tuned on the gas and put the kettle on the stove to boil some water for tea and waited until three-thirty. I made tea as I knew that she would be coming in at any moment.

After ten or fifteen minutes, I heard noises just outside the door. I opened it and found Mahsa struggling with her keys; her hands were full of bags, so I grabbed some from her. Breathless, she said, "Thank God you are here! I knew you were here as soon as I came up." I asked, "How did you know I was here?" Mahsa smiled, "By your smell. As soon as I got to the elevator I knew." I was surprised, "Oh great, now I am smelly?" She said, "No dummy everybody has a unique smell especially their skin and hair. Sometimes you can tell who it is. But it does not necessarily mean that the smell is bad. Please don't think like that."

Mahsa started sorting through the bags, "I went to the market and bought some things I thought we would need." We took the bags into the kitchen and put everything away. When we finished, she suddenly pushed me to the sofa and climbed on me saying, "Just shut up and undress me!" I did so as she undressed me too. We spent a long time making love on that sofa.

After a while, Mahsa got up and grabbed my hand to pull me up too. Then she went to the bedroom to put on her robe as I went to the kitchen, poured tea into glasses and brought them to the living room. I went to the bedroom to change into my robe. We sat next to each other on the sofa. I leaned over and kissed her saying, "Hi Honey Bunch!" She replied, "Hi Chubby! How was your trip and your family?" I answered, "Everything and everyone was fine. How about your trip with your brother?" She smiled and said, "It was okay, but I think that it was probably not as much fun as yours."

CHAPTER 12

The Party

Two days went by and by the third day I was really going Mahsa turned to me and asked, "Are you ready for the big charity party?" I swallowed hard, "Yes but are you sure it's okay?" She answered, "Yes of course. I made sure that there would be no problems. But only thing is that we have to go shopping." I winced, "Shopping for whom; you have everything." She rolled her beautiful eyes at me, "No, not for me, dummy! We must go shopping for you. I don't know why sometimes you act like such a dummy." Defensively, I said, "Why? I have a black suit." Laughing at me, Mahsa said, "You need a different type of black suit – a tuxedo. You will be able to tell the difference and please don't say anything, O.K?" I mumbled, "Okay." Then I said, "You are going to kill me aren't you?" Mahsa grinned wickedly, "I'd love to; and then I wouldn't have to argue with you every time. You would be mine and mine only."

I bravely asked, "When is the charity party?" She replied, "The end of this week, so we don't have much time to play around. Do you understand what I just said?" I felt like a small child being scolded, "Yes I understand completely." "Good." Mahsa continued, "Maybe tomorrow or the next, we can go shopping. But we have to do it these next two days for sure."

I took a sip of tea and noticed that our tea had gotten cold; so I got up and got us both some fresh tea. As soon as I returned from the kitchen, Mahsa grabbed me and said, "Oh Chubby! Please don't be upset with me. I love you so much and I want you to look your very best, but I don't want you to get upset with me over it." I said, "I am not upset." Then she said, "I can tell by your voice that you are. Please don't be!" I held her and put my head on her shoulder and suddenly I lost all control and burst into tears. I told her, "I love you so much and I know you love me the way I am, can't you just let me be?"

She lifted my head with her hand on my chin and kissed my face and lips, saying, "I love you to death and I don't ever want to change you. I love you the way you are. Why would I want to change you? You have to be yourself and if there is anything you don't like, then just

BE HIDDEN LOVE

tell me that you won't do it. If it is so hard for you to come with me then don't because I want you to be happy, that's all."

I told her, "But you keep buying things for me and it's gotten out of hand." I sniffed, "I know that I will never be able to give back to you. I cannot afford to buy anything I might want for you. Because the things I would love to get you I cannot afford and the things I can afford I don't like." I felt so miserable, "I don't know how that's become my life with you, my love and that's what makes me upset."

She hugged me again and tried to soothe me, "I don't want you to buy anything for me. You are the richest guy I have ever met. I know how wisely you buy things and that's what makes you rich. You are richer than any one of us. I want you for you only, not for anything else." She gave a great sigh, "Oh my God, you're going to kill me with the way you treat me. You are somewhere I cannot reach. Please come down and help me to understand you."

I hugged and kissed her, saying "I love you Honey Bunch! I love you so much - I love you to death and I will do anything to make you happy, just bear with me. I don't want to be too hard to handle. I just don't want you to think of me anything that I am not, that's all."

Mahsa looked at me thoughtfully, "Well, if that party is going to make you that upset, then I am not going either. I just wanted you to be with me, that's all. Is it too much to ask?"

I gazed into those beautiful eyes of hers; those eyes that were full of tears. I felt even worse as I rested her head against my chest and said, "Please don't worry, I will come with you to the charity ball. It will be my pleasure to be with you for something that is important to you. I love you too much to not come. So yes, my sweetie, I will accompany you."

After she had stopped crying, Mahsa got up and went out to the balcony then called me to join her. As I stepped out, I was rewarded with a view that was beyond compare. It was one of the most beautiful sunsets I have ever seen or to ever see again in Iran. Mahsa wrapped her arms around my waist and rested her head on my shoulder as we watched the sky burn with vivid colors of red, gold and orange.

Later that evening, we went out for dinner at Sorrento and ordered two juicy New York sirloin steaks with baked potato with a bottle of wine. When the waiter brought us the wine, he also left us appetizers of bean dip and chips. We raised our glasses, saluting each other and just sat there in silence, enjoying each other's company and the wine. Neither of us said a word, until the waiter returned and asked if everything was all right? The spell broke and Masha looked up at him and said, "Yes, everything is fantastic." I chimed in, "It couldn't be better." After he had left, she looked at me and said, "What do you think?" I nodded, "Yes, absolutely. But I really don't know what the absolutely is for." At that, we both burst out laughing.

The food was brought out and those steaks were enormous. Even I couldn't finish it all. We successfully finished the first bottle of wine and Mahsa promptly ordered another one. I shook my head, "Mahsa, what are you doing?" Smiling at me, she replied, "I want to drink good wine tonight, don't you?" They took away our plates and the second one which was finished too. The waiter asked us if we would like anything else. Mahsa ordered some Italian fruit ice cream and I said that I would have the same. We laughed and talked our way through dessert and we both were too full to move for a while. I motioned the waiter to bring the check, which I paid without any assistance.

As we walked out, Mahsa took my arm and asked, "Yousef, can you drive?" I put my arm around her and kissed her, saying, "Now don't worry we will be okay." I think it was more to reassure myself than her. I took the keys, opened the door for her to let her in and I went to around to the driver's side. Thank God it was late and there was almost no traffic. The streets were almost empty. I started the car and very carefully pulled out of the parking lot. I drove very slowly until we got home. I helped Mahsa out of the car and upstairs. When we got in she asked me if I can make some coffee I agreed, thinking that it would be good for both of us to have some. I went to the kitchen to brew a pot, then headed for the bedroom to change. Mahsa was there and had already changed into that gorgeous silk robe that I loved so much. I changed into my robe and we went out to the living room.

Mahsa made herself comfortable while I brought out the coffee. She took a sip and said, "Well, chubby, I see that you can brew a pretty good coffee too." I replied, "Anything for you."

As we sat drinking our coffee, we said nothing for several minutes. Mahsa broke that silence, saying, "Come sit next to me my darling, my sweetheart. I want tell you something very important."

I sat down next to her, took hold of her hand and said, "I am here, what's the important thing you want to say to me?" Mahsa gazed at me for a while before speaking. She took a deep breath and said, "Do you know who the most important person in my life was? My father. We were very close. As you realize, he left me to handle everything instead of my brother. After he passed away, it was so hard for me and I fell into a very deep depression. Mama had to take care of me for a while. Then my kids became important in my life until I met you. When I got involved with you, I was warned not to get too close to you by a lot of people including my friends and my auntie. And that's all because of your family and the way they think." She took another deep breath and continued, "I don't mean that they are not bad, no they are very good people, but they don't understand what it is with us. You and I are living in two different worlds. But I refused to listen to them because of my feelings for you. My heart was telling me to think differently. I got closer to you and so deeply involved that now you have become the most important person in my life." Mahsa took both my hands in hers, "I don't ever want to lose you at any price. Do you understand what am I saying? I might be drunk right now, but I know what I am saying. I want you to listen to me carefully; you have become the center of everything I do. My love for you is with me every second of every day. With you in my life, I am never alone."

I hold onto her very tightly and said, "How could I ever leave you alone? When you are the only one who could give me a new life, new spirit and almost new everything. How can I leave you alone or not want to be with you? It's all I want - to be with you and love you that's all!"

She wrung my hands as if trying to physically squeeze

her thoughts into me, "You know Chubby, I am very proud to have you as a partner, friend and husband. I am proud of who you are. But you are trying to take away the one thing that it the most fun from me and that's to shop for you. You don't know how proud I am that when we go shopping together that you start nagging 'don't do it, don't buy it' Please don't take that fun from me. Is it that much to ask?"

She continued, "You know me, my love. I know how you perceive it, but sometimes you think incorrectly. I love to do these things for you and it is my pleasure to do them." She looked at me as if begging, "I know you are the same way when comes to buying things for me. But I believe my feeling is much stronger than yours because I am a woman and naturally enjoy shopping. Please don't take that pleasure from me!"

Mahsa started crying again and looked pleadingly into my eyes. I completely melted at that sight as I massaged her hands and promised her that I would not take away the thing she really loved doing from her. It was a very tough decision and it made me uncomfortable; but I was resolved in accepting anything that was that important to her and I didn't care what it was.

She wrapped her arms around me, kissed me and said, "Are you sure?" Nodding, I said "Yes my dear, I am sure." She kissed me again and again, "Thank you, thank you. You know what you just did? You gave me a new life. I feel like a woman again! Thank you Chubby for understanding. I don't know why I am saying all of these things to you; maybe it's because I had little too much wine. I hope you forgive me if I said something I am not supposed to say." She hiccupped, "But thank you again for listening to me." Then she kissed me again, but this time was different and it lasted a long time.

I got up, stretched and went to the kitchen to see how much coffee was left; I saw that we had enough for two more cups. I called out and asked her if she wanted another cup. She didn't answer, but when I turned around she was standing right behind with our cups; she smiled and said, "Yes please and thank you." I refilled our cups and turned off the coffee machine and we went to the bedroom. We sat on the bed, drinking our coffee, when Mahsa suddenly gave me a strange look; she whispered, "Chubby I want you make love to me." Again, it was like she was begging, "Yes make wild love to me. You are a tiger aren't you?" Surprised, I just stared at her, but she was serious, she wasn't kidding, so what could I do but oblige her? I slowly removed her robe out and pushed her down on the bed. We got really wild and it was a wonderful release from the evening's heavy emotions. The next morning, however, I discovered just how wild we got with so many scratches all down my back and there were also some in front.

We got up together and poor Mahsa had bit of a hangover and didn't remember much of last night. I felt a little strange about the whole thing; the whole conversation and the lovemaking – all gone, nothing. I told myself 'Maybe it's better this way. Why should I have to tell her anything; but I will keep my promise no matter what happens and I did.

We were both starving, so we decided to go out for breakfast and then we would go shopping. First stop was a men's shop in the Hilton lobby and then to a street near the Hilton. We searched and searched until she found the exact one she was looking for. She bought the tuxedo and a very nice shirt but the suit had to be altered. The tailor told us that it would be ready the day after tomorrow and Mahsa was pleased. She then asked me, "Do you have nice black shoes?" "Yes" I said, "They are at the house, we can look at them to see if they are the right ones." Mahsa agreed, "Yes Chubby, you're right we will look at them tonight and see."

From there we went home and she asked me to show her the shoes, I brought them out for her and she approved, "These are okay, we don't need to buy shoes."

Then she stopped and stared at me, "Now wait just a minute! What happened last night? You were very easy on me today, so you tell me what happened." I shrugged, "Nothing very important happened, but I did promise you that I would be more understanding than before that's all." But Mahsa was unconvinced, "I think there was much more than what you're saying. But okay, you can tell me later on. I can wait until you are ready to tell me yourself."

On the day before the party I stayed there until late and Mahsa urged me to go, "You should go and get your hair cut tomorrow before you come here." I promised her that I would and when I got home, I promptly called my barber and he gives me an appointment between three and four-thirty. I thanked him for fitting me in on such short notice.

The next day after school, I stopped for a quick burger then I went to the barber. He knew exactly what needed to be done. He cut and washed my hair then he styled it. He was finished by four-thirty, perfect timing. I headed straight for Mahsa's place and as soon as she saw me, she beamed with pride, "That's my guy, beautiful!" In the meantime, she picked up my suit, so everything was ready. We started getting ready for the ball; Mahsa took a shower and I put on that suit but couldn't figure out how to tie the tie. Giving up, I asked her to do it for me. First she said, "Sit down here and let me do something. She worked on my face for almost half an hour then fixed the tie and said, "Now put on your jacket and take a look at yourself in the mirror." As soon as I pulled on the jacket and straightened everything, Mahsa gasped, "Oh myyy

God! You look so good. Now go fix your tea and let me get dressed. Grinning I asked, "Can I watch?" She waved me off, "My sweet God, you ask too much! Please go fix your tea; you will have enough time to look at me later. Go, go!" and out of the bedroom I went.

I fixed some tea and had a glass that was followed by a second, this time with a cigarette; then Mahsa finally came out. My God, who was this princess who was standing before me? She looked absolutely stunning in a long black silk dress with hand embroidered stones and gold thread. Mahsa told me that it was old dress that she had refashioned, I shook my head in amazement and she asked me if the tea was ready and if I could get her one. It was very difficult for me to tear my eyes away from her, but I said, "Yes, I will get you a glass."

I don't know how to explain just how beautiful Mahsa looked in that dress wearing high heels. Before we went to the ball, I took a picture of her and she took one of me, then I put the Polaroid on automatic and snapped a picture of the both of us together.

We arrived and Mahsa handed over the invitation to the door man and went in. I was very nervous because this was the first time we would be seen together in public. I was hoping that perhaps no one would recognize me on account of what she did to my face that make me six or seven years older. Her makeup, however, did the opposite made her look several years younger. As we made our way through the crowd, I couldn't help but notice that everybody was dressed in their very best. Mahsa picked up two glasses of white wine and gave one. We were standing near a corner talking when suddenly I heard the voice behind me that stopped me cold. "So" the voice said, "Is this *The* Ms. Doctor? The voice belonged to my older brother. "Shit!" I muttered under my breath and turned to face him. Oh yes that was my good old brother.

We both turned and I introduced Mahsa to my brother. Trying to keep my cool I said, "Mahsa this is my older brother." I nodded to my brother, "This is Mahsa, or who you know as Ms. Doctor." My brother leaned forward and kissed her hand as Mahsa made a small curtsey. My brother then said, "I asked Yousef to arrange a time for us to meet, but I think he has been too busy to do so." Mahsa was so thrilled that she invited him for dinner the following week right on the spot. Smiling, my brother agreed, "I can come on Wednesday." So it was set it for us to meet on that day at the restaurant in the Hilton. My brother said "Okay, great. You guys have lot of fun, I am around if you need anything." Mahsa blushed and said, "Thank you and it was so nice to finally meet you." My brother clapped me on the shoulder and walked away.

As soon as he left, Mahsa buried her face in her hands, "Oh God! We fucked up didn't we?" Strangely, I felt calm and said, "No, not exactly, I think he is okay. But I will talk to him." We put on our brave faces and went on with the party. Mahsa whispered in my ear, "Please stay close to me, because here people ask a lot of questions and you don't know a lot of the answers, so just stay with me." I did not leave her side the entire time.

We mingled with the others, shaking hands, saying hello and making small talk. The last person I met that evening was an elderly lady wearing a very beautiful dress and seemed to be in very high standing. I kissed her hand and she asked me my name and I give her my name, but only my first for sure. When she asked me, "So Yousef, what do you do?" Mahsa deftly stepped in saying, "He is in management Ma'am." I bowed my head and said, "It was very nice to meet you Ma'am." To my surprise, she winked at me and said, "Have fun you two."

We went back to same corner where we had met my brother, got two more glasses of wine and talked for a little while. Mahsa's eyes gleamed as she said, "This is our night, Yousef and we are the center of attention. Especially you. Everybody wants to know who you are and who invited you. Believe me; many of these ladies would love to catch you, because you are so sweet." She pecked me on the cheek, "Sweet enough to eat."

Her words made me uncomfortable, so I asked, "What am I doing here and what is this charity all about?" She said "First and foremost, you are with me and you are everything to me. This charity is for orphaned kids who need foster homes and a children's hospital." She handed me an envelope and said "When they bring the basket around, just put this in. They will most likely ask you for your name, phone number and address. Just give them the penthouse information and that's all." She patted my arm reassuringly.

Mahsa gazed at me and together we scanned the room as she said, Don't worry, I am here, just stay with me. Do you see those women over there? They would love to get their hands on you." Shocked I asked, "Why?" She giggled, "It's because you're young, beautiful, and handsome and they don't know you. They would absolutely die to find out who you are where you come from." I could tell that she was enjoying herself at their expense.

Mahsa then added, this time with a touch of contempt in her voice, "Do you know what those women really do Chubby? They pick a young guy and keep him as a plaything for a while until they get bored with him. Then they dump the poor fellow. That's what they do and they would love to get you." Then she said, "Now it's my turn to have a little fun. I want to spread the word. She called somebody's mane and the woman turned. They greeted each other and Mahsa said, "Why, long time no see! Where have you been?" The woman answered, "I have been traveling to London and New York for a while." Mahsa then asked, "How is everything?" It was the usual congenial reply, "Oh everything is fine. By the way, who is your friend?" Mahsa beamed a bright smile, "Oh this is Yousef, and he is in management. We were just talking to see what can be done with my business. He might consult on some things." They shared other niceties, until the woman said, "Mahsa, it was nice seeing you again." She then shook my hand and said, "Yousef, it was a pleasure to meet you." and left.

Shortly, we were called in for dinner. Mahsa instructed me to wait for a moment "Let the others go in first, we'll go in later." In the meantime, I looked around to see if I could spot my brother. But I didn't see him. We waited for five or ten minutes, then we went in to find that everyone else was already seated. She said, "You see? Now relax, we can pick whatever we want without all the pushing and shoving." We got our dinner and walked out; but on the way, I notice that people were watching us and talking. I whispered to Mahsa, "You were right about what you said about them. We are definitely the subject of their conversation." She scoffed, "Let them be for now. They really are dying to know who you are. But they are not going to find out unless your brother screws us up." She cast a sidelong glance. I felt defensive, "I don't think he will. He is smart enough not to do that." Secretly I hoped I was right.

After dinner they passed around the basket and I did as I was instructed. Then music started and people flocked to the dance floor. Mahsa and I caused a stir when we danced. One was a jazz number and at the end I kissed her as I thought I should. My kiss startled her and she asked, "Why did you do that?" I apologized, "I thought we have done something like that, I didn't do something very bad, did I?" Now I was worried. We were causing enough of a scene; I didn't want to make things worse. Mahsa said, "Don't worry baby. It's no problem really, it's okay. We passed the test, so don't worry."

We stayed until one then went home. But on the way we had such fun talking about them and laughing. Mahsa said, "We did it to them!"

We got home and went straight to the bedroom. Mahsa struggled to get out of that amazing dress; I asked her if I could help. "May I undress you?" She glanced at me and said, "Of course it's would be my pleasure for you to undress me." I unzipped her dress very slowly and carefully. I enjoyed removed each piece of her clothing. When I finished, I paused long enough to put that dress on a hanger. Mahsa in turn began to untie and undress me. Then we made fantastic love, the slow, gentle kind that allowed us to enjoy every moment. Afterwards, she wrapped her arms around me and said, "I am really proud of you. You did so well and have so much more class than many of the other people there. I wouldn't change a single thing this evening for millions. Jokingly, she added, "By any chance, are you related to last dynasty? You are not prince aren't you? I laughed and said, "No but...." Mahsa demanded, "But what?" I coughed a little and said, "I will tell you another time...." "Oh come on! Mahsa pleaded, "I cannot go to sleep now. Please tell me!" I told her the story about how my great, great grandfather was king of an island in the Persian Gulf. "Ohhhhh." She said, "It's no wonder you are like this."

We held each other close and Mahsa whispered, "Thanks for a beautiful night." I whispered back, "No thank you for giving me the opportunity to be with you."

We curled up in the comfort of each other's arms and fell quickly to sleep. The next morning, Mahsa got up before me and took a shower, then came back to bed, wrapped arms around me and whispered, "Oh Chubby Prince, wake up!" As soon as I heard those words, I opened my eyes and smiled up at her. I kissed her, saying "Good morning my princess!" She gave me a big kiss and said, "Get up, it's almost noon. It's getting late." I got out of bed, washed up and went out to the kitchen.

When I came in, Mahsa asked, "Do you want to eat out or make me a good breakfast? I shrugged, "I don't know, what you would you like?" She thought for a moment then said, "Let's go out to a hotel where they have those amazing brunches. I like the sound of that, "O.K." We got dressed and went to a nearby hotel, I don't remember which one it was, but I remember how beautiful it was. On our way there, I asked her what a brunch is because I never heard that word before. She explained to me what it is.

When we got there, we saw a sign that said 'Brunch Served Until Two P.M.' we had gotten there just in time to order. We ordered different things so we could share. The meals were enormous; starting with orange juice and coffee and seemed to go on and on with endless amounts of food. We stayed until three then we walked through the hotel lobby for some window shopping then went to our car.

We spent the rest of the afternoon outside. At six-thirty I asked her to drop me off at my cousin's and I said, "I will call you later and let you know what happens." She replied, "Call me anytime. I will stay wake until you call." I smiled, "Ok, I will definitely call you." We kissed and I got out of the car.

I walked in my cousin's house, but he wasn't home. I had tea and talked to my other cousin (I mentioned earlier that two of my cousins got married to each other). As I was talking with her, there was a knock at the door and it was my eldest brother. As soon as he saw me, he smiled but didn't say anything. He sat with us for almost ten minutes; then asked me to come outside with him.

I opened my mouth to say 'Hi, what's up?' when he turned to me very angrily and said, "Yousef, are you out of your fucking mind?" I didn't say anything, and he continued, "Do you know who *she* is and do you know how powerful she can be? Plus, do you have any idea how old she is and also just how wealthy she is?" I just blinked and still said nothing. Then he said "Answer me!" I took a deep breath and answered calmly, "I know all of that; is there anything else?" My brother's face turned bright red, "Yes, there is one more thing. Do you know how many men are after her? If they find out about you, you are dead meat!" I remained calm and replied, "No I didn't know that, but it's okay."

My brother looked at me hard and just shook his head, "But all these things aside, when I saw you last night, I was at first surprised and angry. But as I watched you with her, I was impressed at how much of a gentleman you were and then I was just happy for you." He looked down at the ground, "I always thought you were worthless because I didn't see much in you. You always screw up in school and get into trouble outside, so I never thought much of you until now." He looked at me and smiled, "Anyway tell me what happened and how the hell did you manage to meet her? You must tell me all about it. So I did, I told him every single thing right up to the previous night at the charity ball. At that point, my brother held up his hand and said "Now wait just a minute! You managed to pull all of this off? That was a very smart move." I then told him how Mahsa set up the charity ball. He shook his head again, saying, "You both are crazy! But I think she loves you too much that she cannot turn back now. But it's her choice and nothing can be done about it…." Then it dawned on him, "Hey, that was her son who went to London!" "Yes." I said, "But he was my friend before we became involved." When he heard that he burst out laughing. I looked at him, "What?" Still chuckling, he said, "It's nothing, but I am proud of you. I really didn't know you my little brother and for that I am truly sorry. I promise that things will be different between us from now on. You keep doing what you're doing and if you need anything just call me okay?"

"Ok." Quickly I added, "Please don't tell anybody, not even our other brother." He nodded, "I won't, don't worry your secret is safe, just be careful."

We went back inside and my cousin took one look at us and said, "Now wait just a minute; how is it that you two became so close just from going outside and talking to each other for almost half an hour?" He had a point; my brother and I didn't get along very well and normally after about a half an hour we would start arguing. But my brother stepped in and simply said, "We were just talking about his friend who had a problem and I was just giving a little advice. That's all." He changed the subject about something else and the matter was forgotten.

I couldn't wait to get home. But they started a card game and talking about stuff that really didn't interest me; so I sneaked out to the hall and called her. I had talk in a low voice as I told her everything that went on between me and my brother. At one point, she laughed so hard. She then said, "Yousef, I think everything is okay." I agreed. Mahsa asked, "Did you tell him about the Hilton? I said, "Oh no, I totally forgot! I will tell him later, I promise." We said good night and hung up.

Later that night I told my brother about meeting us at the Hilton and he promised to be there. Days passed and Mahsa and I spent as much time together as we could as my other brother wasn't in town. On Wednesday we went to Hilton at a quarter to seven, got seated at our table and waited for him. A few minutes later, I saw my brother at the entrance. I swallowed hard and whispered to Mahsa, "He is here!" We stood up and waved him over to our table. He kissed Mahsa's hand before sitting down to join us. His good nature put us all at ease and in no time at all, we were talking about all different things. Mahsa thanked him for helping Assa. He said, "Oh, it was my pleasure, don't mention it." We stayed until past eight until he said he had to go. He called the waiter over and paid for dinner. Mahsa tried without success to change his mind; he wouldn't hear of it. My brother then said good-night and left.

After he left, Mahsa turned to me, "Why didn't you say anything?" I shrugged helplessly, "I know him and I know you; I decided not to get in the middle." I explained, "He's like that, but you know what we can do? We can invite him over for dinner some evening. I think he would like that." To that, Mahsa nodded in agreement.

It was getting late and we got ready to leave. I suggested that Mahsa drop me off at my cousin's. I knew my brother would be there. She looked uncertain and asked, "Are you sure?" "Yes" I said, "I will call you as soon as I can." Mahsa dropped me off and left. When I went in, I was right in thinking that he would be there, sitting with my cousin making small talk. I got myself some tea and went out to the balcony to smoke when he joined me and said, "It is just as I said before; you both are crazy to go out together as openly as you do. You have to be careful! You have to think about what would happen if you got caught. Then what will you do?" I then told him what I did and he couldn't help but shake his head and laugh, saying, "You son of a gun! You did that because of him didn't you?" I answered, "I would do it again too." My brother shook his head again, this time he was serious, "You do know that this relationship is nearly impossible to keep." I said, "Nothing is impossible. Anything can be possible, if you put your mind to it!" He looked doubtful,

"We will see; just be careful and if you need anything, just call me. Do you understand?" I nodded. There was nothing more to say and he went back into the living room and returned to whatever he and our cousin were doing.

I waited for a little while to call her and tell her all about our conversion. We said 'bye' and hung up.

Days flew by and before long; it was the anniversary of the night we met one year ago. Mahsa told me that she wanted it to be a very special night for us. She made dinner reservations at the Hilton (it was her favorite place). I bought my usual bouquet of roses, but this time I arranged to have two white and five red and gave it to her. Dinner started with a champagne toast and hors-d-oeuvres. The meal was wonderful and at the end, there was a cake with a single candle and 'Happy Anniversary' written on it. It was all so very romantic. We kissed and said "Happy Anniversary" to each other. Mahsa kissed me again and said, "I love you Chubby! Everything I have is yours." She then picked one of the roses out of the bouquet and gave it to me.

After dinner, we went back home, went into the bedroom and changed into our robes. Mahsa turned to me and said, "I want to show you a movie. Have you ever seen an adult movie before? Smiling, I nodded. She looked at me coyly, "And where did you see it?" "With a bunch of guys." At my response, she said, "Well, this is not like any of those. This is a 'mature' movie and I think you will like this one because it is very close to our own story." Now she had my interest. Without another word, she set up the projector and started the film.

We snuggled up together in bed to watch the movie. It was made in Germany with subtitles in English. Luckily, Mahsa knew English so she had to translate for me.

The story was about a teenaged boy and a young, tall and beautiful school teacher. He was almost eighteen and in his last year of high school. During class, the teacher could not help but notice the way his eyes were all over her, tracing every single detail of her body. It did not matter what clothes she wore, or where she stood in class; the young man never took his eyes off of her. This went on and on for quite some time it seemed and the teacher didn't seem to know what to do about it. Then one day after school, she noticed him walking home, stopped her car and offered him a ride. Of course he got into the car. She drove out of town and he didn't say a word, just watching her the entire time. They arrived at a park and she stopped atop a hill and they both got out of the car. After walking for a little while, she turned to him saying, "Do you want me? Well here I am, come get me!" The teacher then reached out and took his hand but he pulled his hand away in shock, speechless. Then he turned and ran away. She waited for a few minutes, but he didn't come back, so she left. However, the next day in class, it was the same; his eyes were all over her. But as soon as she turned to face him, he looked down. That's when she knew she had gotten him good!

Later that afternoon she picked him up and they went back to the hill in the park. As soon as they arrived, the young man broke his silence, confessing everything, "I'm sorry about yesterday." He said, "I was speechless, I just didn't know what to say." He continued breathlessly, "I am in love with you and want to be with you no matter what." The teacher took him in her arms and they made unbelievable love. Then they watched the sun set and she gave him a ride back into town.

Their relationship went for a while until the boy's parents found out about it and brought matter to the school principal. The principal then demanded that the teacher stop seeing him or she would be dismiss. Right then and there she resigned from her job because she would not give up her relationship. In the meantime, the boy left his family in order to be with her.

The teacher had to move to other town and the boy stay with a friend until he turned eighteen when he moved in with her. She got another job and he went to college.

When the movie had finished, Mahsa asked, "Well, what do you think? Should they should have done what they did?" I thought hard, "I don't know because I don't have a son in order to better understand the entanglement. But the story was very close to ours and I don't want to let our relationship go, no matter what the price is." Mahsa agreed, "I feel the same way, but I cannot comment on that because I am a parent and wouldn't want my son to get hurt. But as you said I don't want to lose what we have, no matter what the cost may be."

We held each other like we had just found each other and gazed at each other like it was the first time. That night was really special because it was our anniversary and also because we saw that movie and we both felt like we were not alone. We weren't the only ones in this situation. Yes, Mahsa might be older than me and yes there are a lot of differences between us. But none of this mattered, what was most important was how we felt about each other. As a perfect end to a perfect evening, we made unforgettable and unbelievable love that night. That night was to become the centerpiece of my memory; I always remember events as before or after this night. After making love, we held each other and gazed into each other's eyes. I don't ever remember falling asleep. All I remember was in the morning when Mahsa was calling me from bathroom until she came out and kissed me then I woke up.

She cooed in my ear, "Good morning sleepy boy! Why do I have to beg you every time to wake you up? Please get up." She kissed me again and tousled my hair. I kissed her in return saying, "Good morning sweetie. I am awake." "Well, thank God for that!" she smirked over her shoulder as she left the room. I got up, washed and headed to the kitchen. Mahsa must have been up early as she already made breakfast. Smiling, she handed me an orange juice and had poured a glass of milk for herself. After breakfast and tea, we washed the dishes. I brought tea out to the living room, lit our cigarettes as we relaxed on the sofa.

I rested my head in her lap and teased her, "I hear your tummy talking and it has a lot of things to say!" Mahsa rolled her eyes, "Well, I just told her to shut up." I continued, "No, just listen; what do you think she is saying?" Mahsa turned serious and said "I know what you want to hear. But there is nothing because I don't want to." I looked up at her in earnest, "No? No chance? Not even a little one?" She said, "No not now. But if I should stop taking the pill, then, yes, there would be a chance." Her face was dark, "But I do not want to get pregnant, although I wouldn't want to lose it, but it would make things very difficult for us. Do you understand me?" I was shocked, but I persisted, "Yes but if you have a baby, it would be *our* baby. But the way you put it, it's all yours and that's not right." She looked down at me and sighed, "No the baby would be yours too, but I have to protect both of us."

I felt betrayed, "So, you control everything right now, is that true?" She said, "Yes, I do control this decision, because our situation isn't stable enough to let such a thing happen. We have to be ready for it." Her face softened, "Yousef, I would love to have your baby. That would be one of the most beautiful things that could happen to me."

I sat up and looked deep into her eyes. Suddenly Mahsa closed her eyes and whispered, "That's enough, please stop it." "Why?" I asked. She replied, "I get so afraid when I am alone, because I see how things are around us. And then I see you looking at me this way and I can't, I just can't." I said, "Well, let me tell you…" "Please!" She cut me off, "Not now, not right now maybe some other time. Thank you for understand me." I could tell by the look on her face that this was not the time for such talk, so I let the matter rest.

I lay back down resting my head in her lap and she whispered, "Yes baby, try to relax, I have to tell you something." I tensed fearing the inevitable. Mahsa continued as if she hadn't noticed, "I've decided to return to Shiraz next week until your exams are finished, then I will come back." Now I was upset, "Why, what's happened? Why do you want to go and leave me alone right now?" She said, "You have to study and while I am here, there is no way you will study as hard as you should. Plus, I have lot of things I need to take care of in

Shiraz. You must understand that I left everything unattended that I cannot do from here. I have to go back and you have to promise me that you are going to study and study hard the way I like it. I want you have to pass every single one in the spring. You have to promise me that!" I shook my head, "I cannot promise you that because there are some subjects that I don't know at all. There is no way I can pass them all. I am sorry; I'd love to, but cannot." Mahsa looked exasperated, "Then promise me that you will at least study as much as you can, no matter what. Can you do that? For me?" I gave in, "Yes my love, I will do my best. And I'm sorry that I cannot promise more, but I don't want to lie to you."

Soon, Mahsa left for Shiraz and I was alone again. But I was resolved to keep my promise and tried to study much as I could. Unfortunately my best wasn't good enough because I didn't pass all of the exams. Word arrived two days later.

The school principal called my sister and gave her the news. Somehow I got screwed, but I didn't give up, I promised myself, 'I will do it again in September.' Everything calmed down after a few days and I waited for Mahsa to call and tell me when she planned to return to Tehran. A few days later, she called me to check and see when my brother would be leaving for his two week work schedule. I gave her the dates and she arrived two days later. I rushed to the airport to pick her up.

It was a beautiful day nearing the end of spring. I waited for her at the baggage claim; as soon as we saw each other, we flew into each other's arms. I missed her so much and couldn't resist giving her a huge kiss. We picked up her suitcases, caught a cab and went home. The doorman brought up the suitcases and Mahsa tipped him.

As soon as the doorman left, Mahsa pushed the door closed with her foot and jumped on me. I held her so tightly. In each other's arms, we didn't speak, there were no word only the feeling of our hearts beating together as we got lost in each other's eyes. It seemed that we dissolved into each other as Mahsa kissed me over and over again until we were both out of breath.

When she had finally caught her breath, she said, "Hi Chubby, I missed you so much!" I was out of breath too, "I missed you so much, Honey Bunch. I felt so alone, you cannot imagine." Her eyes bored into mine, "Oh yes, I can because I felt that alone as well." We went into the kitchen and made coffee. We took our mugs outside to the balcony and told each other everything that happed while we were separated. She explained to me what Meetra had told her. "Mom, why are you coming here when you know how miserable you will be? Why don't you arrange to have him come to Shiraz with you?" I then told her how about my exams. Mahsa scolded me gently, "I told you to study!" I held up my hands helplessly, "I really did try, but there are some that I just didn't understand. What could I do?" She tried to reassure me "Don't worry Chubby you will pass them in September." She touched my face with the back of her hand and smiled, "In the meantime, I arranged some time for us to go up north together for three or four days. We will leave this Wednesday." I was surprised, "This Wednesday?" "Yes, do you have a problem?" "No, it's just that I will have to let my sister know." Then I asked "Where are we going?" "Ram-sar." She replied. (Ram-sar is a very famous resort town up north where many rich people have summer homes.) Mahsa saw the look on my face and laughed, "We will be staying in a hotel. It will be wonderful, I promise!" She told me about the arrangements she made, so we could make the most of our time there. I kissed her and thanked her for being so thoughtful. Mahsa smiled, "Don't mention it Chubby. You know that everything I have is yours. You still don't realize just how important you are in my life. But I think you will get it soon."

We spent the afternoon on the sofa, making love and talking. We made love without having sex and enjoyed ourselves so much. We were so caught up with each other that we didn't notice how fast the time flew by. Suddenly, Mahsa sat up and asked me if I knew the time. I checked and we were amazed that it was almost ten! We then realized that we were starving, so Mahsa ordered pizza. After dinner we went to bed and what a night it was; so beautiful and romantic. The next day, I told my sister about my plans for going out of town. She smiled and said, "Okay, Yousef, just call me wherever you are. I want to know that you will be all right." I promised her that I would.

CHAPTER 13

Shared Stories

On Wednesday, we started bright and early to head up north. Along the way we saw some beautiful sights like Dry Mountain and the verdant slopes of Green Mountain. We stopped for a light lunch in a small village. It was truly a beautiful day. When we arrived at the hotel, my jaw dropped, it was so beautiful.

Mahsa checked in while I waited next to the car. She returned shortly with a valet who took our suitcase to our room. The room was amazing; we had a gorgeous view of a courtyard and beyond that, the ocean. When we had gotten settled, the valet asked Mahsa if we needed anything from downstairs. She ordered champagne and caviar which were brought up in no time.

As the champagne chilled, we unpacked and changed into robes. We decided to have our champagne out on the balcony. We made ourselves comfortable and toasted each other and to our love. Mahsa then busied herself fixing the caviar drizzling it with butter and lime with crackers on the side, and served me. I had never had it before and hesitated. Mahsa smiled at me, "Go ahead, eat it. It is different from what you've had before, but I know you will like it." She was right, it was delicious! She made more for me which I relished greatly.

After a couple glasses of champagne, we lay down on the bed and talked for a while. Our conversation revolved mostly around our plans for the future. We then changed into swim wear and headed down to the beach. We walked along the seashore as though we were the only people on the planet; we laughed like children, splashed each other and stood waist-deep in water holding each other and kissing. After we grew tired of playing in the water, we walked back toward the hotel, found a bench and sat watching a brilliant sunset.

Back at our room, we finished the remaining champagne and caviar as we got ready to go out for the evening.

The hotel's dining room was beautifully decorated. We both ordered fish, although they were different and a bottle of red wine. We shared our fish, but only drank half of the bottle. We stayed there for a couple of hours, talking, laughing and enjoying our meal, which was wonderful. When the waiter brought the bill, Mahsa wrote something on it and gave it to him. She then took the wine bottle, our glasses and turned to me, "C'mon, let's go up." I motioned to the bottle and she said, "Oh, it's okay, everyone does this." And she was right.

So we went upstairs, changed back into our robes. Mahsa filled our glasses with wine and we toasted each other once again. As we got comfortable, Mahsa threw me a conspiratorial look and announced; "Now it's time for us to share our deepest secrets with each other." I was game, "Absolutely let's do it!" Mahsa went first.

"I was the only girl and the baby of the family. I have one brother who is older than me. From when I was baby, or at least as far as I remember, there was a big difference in the way my parents handled my brother and me. My brother was the son and that was very important to them. I was the girl and as Iranian tradition goes, everything would go to him and I would get only a little when they passed away. But when nobody was around, my father had a completely different attitude. Whenever he and I were alone together, he always showed me how much he really loved me. He would always tell me, "You are my favorite and you need never worry, I will always be there for you and take care of you." There were times that he hid his love for me, but I knew how much he loved me. So you see, he had two different attitudes toward me; the one who loved me best when we were alone and the other in front of everyone else, even in front of my mom or my brother. I remember that when we were alone together it was wonderful to have him share things with me that no one else knew. I knew that my mom loved me too, but she never really showed me; she was much closer to my brother. But she also kept some distance from him as well. So that was the atmosphere I grew up in."

Mahsa took a deep breath and continued.

"As my brother and I got older and bigger, he would always tease me and give me a hard time; I think all brothers and sisters fight like that. I knew he loved me, but being the only girl, I often felt alone, had to take care of myself and be strong. I knew that it wasn't my parent's fault in the way they treated me; they were raised like that and they became exactly the same as their parents. I couldn't blame them because they didn't know any better."

"When I was ten or eleven, my father and I were closer than ever. One day he sat me down to talk and we decided that I should go to school somewhere far away and get the best education. My father wanted to give me the best of whatever he could and let me go out and see the world, not just stay stuck at home and in that small town. We picked London and when I was fourteen, I went to an all-girl's boarding school. In the years that I was in school, I would come home to visit and somewhere during this time; my late husband saw me somewhere and liked me. His family came to our house to talk with my folks and ask for my hand in marriage. My father took me aside and said, "This is totally up to you and there is no one forcing you to make a decision." I asked my father to let me sleep on it for couple of days and he replied, "Take your time, my dear this is something you need to think about and go with what you feel deep inside." Two days later, I gave them my decision that I would marry this guy. Two months later, we were married and went back to London together. I moved out of my flat and we got a very nice house in a suburb of London. Less than a year later, I gave birth to Meetra and two years later, Assa was born. In the meantime, I got my bachelor's degree, then my master and was so close to finishing my doctorate when we moved back to Iran. Fortunately, I was able to complete that some years later. My husband was a very good man and a gentleman; he made life very easy for me. He and his family were considerably richer than my family. But that was never an issue between us and we had a very good life together. I never really loved him, although I cared for him very much. I married him because I felt that he was the safest bet for my future plans and my instincts were correct. He was a good husband and a wonderful father. We were a happy family until the accident and he passed away. I fell into a deep depression and started seeing a psychiatrist for over a year. Slowly but surely, I started feeling better, but never really had any interest in meeting someone new. Until one night - I saw someone so different and so out of place in this world. The first thing I saw was the eyes; those eyes drove me crazy! I couldn't tear my eyes away from them and suddenly my body became so hot, like it was on fire. All because those eyes were traveling all over my body and finally met mine. Those eyes were your eyes, Chubby and that night changed my life completely. And the rest is history."

I took her in my arms, kissed her and said, "Well, my goodness, how similar our lives are?" Then Mahsa pulled away and said "Okay Chubby, it's your turn to tell me secrets that you've kept to yourself for so long."

My story went something like this. "First I have to tell you that somehow I can remember things that happened since when I was one and a half years old. I am the youngest of six children and was the baby of the house. When I was very small, until about six or seven; I had a rare disorder that whenever I cried very hard, I would stop breathing. Once that happened, I wasn't able to start breathing again on my own and would start turning blue. My parents would have to perform CPR until I started breathing again. If no one was around to help me, I could have slipped into a coma and there was a very slim chance that I would ever come out again. So out of fear of my condition, everybody was very easy on me and as a result, I became very spoiled. When I was born, I was named after my grandfather, and maybe that's why my father put up with me for so many years. My youngest sister, the one who now lives in Tehran, took care of me until she got married and left home. I would always put my head on her lap and she would tell me stories until I went to sleep. I owe her so much because she was the one who seemed to love me the most. She made up for the love that I just didn't seem to get from my mom. I never could do the same things with my mother as I did with my sister. For example I could never have rested my head on her lap and go to sleep; she would never allow it. I knew that she and my father loved me, but neither showed me much affection and I was very sensitive kid. That much I knew from a very early age."

My mom was very active publicly and was out much of the time. She also didn't want me to be a spoiled brat more than I already was. On the other hand my father was often as distant; from time to time he would show his love for me in small ways, but indirectly.

When I was about seven, my sister got married and when I learned that she would be moving away, I got very sick for two months. She sat next to my bed for the entire time until I got better. My sister then promised me that she wouldn't move that far from our family's home. I had to believe her because I didn't know how far away the town they moved to was until I was much older. I was brokenhearted after my sister left; my mom decided to drop some of her activities so she could spend a little more time with me and eventually, she and I became much closer. But I still missed my sister terribly."

Even as a little kid I was very hyper and my breath-holding disorder made discipline all that much harder for my family. In those days, it was considered an embarrassment to have any family member undergoing any kind of psychiatric help. To add my family's notoriety, it was unthinkable for them to take me to see a 'shrink'. As a result, I grew up a spoiled brat who was unmanageable and a trouble maker."

It didn't take me long to get into trouble when I started going to school. I started smoking when I was about eight, stealing cigarettes from my parents. Because I started at such a young age, I haven't been able to quit. Such habits like smoking have become a big problem for many family members like my sisters and aunts."

To make a point, I lit a cigarette and continued.

I made my way through elementary school, started junior high and that's when my problems really started! I didn't like any of the other kids, or the teachers or the classes and couldn't be bothered to learn anything. I didn't see any reason to."

"My heavy smoking and nasty attitude toward people especially at school was becoming more of a problem. The school faculty tried talking to me in a vain attempt to figure out what the problem was. It got to the point that my sister and aunts didn't want my cousins and nephews going out with me. I didn't pass my exams in my first year of junior high, a fact that didn't bother me in the least. But for my family, it was the end of the world and for me it was beginning of a long fight. Throughout all the family tension and problems at school, I became more isolated and no one could do anything to reach me. The harder everyone tried, just added to more problems. Everyone thought they were helping me, but instead they just made things worse.

I didn't have any friends in school with the exception of Assa, your son. For nearly two years, we were buddies, but after a while he and I drifted apart. After losing my only friend, I became more hyper and a trouble maker than ever before. I didn't know what to do about all my conflicting feelings and felt lonelier than ever. Anything that went wrong ended up being my fault; it didn't seem to matter if I was there or not. So I decided to get involved with other things; but I still missed having personal contact with people, especially my own family. I just didn't know what to do about it. I forgot to tell you that in my last year of elementary school, my second eldest brother left Iran to study in the US and that was another reason why I felt more alone than ever.

In my third year of junior high, my second brother promised me if that I passed all my exams in the spring that he would take me with him to the US; but he didn't keep his promise. That left me feeling betrayed and even angrier toward my family. I spent the majority of my time avoiding the house everything and everyone close to it and felt even more alone.

That summer in Tehran was the same as any other summer. When I returned to Shiraz, everything was different, I felt so disconnected and more distrusting of my own family."

"By the time I returned to Shiraz, school had already started; I was coming in about a week late. When I showed up, it became clear that no one was happy to see me; they were hoping that maybe they wouldn't have to put up with me that year. That year, things were different, I kept very quiet. Everyone thought I had become more mature over the summer, but they were wrong. I simply withdrew, closing myself off from the outside world. I read more books than ever in my whole life. That year was passing so slowly for me until I saw your son (Assa) again after three years when he was with your daughter and they begged me to come to her birthday party. Meeting you that night changed everything in my life."

Tears welled up in my eyes.

"You see, not only did you give me my life back, you gave me a whole new and beautiful one. I was just starting to get to know myself again before meeting you. I was trying to mold my personality with what I saw and experienced and tried doing this with a different perspective. You know sweetie, it was then that I realized that I was in the right place at the right time. For everyone else it seems to be the wrong time and place. I learned a lot in experiencing all this. I've always told myself that whenever I'd get close to someone and get married; I would do it with a love that I have never had for anyone else. I never liked the way people treat each other. I hated being blamed for things just because I found my own way of doing things and living life my way. People think I'm wrong, but who are they to judge me? I don't want to live with what they believe and that's one of the main reasons that I don't get along with many of my family members. Yes sweetie you were the only one who has had any effect on me, my life and beliefs. The rest of my story you already know very well."

Mahsa gave me a long look, "So why did you try so hard to be that different from everyone else? Were you rebelling against something? I know why I did what I did; it was because I was a girl and you know how hard it is for people to recognize us for what we can offer." I responded, "That is exactly my point, why me?" Everybody I know has asked me the same question; I've never answered them but I will answer you because I love you and I know that you understand me. So I answer the question with a question. If everybody around you thinks that you are crazy and that there's something wrong with you mentally, then what do you do?" She looked at me in surprise, "Who said you were mental?" I shrugged, "Just about everybody in my family." Mahsa's eyes narrowed, "Well, first of all, they are the crazy ones and secondly, I would have done exactly the same."

She took my head and rested in next her heart and whispered, "No wonder you always put your head on my lap; I get such a strange and wonderful feeling and whenever I massage your hair, feeling changes. She kissed me and said, "Please know that you are not alone anymore." My eyes filled up again, "How could I ever be alone when you are in my heart, whether or not you are next to me or across the country. I know that I am no longer alone!" I kissed her long and hard, saying "Thank you for understanding me." We held each other for a long time and just cried. Not for her, not for me, but for the both of us, knowing that our loneliness was gone and that we had found each other at last. After wiping her eyes, Mahsa promised, "We will be together forever, no matter what."

Y. JOSEPHSON

We finished the last of the wine and made amazing love. I still can remember every move, every emotion and every word from that night. Our shared experiences had strengthened our bond even more. We fell asleep holding each other tightly were holding each other tightly until noon. Mahsa called me sweetly out of my dreams until she had to come back to bed to kiss me awake, saying "You really are spoiled." I opened my eyes and kissed her; getting out of bed reluctantly to take a shower. It was too late to go down for breakfast, so we ordered room service.

Later in the afternoon, we went to the beach and enjoyed a refreshing swim in the ocean. The sun, sea and fresh air can truly make one feel alive. After our swim, Mahsa told me that she wanted to get tan and asked me to lay out with her. She rubbed that awful smelly raw olive oil all over my body and asked me to rub some on her too; I did it only because I love her and that she asked. We remained on the beach until sunset then returned to our room, took a nice nap; then got cleaned up and ready for dinner. We discovered that there was a band playing in the grand dining hall, so we spent the night dining on sumptuous food and dancing. By one-thirty, we were exhausted. Once back in our room, I don't remember changing into pajamas, climbing into bed or holding each other tightly as we fell asleep. All I remember is Mahsa waking me up at ten after a blissful and dreamless sleep. After a hearty breakfast we went into town and enjoyed the sights, the beautiful weather, had a very good lunch and didn't get back until sometime around nine-thirty.

We decided that we weren't really that hungry around dinner time, so we ordered one plate of food with a side of fries which we shared and that was just right. Then we went outside to enjoy the music and dancing. We were having such a good time that we didn't realize how late it was getting and how tired we were. By one, we were ready to go up to our room.

We changed into robes and went out on the balcony to look at the moon which was almost full; it was such a beautiful night. We sat out in the mild air, arm in arm and reminisced about our first night together. Mahsa silently took me by the hand and led me back to the room, wrapped her arms around me and whispered in my ear, "Oh Chubby, do you know what would be the perfect ending for tonight? I had an idea, but decided to play along, "No, sweetie, what is it?" "Let's be wild like tigers and hungry like lions." As we fell onto the bed, "That's what I was thinking!" We had the wildest love making ever. Two hours later, we lay thoroughly spent in each other arms, savoring our cigarettes. I noticed some red spots on the linen bed sheets, so I asked Mahsa to look at my back. She looked me over and gasped, "Myyy God" What the hell did I do to you?" I winced, "What is it?" She jumped out of bed, "Don't move a muscle." She commanded as she hurried to the bathroom for the first aid kit. She patched me up with some ointment and a bandage. Then she kissed me and said, "I'm so sorry baby, I scratched your back pretty badly. Some of them looked deep, but you should be okay." She gave me her best guilty face. "I will check on them for you tomorrow." She promised as she kissed my wounds. Then we looked around the room; what a mess we made! Everything was on the floor, pillows were scattered all across the room; there was one all the way by the door. The blanket lay crumpled in a corner, the comforter was under the bed, and the top sheet was nowhere to be found. We looked at each other in amazement and burst out laughing. We put everything back in their places and then curled up together back shoulder and fell into such a sleep that only great sex can give you. This was the last night of our stay in Ram-sar and next day we had to go back to Tehran. We got up around ten. Mahsa kept her promise and changed my bandages; the scratch marks seemed to be healing well, she reported. We went downstairs for another amazing breakfast then it was back upstairs to pack and get ready to check out. Mahsa went to front desk to pay and I went out to wait for her. By the time she came out, the valet had brought our car around then we headed home.

We took our time driving back to Tehran, there was no hurry. We stopped at a couple of markets along the way and bought some fresh food like butter, cheese, yogurt and some other things. We got back sometime in the mid afternoon. We were a little tired after the trip, so we took a short nap.

As soon as we awoke, Mahsa got up and the only thing she said was, "I want my coffee!" And headed straight for the kitchen. Shortly after, the smell of freshly brewed Italian coffee wafted through the house. From the kitchen, Mahsa called out, "Chubby do we have the chairs outside?" I checked, "Yes we do." She brought the coffee outside; we sat enjoying the mild weather and smoked a couple of cigarettes. Mahsa asked me if I had enjoyed the trip to Ram-sar. "How was it for you?" "I loved it and thought it was great." We stayed out on the balcony until sunset.

We got dressed and went out to one of the local hotspots in Tehran. The place was full of people having fun on a Friday evening. We snacked on barbecued corn-on-the-cob and some Italian gelato until eleven when we picked up a pizza and headed home.

We got ready for bed just after midnight, when Mahsa turned to me and said, "I want you like last night." I was shocked, "My goodness another crazy love fest?" She laughed, "No Chubby I mean that I want to hold you just like we did last night." "Oh, well, that's okay, I enjoy that too." We lay close to each other as she massaged my back and shoulders and kissed my wounds over and over again. It was a tender night indeed.

The next morning as we were having breakfast, the telephone rang and when Mahsa picked it up and started talking, I knew right away that it was Meetra. I stiffened, expecting bad news. From where I sat, I could see Mahsa's face turn serious, and her voice became grave. After she got off the phone I asked, "What's wrong?" She averted her eyes and said, "Nothing". "That's BS!" I said, "I can tell by your face, eyes and voice that something's wrong. Please tell me what's wrong." Mahsa turned toward me with tears in her eyes and said, "Assa had an accident. He has a broken leg and arm." She looked so upset, "I'm sorry Chubby, but you must understand that I have to go to him." "Of course you have to go!" I said, "He is your son and my best friend." Mahsa picked up the phone again, and said, "Chubby, can you look in my purse and find the business card for the travel agency? Thank you." I replied, "Don't mention it."

She finally got through to the hospital in London and was able talk to Assa. He was okay, but was in some pain and couldn't walk. Mahsa reassured him that everything would be all right, saying "I will come as soon as I can get a flight." Assa said, "I am okay, but please get here as soon as you can." After getting off the phone, she put her head on my shoulder and sobbed. I just let her cry as I stroked her hair and said, "It's okay, it sounds like he is all right. Try not to worry baby. Assa is O.K. Thank God."

After her tears subsided, Mahsa took my face in her hands and kissed me, saying "You are so good to me! You always seem to know what I need whenever I need it. Thank you Chubby, I love you to death, I hope you know that."

I kissed her in return and said "Yes, and I hope you know I would do anything for you, don't you?" She smiled, "Yes, of course." Then I gave her the business card for the travel agency so she could call to make her arrangements. The agent told her that she would do some research and would call back. She called back a half an hour later with an available flight within the next couple of days.

I went home late that afternoon to make an appearance and went back to Mahsa's first thing the next morning. We went out shortly after I arrived so she could run errands like banking and other tasks. We stopped at a market and bought some sun dried fruit that she knew Assa loved and probably missed in London. I stayed with her that night which we spent making fantastic love. Afterward, Mahsa said "I will take this feeling with me when I go. I needed it very much. And you should keep this feeling because you will need it too." We didn't sleep at all that night so we could enjoy every single moment together. Mahsa had to be at the airport by five am; her fight was at eight. She let me go with her to the airport, but only under one condition – there would be no crying when we parted. Mahsa said, "I cannot take the emotional turbulence anymore!" I promised her that I wouldn't break down and I kept my promise; at least until after she had departed, then I lost it. I waited until the plane took off, went straight to the bar for a shot of scotch and then went home.

As soon as I got home I got undressed and crawled into bed. I slept until five and when I woke up; I decided to go over to my sister's. But no sooner did I set foot in the door, my sister started in, "Where have you been? Why you do these things?" And she went on and on. Finally I held up my hands and said, "I am here now and am not in a good mood! Can't you let it be? I will stay for dinner." While there, I waited for Mahsa's call and I couldn't help but pace back and forth until my sister said, "What is wrong with you today?" "Nothing." I mumbled, "I'm just waiting for an important call from a friend." Suddenly as if on cue, the phone rang, I ran to pick it up; it was her! Breathlessly I said "Hi it's me. Did you get there all right?" She sounded tired, "Yes and I know that you cannot talk, so I will call at your house around midnight. Will you be there?" "Yes." I said, "Talk to you soon." My sister whom I knew was trying to listen in on my conversation asked, "Was that the call you were waiting for?" I answered, "Yes that was the one." And I went into the other room.

I got ready to leave, despite my sister trying hard to get

me to stay longer. I refused, saying, "No I have to go". I got home by eleven-thirty actually running most of the way because I didn't want to miss her call and we didn't have an answering machine. I got ready for bed and laid down on bed to wait for her call. The phone rang shortly after midnight. As soon as I heard her voice, I said "You wouldn't believe just how much I miss you." Mahsa sighed, "Yes, I know dummy I miss you just as badly. But you have to be strong." I asked "Where are you?" "Right now I am in a hotel, but Assa is going to give me the keys for his apartment tomorrow, so I can stay there." She then gave me the phone number to the hospital along with Assa's room number and his home number as well. She instructed me not to call her. "I will call you, but if you have to call, you know what to do. Just go to the penthouse and call from there." I swallowed hard, "Okay, I will." I then asked, "Are you alone?" "Of course I am alone." "Good." I said, "Can you feel me?" Mahsa replied, "How can I not?" I said "Put your lips to the phone." "They are already there." Then I kissed her and she said, "Oh my God, I felt that all this way! But please don't do that! Don't drive me crazy; just let it be for now thank you!" I pretended to sound hurt, "I just wanted to kiss you, that's all." We continued talking for another fifteen minutes, then said our good-byes. I went to sleep, if that's what it could be called; I kept waking up every single hour to see if she was there with me, but she wasn't and I would try to fall asleep again.

She called me almost every day until one day I went up to the penthouse and called the hospital, Mahsa picked up and said, "I think someone is in my house!" I said "Yes I am." We talked for a little while and then I asked her to let me talk to Assa. She handed Assa the phone, I said "Hi crazy guy! What are you doing?" He said, "I am having so much fun." At that point I knew he was okay. I asked him, "How are you?" "I am doing all right. Just two feet and a bad arm, you know. It's nothing." Assa paused, "I want to thank you for taking care of her for me." I said "Don't mention it. It is my pleasure." Wrong thing to say! He snapped, "Oh, shut the f-up!" Then he changed the subject, "So, tell me how are you? Did you finish school? When can you come to London?" "School is okay, but I haven't finished yet. I don't know when I will be able to visit you. I will have to see what will happen this year." Then he said, "Yeah, we will see." I said, "See you when I see you." To that, Assa responded, "Not if I see you first!" and gave the phone back to Mahsa. She said "Okay, baby I will talk to you later." and hung up. Later that week, I felt so alone and frustrated, that I went to the penthouse and spent the night. I went to the bedroom where her scent still lingered in the air. I went to the closet took out a white dress and laid it on her side of the bed. Looking at the dress lying there, I couldn't stand it anymore, so I called her. When she answered the phone, she sounded surprised, "Is that you?" I said "Yes it's me, I am at your place." and I told her what I had done by laying her dress on the bed next to me. Intrigued, Mahsa asked, "What are you going to do?" "I am going to make love with you over the phone." "You are out of your mind." She was giggling uncontrollably, "You are crazy!" "Yes I am!" I replied, "And I am still going to make love with you." Mahsa was still laughing, "I love you crazy guy; where do you want me to be?" I had no other answer, "In my heart." I started by saying, "I am in bed holding your dress and I love to touch you." then I described to her where on her body I was touching. We went on and on like this until we both reached our peak. I stopped and lay there just listening to her breathing over the phone. Mahsa sent me kisses and after catching her breath, said, "You took me so and drove me crazy! I really needed that. I thank you and love you to death." Smiling, I replied, "I love you to death as well and I thank you, I couldn't have done this without you." After we both felt like we were back to earth again, we talked about more serious matters. I said, "I cannot take being alone anymore, I am going to visit my other sister in the south country that borders Iraq. Mahsa was surprised, "At this time of year? Are you crazy?" I shrugged, "I already have my train ticket, I will be back in four days." "Okay, just be careful! It's too hot down there; don't go out during the day. I will miss you!" I could hear the sadness in her voice, "I will miss you too." Then we kissed each other and said good-bye. The next day, I was off to see my other sister.

A few days after I had returned from my trip, Mahsa

called to say, "I will see you at the airport." She took my surprise, "What did you say?" "I will see you at the airport!" I was so thrilled that I gave a shout and asked, "When?" "I arrive in three days." She gave me the arrival time and the flight number. I said "Thank you God, thank you!" She answered, "You're welcome." To that, I replied, "Yes, you are my God!" "What did you say?" I decided it was best to keep that one to myself, so I said, "It was nothing, absolutely nothing."

I don't know how Mahsa always managed to arrange her arrival times to coincide with the days my brother was scheduled to leave for his job out of town; which meant that I would have plenty of time to be with her. The next three days passed by so slowly and all I could do was anticipate her arrival. The day finally came; and her flight was at night. Earlier that afternoon, I stopped by the florist and bought my usual bouquet of six roses - five red and one white.

I waited outside of the arrivals area when I saw her. She hadn't spotted me as she headed for the baggage claim. I took a step back and accidentally bumped into a guy who asked, "Have you seen yours yet?" I nodded, "Yes I see her." He followed my line of sight then said "Well, why are you still standing here? Go up front and call her!" I replied, "She doesn't like it when I do that, so I will just wait for her out here." He looked at me and said "I see; good luck!" "Thank you." I answered, A half an hour later she came out and saw me standing there. As if pulled by a huge, unseen magnet, we headed straight into each other's arms. I picked her up and swung her around. We were both laughing when the attendant who was carrying her bags waved to get our attention wanting to know what we planned to do. I gave Mahsa the flowers, turned to the man and said, "I am so sorry, please help us out to the taxi stand. I gave him some money and put the suitcase in the cab. All the way home we held hands so tightly as though someone might tear us away from each other and kissed each other over and over.

When we got in, Mahsa put the flowers in a vase on the counter; then flew back into my arms and kissed for a long time. I whispered to her, "Welcome back!" She whispered in return, "It's so good to be back!" She kissed me again and again. Mahsa went into the bedroom to change as I brought her suitcase in for her. She turned and asked, "Why you don't change?" "Just give me a moment and I will." As I changed, she went to the kitchen to make coffee; she said "I really missed our coffee. Over in London, the coffee was just awful." As the coffee brewed, she called for a pizza and requested it with extra, extra cheese. We sat on the sofa with our mugs of coffee. We just sat looking at each other and Mahsa said, "Oh Chubby, it is really good to see you again! I missed you so much and I know you missed me too." She continued, "Why don't you come here and sit next to me? I want to feel you." I jumped at the offer, "I want to feel you and be close to you as well." I moved to sit next to her.

I laid my head on her lap and Mahsa sighed, "Oh yes I really missed this." As she caressed my hair, face and neck. I kissed her hand, saying, "Thank you very much, I feel alive again..." I was interrupted by a call from the front desk; our pizza had arrived. As she paid the delivery man, I took the pizza into the kitchen and was putting out the plates, when she said, "No, we don't need them. Let's just eat from the box." That was new. Although it was delicious, we couldn't finish it all. Mahsa suggested that we put it away for later. I knew that she must have been hungry. After dinner and tea, we went back to the bedroom so Mahsa could unpack. She asked me, "Which one I should open first?" I pointed, "The big one." "Why is that?" I shrugged, "No reason, just open it." It was mostly filled with her old clothes with the exception of two new beautiful dresses. She then opened a small one. I said, "What about that one?" She threw me a conspiratorial look and said, "Just wait; I will open that one too." The smaller suitcases were mostly filled with shoes and nightclothes. I noticed two pairs of very beautiful new shoes. I mentioned it casually, "Those are beautiful new shoes you have there." "How did you know that I bought these two, I've been wearing them." I explained, "I know very well what you took and that those are new along with the two dresses..." Mahsa cut me short, saying, "You know what exactly I took?" "Yes I know what you took. She kissed me and said in amazement, "My God, you're good, you pay such close attention to me. It's no wonder that I love you so much!" Then pointed to the third suitcase, "That one is mostly for you." Now it was my turn to be surprised, "For me? Why?" She answered, "Just because. Now open it!" Inside were two pairs of jeans, one fitted and the other was straight leg, there was a very nice polo shirt, some socks, underwear, T-Shirts, a beautiful jacket to match the jeans and a very nice belt (which I still have). There were also a couple of dresses, a pair of shoes and some under wear for Meetra and a couple things for Mama.

Mahsa looked satisfied, "Now you have enough underwear so you can throw out the old ones. I asked her if she would model one of her beautiful new outfits for me which she did. My God she looked so beautiful in that gorgeous dress especially with those high heeled shoes. Not to mention that she had impeccable taste in fashion; not only for herself, but for me as well.

After the private fashion show, we put everything away and got ready for bed. I was already keeping the bed warm by the time Mahsa got in. She smiled at me and said "Well, well this is new!" I was confused, "What's new?" She replied, "That you are in bed first. That is what's new around here!" She snuggled into my arms as I kissed her, saying "Welcome home baby." Mahsa gazed into my eyes and said "It's so good to be home with you baby."

We talked for a while about her trip to London and about Assa. Suddenly Mahsa said "Wait a minute, what did you promise Assa that you would take good care of?" "Oh sweetie!" I said evasively, "I told you before." She tried to look angry with me, "That means you don't want to tell me or that you are going to lie to me." "No!" I said "I would never ever lie to you!" "Then you have to tell me what you promised Assa." She demanded. I gave in, "Okay, but I will only tell you under one condition; that you swear to me that you will never ever mention this to anyone!" "I swear to you that I am not to repeat this to anyone." Then I told her about when Assa originally wanted to go to London, "Just before he left, he whispered in my ear, 'Take good care of my mom, I worry about her.' that was all he said, because he loves you so much." Mahsa stared at me, "You son of a gun, both of you kept this to yourselves.

She hugged me and said "Do you remember the day you called me and did that crazy thing?" Giggling at the memory, I said "Yes I remember every minute of it." Mahsa continued, "All that time I felt it with every part of my body. I want that feeling again, physically and mentally." I kissed her and promised, "I will do it with all my love, and everything I am: veins, bones, blood and nerves." We made love with that promise to each other and what a night of love it was. I'm sorry, dear reader, but I am not going to go to details of that night. I will leave it to your imagination and keep it a secret that only Mahsa and I can know. All I will tell you is that from that point on, our love was all the stronger. . .

We didn't wake up until noon. Mahsa kissed me and said "Wake up Chubby, wake up!" When that didn't work, she then tried kissing me awake. I wrapped my arms around her neck, but didn't make any further movement to get up; so she worked her tongue between my lips and gave me a deep, sensual French kiss. That woke me up fully. Flopping back down on the bed, she murmured aloud, "I just don't feel like it..." I replied, "Neither do I..." She looked at me and said "What are you talking about?" I stretched and said, "I don't feel like taking a shower either." "Now wait just a minute, you can now read my mind too? No way!" Then she ventured, "So why don't you like to shower in the morning?" "Because." I said, "I get wet, that's why."

We made our way to the kitchen and Mahsa had already made coffee, so I fixed breakfast. After eating, we took our coffee and sat down on the sofa. I laid my head on her lap and thought to myself 'Yes she is back! She is with me, now I have somebody to be, somebody to talk to, somebody's shoulder to put my head on and finally I have somebody to love. I don't have to feel alone. I hated all those parties and gatherings because I was alone. Yes I have her now.' After a moment Mahsa gave me such a nice hug and asked, "Are you as tired as I am?" Then we shared, one by one, all the things we were tired of. We both were tired of lying, pretending, suffering, watching our every move, carefully planning our next time that we could see each other, and we were especially tired of not being counted as a married couple, Yes, we were tired of all those things; these limitations put upon us by Iran's social structure, our family differences both social and religious. I told Mahsa that if she wanted to, I can change everything and make our marriage official. The only thing I would have to do read all the fine print and make a couple of small changes. Mahsa shook her head, "It is not that Chubby, I want a perfect wedding! I want to see you in a black tuxedo and I want to see myself in a beautiful wedding dress. I want a wedding that is full of love and people there who will be happy for us." She continued, "Yes I already had one wedding, but it doesn't count for me, because I wasn't in love with him. I want this one with a huge ceremony. But it's more than just a marriage. That's what I am waiting for.

Desperately, I begged her to tell me what I could do. She looked so sad, "Oh, oh my beautiful Chubby, I wish everyone could be open and understanding like you - so full of love inside. No, no Chubby you cannot do anything about it. Truth is that neither of us can do anything. Only God has the power to help us go through these things. That is all we can do my baby."

She held me so tight and I noticed tears in those beautiful eyes of hers, welling up and running down to her face to linger on her chin. I kissed her tears away and wished fiercely that I could kiss away our problems too. Mahsa squeezed me tighter and kissed me.

After that conversation, there was nothing more to say; we just looked at each other in silence. Being held in her gaze made all time stop for me. There was nothing else that mattered. Finally, Mahsa spoke, breaking the spell, "You probably should go soon." She sniffed, I shook my head, "Not really, there is nobody is waiting for me except you. No my dear I will stay with you. This is the only place I want to be."

She smiled at me and said, "It's true, we are two of a kind, aren't we? Neither of us has any place we would rather be than together and that's good." She pressed on, "But you do have to go and show yourself to the family at least for couple of hours. I have to take my pill and once I do that, I will be out for two or three hours. Maybe it's a good time for you to go." "Okay" I said, "But I will be back soon. I don't want to miss you anymore than I already do." Mahsa kissed me, saying "Yes Chubby, go my baby go and come back. I will be waiting for you. And never forget that I love you to death."

Mahsa went to bed and I went over to my place and turned on a couple of lights and the radio; left them on and then headed over to my sister's. She started in right away, scolding me, "Where have you been? I called couple of times but you don't pick up the phone." Putting on my best innocent face, I shrugged, "Maybe I was asleep. I never heard the phone ring; perhaps the ringer is set too low." I stayed for about two and a half hours at which point I excused myself, "I have to go." Again she was suspicious, "Where do you have to be?" I answered, "Well I have lot of things to do and plus I need to study so I am very busy. I will see you later." I left my sister's house and made a straight line to our house.

I opened the door as quietly as I could. I looked in on Mahsa and she was still asleep. I went to the kitchen to make some tea. I was sitting in the living room when I heard a noise from the bedroom, I walked in and yes, my sleeping beauty was awake! I kissed her once then twice. She smiled, "It's no wonder that you were looking for that second kiss, it felt so nice." I asked her if she would like anything and she thought for a moment, "What did you have?" "I just made some tea." "That sounds wonderful, I would love some tea." I asked, "Would you like your tea in bed? I'll bring it to you." "Hell no!" Mahsa said, "I have to get up. I will be out in a moment." She joined me out in the living room for some tea and cigarettes. It was getting late and we discussed options for dinner. Mahsa suggested that we order out as there wasn't much food in the house. I said "Whatever you want is fine with me."

That evening, Mahsa was like an angel who swooped down and took me straight to heaven. I will never forget the beauty she showed me. Later that evening as we lay in each other's arms, she asked "What plans do you have for tomorrow?" I shrugged, "What do you have to do?" She sighed, "I have lot of things to do tomorrow, so I have to be out early. What are you going to do?" It was my turn to sigh as I said I'll go over to my sister's to study." Mahsa nodded in approval, "Yes you should do that, it's very important to me. I hope you know that." "I know." I grumbled, "I will go and study, don't worry." She gave me a hug and a kiss, saying, "I don't know what to do with you. You have become the most important issue in my life. I care about you and want you to pass your exams."

The next morning, Mahsa dropped me off near my place and went on her way. I picked up my books, went to my sister's. She was thrilled to have me and helped me with my math then left me alone to study other subjects. I was there for almost six hours when I decided I'd had enough of my sister and my books. I headed over to Mahsa's. When I went there, she wasn't home yet so I fixed some tea and had just started on my cup when she got home. I heard her at the door and went to open it for her, but she beat me to it. She had a lot of things with her, so I grabbed some from her and took them to the kitchen and came back to help her with the rest. After we had gotten everything in, I turned to her and said, "Why didn't you have me to help you bring all of this home? It's too heavy for you! You shouldn't tax yourself like that." "I know" she said, "I went to the market and stocked up on things we didn't have and totally forgot about you. I'm sorry." I said "Don't be sorry, but it's not good for you." Mahsa relented, "Okay, okay, next time we will go together."

Exhausted, she plopped down on the sofa and I brought her some tea. She said, "Ah that's why they call it love." She then asked, "Now tell me, did you go to your sister's and study?" I said "Yes I did." Mahsa looked pleased, "Did you bring your books here with you?" "Yes of course." "Good." Mahsa got up and went to the bedroom to change. When she came out, she asked for some more tea, which I brought out fresh cups for both of us to go with our cigarettes. After Mahsa refreshed herself with tea and cigarettes, she said "Go get your books and let me take a look at them. As she looked them over, I went to the kitchen and began making dinner. Hearing me in the kitchen, Mahsa asked, "What are you doing in there?" I called back "I am fixing dinner." "After you're done with that, please come here." "O.K." I really didn't know what she had in mind. I got everything ready and put the pot on the stove to simmer and went back to where she was sitting.

She had one of my books on her lap and said "Tonight we will study this subject." I rolled my eyes, "Look I studied nearly six hours today. I am tired." She looked at me levelly, "Just do it for me." I couldn't say anything after that. We studied for almost four hours and I was surprised to discover that I didn't get as tired as I usually got studying by myself.

After dinner we went straight to bed, held each other close and fell asleep quickly.

I woke up the next morning to find Mahsa already showered and fixing her hair in the mirror. She heard me stirring and turned to me saying, "Wake up Chubby. Wake up!" She then came over to me and kissed me twice "Now you don't have any excuses. Now get up!"

She added, "I already made coffee. Can you please make me a light breakfast? I have to go soon." "For sure." I washed up and went to the kitchen and by the time she was ready breakfast was ready too. As Mahsa ate, she asked, "What are you going to do today?" Tentatively, I said "I will stay here and study until you come back." It was a good answer as she kissed me and said "See you later…" "…alligator!" I answered back as she left.

I kept my promise and studied all morning and for a good part of the afternoon. I felt myself growing sleepy and thought to myself, 'I'll just close my eyes for a little rest.' The next thing I knew, Mahsa was kissing me, saying "Hi my Chubby. Hi sleeping beauty, hi." I sat up, rubbed my eyes and said "Hi Honey Bunch! When did you get home?" "About five minutes ago." she said "I see that you are very tired. Come on, let's get changed and go someplace nice." On her way to the bedroom, she made a quick phone call. She called to me from the bedroom, "Why don't you wear those tight jeans I got you and I will wear the ones that you love." Now I was curious, "Where are we going?" Mahsa gave the name of this place just northeast of Tehran; it was a very nice place surrounded by beautiful gardens. We both wore jeans and Mahsa promised me that it was okay to dress casual for this place. I came out wearing the new jeans and Mahsa was delighted, "Wow, they fit perfectly and look great on you. I love it!" She wore her jeans with high heels and she looked gorgeous as Hell! Secretly I didn't want to leave the house.

After a short drive, we arrived at a big gate. Mahsa tooted the horn a couple of times and someone came out and opened the gate to let us in. A woman came out as we drove up. As we got out of the car the woman gave me a strange look; I said hi and she courteously replied, "Hi sir, come on in." As we went in, Mahsa introduced me to the hostess, "Although you don't know him, this is Yousef he's my husband." The woman's eyes opened wide in surprise, "What, what are you talking about?" There were some children running around who she quickly sent to their rooms. Turning her full attention back to Mahsa, she asked again, "What are you talking about? You got married? No kidding, married?" Mahsa laughed and said "No I am not kidding!" and proceeded to tell this woman all about us. Then she put her arm around me and kissed me. The woman looked me up and down, saying "And who are you to push her into doing a crazy thing like that?" I didn't quite know what to say, I said simply, "I am nobody really, just Yousef and I love her, that's all." The woman started telling me how she and some of Mahsa's other friends tried so hard to get her to go out and make some new friends, but she would always refuse. The hostess then said "My God how is that possible that she met you and is now *married*!" I said "Well, there a little thing called destiny. I think that we were destined to meet and that Mahsa would be ready for our life and that's it."

The hostess took me by the arm and asked, "Do you know how to make ground beef kebab?" I smiled, "Yes I do." The lady motioned to a grill already smoking and said "Here you go. There is fresh beef, onions and spices. Let me know if you need anything." The grill was in one corner of an enormous balcony and that seemed to be where the party was. I prepared the kebab and put them on the grill. I motioned to the hostess, "I will need more charcoal." She said "I will get some right away for you. Thank you Yousef." I nodded at her, "You are more than welcome."

We had fresh kebab for dinner and I have to admit that I did a good job, everyone seemed to enjoy it. The hostess took Mahsa aside, "Well, now I have to throw you a party and tell everybody the good news!" Mahsa shook her head, "No, no! I have to say no because no one in either of our families know about this." The hostess looked disappointed, "But what about the kids?" "Yes, they know, but not the others."

CHAPTER 14

Back to Shiraz

Two days went by and by the third day I was really going We had a lovely time that night. But the following morning, Mahsa was firm in telling me that I wouldn't see her that much as she was going to be very busy. She also pushed me to study more but it still wasn't enough. I fell short on three subjects. My sister and cousin went to the teachers to see if I could at least get a (D) (passing grade). One of them, my English teacher asked my cousin "How I can give him a (D) when he wasn't even awake in my class? He was either asleep or wasn't in class mentally." My cousin then gave him a story, "But he is sick, he is diabetic. If you could at least give him that (D) you really help the sick fellow out. But that's totally up to you." My cousin was very good at winning arguments. Finally they decided to give me all (D's) so I could pass onto the next grade. But the principal of school had the last say; a demand that I had to go back to Shiraz for my next year of school. My family agreed, I had to go back to Shiraz, so be it.

When I told Mahsa all that happened at school; she laughed a little and then shook her head sadly, saying "Chubby, Chubby look what you've done! I told you to study but you are too stubborn and wouldn't listen to me. I don't know why you didn't do as I asked."

Shortly after the whole mess at school, my second brother tried to talk to me but I couldn't help but I think that he went little too far. He kept telling me from now on you have to do this and that and you don't know what responsibility is and so on. I got mad and lost my temper. I started shouting, "It's none of your fucking business! I know what I want in my life and it's my life. If I want to screw it up then that's my business." I kept going on and on. I stormed out of my cousin's house and slammed the door behind me as hard as I could. There was nowhere else for me to go but to her place.

It was late, so I knocked on the door first then I unlocked it with my key. "Mahsa it's me." I spotted her in the dark holding a wooden cane high over her head. I stopped in my tracks, "My God, what are you doing with that cane?" She let it fall, "I was going to beat you with it. You scared the shit out of me! What the hell are you doing here? Do you know what time it is?" I didn't say anything as I pushed past her into the living room. I sat down on the sofa and burst out into tears. Mahsa suddenly became very concerned, "Let me call your family to make sure that they are all okay." "Everyone is okay except me!" I buried my head in my arms and continue sobbing. She sat next to me, put her arms around me and kissed me, saying, "Chubby my baby, please tell me what happened." Slowly I calmed down and told her what happened. She cradled me in her arms and said, "Don't worry, I am here for you. It was good that you came here. I love you so much and cannot help but love you more now. Nobody can force you to do anything that you don't want to do. Just stop crying please, for me just stop. I cannot bear to see you like this." She kissed me again and again until my tears finally subsided. Mahsa said. "There, that's better. Now listen I don't know why you got that mad because we did talk about this and you yourself decided that it was best to go back to Shiraz. Why are you acting like this and making yourself miserable?" I sniffed, "Going back to Shiraz isn't the issue for me, it's the way my brother kept telling me that I was wrong and it made me mad." To my surprise, Mahsa laughed, saying, "Well, then, I will have to watch myself." Shocked I asked, "What for?" "So I don't make you angry." I shook my head, "You would never do that because you don't see me like they do." I felt my face get hot again, "They think they own me! But they don't know me. Nobody owns me, nobody!" Mahsa sat back and crossed her arms, "Not even me?" I was flustered, "Don't do that, you are different. You own my heart and soul. I don't know how to explain it, but it is different with you." She smiled at me, "I am just teasing you; of course it's different between us. And my heart is yours as much as yours is mine."

We sat for a while longer as Mahsa held and kissed me. Finally she released me and said, "Go call your sister and tell you that you are all right. She will be worried. Go on call her." I hesitated, "No not tonight. I will call her tomorrow. Mahsa just looked at me and shook her head, "My God you are such a stubborn guy! You should be saying to me, 'Yes dear, whatever you say.' Ha!" I was stubborn, "Not everything. I will call her tomorrow, but only because you want me to." She gave me a hard look and said "Oh shut up! Don't talk like that, I don't like it! She is your sister and she loves you, I think probably as much as I love you. You shouldn't talk like that." I didn't answer; I just put my head back on her shoulder and started to cry again. Mahsa softened, "Why are you crying again?" I sniffed, "It's nothing. I am just tired. You know, just tired of everything."

She hugged me and said, Okay, let's go to bed. If you're not going to call your sister tonight, at least let's get some rest." Then she stopped and said "Wait a minute, nobody knows where you are!" I nodded, "Yes that's it and you have to promise me that you will not call them either."

Her eyes narrowed, "Are you sure there isn't someone I can call? Who can I call?" I still refused, "You have to promise me that you won't." "Okay!" she said "I promise!" "Good" I said, "and don't forget that you promised." "All right, all right!" Mahsa gave up. "Go to bed, crazy guy go, go! You've gone totally crazy tonight. I don't know what to do with you. God help me!"

As we lay in bed she put her arms around me and said, "Look at me and listen to me for once." I turned to look at her as she continued, "You have to be better than this. Tonight you were not the Yousef I know. I believe you should be much better than this. I don't know what they did to you baby, but you have to forgive whatever happened. Oh, and you *will* call your sister as soon as we wake up. Okay?" I was too tired to argue, "Whatever you say, I will do." She hugged me tight and said "Yes this is the Chubby I know and love. I don't ever want to see you that angry again. I am glad that you are here and that you are safe. I know you know this place is yours and I love you so much more for coming here." She kissed me and said "Put yourself next my heart. I want to sleep heart to heart tonight."

Even if she didn't know it at the time, Mahsa really empowered me that evening. By supporting how I felt, even if she disagreed helped boost my self-confidence. As usual, she was up before me the next morning; she called me, kissed me twice and said, "Come on wake up!

I feel so alone!" Rolling over, I grumbled, "I am awake. Give me a minute, will you?" She headed off to the kitchen to undoubtedly make coffee. I followed soon after, saying good morning when I walked in. She kissed me again and said "Good morning Chubby! How are you this morning? Are you feeling better?" I woke up feeling refreshed, "Yes, thanks to you I feel much better." She smiled at me, "Don't mention it." After breakfast though, she held me to task, "Go and call your sister!" I spoke with my sister briefly just to let her know where I was and that I was all right. She asked repeatedly, "Are you okay? Are you sure?" I reassured her, "Yes I am fine, don't worry. I am with a good friend and I will see you tomorrow."

Mahsa had to run more errands that day. Before she went out, she asked, "What will you do today?" I was unsure, "Maybe I will go out later, or just stay here. I'm not sure what I will do yet." Mahsa kissed me and said, "The only thing that I want to ask of you is to think about what happened last night. Don't just do it for me and but for yourself. Please don't make life more miserable for yourself and me. Okay Chubby? I love you and you know that."

I spent the day alone, I didn't see anyone or talk to anyone; I just stayed at home by myself. But what I experienced was a completely different kind of loneliness. Maybe it's better to call it solitude and I felt good about it. Perhaps I just needed some time alone to think. I fixed some tea and just sat there with my thoughts and my tea until Mahsa returned home.

She knocked on the door and I opened it for her. With a hug and a kiss, she said "My God, that's a good feeling to come home to. Thank you!" I squeezed her tight and kissed her several times, replying, "No thank you for allowing me to be in this position." I brewed some fresh tea for her while she relaxed. Then she asked, "Would you like to go to my friend's house again this evening?" "Sure" I said "Why not, she is good friend to you. And we had such a good time there the other night." Mahsa jumped up to call her friend. I could hear from the other room, Mahsa telling her that we would be there; she sounded so happy.

We had such a wonderful time and stayed until about ten-thirty. On the way back home, Mahsa turned the subject to more serious matters concerning how I should deal with my family. I was planning to stop at my sister's the next day and would see my brothers and cousin. Mahsa suggested, "It would be best that you apologize to them for your bad behavior…" I cut her off, "But it wasn't my fault, it was him…" She interrupted me in turn, "I know my sweetie I know. But it would make things better if you did that. You will be the better person for it and they will know who did what." She continued, "Now you realize what happened wasn't your fault, it shouldn't be too hard for you to tell them. If it is, just imagine that you're talking to me. I know you can do it!" I put my hand on her shoulder, "You are too good to me and I don't know why." Mahsa smiled, "You will know soon enough my dear."

We got home, changed into our robes on and sat for a while out in the living room, I asked, "Do you want anything?" She shook her head, "No, just come and sit next to me. I want to talk to you." She took a deep breath, "I just want you to know that I understand what's going on between you and your family. Each of you is right in your own way. But you, Yousef, are more right than they are, because this is about your life. Unfortunately that's the way it is in this crazy world. Sometimes, it is more important how you fight than what you fight about. I know it seems that everything is against you now. Yes my Chubby, I think that it's better that you face them and try to resolve the issues at hand so you can start fresh. I think it's more helpful than just continuing with all these hard feelings. Trust me, you will see." She rubbed my shoulder reassuringly, "Now I want you to promise me that you will take care of this tomorrow for sure." I sighed helplessly, "How can I not do it when you ask me to? Yes I promise you that I will do it."

Mahsa stood up took me by the hand to the bedroom and said "Let's forget about all this nonsense and lets go somewhere we've never been before!"

That night we made the most incredible love imaginable. We flew together to heights we had never reached before. Our experience was so beautiful and it's one that I will always remember. I carry all of these precious memories inside myself. Two hours later, we lay thoroughly exhausted, held each other so tightly and fell asleep.

Mahsa as usual was up first, but instead of calling me, she lay next to me and repeatedly kissed my face and lips, saying "Wake up my sweet Chubby! Wake up. I don't like to be alone." I opened my eyes and the first thing I saw was that beautiful smile of hers. I yawned and said "Good morning Honey Bunch." To that, she replied, "Good morning Chubby." I got out of bed, washed up and met her in the kitchen for breakfast which we made together. After breakfast, I made tea and we went to the living room.

We cleaned up the kitchen and put everything away and it was time to go. Mahsa dropped me off about three-quarters of the way to my sister's and I caught a cab the rest of the way.

As soon as I got in, my sister ran up to me, threw her arms around me, gave me a kiss and said, "Please don't ever do that again. I was so worried about you!" I knew she meant well and Mahsa's words echoed through my mind. Looking down at the floor, I said "Okay." I looked around and the house was empty, "Where is everybody?" I asked, my sister replied, "I don't know but tonight everybody will be at your cousin's house." I shrugged, "Well that's good." My sister tried hard to get me to meet her eyes, "You know that you have to apologize to them - to all of them." I finally raised my eyes to meet hers and said, "Yes, I know and before you go any further, I want you to know that I've decided to go back to Shiraz. Tehran is good for you guys, but I don't want to be here anymore, it's all yours."

My sister seemed surprised at my calm attitude, she smiled at me and said, "That's good my boy, this will be much better for everyone." I nodded, "Yes I think so too." Later that evening, she and I went to my cousin's house. Everyone fell silent when I walked in the room; it was very uncomfortable for me. I first apologized to my cousins then quietly walked up to my second brother and held out my hand. He threw his arms around me and we both broke down in tears. Regaining his composure, my brother stepped back and said "I am sorry that it all came out that way, but you have to understand my situation. I also can't keep that apartment anymore because I am hardly around. And on the other hand, you didn't keep your promise either. You were supposed to study hard and get passing grades. But you didn't, so perhaps Shiraz will be much better for you. I don't want you to think that I dictate anything in your life; but you have to be more responsible in your life. You are no longer a child, but a man now." He continued, "And where you have been these past two days? You know our sister is sensitive and she was so worried over you!" Suddenly my eldest brother burst out laughing and said "You son of a gun! 'Where' is a good question indeed…" but he stopped and said nothing more. Later when we were alone, he asked, "How is Ms. Doctor?" I said she is okay, I haven't seen her in a while." I fed him a small hint and continued, "Anyway, I will be going to Shiraz soon, perhaps in the next couple of weeks." It was settled, now everybody knew that I would be leaving soon. We had nice night as a family and I stayed the night in my cousin's house because the other place wasn't available for me anymore. Later that night my eldest brother asked me "Did she change your mind?" "Maybe…" He laughed "You son of a gun, you are really in love with her! What should I do with you, except love you more than ever?" He continued "Hey you, when you get back, give me your bank account number; I will send you some money every month." I opened my mouth in surprise, but he held up his hand, "Just shut up and listen! You will need it and I don't want you to feel like you're less than she is. You got it?" I felt so humbled, "Yes thank you. I don't know what else to say." My brother smiled, "It's nothing, just enjoy and be happy. But remember, things don't always work out the way we want them to, so enjoy it as much as you can."

The next day, I went over to Mahsa's place but she wasn't home. I waited until she finally arrived. She knocked softly at the door and I ran to open it. Delighted, she jumped into my arms and said "I love it when you open the door for me." Perplexed, I asked "How did you know that I was here? Did the doorman tell you?" She shook her gorgeous head, "I didn't see the guys. I could smell your cologne all over the place. That's when I knew you were here and I got so happy. That's why I knocked on the door, my sweet, sweet Chubby, you really made my day!"

We sat down on the sofa and talked about last night. I said "Everything went really well with the family. What I really missed was you and your beautiful smile and your warm arms. I think I missed the last two the most." I continued, "Now we can go." Mahsa gazed into my eyes and said "What date should I buy the tickets for?" I gave her the date and added that we could be flexible; the day before or after would be fine. She called the travel agency and gave them the date.

Mahsa hugged me and said "Don't worry, this time Shiraz will be different." I said "I know for sure that it will be different because we will be together."

The day before our flight, I got all my things together and then left for my sister's house. The next day around noon I said good-bye to everybody and as I left the house, my sister asked, "Do you want me to call a cab for you?" I said "No I am going to a friend's house first and will go from there." My sister shook her head, "With those two big suitcases? You are crazy!" I said "I will be okay. I'll see you soon." I caught a cab a block away and headed for the airport.

I looked around and saw her from a distance. I went to meet her, we kissed and she said "Hi sweetie, you're late!" I said "I'm sorry; I got here as fast as I could. Is everything okay?" Mahsa laughed, "Yes, of course. Everything is more than fine. I am just joking with you. Let's go in." We checked our bags and got our boarding passes. The flight was uneventful and we got into Shiraz around two in the afternoon. We got home very quickly and found Meetra and Mama waiting there for us.

Mama and Meetra greeted us at the door Meetra gabbed Mahsa and kissed her "Welcome back home Mommy!" then she gave me a hug and a kiss on the chin. Mama hugged and kissed us too, saying, "Welcome back my babies, welcome back!" The four of us trooped into the kitchen where Meetra brought out a bottle of champagne and with an OK nod from Mahsa, popped the cork and filled our glasses. We drank a toast to a new beginning of our lives. We quickly finished the first bottle and Mahsa opened a second. Mama asked Meetra to set the table; lunch was ready. She had made my favorite rice dish which was saffron rice with chicken and yogurt. We call it <u>Tahcheen</u>.

After lunch, Meetra excused herself and went out. Mahsa and I took our champagne out to the side garden. We stayed outside for about an hour there then went back in and took the suitcases upstairs. Mahsa asked, "Do you want to unpack now? It will take the entire afternoon." I said "What do you want sweetie? Just tell me." She pointed to the closet, "Could you fix it like it was in Tehran?" "It's my pleasure to do that, but I will need your help."

Working together made it much easier. We got almost everything organized in the closet and set it up very nicely; starting with sportswear to nightgowns then shirts, underwear and last but not least the shoes. It took us three hours to finish the job. Mahsa had an amazing closet and it was huge; it measured at least 9x12 feet! With that job done, we went down for coffee and the smell of pie wafted throughout the house. Mama beamed at me and said, "I made it just for you!" She brought us two huge slices with her amazing Turkish coffee. The memory of that wonderful pie still makes my mouth water even to this day!

As if drawn home by the aroma of fresh baked pie, Meetra came in and joined us at the table. "Where is mine?" she pouted at Mama. "I am so tired!" Mama called back, "Just a Minute baby." and brought Meetra pie and coffee and asked, "Where did you come from? You weren't in?" Meetra shook her head and said "No

Mama, I just got in and thank you for lovely coffee. I am very tried and really needed it."

Mahsa told Mama "Yousef fixed my closet and he did such a wonderful job." Mama was surprised and said "You never let me do that. Let me go up and see what you guys did." She came back down, put her hand on my shoulder and said "You are really quite a guy. The man with special powers. I love what you did; we really need a man around here." Mahsa confided in me later, "Mama has tried to fix my closet but never stayed that way for long. But this time I will keep it like this."

We hung out in the kitchen for a while and Mama asked us what we wanted for dinner. Hamburger seemed to be the unanimous vote. Meetra suggested to Mama "Make those fantastic burgers of yours with the big fries. I love those!" Mama patted her cheek, "I will be happy to make that for you my baby." Meetra was right, Mama made a fantastic burger with fries.

After dinner Mahsa and I went up to our bedroom and after we both washed up; she jumped on the bed and with her finger, motioned me to come to her. I was not about to refuse that invitation. As soon as I got close, she grabbed me and wrestled me onto the bed where we made love. Mahsa whispered in my ear "Welcome back home baby. We will have good times here too. Try not to worry about anything. Shiraz will be different for you from now on. You'll see." She was right.

After making love, we wrapped our legs around each other and snuggled close together. We quickly fell asleep in that amazingly comfortable bed. We awoke the next morning to the sound of Mama's voice calling us from downstairs, "Are you coming down for breakfast?" Mahsa got up, took a shower and when she came out, she walked over to the bed. I was awake, but just lounged in bed and smiled at her. Mahsa said, "Why you are still in bed?" She came over and kissed me and I said "Good morning to you Sweetie Bunch!" "Good morning to you too Chubby. Now get up, it's late and you have to go don't you?" Groaning at the thought, I said "Yesssss" then got up, got ready and we went downstairs for breakfast. Mahsa suggested that she call me a cab. "With all those things you have, it would be better for you." We hugged and kissed until the cab arrived. Mahsa waved, "I'll see you later alligator." I replied, "I'll see you, but I'd rather be you." I said bye to Mama and left for my parent's house.

I asked the cab driver to help me with my things. I knew him as he was the guy we usually called for. He even took everything up to my room. I paid him double for the extra service. He gratefully took the money and said, "God bless you and keep you!" My father and mother were waiting for me. My mom flung her arms around me, kissed my head and said "Welcome back baby!

Welcome back." My father approached and I kissed his hand. He then took me in his arms and kissed me, welcoming me home. I went up to my room.

I took a short nap and my mom woke me up for lunch. We had lunch with my father as usual and we talked some. I went back to my room and flopped down on the bed. Yes I was home in my bed and my room, but the atmosphere of the house was somehow different. I felt more relaxed and calmer than before. Later that afternoon, some of the kids of very nice neighbor who would sometimes help my mom, came to our house. I heard them calling for me from my window. I waved back and said "I'll be down in a minute." I ran downstairs and let them in; we went to my mom's room because my room was off limits. They were happy to see me and welcome me back to town. They stayed about an hour and we had a great time catching up. As soon as my neighbors left, my nephews stopped in and they ended up staying for the night. We had a lot of fun together, but I had no time to call Mahsa and that was too bad.

I finally had some time the next day in the afternoon to get out of the house to see her. I told my mom that I would be going out and not be back until later that night. She stopped me short, saying, "Please don't come home too late. Your father gets worried." My heart sank, "I will be back before ten, how is that?" She nodded, "That is fine." I said bye and ran out the door.

Y. JOSEPHSON

I went over to my other home and knock on the door. Mama let me in and whispered to me, "She is upstairs and has been kind of tired." I went upstairs into the bedroom and found Mahsa lying in bed. Concerned I asked "What's wrong?" She said "It's nothing really, I don't know, but I am just down for no reason." Then she threw back the covers and said "Come in and join me, you are my energy. Come to me." I took my shoes off and climbed into bed and held her. I was startled to find her feeling cold, so I held her more tightly, rubbing her arms and shoulders while kissing her. After a while, I urged, "Come on, get up from this bed and let's sit next to the sliding glass door. The sun is shining and you could use a little sunshine!" I called down to Mama to bring us some tea. We sat in the sun drinking tea and I said thoughtfully, "You know that just because we are now in Shiraz, our problems are still the same as before." I sighed "But I will try to see you every day no matter what. I promise." She squeezed my hand and said "Promise me?" I put her hand over my heart, "I promise. I will see you every day unless something happens and that's out of my hands or anyone's for that matter." She leaned over and kissed me, saying, "Your promise is enough for me. I woke up feeling so down this morning and I kept thinking, 'Is this our future?' and I got so upset. I asked myself over and over, 'Why do we have to go through all of this? It's not fair!'" I tried to reassure her, "I know it's not fair now, but it's not going to be like this forever and this too, I promise you!"

BE HIDDEN LOVE

Little by little, Mahsa's mood lifted and when she was feeling better, we went downstairs. Mama later confided in me that she hadn't seen Mahsa that depressed in a long time. She also said, "Try to hold onto her and be with her as much as you can. She has become very attached to you and really loves you very much. It really hurts her when you are apart." I replied, "Yes Mama, I know how much she loves me. I will try to stay with her as much as I can."

Mama brought us coffee and some of her amazing apple pie. Mahsa was on her way back to her old self again. Mama reminded her, "Did you take your medication today?" Mahsa squeezed my hand and smiled, "Yes, and it has been so effective!" We knew what she was talking about. After finishing our coffee, I bundled her up and took her outside for a little fresh air. It was chilly out, but she seemed to enjoy the brisk weather. We stayed out for more than an hour. The time flew like crazy; I looked at my watch and was dismayed to discover that it was already past eight. I had to break it gently to Mahsa that I would have to go soon. She clutched my hand as if I would disappear right that moment and said "Can't you stay until nine?" I was torn, but agreed, "That's fine nine will be okay." She pulled my hand, "Then let's go in and to the bedroom, so we can relax for the time we have left." A whole army couldn't have kept me from saying, "Okay, let's go!"

As soon as we got into the room, she pushed me down on the bed and began unbuttoning my shirt; breathing in my scent and kissing my chest. She buried her face in my chest and we just lay there, being with each other. We lost track of time until Mahsa sat up suddenly and said "Chubby, my sweet Chubby it's time for you to go." My heart failed me, "I don't want to go and leave you alone!" But she was physically pushing me to move, "No you have to go. Your family loves you too and they want to see you. Get ready, I am calling a cab. Yes you are taking a cab, there is no time and don't say anything."

I wrapped my arms around her and kissed her, saying "See you later alligator." She snapped back, "See you later and let me bite you." "Sure anytime you want!" She rolled her eyes "You are a sick person." She gazed heavenward "I got a crazy guy as my love! I don't know what to do but I will find a way!" I kissed her once more and headed back to my parents.

As promised, I got home before ten to find that my mom had made one of my favorite dishes; a red bean stew and with toasted bread just the way I loved. We dined with my father and he welcomed me back and made a point to tell me that on no uncertain terms that this was my real home and not anywhere else. I agreed with him although secretly in my heart, home was across town. We talked a little over dinner; I heartily enjoyed the stew while my parents had a simple meal of bread and milk. After dinner, I had the task of feeding the three or four cats that came around evening time.

I said goodnight to my parents and went up to my room. Later, when I was sure that my parents had gone to bed, I called Mahsa and we talked for a while. It was getting late, so I went to bed with her picture next to my heart. In the days that followed, Mahsa and I managed to see each other every day. One bright and sunny Thursday morning, I said to my mom "I won't be coming home tonight. I promised a friend that I would stay with him. I will be back tomorrow afternoon." She frowned at me "Just be careful! Please don't do anything crazy. Remember that you are back in Shiraz. I reassured her "I know mom try not to worry so much. She then asked, "When will you be going back to school?" "I start on Saturday." She seemed pleased with that answer, "Very good, my boy, very good."

After lunch I went straight to Mahsa's place and knocked at the door. Mama let me in. I said hi to her and she replied, "Hi baby, she is upstairs." As I headed up the stairs, Mahsa emerged from the bedroom, wearing that gorgeous smile on her face. I met her at the top of the stairs, and she pulled me in the room. She took my face in her hands and gave me one of those kisses that instantly set me on fire. Then I gave her the good news, "I am staying with you tonight." As soon as she heard that, she jumped on me; wrapping her arms around my neck and locking her feet behind my back. She kissed me again and asked, "Is this for real?" I kissed her in return, "Yes it's for real. I will find a way to stay with you at least two nights a week. I will keep my promise to you baby, my sweetie."

Mahsa sat on the bed and looked up at me, "So, what we should do? I have to go out of the house because I am so tired of these four walls! I haven't gone out since we got back. Where do you want to go? I thought about it for a moment, "Táchira would be nice." Without hesitation, she called to reserve a table. When that was said and done, Mahsa hugged me tight and said "I love you chubby; love you so much."

We started clowning around and I tried to carry her down the stairs. We both started laughing so hard that I could barely stand. Mahsa wriggled out of my arms "Put me down, you crazy guy! I am heavy and there are too many stairs. There is no way I will let you do this. Still laughing, she grabbed my hand and said "We can go down together like this. See, isn't this better?" When we reached the bottom of stairs I scooped her up and carried her to the kitchen then put her down in her chair. She smiled happily and asked, "Are you satisfied now? Here, sit down next me, I can't bear you being too far away from me."

Mama came out from her room and asked me "Did you

have lunch yet?" I answered, "Yes, I already had lunch, but I would love some tea." So she brought me a large glass asked if it was dark enough. I checked and said "It's perfect." Satisfied, Mama busied herself getting lunch ready for Mahsa.

As we sat in the kitchen, Mahsa gazed at me, smiling. I loved that smile of hers; I let go her hand and stroked her thigh under the table as she ate.

After Mahsa had finished eating, Mama brought us more tea which we took back upstairs with us. We lay down on the bed and ever so slowly, Mahsa removed my clothes and I removed hers in turn. We made sweet and tender love. Oh God, it was so beautiful. Yes, I think that afternoon was the best I ever had in Shiraz in my life. When I told her that, she said, "I told you that Shiraz would be different for you from now on. Don't look at it the same way as before. Now we have each other and that's what makes it so different. Is it not true?" I couldn't have said it better myself, "Yes it is true and I think that Shiraz is different for you too, isn't it?" Mahsa nodded, "Oh definitely, it is very different now, thanks to our love that made it possible."

We stayed in bed all that afternoon then went down later for more tea. Meetra came in and joined us for tea. She seemed upset and we started talking. She turned to Mahsa, tears glittering in her eyes, "I have to tell you something. Something happened today in the cafeteria at lunch. I walked in and saw him with another girl. They were talking, then they hugged and he kissed her on the chin! When I walked up, he didn't even bother to tell me who she was, or what he was doing with her anyway."

I asked Meetra, "How long have you known this guy?" Maybe nine or ten months." Then I asked her "Did you do it with him?" Mahsa cut me off sharply, "What are you doing?" "I am trying to help her, so I have to know these things. Believe me, I am a guy. I know what I'm doing." Mahsa let me continue and Meetra said, "We did make out a couple of times, but no we haven't had sex." I then asked, "Did he want to have sex?" Meetra rolled her eyes "Yes, all the time and I kept saying no." I asked her bunch of other questions about him. Then we made a plan to get him and see how much he really loves her.

Meetra said "We are supposed to meet for a date on Saturday around twelve-thirty in the afternoon. I told Meetra, "Don't worry, we will find out the truth once and for all." Mahsa was amazed. She told Meetra, "It's no wonder that I tell Chubby that he can solve whatever problems are around him. Yes, baby, don't worry. Chubby will find out exactly what's going on with this guy." I reassured her "Yes Meetra, I will try my best to find out what's really going on."

Meetra looked at Mahsa and said "Can you solve this

BE HIDDEN LOVE

puzzle for me?" Mahsa said "What is it baby?" Meetra motioned at me and said "Can you tell me how he can talk and act like my father, but he's almost the same age as me?" Mahsa shrugged, "You got me on that one baby. I really don't know, but as you see, it's in his character. I don't know how he knows all these things, I guess it's just God's gift that he has." Then Meetra turned to me, "How is it that you know all these things? I think it is impossible that you could have read that many books to learn all this. But I would really like to know how you do it?" I answered, "Well, my dear, my house is much different from other people's houses because so many people would come to my father for advice on how to solve their problems. He would sit and listen then give them the advice that he thought was the best to help them. Sometimes it's best to listen and not just talk. You can learn a lot that way. I would often hide behind a door and just listen to people's discussions. Sometimes I see those problems right from the beginning. I also have a photographic memory. You see everything I hear or see, I remember. Unfortunately, the downside is that I am very bad with remembering names. I think I got it from my father; his mind is like a steel trap!" I added, "I think that I talk like an older person because I am the youngest in my family, so it was the way I was taught. Everyone in my house is older than I am, so that's how I learned."

Meetra sighed, Poor mommy!" Surprised at her remark, I asked "Why poor mommy?" Meetra replied, "More precisely, not just mommy, but all of us; we have to watch what we say because you will remember it all! No, I was right the first time - poor mommy." Mahsa laughed and said "Chubby is a good guy; I'm sure he will forgive us if we say something we're not supposed to. Isn't that right Chubby?" It was my turn to laugh. "You guys are wonderful! What more could I want from you? I will never ever forget everything you've done for me. That day when I needed someone badly you were there for me. How can I forget that? You know what day I am talking about; the day that Assa and I got into that huge fight?" I looked at Meetra and continued, "It was you who stood up for me to your brother. For that, I will always be grateful." Meetra looked long at Mahsa and said, "I was right, poor mommy." Meetra leaned over and surprised me with a kiss, "I am just joking with you. I love you both."

We left the house around 9. Mahsa ordered a bottle of wine; we sat back and enjoyed it. After ten, the dance music started and we did some dancing to work up our appetites; the restaurant made an excellent barbecued chicken. Time flies when you're having fun; much to our amazement, it was already past two in the morning. But Mahsa wasn't ready to leave just yet, she said, "I want to dance the next songs and then we can go." I was having fun and said "Fine, no problem." She then ran over to the DJ and asked, "Can you play a nice slow song? My sweetie and I are leaving soon." He nodded "Yes Ma'am, just for you." When I tell you that Mahsa was beautiful and that no man could refuse her - believe it. He played a beautiful Italian song, which was also very long; to that we danced, finishing a splendid evening out.

It was well after three when we finally got home. As Mahsa opened the door, we made sure to be as quiet as possible. Before she walked in, I stopped her, "Your heels will make a lot of noise." "You're right!" We both took our shoes off, tiptoed giggling like two teenagers sneaking into the house and made our way upstairs. We fell into bed and held each other tight. When I awoke the next morning, she was still asleep. I just lay there staring at her; she was sleeping like an angel or a baby. Her face was perfect and her body looked as if it had been carved by a master sculptor. Slowly, gently, I stroked her hair and let my fingers caress her neck. Mahsa opened her eyes, those intense sea-green eyes and she smiled sleepily at me. "Good morning" she murmured. "Good morning to you too." I answered. She asked what time it was. I replied, "I don't know and I don't care."

Mahsa turned to rest her face to my side and she started to play with my ears and to bite them. She knew I loved it and that it would turn me on like a light switch. That's when she jumped on top of me and massaged my chest and belly. There is nothing better in the world than morning lovemaking. We went so high as if we had wings. Is this how angels made love? I could only imagine. Then things got pretty crazy as Mahsa locked her legs around my back and used her toes to massage my lower back while using her hands to rub my upper back and shoulders. We both got so hot; I could feel her hands burning my flesh and could feel her touch all the way inside my body, all the way to my bones. I felt as though my ribs, lungs and heart would explode from the heat. I tried to move with but not only was she much stronger than me; she had extra leverage by being on top of me. I couldn't move an inch, so I held onto her so tightly. My climax intensely powerful with the added sensation of Mahsa's toes and hands massaging me in unison. It felt like I had become a star and went supernova. Mahsa kissed me nonstop as we both came down to earth, she flopped back down on her side next to me. We both lay there breathless as I wrapped my arms around her and whispered, "Thanks." Mahsa replied, "No thank you for making my day!"

Mahsa ran her hands up and down my back and I felt a sting. I asked her to look at my back to see what it was. She looked me over and swore, "Shit I did it again!" She kissed my shoulder and apologized for the damage. I kissed her in return and said "What are you sorry about, I love it and enjoyed every minute of it. There's no need to apologize. But I think your back might be the same. Let me take a look at it." She turned and I was shocked to find her back had big bright red blotches all over, looking very much like bruises. But at least there were no scratches on her skin. I told her what I saw and she hugged and kissed me again, saying "Anything that comes from you is worth more to me than diamonds." I rubbed my raw shoulder, "Then mine must be diamonds too." Mahsa went to the bathroom and got the ointment which she applied to my back and covered it with a bandage. She hugged me once more, saying, "How crazy are we to enjoy the pain?" Mahsa put on her robe and went out to see if anyone was around, but nobody answered her call. She then called downstairs; Mama picked up the phone and said she was out in the yard. Mahsa told her that we were awake and would be coming down in a few minutes.

After we finished our breakfast, we went out to the garden for a walk. After about an hour, we went back in and talked with Mama for a while. We went up to take our showers. After my shower, Mahsa looked at my war wound and put on a fresh bandage for me, saying "Keep it on for two more days, but if you can change it, that would be best." The afternoon flew by and it was already five o'clock and I told her sadly, "I have to go." Mahsa was dismayed, "Why, what time is it?" "Five" "Well, can't you stay until at least five-thirty or six?" I didn't have the heart to leave either "Yeah, okay, it will be fine." She shook her head, "I didn't know that was five already, I thought maybe it was four so we could have another hour to be with each other. But when you told me it's five I didn't want to believe it, but it's true." I stayed until six and then I had to leave. On my way home, I ran into the old cab driver, who was a very nice guy. He told me something that I will never forget, "Young man, if you are in love, hold onto it with all your might and don't ever let it go; because if you think you can any better than what you love now, you are very wrong." He shook his finger at me wisely, "I know, I've been there, I've been in love and then lost it. Don't lose your love at any cost."

I got home, headed straight to my room and lay down on my bed, thinking of the old man's words. I must have fallen asleep because when my mom called me, I didn't hear her until she knocked on my door and told me that it was time for dinner. I went to my father's room to eat with him. My mother had made a delicious rice dish. As I ate, I noticed that my father was not his usual self. I asked him if anything was wrong. He sat silent for moment then answered, "No, but I am worried about you and your friend." I opened my mouth to speak but he continued, "I have many dear and good friends. For the most part, they are good people but they only show themselves as friends because they want use people for their own purposes. In the end, they are not true friends at all." He went on and on about the topic for almost an hour, until I finally spoke up, "Don't worry so much about me! I am not stupid; I don't hang out with bunch of zombies. I know who in my life is a true friend or not. I have my own ideas about things. And for that matter, the guys I go out with, you know their fathers and families such as so and so. The couple of guys you don't know are students in university, they are not complete losers. I promise you and swear to grandma I never ever get involve with questionable people." I continued, "You know how I think and sometimes we don't agree with each other, but that's the way I think. I believe that I am mature enough not to get involved with anyone who just shows up at the door. I promise you and swear to God I am not doing anything to endanger our family name and that's all I have to say on the matter." My father leaned back in his chair with a satisfied look and said "Well done my son, I am not worried anymore. Just let us know where you are."

We finished dinner in a lighter mood and my mom brought me tea and said to my father "He's good guy and doesn't do anything bad, someday you will see. He's going to be better than anybody else." My father nodded, and agreed, "Of course he is. I am just saying this for his benefit. These are tricky times and there is a lot of trouble out there." I stayed another half hour then went to my room to be alone with love.

The next thing I knew, my mom was knocking on my door to wake me up for school. I went to the school office to check in. On my way to class, I took my time saying hi to everybody. I was starting my classes three weeks late and that was a record in my high school history. When I walked into the classroom, everybody gave me a round of applause, welcoming me back. That was a one and only performance and they didn't do it for just anybody; they knew me all too well. Also at that time, they trusted me and that was a big deal for me in those days.

After my morning classes, I went to my sister's for lunch and to see my nephews. They begged me to come over next Thursday night and I just couldn't say no. I went back for afternoon classes and after school let out, I called Mahsa who said, "Where can I pick you up?" I was surprised, "What?" "Don't 'what' me!" She snapped, "I'm not repeating myself." I said "Okay, you can pick me up at the usual spot in the square in half an hour." "Great!" she said "Love you, see you." I then quickly called my mom to let her know that I would be home around nine-thirty, ten.

I went to our meeting place at the square and Mahsa arrived five minutes later. I jumped in the car and she sped away quickly. She asked, "Where do you want to go?" "Táchira?" "No' she said "I am tired of that place, let's go somewhere else." I glanced at her, "Is it safe?" Thinking about it, she said "I don't know." Then she reconsidered, "Let's go home for tonight, we can decide where should we go next time."

It was so nice to be at home together, but it was short lived. Around nine, Mahsa sadly called for a cab to take me home.

In the meantime, I had made arrangements with Meetra to go to her school and act as her boyfriend. While we acted out our play, the guy in questions didn't seem have a reaction, but I am certain that he was careful to keep whatever his feelings were to himself. I made sure to ask Meetra about it the next time I saw her.

When I was at their place the next day, Meetra was home, I asked about the guy, Meetra reported that he was really pissed off and wanted to know who I was. "I kept telling him that you are my friend." Meetra continued, "I finally got him to tell me that the girl he was talking to and who he kissed was his cousin. That's when I told him that I didn't like it when I walked in that he didn't even acknowledge that I was standing there." She looked triumphant, "That's when he admitted that he was so busy talking to her that he didn't notice me. I told him 'That's nonsense, you should notice when your girlfriend walks in the room, because it is very important to me!' He apologized a number of times and said that he would be more considerate in the future."

Meetra turned to me, "So what do you think?" I thought for a moment and said "Well, I think it's best that you get to know him better first and that way you can understand his habits. That's very important in a relationship." Meetra nodded, "I will do that, thank you for your help. I owe you one." I smiled "You're welcome but you don't owe me anything, just remember my advice, that's all."

I made plans to see Mahsa every day; it didn't matter for how long, as long as I got to see her. One day, I called her after my afternoon classes and she sounded so down. Concerned, I said, "I am coming over." She said "No I don't want you to see me like this." But I was so anxious about her that I had to see her and find out what was wrong with her.

I caught a cab and hurried over. When Mama let me in, she looked very worried, "She is not good at all, please see what you can do." I went upstairs and found her in bed; her face was ashen and when I took her hand, it was ice cold. I almost broke down in tears. I didn't know what to do and it broke my heart to find my love in this state. Then I remembered when I was little, my mom would give us melted sugar that tasted like caramel. It had a soothing taste and we kids would perk up after a dose of that sweet goodness. I went downstairs and asked Mama if she could make some. "Yes" but she hesitated, "But I am not sure if it will help her." I said, "Don't worry about that, just make some and I'll do the rest." I took it up, helped Mahsa to sit up and gave her the cup and asked her to drink it. She asked "What is it?" "It's something good for you." "Are you sure?" I just looked at her, "Have I ever tried to offer you something bad?" She shook her head slightly "No" I pushed the cup toward her again, "Then just drink this, it's nothing more than just hot syrup." Reluctantly, she took the cup from me and took a sip. Mahsa made a face of disgust and tried to hand the cup back to me, "It's too hot and sweet!" I smiled at her, saying, "Just like me! Please drink it for me?" She took the cup back and drank down the syrup, all the time with an expression of an unhappy child. After she finished, I took the cup from her, satisfied. "What did you just say?" she asked. I replied slyly, "You said that it was too hot and too sweet and I said 'just like me.'" Mahsa smiled and said "You really like yourself a lot don't you?" I countered, "But not as much as I like you." Then she rested her hand on top of my head and said "Oh shut up, you crazy guy."

I held her close against my heart and whispered, "It's nothing my baby, you will feel better very soon. I promise." A short time later, Mahsa began to warm up and the color was returning to her face. I ran downstairs to get her a glass of cold water and Mama asked "How is she doing? Did she drink your concoction?" I smiled at her, "Yes she did and she is doing much better now. I will bring her down when I can." Mama looked so relieved, "That's wonderful, I am so happy!" I took the water up, gave it to her and instructed her to drink. She looked at me suspiciously, "What is it this time?" Laughing, I said "It's just water my dear, just water." and she drank it down without further comment.

After some time had passed, I asked Mahsa if she would like to go down to the kitchen for a nice cup of tea together. She was resistant, "I cannot, I am too tired." But I persisted "I will help you, come on let's go." Mahsa sighed "What am I going to do with you Chubby? I cannot say no to you, so let's go." Leaning on my shoulder, Mahsa and I made out way downstairs to the kitchen.

When we got there, I helped her to her chair. Mahsa asked Mama "Do you know what Yousef gave me the first time?" Mahsa shot me an accusing glance, "Because he won't give me a straight answer me." When Mama told her what the mysterious syrup was, Mahsa turned to me "Chubby how did you know about that?" I shrugged, "I just remembered what my mom used to give me when I was like that, and I remember how much it helped."

She turned to Mama "Do you see what I have to put up with? Ha!" Mama chuckled, "I really don't know what to tell you, Ma'am." Mahsa took my hand, pulled me to her and kissed me hard, saying "That's it, that's all I can do. My heart soared like an eagle, "That's worth millions for me and there is no substitute for it either."

I stayed until nine, and luckily Meetra got home just after eight. When she saw her mother, she was shocked, "What happened?" I tried to reassure her, "It's nothing serious; she just had low sugar. But now she is okay."

BE HIDDEN LOVE

Meetra ran upstairs and returned with a blood pressure machine and checked Mahsa. Her pressure was still a little low: 90 over 60. Surprised, I asked Meetra "How do you know how to use this?" Meetra beamed at me, "I know how to do lots of things. Would you like me to check you as well?" Stepping back, I said "No thank you! I know that mine is high right now. Let's just leave it at that."

It was time for me to go and I headed home with a heavy heart; all my thoughts were with Mahsa. But God knows that I couldn't stay although, I wished to God that I could. I called her later that night, but Meetra picked up and reassured me that Mahsa was okay. She is getting ready for bed now. I will tell her that you called." We hung up the phone and I lay down to try to get some sleep. But sleep refused to come and I knew that I couldn't call her again, so I had to suffer until the morning when I could call and check up on her.

I was in a lousy mood that morning and after breakfast; I complained to my mother that I needed a little time to myself before heading off to school. Around ten, I stepped outside for a smoke and to call Mahsa. This time, Mama picked up and gave the phone to her. We talked briefly and before hanging up, I said "I will see you this afternoon." She replied, "See you then."

I then phoned my mom to tell her that I would not be

coming home tonight and that I was going to 'so-and-so's' house to spend the night. My mother didn't say much, except "God be with you, watch yourself and be careful!" I promised her that I would.

Straight after school, I ran over to her place. Everybody was home and Meetra opened the door for me and they were happy to see me. I cracked some jokes and teased Meetra about her boyfriend. I asked if he was still jealous of me. We all had a bit of fun for a while. I asked Mama "What do you have for me tonight?" Mama beamed at me "Are you staying for dinner?" "Yes I am." "Well" she said "I will have to cook you something very nice!" Meetra pouted playfully "But Mama, how come we don't count? You never asked us what we want for dinner." Mahsa cut in "Wait, wait.." she turned to me, "Are you serious or joking? I cannot tell whether you are serious or you're joking today."

I met Mahsa's gaze, "No I am serious, I am staying for dinner." Looking uncertain, she asked, "How did you pull that off?" I shrugged "I don't know, I just did it and they let me." Then I dropped the bomb "And I think I will stay tonight as well." Double surprise! Mahsa was delighted, "Oh yes, double surprise indeed!" I told them about the conversation I had with my mom.

We had such fun that day. We had a p perfect dinner, thanks to Mama. After tea, Meetra went to her room and

Mahsa and I went to our room. She sat down on the bed and motioned me to sit next to her. Very seriously, Mahsa said "Yousef, I want talk to you and this is very important to me. If you love me, you will have to do as I tell you. Do we have a deal?" I sat close to hear fully attentive, "What is it? Anything you want I will do and that is a promise."

Mahsa took a deep breath and began "Look, I know how much you love me and I definitely know how much I love you; but the fact remains that your family lies between us. They are your parents and you have to respect them even more than you respect me. By design, I am both mother and father for my kids. I know how they feel and I know that they want the best for you as much as I do." She looked my directly in the eye and held my gaze. "So Yousef I don't want them to be upset with you because of your relationship with me. If at any time you see there is a problem or if they are upset, I don't want you involved. You have to take care of your own family first and foremost. Do you understand?" I felt as though she had just slapped me "You are serious aren't you?? She gave me that look "Yes very much." Then I told her "You have put me in a very bad position. Because of my relationship with you, I have a whole new life and hope for the future. My family doesn't understand me and they want me to be just like them. That's not who I am. If I understand you correctly, the way you want me to act around my family and yours makes things a lot more difficult and I think you know that." I sighed in resignation "Okay my dear, I promise to do as much as I can. But you must let me take care of my family matters my own way, because you don't know a lot of things about my life. And if I were to tell you absolutely everything, it would take several days to explain."

She hugged and kissed me, saying "Okay, please try to do as much as you can especially things concerning me." Then she added, "Yousef my love, please know that you're doing this means a great deal to me. What you do is very close to my heart, please don't disappoint me, you haven't yet and I hope you never will."

I held her tightly against my heart and kissed her, replying "I promise never to do anything to disappoint you, and you know that. I understand your point of view, but believe me when I say to you that sometimes it's almost impossible for me to do everything that everyone wants. But that's nothing new to my life; it's been that way for a long, long time. I will do it for you because it means so much to you and your happiness is everything to me." Mahsa hugged me tight in return and kissed me back, saying "That's enough for me and I am very sure you can do it." That was the end of that discussion as we both got ready for bed.

Mahsa later told me that night "My relationship with you is the most beautiful thing that has ever happened in my life." But it has some unique problems too…

From Mahsa's diary:

I am very confused about my relationship with Yousef. You know, Diary, that I love him so much! I love him to death and he has become everything for me, which makes him very unique. I know that within his own family, he completely alone, because he is nothing like them. Now he runs my life, he's a very strong man and I have never met anyone like him before. I have only one problem with this relationship which really doesn't have anything to do with him directly. The problem is that 97% of the time, I love him as my lover, my man, my protector and my husband. But there are time when I love him like a son; he becomes almost like Assa to me and that's the time when I cannot touch him; I can only talk to him or take him to dinner and that's really bothering me. But I love him with all my soul, flesh and blood. I must not let such as small thing separate me from him.

She never told me what the unique problem in our relationship was; but I found out years later from her diary. I only wished I had known at the time. Perhaps things could have been different.

When Mahsa reached for me that night; it was unlike any other experience we shared together. The feeling that came over our lovemaking was completely different – something very deep and indescribable. The way we touched each other, the way we kissed was different but beautiful. It's hard to describe in mere words. After two hours of intense emotional and physical sharing, we flopped down on the bed side by side, facing each other. We held hands and occasionally, one of us would kiss the other's hand. Mahsa and I curled up close together and fell asleep. The next thing I knew, Mahsa was calling me to wake up for school. I really didn't feel like going to school, but knew better than to have that argument with her.

I spent the weekend with my nephews, studying Persian literature, spanning the classics to contemporary works. We read poetry by Rumi, Hafez and many others. This was not for school as much as for our own enjoyment. We immersed ourselves so deeply on these works that we forgot where we were and what time it was. It was if the three of us were in our own little worlds. It was great that we could spend this time together; it had been so long since I had been out of town. I even managed to find some time to call Mahsa a couple of times over the weekend. One time I got very close to being caught on the phone, but got lucky. They stayed with us until Saturday morning and we went to school together. After school let out for the afternoon, I went to my other home.

When I got in, Mama informed me that Mahsa was very tired and had gone upstairs for a nap. "Any problems?" I asked. Mama seemed relieved, "No, she went to the office today and came back around three. After lunch, she went to lie down." Mama hesitated, "But she did ask me to wake her when I arrive." I shook my head, "No let her relax for a little while. I will stay here with you until she wakes up."

CHAPTER 15

Rumi Nights

Mahsa came down around five-thirty. When she saw me, she gave me a hug and said "What time did you get here?" "About an hour ago." Mahsa turned to Mama, but I interjected, "I told her not to wake you up." Letting the matter go, Mahsa sat down next to me and looked over my shoulder, "What you reading?" "Rumi." She leaned in closer, "Can you read a little louder so I can hear too?" Smiling, I said "Sure." I started over and read aloud one of my particular favorites, then I began to explain the poem from two different perspectives: one philosophical and the other, Gnostic.

I was really in that zone and went on and on and on that night about Rumi's poetry and the many different levels of meaning that can be taken from a single poem. When I was done, I added, "We can have a 'Rumi night' if you like?" Delighted, Mahsa agreed, "Yes here with you?"

BE HIDDEN LOVE

Catching herself, she laughed and I laughed too as we both shared our private memory.

In middle of my recitation, Meetra came home and headed straight to the kitchen to see what was going on. Mahsa said, "Ah Meetra, you picked the right time to join us. Yousef is reciting Rumi tonight. Come sit down and listen. He is something! When Meetra had gotten settled, Mahsa asked me to please continue, which I did most happily.

I handed a book to Meetra and told her to open it. Then I asked, "Can you read it for us?" She said "Of course I can, what do you think?" After she finished the poem, I asked, "Do you know what that poem means?" Meetra looked proud "Yes, it's so obvious." She went on to explain exactly what the poem meant and she was right! I decided that I would challenge her, "Do you think that this poem might have another meaning?" She looked it over gain "Maybe but I am not sure what different kind of meaning though." I went on to explain the different layers of the poem from both philosophical and Gnostic perspectives.

Meetra just sat there; amazed and asked again "How is it that you know these things?" "My father is an avid reader of Persian literature. He taught me everything he knows. He was very good at teaching me how to decipher these poems on many different levels." Meetra was excited, "Can you teach them to us as well?" I shook my head, "I don't know how to teach that well, but if you really want to learn, I can arrange to have a guy to come and teach all of us. But it would be best if we could have a group people who would be interested. If I know that there is a group, it will be much easier for me to convince him to do it." Meetra said "Don't worry about that. I can certainly get a group together, but it won't be a lot of people." "That's okay." I said, "A small group is better. Do you want me to contact him?" Meetra said "Yes, please talk to your guy and I will get the group together." Mahsa cut us off, "Yousef, do you know what time it is?" Reluctantly I said "No, I don't." "It's nine now, it's time for you to go. Let's talk tomorrow okay?" I said "Okay, whatever you say." She called the cab for me, gave me a hug and a kiss, saying "I'm sorry baby. I love you!" Then she admonished me "It's too bad about this afternoon but that was your fault, you told Mama not to wake me up." I smiled at her "It's okay. I'd rather you have your rest. I will see you tomorrow baby." Mahsa kissed me repeated until the cab arrived and honked its horn. I had to leave.

Even though I got home before ten that evening, I couldn't help but notice that my parents were not happy about my going out every night. This was going force me to come up with a different plan.

I went to my room after dinner and lay down on my bed and thought hard for a while. Suddenly it hit me; I found the answer for my problem, and I went to sleep happy. The next day at school, I sneaked out for a smoke to call Mahsa and asked her if she would be home later today around noon. Mahsa replied, "I won't be home by noon but definitely by one or one-thirty. Why do you ask?" I said "I will be coming over for lunch and I need to talk to you, it's very important." "I will be more than happy to see you, but don't forget your promise." "I haven't" I answered, "That's why I want to talk to you." "Okay then, see you at one baby." I said "See you baby. I love you." Then I called home to tell my mom that I wouldn't be coming home for lunch, but that I'd be home by seven. She said "That's fine baby. Thank you for calling and letting us know."

After morning classes let out, I headed over to Mahsa's. I got there around twelve-thirty and Mama let me in, saying "Hello, it's nice to see you. Are you staying for lunch?" Her eyes twinkled, "I made something very good." Mama chatted with me as she puttered around the kitchen, "You know Mr. Yousef...." Laughing, I held up my hand to stop her. "Forget about the 'Mr.' please!" Mama laughed too and continued "You know Yousef, I've met many people throughout my life, but I have never come across a man like you. You are completely different from other guys. It's your attitude, the way you talk and the way you do things that sets you apart from all the others." She looked at me levelly "I like what I see in you and I know that she is crazy about you. I am not supposed to say anything, but I think she has plans for the both of you." Mama leaned over to look me in the eye, "Tell me something; why do you do what you do and who are you? The reason I ask is that because most people don't behave like this. You are something else." Then I said "No Mama I am who I am. I am a 'lovey' guy and I am in love with her, crazy in love. I love her to death I cannot bear to see her upset or struggling. That's the way it is and that's the way I am."

Mama patted my cheek "God bless you and may he help you with these things. Just remember I cannot see her heart as you do. Do you understand what am I saying? This conversation is just between you and me. We are two people who love Mahsa very much." I nodded, "Of course Mama, I won't say anything about what we discussed. My mouth is a dead end."

Mama brought me a big mug of Italian coffee, winked at me and said "Mama's mouth is a dead end too." I said "This is perfect, believe me I feel the same as you about her that all I want to say." "Thank you" Mama replied, "Now I can be at ease. God bless you and God bless her. You both are my babies!"

There was a soft knock at the door; it was Mahsa. She gave me a kiss and sat next to me with a look of concern, "What is it baby?" I took a deep breath "When I got home last night, I got the feeling that my parents are very upset with me. I think it's because I stay out late every night and they don't really know where I am. That's very important to them. So, in keeping my promise, we need to discuss this because now there is absolutely no way that I see you every day." I saw her face drop with those words and I hastily continued. "I have to see you; so here is what I am thinking. There are some days that I don't have afternoon classes. Those days I can come here for lunch and stay with you until six. The other days stay the same. My family shouldn't be too bothered about a couple of nights a week." Mahsa kissed me and said "Thank you for being so thoughtful." Her brow furrowed, "But aren't there some days when you don't have any classes?" I said "Not really, I do, but they are not very important. One of Mahsa's eyebrows traveled upward in an arch "Such as?" I answered "Gym class, S.P classes (shop and metal work) and history." Mahsa still looked doubtful "Is that really true?" I felt childish, but nodded yes. Mahsa looked satisfied "Well, in that case, you're on!" "I will have to check with my family and let you know about those days without afternoon classes, but not today. I've already taken care of today."

Meetra came in for lunch and when she saw me she asked "What are you doing here? Don't you have classes?" I winked at her, "Not this afternoon." "Well" she said "How about that!" I admitted "Actually, I do have classes this afternoon, but only gym and S.P. No one really shows up for them though. I'm sure you know that." Meetra gave me a hard look, "No way, we had to go to all our classes." She jerked her head in the direction of Mahsa's voice coming from the kitchen, "She was worse than the teachers!"

Mahsa walked into the room and thankfully Meetra dropped the subject. To ease our secret transition, I asked about her boyfriend she replied "Well, he is still mad about that day and really wants to know who you are. We talked about it and I told him that you are friend of Assa's and like a brother. I told him that I asked you for help and that's why you did what you did. But then he got so mad and wanted to know why I tested him like that. I reminded him about his date with that other girl and that I had to do something. He said over and over again that it wasn't a date and that the girl is just his cousin. Anyway it's okay for now; I have to wait and see what going to happen in the future.

After lunch, Meetra went to her room, while Mahsa and I lingered downstairs for a little while before going up to our room. As agreed, I stayed until six then went home. But before I left, I discussed with Meetra about our 'Rumi Night'; she said "I have eight people who are interested, and counting mom and all of us, we will have more than thirteen in totals." "That's a good number." I told her.

That day I made sure that I got home before seven. I went to my room to change, grabbed one of my Rumi books and went to my father. Looking up as I entered, he asked "What is that you have in your hand?" (My father couldn't see very well because of blood clots in his eyes) I said, "It's a Rumi book." He chuckled "Well, well, would you like to start again?" "Yes" I said "I'd like to continue from where we left off." He smiled at me "I think we can do that." I opened the book and started reading some poems and then he would explain to me the many different meanings to each one. We studied together until dinner and continued afterward as well.

My mom was so happy to see me with my father, reading for him and keeping him company. By eleven, my head was filled to overflowing with Rumi poetry and interpretations which left me exhausted. I went to my room and straight to bed. I curled up with her picture and the next thing I remember was the voice of my mom calling me for school.

Now it was time to try the new schedule, I went to school, came home for lunch and went back for afternoon classes and then headed over to my other home. I stayed until eight and returned home.

When I got home I called a guy who was a friend of my father's and told him about our plan to have a Rumi Night. He said "I will give you a number for a man who is very good. He was one of my best students, so he should be able to help you guys." I thanked him and called the guy whose number I just got, but he wasn't there. I said to myself 'I will call later tonight.' I finally reached him and he said "I will be more than happy to help you, but I only have two nights that I would be available. It's your choice of either Tuesday or Friday." I didn't want to lose the chance, so I said "You can put us down for Tuesday night and if anything changes, I will call you."

The next day after school, I went stopped by and informed Mahsa that the gathering will be on Tuesday nights. "Please tell Meetra to let her friends know." Mahsa was pleased, "That's fine, I will tell her tonight when she gets home." She and I had a lot of fun that evening; we read some poetry then I recited for her an old school essay about some dry leaves under a tree and what they would say to us.

In the springtime, I was fresh and green. You were happy to see me; you gave me some water and took care of me. When I got bigger, you would picnic under me and enjoy the protection of my shade from the sun. The summer months passed and I gave you lots of nice fruit which you enjoyed greatly. Not long after, my colors turned from green to gold and red. You would come with friends to admire these colors and take many pictures of me. Together we had a lot of fun, but now I am old and dry. My colors have faded as I wither and fall to the ground only to have you walk on me and crush me. Why do you do that? Once I had value to you and now I am just litter. But I can still be of more use to you. If you rake me up and turn me under the soil, I can then serve as fertilizer for your new trees and plants. Or if you wait patiently, I will return next spring in all my leafy glory. [..]

As I read, I became aware that Mahsa had laid her head on my shoulder and that she was crying. When I had finished, she asked "Did you really write that?" "Yes" I replied, "I wrote it for an eighth grade assignment." She asked "What mark did you get for it?" "The teacher gave me an (A) for essay, but I included some illustrations, so he gave me an A+."

Mahsa then inquired "Do you still have that piece?" "I sure do, I keep everything." "I would love to see it." "Sure, I will bring it for you as soon as I find it." I gave it to her a month later. I kept a copy of the essay but without the illustrations.

Mahsa hugged me, saying "So, you were always a romantic and sensitive guy, weren't you?" I smiled "Yes I was and still am." She kissed me "I learn more about you every day that passes and it makes me love you much more than the day before. I often wonder how far we can go."

I stayed until eight-thirty and Mahsa drove me crazy for more poetry and things that I had written. I promised her that when I remember them that I would share each one with her. "Don't worry; you will be the first one to know." I reassured her as I got ready to head home.

Let me also mention, dear reader that at one point while I was at university in the U.S., I rewrote and translated that essay for English 101. I submitted it in a final exam and the professor gave me an A+ as well. It was very difficult writing it again because every line I wrote, I cried because the last time I had read it was for Mahsa.

The following week flew by; Mahsa and I enjoyed every stolen minute we could get. I couldn't stay overnight at all that week. I had plans to stay with her on Thursday night but my nephews came over and there was no way I couldn't escape. I called to tell her about the disruption to our plans; I was really pissed off but couldn't do anything about it. As we talked, Mahsa advised me "Don't take it out on them. Just be there with your family and have some fun. We can see each other some other time, just please don't be miserable! You know I don't like it when you get like that, so just let it be until next time." She kissed me and hung up. I felt a little better than before, but it was still hard for me.

That night we did have fun, spending most of the time in my room reading the poems and love stories from classical and contemporary Iranian literature. My older nephew turned to me and asked "Are you in love?" How ever he knew I was but taken me by surprise at his overly-candid question, I returned, "Why do you ask?" "Because all you read is about love and romance. Are you?" I really didn't want to get into this discussion with him "Maybe" Frustrated; he kept pushing "What do you mean 'maybe'? It's either yes or no!" Again, I said "Maybe" A look of realization came over him "I got it." and politely changed the subject. But not until my younger nephew caught wind of the topic and started in as well "Are you really in love? What is it like? Please tell me!" Avoiding his eager stare I said lamely, "I am not, but I can describe for you the feelings...."

Then suddenly, my mom called us for dinner and we went to join the rest of the family while I silently praised her excellent timing. After dinner, my nephews and I trooped back to my room. By then I was able to think of what to tell the younger one about what love feels like. Both listened attentively, but didn't ask me anything about it any further.

The three of us stayed up until two in the morning, practically falling asleep on our books. The next day, however, I was dying to go see Mahsa, but was afraid that if I told my nephews that I was going out, they would want to come with me. I had to keep quiet until I could come up with a plan. I made phony call and quickly changed clothes. I announced to everyone "I have to go. I just called a friend and found out that he is sick. I have to take him to the hospital to see what is wrong with him then I will be back." My younger nephew asked "When are you coming back?" I tried to keep my answers vague "I don't know, I have to go see what is what. Maybe I'll be back late or maybe I won't come home at all. My nephew was amazed "What do you mean by you won't come home at all? You stay out for the whole night? How is possible?" I said "Anything is possible; you just have to work on it." I went to say bye to my father and my older nephew, who was busy reading a book for my father. My father looked up at me and asked "When are you coming home?" I said "Maybe later." "Then I will see you later." I left the house and headed over to Mahsa's, but made sure not to take the usual route. I went a different way to the main street.

When I arrived at my other home true home – the home of my heart, soul and everything I treasured -- Mama opened the door for me. She told me that Mahsa wasn't up yet. She whispered to me "If you want, you can go up and wake her. I am very sure she would love that!" I said "Okay, but if I could get some of your wonderful coffee first." I followed Mama to the kitchen where she brewed me a cup. I went up and found Mahsa sleeping like an angel. I just stood there a moment, taking in her glorious beauty as she slept. Then I went to her side, took her hand and stroked her luxurious hair. At my touch, she awoke, just like a princess in a fairy tale. She opened those ocean blue eyes and when she saw me she gave me one of those smiles that imprinted itself in my heart forever. I kissed her sweet face and said "Goooooood morning Sleepy Beauty!" She yawned "Well, good morning sweet Chubby! What are you doing here?" I kissed her again and said "I came to wake you up!" Her laugher filled the room like sunshine as she got up and went to the bathroom. After washing up, she put on a little bit of makeup and together we went downstairs.

We discovered that Mama had already laid out breakfast for us. As she served us, I held up my hand and told her that I already had breakfast. Mama looked at me shrewdly "What time?" I said "Around ten." "Well" she said "You can have a little something now. But you want some more coffee, don't you?" I said "Of course I want my coffee!" I should have known better than to tell myself that I will only have a 'little something' when it comes to Mama's cooking. She brought us a veritable feast and told us to eat. And we sure did eat! I didn't think I could eat that much but when I am with Mahsa, everything tastes so much better.

Mahsa asked Mama if Meetra was up. She said yes she is in her room. Mahsa called for Meetra to come down for breakfast. The first thing Meetra said when she came in was "What is this devil doing here?" I quipped "Well, I came just to say 'good morning' to you that's why I am here." Meetra laughed, she sounded so much like her mother when she laughed. She joined us at the table and Mama brought her breakfast. That was a morning when I really felt we were a family, a good and happy family.

After breakfast Meetra went back upstairs then came down again all dressed up. Mahsa looked her up and down and asked "Where are you going on a Friday morning?" I jumped in, saying, "Ah, excuse me, but it's Friday afternoon." Mahsa laughed and corrected herself "Yes, the devil is right – afternoon, so where are you going?" Meetra answered, "I am going with my boyfriend to an afternoon party. After that, I'll come home." Then she pointed at me "Why you don't ask him what he is doing here, going around and waking everybody up? Ha!" With that remark, Meetra left.

Mahsa and I went to the side yard. As we walked she sighed "I am so sorry about the way Meetra talks to you." I said "Don't worry, it's okay. We understand each other." I paused, "Or at least, I understand her I know why she sometimes talks like that. It doesn't bother me, so don't let those little things bother you. I think that's just the way she is."

We had brought our coffee with us as we walked to the far end of the side yard. We sat on a bench and talked. I told Mahsa "The only thing I believe that can really change everything in our lives is destiny. I believe it deeply because of things that I have seen in my life that helped me to that conclusion."

BE HIDDEN LOVE

Mahsa just stared at me for a moment and then burst out laughing. Now it was my turn to stare at her "What!" But she laughed harder and harder. I tried again "I am sorry, but I don't know what is so funny." Finally she stopped laughing, took my hand and kissed me, saying "I am so sorry baby, I really couldn't help myself. Maybe it was because of the way you said it so seriously that made it so much funnier that it really is." Then she stopped, thought about it and said, "Now wait just a minute, you son of a gun, you are only eighteen and you talk like that. Where do you get these ideas? You have to tell me, please open yourself up to me, I can take it, I promise." I was a little reluctant and said "Now sure how you could from five minutes ago. It's okay, I am used to it, don't worry you are not the first one." Taking a deep breath, I continued "But I really didn't think that you would laugh at me. I thought you knew me better than that. I can't help but think that maybe I made a mistake. It seems that you are just like everyone else in our society, but that's okay. I understand and there are no hard feelings."

Mahsa face turned bright red and she gave me such a look as if I had slapped her. I never saw anything like that before. She threw her arms around me and kissed me, saying "I am truly sorry I didn't mean to hurt you. Yes I am beginning to understand that I might not know you that well, but that's your fault because you haven't let me. You keep everything inside yourself and you don't let anybody get too close." Her lips trembled and she seemed on the verge of tears, but she continued "That destiny you were talking about; is it real?" I nodded "It is as real as we are. We are living with it throughout our entire lives and we don't even realize it."

Mahsa's attention was rapt "Please talk to me I am listening!" I gave her a hard look "Are you sure? I do not want you to laugh at me again. I don't care about anybody else who may have laughed at me before; but not you, especially you. Maybe it's because you told me that you know me and you understand me and now is the time to prove that. I love you. I know you and I understand you, until now, I shared something very precious and personal of myself, now I want the same from you."

I went on to explain as Mahsa sat in silence "My dear, my love, everything we do may change our destiny. But by definition, we cannot make our destiny. You see some of the things in life are in our own hands but many other things are out of our hands. Can you change the season here right now? No it is not possible. But you can go someplace where it is springtime or the middle of winter right now, but you haven't changed anything, you just moved yourself. And that is what I am talking about.

"Yes my love, my sweet, sweetheart I brought up this topic for a reason; I want you to know nothing can tear us apart except destiny and that is exactly what I am so very afraid of. Sometimes when I think about it, I drive myself crazy, I don't know what to do and deep down, I know that I cannot do anything except to take life day by day. I want you to be very aware of what I am doing because this has become part of my everyday life." I kissed her and added "I love you too much to let anything happen to our love and our life together."

In tears, Mahsa threw her arms around me and held me to her heart, saying "Oh my dear, I am so afraid of that too." She kissed me and said "I am so sorry about laughing at you before. Again you are right; I have to take the time to get to know you better. But every time I learn more about you, then I love you more and I get so afraid sometimes." She paused and bit her lip as if considering her next words "Sometimes I have terrible dreams, and when I wake up in the morning I am like a zombie until I see you again. Only then it goes away. Yes dear, I sometimes worry that maybe you might think that I don't understand these things that you are saying but I can feel your words deep down."

We sat in silence in garden for a while until Mahsa spoke "Enough of this for today. I am really confused now and it's making my head hurt. Why don't we let it be for another time? Come with me, let's go in." She took me by the hand and we stood and held each other before going inside.

Mama came out of her room to greet us and asked me if I would like more coffee. I said "Oh thank you yes I'd love some." Mahsa and I sat in the kitchen without saying a word as we just looked at each other. It was Mama who broke the silence "What time you would like to have lunch?" Then Mahsa looked at me questioningly, I said "Whenever." "Great" Mama said "Lunch will be ready in ten or fifteen minutes." I replied "That's fine, Mama thank you very much."

After lunch Mahsa and I went upstairs. I asked "Do you have any old Iranian albums?" She thought for a moment "I don't know. Anything that I might have would be in that box." I looked and discovered to my delight that she did have may beautiful cassettes. I took one of the tapes and put it in tape player and it was a lady from a long time ago (the 40's or 50's). As we sat listening, I told Mahsa "This lady did this before either one of us was born. It's wonderful!" I took my clothes off, lay down on the bed and rested my head against her breast. I must have drifted off to sleep, because when I opened my eyes, I was alone. Then I heard someone coming up the stairs and I knew it was Mahsa because of the way she walked.

She came in and I said "I fell asleep, didn't I?" "Yes you were out only a few minutes after you started the tape. I stayed here until you moved. I didn't want to wake you up." She smiled at me, "You slept like a baby. I watched you sleep. Then you made a noise, like you were dreaming, but it was beautiful my sweetie." Suddenly we heard the doorbell. Mahsa went to see who it was. When she opened the door, I could see who it was from the top of the stairs. I also saw Mahsa's look of surprise when she realized who it was. She ran back upstairs, changed quickly and muttered angrily, "How stupid of her to bring him here. Especially today! She knows better than this." Without a word to me and she hurried down to the family room.

I got up and pulled on my clothes, trying to decide how to best handle this dilemma; it would be improper for me to go downstairs directly. Making my decision, I headed for her bedroom balcony and with some difficulty managed to shimmy down to the ground. Catching my breath and straightening my clothes, I went around to the front door and knocked on the door. Mahsa opened the door and was shocked to see me. I winked at her and she got the message. "Yousef, come on in please!" When I walked in, there was Meetra sitting on the sofa looking pleased with herself. She turned to the guy sitting next to her and introduced him as her boyfriend, motioning to me, she said "And this is Yousef!"

I sat down next to him as Meetra said to me, "Would you please explain to him what we have planned for Tuesday night's here?" I was relieved, "We are going to have a man who is well versed in Iranian literature come here to discuss the works of Rumi and some Hafez, but mostly

Rumi because we're calling it 'Rumi Night'. Meetra's boyfriend rolled his eyes, "Oh my God, that's going to be boring!" I just looked at him "Have you ever been to a reading session before?" "No" "Well" I said, "Then how do you know that it's going to be boring?" He shrugged "Sounds like it would be." I didn't say anything but Meetra turned to him "Perhaps you should come and learn something that is an important part of our culture. I don't understand why you say it would boring." At that point, Mahsa put up her hands "Why are you guys here and not at the party?" Meetra replied "We went to the party but got the time wrong, we were too early. We got some lunch and decided to come here. Anyway, the party will be starting soon, we should get going." They stood up, said good-bye and left for the party.

After they left, Mahsa looked me over, saying "Are you okay?" "Yes, I'm fine." "You're sure you are okay?" I nodded. She landed a light punch on my arm "What the devil did you do that for? And how did you get down without killing yourself? It's amazing, you have to tell me!" I simply said, "I just jumped with a little help from your tree." Mahsa shook her head "You are a crazy man."

Mahsa wasn't convinced that I was all right until she checked my hands, feet and my back. Still she was amazed "Well, you seem fine, but you don't know what a shock you gave me when I saw you at the door. Man, I thought I was losing my mind! Don't do that to me please! You say that you don't like surprises, but think before you do it to someone else." I stifled a laugh "I am sorry, I thought that I was doing the right thing. I didn't know you would get that upset. I'll never do it again, that's for sure."

We went to kitchen to see Mama. Mahsa changed the subject "Did you see that guy Yousef? He must be older than you by two or three years. You saw him, right? He seems like a normal guy, but he is going out with my daughter. He hangs out with young people and goes to their parties. It seems like he just wants to have fun; he likes the action, the music and dancing. He doesn't want to sit around and read Iranian poetry, much like any other normal guy."

Then she said, "But you come here to be with me; a woman who is fifteen, sixteen years older than you. You go out with me to my friends' house, my aunt's house and to some places where sometimes I get bored, but you don't. You socialize with my people, you listen to my music and you enjoy everything that I enjoy. I don't understand it." Mahsa looked at Mama for help "Mama, do you understand him at all or are you just as confused as I am?" Mama shook her head "No I don't understand him and always had the same question in my mind. But felt as though I couldn't ask because of my respect for you." Mahsa and Mama both turned to me as Mahsa said

"Can you really tell us way you are like this and not like that 'normal' guy?"

I did my best to explain why I was like that. "I am who I am and I cannot change that. But I can tell you how I came to be like this. You are absolutely right, I am not 'normal' or like other guys my age, but I am proud of being different. You see, where I grew up things were different; I grew up alone without other kids my own age around so I was always with people older than me. After my sister left, I really didn't have anyone to rely on, so I naturally learned how to talk as though I was much older. When I was about twelve, my second brother moved away as well and I became more isolated. Even though he and I weren't that close, at least there was somebody around I could relate to. But when he left for Tehran and then the U.S. I was pretty much alone. My choices were rather limited. I could go to school and try to fit in like everyone else or try to stand out and be different. I chose be different and I enjoyed it. I liked having contact with older people, I found that by talking with them and having them share their experiences and offering suggestions that I could learn more from them than people my own age. Guys my age always need someone to talk with to help solve their problems and they would always come to talk to me. What made it harder is that fact that my family is so prominent, so I couldn't be friends with just anyone. My friends had to be in the same class range as my family, much like your son. But most of the upper class kids were in better schools and as you know I went to public school all my life. And in public school there are mostly lower class kids that my family did not approve of. Members of my family also didn't want their kids hanging out with me because I was considered a trouble maker; those family members included my own sister and my aunt."

"There was this time when I was in junior high and I complained to my father that this school was not for me and if we could look for another one. He talked to a couple of his friends who also had children in that same school and they told him 'Your son talk's nonsense, this is a great school!' My father sent me there anyway, against my wishes. So I grew up thinking that I had no one to rely on and that I was pretty much on my own. That's when I decided to be different. And because of my father's notoriety, they couldn't touch me; I knew that and used it to my advantage. That is why I have a lot of older friends, rather than guys my own age. The only exception is my one true friend, your son, Assa."

Also my dears, at my house also each of us had to be able to talk to anyone from the maid to governors, mayors or heads of universities. Perhaps that's why I really enjoy being with you. I really did miss my childhood and early teenage years. I didn't notice them at the time perhaps because I didn't know any better. I wish I knew then what I know now. But I am happy because throughout the years, I have gained many things that none of the other kids have. And that is what it is like to be me, Yousef."

I continued "But I do have problems. The first one being that I have a hard time starting a conversation or relationship. As you remember my sweet dear, I was sitting on that sofa by myself and yes, I fell in love with you at first sight. That moment when I caught your eye from across the room, I couldn't talk. If you remember, all I could say was 'Yes Ma'am' or 'No Ma'am' until we went out on the balcony. Only then in private, I could talk. You started the conversation, the whole thing really, whereas I could not say a single word. But I can pull a plan together perfectly as you know. My dear that night I had a choice: I could have picked up my jacket and went inside to join the others or come with you and continue the relationship. Yes I had a choice and I am very happy with it."

Without a word, Mahsa rushed toward me and hugged me so hard, which I enjoyed very much. She then kissed me, saying "I will never ever question your love. I know now how pure and unbelievable it really is." I turned to Mama "Can you get me something to drink, my mouth is dry." Mama got up from the table "You bet. After that much talking, it's no wonder you're thirsty. But at least we know you much better." I excused myself saying that I needed to call home. I told my mom that my friend was very sick and that he would feel better if I stayed with him until the next day when a family member would be stop by. She said "Yes baby stay there with him. Where are you now?" I said "I am at a payphone on the street next to his dorm." I said bye and that matter were settled.

Mahsa was standing close by and asked, "Yes or no?" I said "Maybe" "My God can you ever give a straight answer? I always have to guess. Now you tell me yes or no. And who is this poor guy you are always taking care of?" I said "He is the son of one of my father distant cousins, so he knows them very well. And this guy is a very cool guy, I should bring him here. I think Meetra knows him."

Mahsa called to Mama "Yousef is staying; please make him a nice dinner." Then she turned to me, saying "You son of a gun, the answer is yes!" I smiled at her "Yes" She shook her fist at me "My God you are so difficult." "What did you say?" Mahsa just looked at me and "Oh shuuut up you!"

Mahsa told Mama about my afternoon adventure "Would you believe that he jumped down from the bedroom balcony into side yard?" Mama shook her head "Yes I saw it and I said to myself, 'He must be crazy! He could break a leg pulling a stunt like that.'" I said to Mama "Don't worry; I've jumped from places higher than that. But you are right; it was a stupid thing to do."

Mama slapped me on the back, smiling all the same as she said "You deserved that!"

Mama made us a very nice dinner indeed and after eating, Mahsa and I went up. We undressed and sat on the bed across from each other, kissing, smelling and massaging each other. We made the most amazing love and got a little crazy too. We made quite a lot of noise on our way to ecstasy. Mahsa panted in my ear "It's okay, Meetra is not home and Mama is in her room all the way in the back of the house, she cannot hear us either." Her words put me at ease and we continued unfettered by worldly cares. I had never been that crazy before or after that. We did it twice in a row then after we lay exhausted, holding each other tightly. Mahsa sighed "You son of a gun, what are you doing to me? You drove me crazy!" I replied "But you did it to me too." I added "We did it with our absolute joy didn't we?" "Yes" she said "Yes baby we did and I am proud of you, whoever you are. You are my king! You are everything to me, don't ever forget that. I never felt like this about anybody, but you are something else. I know that with you I don't have control of anything." "I understand completely." I said "Because I am much like you. You are everything to me and you know it very well don't you?" She said "Yes baby I know that."

Mahsa turned on her side and looked at the clock "Shit, you have to go to school!" and set the alarm for seven. I looked at the time in dismay "Are you kidding me, seven? Don't do that to me. Make it eight." Finally she changed it to seven-thirty. We wrapped ourselves in each other's arms and fell asleep. She called me in the morning "Wake up it's already eight!" Panicked, my eyes shot open "Good morning is it really eight?" Mahsa giggled "No baby it's only seven." I looked at her "Well you know that I am not going to school early." "Yes I know but at least we have a little more time together." She came back to bed, put her arms around me and kissed me, saying "I had such a wonderful night last night. That was amazing, thank you. You know you really are something." I said "You are something too and that was unforgettable experience for me as well. I will never forget it. Thank you for the lovely night you gave me, which I will carry with me for rest of my life." We snuggled until about a quarter to eight until Mahsa pushed me out of bed. Reluctantly I got up and got ready for school with her love. I believe you the reader knows when I talk about 'lessons in love'.

I went downstairs and Mama greeted me with a mug of coffee. She also wanted to fix me breakfast, but I said "No thank you, I have to go." I called for a cab, which luckily got me to school very quickly. I amazed that I had got there at a quarter to nine. I went to my classes, but I really wasn't there. Exasperated, one teacher yelled at me "Yousef where are you?" I answered "I am right here." He gave me an angry look and said "Really? Then be here." We had a fifteen minute break between morning classes; I went outside for a smoke to help get me through the next set of classes. I went home for lunch but was so tired that I went to my room and fell asleep for a while until my mom called me for lunch. I ate quickly and went back up to my room and back to sleep. Merciless as ever, my mom woke me up again for school. I changed clothes and left the house. When I got home later that afternoon, Mahsa called me from her bedroom. Finding an excuse to leave the house, I went over to see her. She had a paper on her hand. Curious, I asked "What is that?" Beaming, she handed me the paper; it was written in English which I didn't know at that time. Again I asked "What is it? You know I don't read English." Proudly she said "This is Assa's final exam paper! The university just awarded him with a total scholarship; they will pay all of his expenses including housing!" She continued "You know he doesn't need it, but because he worked hard to become a straight A student; they gave him that scholarship as a reward, so why shouldn't he use it?" She was very happy and I was very happy for him as well. Assa was my friend and always would be. We sat on the bed and Mahsa hugged me, saying "I got it around noon and I just couldn't stop looking at it. I am so proud of him." Mahsa leaned her head against my shoulder "He is a lot like me, isn't he?" I said "I don't know because I don't know what you were like in school."

BE HIDDEN LOVE

She said "When I went to school in London, I was also an A student and also got a scholarship. The same for Assa's father, he was a very smart man." Mahsa looked at me and said quickly "Unfortunately, not as smart as you. You are the smartest son of a gun I know. But you put your energy in other things."

We went back downstairs and I stayed until six. Just before leaving, I told her "I cannot come over tomorrow because we have family coming to our house tomorrow night, so I have to go home straight from school and buy some stuff for my mom." Mahsa looked a little sad and that worried me "Well that's okay." She said "It's like I told you before, she must come first, she is your mom." Mahsa continued "She loves you very much even though she doesn't always show it and you have to remember that always. It doesn't matter whether I am here or am not, she is your mom. She loves you very much, maybe more than I do. As her son, you have to understand it and love her unconditionally as she loves you unconditionally."

At six, she called a cab for me; I asked "What are you doing?" She said "You have to go home. We had our time together last night. Now it is time for your family. Go my sweet heart, be with them and give them all the love you can. You know that you can give them as much love as you give me."

Then cab arrived and took me home. But this time I felt different, because of Mahsa and what she said, yes, all because of her. I got home and changed then grabbed a book of Rumi and went to my father's room. He looked up and I went in and said "Ah you brought another book. "Yes" I said "Can I read it?" He nodded "go ahead, but read slowly and don't rush. There is nothing to be gained by rushing for the things you are looking for." I read a poem slowly and gently. And my father then broke down the meanings for me: word by word and line by line. At times I would get frustrated about a certain line or meaning and he would say "Just wait, we'll get there! Why do you hurry? There is no rush in understanding these things. You have to take the time to understand fully, not just a little. Bear with me and listen, I know it can be hard for you, you want to learn this in no time and that's not going to happen." He said gently "Do you understand what I said?" I said "Yes I do. We continued until my father said, "We have to stop. I have to pray now. Go and come back later." On the way to my room, I saw my mom, who said "Very good, my son. It's very good that you two are finally together, thank God for that. Your father always wanted it like that, but you were never here. Thank God you were here now. Go and rest, my son."

My father and I had a very enjoyable night, but just before going back to my room, he asked "Are you also studying your school books?" I had to be honest with him "Yes I do." He knew the truth "Just as much as you study this?" "No not as much as this." He placed a heavy hand on my shoulder and said "You must concentrate on your lessons, because that's where your future lies, don't screw it up."

Before leaving for school the next morning, my mom gave me a list of the things she wanted. When school let out, I stopped at the market to pick up what was needed. Our house was full of family that night. Both of my sisters came and there were aunts, cousins and everyone brought their kids as well. As crowded as it was, I still felt alone and all I could do was think about Mahsa and wish that she was with me. I tried hard to imagine her there, talking to people and laughing by my side; but of course nobody saw her, they didn't even know that she existed. By the time everybody left, I was mentally exhausted. I hurried to my room and laid on my bed, so life could start again for me.

Falling asleep, I had the most wonderful dream, if only it could be a reality! But it was interrupted by my mom calling me for school. I got up angry, saying to myself 'Damn the school!' I had such a beautiful dream and wanted more than anything to go back to it, instead of going to school. I couldn't wait to finish the day so I could go to her and tell her about my dream.

After school I stopped by Mahsa's place and Mama let

me in. I asked for her and Mama said "She is upstairs taking a shower." I followed Mama to the kitchen where she offered me some coffee. I heard Mahsa come down the stairs. "Here you are!" she kissed me and added "What's new?" That was the cue I was waiting for. Excited, I said "I had the most amazing dream last night! I've been waiting all day to tell you." I went on to describe my dream.

"This is my dream. 'I stopped by and you greeted me at the door, wearing that beautiful white dress with a long white scarf decorated with silver needlework. We went to my parent's house and my mom gave you a white silk chador (A chador is a type of scarf that women use to cover themselves when out in public.) You put it on and we went to see my father. When we walked into his office, he told us to stand away from each other and invited you to sit next to him. He turned to you and said "You are like a daughter to me. I knew everyone in your family: your father, grandfather, all your uncles and I knew your mother's side of the family also. I see that my son loves you in such a way that I have never seen before. Now I want to hear your side of the story and I want to know where you stand in regards to my son's love for you." You went on and on describing every detail since the moment we met. My father held up his hand and said "Okay, I got it. But as you may already know my dear, there is one problem here and that is the difference in age between you." My father continued "I have tried to talk with Yousef about this and he doesn't understand why this is a problem. And I think you are of the same mind." Then you spoke "Yousef is the only love in my entire life. My first husband was a good man and I cared for him very much; but I was not in love with him." My father thought for a moment and said "My dear, this family has rules, but I have to decide to break them. This is very hard for me, but in your case and his, I know that I must do something because I know my son very well. If he loves you as much as he says he does, he will never marry anyone else and I don't want that. I have decided to acknowledge my son's love for you, despite what other family members might think. All you two have to do is grant me power of attorney so I can perform the marriage ceremony right now. Then later on you can have a public ceremony." You and I looked at each other in silent agreement and both gave my father our consent. He performed our marriage ceremony right then and there. After we signed the papers, my mom came forward with a ring and placed it on your finger. You then kissed my father's hand and he kissed you in return, saying "Now I have five daughters!" You started to remove the chador, but I stopped you, saying "No" You asked "Why?" I replied "My cousin is here; just keeping it on for now." After all the other witnesses had left, my father said to us "You are now husband and wife!" We were getting ready to leave the house.....' Then my mom called me for school and I woke up."

Mahsa looked at me sadly and said "Your dream is like you – crazy! So then what happened?" I said "I told you; my mom called and woke me up. That's when my dream ended."

She put her arms around me and kissed me, saying "One day it will happen! Don't worry my baby." Them she said "Mama, look at his face, my God, he looks so sad." I replied "Why shouldn't I be sad? I love you and I want things to be like they were in my dream. It's possible, yes, I am sure it is. It's that the time has to be just right, that's it.

I turned to Mama "Can you get me something to drink?" Mahsa said "Me too!" Mama served us a sour cherry drink. Meetra came in and Mahsa asked "Tell Meetra about your dream and don't leave anything out." I told Meetra about my dream and all the while, she just sat there listening. After I had finished, Mahsa asked her "What should I do with him?" Meetra quipped "Just kill him!" I frowned at her "Thank you very much for your suggestion!" Meetra grinned wickedly "Or you can tie his hand and feet and keep him here next to you." Mahsa rolled her eyes "Oh thank you! Now my house can become a jail." I teased Meetra, "Sorry, but your suggestions aren't any good. You're out!"

Mahsa changed the subject and asked me "Would you stay for dinner?" I shook my head "No because I will be here tomorrow, so I cannot stay tonight." Mahsa hugged and kissed me, saying "It is such a nice dream. Please make it a reality. I love you and I am with you wherever you want to go. Just tell me where and when and I will be there for sure." We held each other tightly and she said "What time do you have to go?" "What time is it now?" "Eight" "Shit I have to go right now. I'm sorry!" Mahsa said "Don't be. See you tomorrow." I answered "See you baby. I love you so much!" Mahsa called out as I left "I love you back."

I got home, went to my room to change, then grabbed my Rumi book and went to see my father. Walking into the room, I said hi and he greeted me in return, "Hi mister, have a seat." I sat down next to him and turned to a page to read. But he held up his hand and asked "Where were you last night?" Confused, I answered "I was here with you." He shook his head "Yes you were here physically, but not mentally. Is there anything I should to know? Is there anything you want to tell me? Tell me before your mom comes in." I replied "I don't know what you're talking about and no I don't have 'anything' to tell you." My father let the matter drop "Okay, then read. Let's see what the book has to say." My eyes scanned the book as I picked a page, but my heart was pounding. I was really scared! How did he know and how could he see me if he couldn't see well. Trying to keep my voice steady, I began to read and all the time, my father just sat there, smiling and shaking his head from left to right. When I had finished, he then explained to me all the different meanings that particular poem held.

After his explanation, I wanted to continue to the next poem. But instead, my father instructed me to close the book and give it to him. He sighs and ran his hands lovingly over the book, opens it, handed it back to me and asked me to read again. Oh my God what a poem that was! That poem opened up entire new worlds for me that went beyond words; my father looked at me and said "You still don't have anything to say?" Back to that, I held my ground "That's right." He shrugged and went on to explain the various meanings of this one. He and I went over several poems that night. At one point during a reading, my mom came in, sat next to me and listened for a while. After our discussion, she said that dinner was ready. After dinner and some tea, I said good night to them, but before I left, my father advised me to spend some time with my school books as well. "Make sure you don't leave them for the last minute. I want you to be ready for those exams."

I went to my room and studied my school books for a little while, but that poem stuck in my mind all night. I told myself 'That poem sure screwed me up. I should do something about it!' Then I laughed at myself; what could I do to a poem from nine centuries ago?

I got up at the sound of my mom's voice and went to

school. After my afternoon classes, I went over to Mahsa's. Tonight was our first Rumi night! Once I got there, I made sure that everything was set for the session. At six-thirty, people started to arrive, our tutor showed up and we got started by seven.

First he showed us a book that he wanted everybody to have, "If you can buy this one, it is very good and be sure to bring a notebook as well." Then he asked "Who wants to start reading first?" Meetra raised her hand and he picked a poem for her which she read very nicely. He stopped her in the middle to explain the meaning of the words and the differences between interpreting the piece literally from the Gnostic perspective.

It was a very nice session and throughout the entire time, everybody sat in total silence as they listened to the tutors. Some even furiously wrote down notes. At the end, he gave each of us copies of two poems, saying "I know that these are very long, but just study them and write down what you think are the meanings of each. I just want to know how much each of you knows." He stood up "Well, that's it for today. Thank you everybody and I'll see you next session." As Mama served pie, tea and coffee, the tutor turned to me "I will need you to help me whenever the others have questions. Can you give me a hand? There are times when you can help explain the meanings as well. Can you do that?" Reluctantly I said "Okay, but I really want to learn from you," He smiled and put his hand on my shoulder "We learn from each other. That's my policy."

One by one, people left. Meetra's boyfriend also left but I didn't like the look on his face; he was too sure of himself. I asked Meetra about it "What was wrong with your boyfriend? I don't think he liked the session." She shook her head sadly "You're right, he didn't like it and kept saying that it's a waste of our time to be here." "I agree." I said "He is absolutely right. For him life is only about drinking and dancing. These old books are more than enough for some of us; that's why we are like this. Every day we can go back in time and then forward again. It's up to us how far we go."

Meetra didn't say anything, she just looked at me. But after a few minutes she commented "But you seemed to enjoy the session. When I looked over at you, it seemed like you were lost in it. Where did you go? I thought about it for a moment "My dear, where should I go when my heart is right here? I didn't go anywhere; I was with myself and my love." Meetra rolled her eyes "Oh my God, you are so romantic! How old did you say are? No you are over sixty. Your mind is definitely out of our range." I asked "What do you mean by that?" She said "You are not the same age as me. Look at yourself; you are a really old guy. I love it! But all I am asking is how do you do it? Mahsa walked in and said "Well, I am proud of him! Did you see when he was explaining things to us that he knew exactly what to say? I have never seen anybody like him before." Mahsa asked Meetra "Why do you say that Yousef is over sixty? He is not even forty! You don't know what you are talking about. I think what you want to say is that you feel he is that old is it not?" Meetra said "What I mean is that he is far away from the rest of us and that he goes much farther than perhaps he should go." Then Mahsa said "Yes maybe he is but that's the way he is. He grew up like this and I am proud of him." But Meetra persisted "Yes from your point of view, absolutely. But my question is still the same – why?" I said to Meetra "You are right. But I personally don't know why I am this way. But as far as I remember I have been like this. This is normal life for me. Maybe that is hard for others to understand, but I am okay with it."

We had dinner then I said "I have to go." Mahsa called the cab for me and we went to the family room to wait. She kissed me and said "Try not to think about it." I said "I am okay, it's nothing; that's the way I think, so be it." We heard a car horn, it was the cab. Mahsa kissed me again, saying "When shall I see you again?" I answered "In the next couple of hours." Everybody laughed and I left with a smile on my face. It was a good night!

I went home, straight to my room and to bed. The next thing I heard was my mom's voice calling, "Wake up! It's getting late." I got up and started my day. I didn't see

Mahsa for a couple of days but made sure that I could stay with her Thursday night and the weekend. (The weekend in Iran begins on Friday so Thursday night is like Friday night in the west) All week I had to come up with a plan. After lunch on Thursday afternoon I said bye to my mom and added "I will see you tomorrow afternoon okay?" My poor mom said "Okay, be careful and God bless!" I said thank you and left.

I finished the day at school and headed over to Mahsa's place. I knocked on the door and Mahsa opened the door and jumped on me, wrapping her legs around me, kissing me nonstop. She said gleefully "Nobody's home; Mama just went to the market and won't back until late." I carried her upstairs and laid her on the bed. We took turns undressing each other. I pulled her up and walked her next to the window against the wall and made love to her. This was new to us both, but she knew exactly what to do; together we went so high we didn't know where we were until we got there. It seemed a lot like what heaven would be. Man that was something I never experienced before, but it was so good, so wild and toward the end we really went out of control until we both screamed with delight. Mahsa pushed me to the bed and got on top of me; squeezing me and kissing me so hard all the while saying "Thank my love. Thank you my Chubby. Thank you!" I repeated the same because I couldn't find any other words except thank you.

We lay gasping on the bed and Mahsa relaxed her grip on me and snuggled in my arms like a teenager. She started laughing and I said "What is it?" She said "Meetra is right; I do act like a teen. You know I didn't really do anything when I was a teenager, because I got married so young and so fast. Now that I am with you, I do feel like I am teenager all over again. Thank you for doing that and showing me what I missed." I replied "I know what you mean; I missed my childhood and early teen years. But you helped me get them back. You see, somehow we both were lacking the same things and I think that is one of the reasons why we've gotten so close to each other." Mahsa thought about it "Maybe, but there are a lot of other things involved too." I agreed "That is true, but I hope we can stay like this. Mahsa murmured back "I hope so too."

Mahsa kissed me again, saying "I love you more than anything in the world. Maybe you know how much I love you." I said "Yes I know because I love you too. I love you so much that I cannot count it. Our love for each other is priceless." We put our robes on and went downstairs. We didn't want Mama to catch us walking around the house naked; she knew our relationship but would probably disapprove of the fact that we were lying around in bed in middle of the day. I made tea and Mahsa ran upstairs to grab our cigarettes.

We sat in the kitchen with our tea and cigarettes, when

Mama came in. She saw us and stopped short "Who made the tea?" Mahsa pointed at me "I didn't do it, he did. You can punish him." Mama laughed, "Why would I punish him, he made tea and didn't wreck my kitchen. Whenever you ladies are in here, you make a mess of the place. At least Yousef cleaned up after himself." Mama flashed me a smile "Thank you for not messing up my kitchen!" Mahsa sighed "This son of a gun knows exactly what to do. I should learn those things one day."

While Mama busied herself in the kitchen, Mahsa and I talked about different things; at one point, she informed me that she had start going back to the office more often and would not be home until two or three in the afternoon. She said "We have to rearrange our plans together. We cannot afford to waste our time together. If we plan carefully, we can be together more." I agreed "Fine I am in."

As I've mentioned before, Mama was a very, very good cook and that night she prepared a fantastic steak dinner. The steak was grilled to perfection and the side dishes were delicious. But I couldn't help but notice that the place settings were very different from what we usually used. The china and cutlery were very nice. After dinner she brought us coffee and her freshly baked apple pie. Mahsa and I were stuffed full of her excellent cooking as we crawled upstairs and into bed well after midnight.

As we lay in bed, I asked her about the fancy plates and knives. Mahsa looked at me in amazement and said "My God you notice everything! You should be in the intelligence agency." (A service like the CIA). Then she went on to answer my question "Well my dear, when my husband and I were in London we lived in a suburb that was a very ritzy area. Many of our friends were very well-off and my husband was obsessed with keeping up with all the latest fashion trends. Our dinner parties had to be impeccable. Mama learned how to set a table for formal dinners and she does that here every now and then. And I must admit that I like it too even after all those years."

She then kissed me and added "I love how you notice everything, down to the smallest detail. That shows how much you care and love me." Then she kissed me again and again, saying "Just please tell me when we can be together as a real family. Please tell me when we won't need to worry about anything and we can go out and have fun like everyone else. Just tell me when." I choked back my tears "I wish I knew when that would be." Mahsa pinched me and said "I wasn't talking to you I was talking to my God. He knows what I want and I was just asking him when I could have it. It is a very simple question and shouldn't be too hard because he knows everything."

Then we talked about having a kid and she said "I would

love to have your baby anytime anywhere." I said "I would love for our kid to have your eyes and body." Mahsa added "I want it to have your lips and your nose. But with my hair. I love my hair!" I agreed "That is a must." Then I added "I want the baby to have our hearts and this is the most important thing; the combination of both." Mahsa agreed with me.

We talked and talked, mostly about ourselves and the children we hoped to have. I said "I would love to have a girl, who would become like you. I would want that baby to be copy of you." Mahsa thought for a moment then said "You do realize that we are going to have problems with Meetra. She will not just sit back and watch; she will want that baby all to herself. She will want to help raise it and take it to school with her. Meetra will fall in love with the baby especially if it's a girl. And it won't be easy to have a little girl because we are both so handsome." I laughed and she continued "But don't worry Chubby, your baby girl will be just fine nobody, not even Meetra will take her anywhere." Then she joined me laughing. Mahsa sighed and wiped her eyes, saying "My poor Chubby look at him he's already mad just thinking about it. Don't worry; your little girl will be all yours!"

Mahsa hugged and kissed me, saying "I love you my dummy." Then she corrected herself, "You are my Chubby and not a dummy. But sometimes you act like one the way you did about five minutes ago. And I know you better than that; you aren't a dummy when you are full of love and passion and I absolutely love that!" She gave me another kiss and we held each other close until it drove us crazy again. Every minute of that night was amazing; it was full of passion and love. We made love over and over again until about four-thirty. We didn't wake up until around noon.

Mama greeted us with a wink and a smile, saying "Good afternoon my babies. We have fresh eggs; how many would you like?" I said "Two for me please." Mahsa echoed "Two for me too." Mama shook her head at Mahsa "You cannot eat two, one is enough." Mahsa put her hands on her hips and pouted "Why can he have two?" Mama pointed "Well look at him, he is big so he can have two. But one is enough for you." Holding my hands up, I interjected "Okay, ladies! How about we go half and half?" Laughing, Mama prepared three eggs for us to split. At that point, Meetra came down and joined us "Hi everybody! What's for breakfast Mama?" She said "Eggs" Meetra said "I'll have one please."

Mama fixed a plate for Meetra. I finished my one and a half, but Mahsa couldn't finish hers. Mama scolded her "I told you that you cannot eat all that but you didn't listen. You have to watch yourselves. If you keep eating like this, you will become fat in no time. Mahsa gave Mama a long look "Who are you talking to, him or me?" Mama said "I am talking to both of you. Neither of you is skinny, so you have to watch yourselves." Now we both felt like scolded children and said "Yes Mama, we will."

Meetra went out after brunch while Mahsa and I we went back upstairs, taking our tea with us. We stayed there until six when I kissed her and said "I don't want to go but I have to as you know. I'll see you soon. I want you to bite me. Punching me playfully on the arm, Mahsa said "Get out of here alligator!"

We made arrangements to see each other every day or at least every other day, but our time together was limited to less than three hours. That was so hard you cannot imagine. I told myself 'There must be a way for us to be together at least for session night. So I spoke to my father about our Rumi night and mentioned the name of the guy who was teaching us. Now that my parents knew about the session night, I was one step closer to what I wanted. I then convinced one of my friends who my father knew as well to come to our Rumi night. That way, I could say that I was staying over with him and my father would have no objections. My friend agreed to call the house and tell my father that I would be staying over with him and a few other friends. My plan worked very well and I got the okay to stay with my friend.

I was so happy that I couldn't wait to run over to Mahsa's house and tell her the good news. I had to suffer through school before I could escape, but something interesting happened in school that afternoon. I had spent most of the day feeling frustrated and bored until I got to my last class which was a literature class. The teacher walked into the room without a word and then opened a book and read a Rumi poem. I couldn't believe it! After finishing the poem, the teacher explained what it meant and I could tell that he was struggling to explain its deeper meanings. Excited, I raised my hand and he said "What do you want this time? And no you cannot go." I replied "This is not about leaving. This is about the poem you're trying to explain to us." Intrigued, the teacher said "Okay, what about it?" I said "The poem does have another meaning. Can you explain the Gnostic or philosophical aspects?" "Sit down, Yousef." He commanded, "That's too much detail for this class." I got up again and asked "Who said so?" Giving me a dirty look, the teacher said "I said so." I wasn't about to back down from this argument. This time I knew more than he did and was determined to prove it. I said "You are wrong. You have no idea how many of us have the ability to understand the deeper meanings of things. But you can be sure that I know about them." He stared at me and said "Yes I know that you know, but how many others? He turned to the rest of the class and asked "How many of you want to hear more about the poem that Yousef is talking about?" Just about every person in the class raised their hands in agreement; with the exception of two guys who didn't like me and weren't about to agree with anything I suggested. The teacher sighed

"Okay guys, you asked for it. But if I cover this material, I promise you that it will also be on the final exam." He took a deep breath and started on an in-depth explanation that ate up the rest of the class. After he finished everyone gave him round of applause and thanked him. At that point, the bell rang signaling the end of school. As my classmates filed out of the room, the teacher asked me to stay. Then he rounded on me "Yousef, are you out of your mind?" Standing my ground, I asked "Why?" "Because three quarters of the class had no idea what I was talking about!" "That might be true." I countered "But one quarter did understand and that's fantastic! Not to mention that all of them loved it. Give the rest a chance and they too will understand. The only thing you need to do is to continue and you will see the results." He shook his head and said "I hope so; maybe I made a mistake." I looked at my watch and said "I have to go, I am late." He scoffed said "Since when do you care if you are late for anything?" Then he softened "Go, you will be late."

I was late and ran four or five blocks, caught a cab and headed over to Mahsa's.

I rang the bell and Mama opened the door. Mahsa was hurrying down the stairs to let me in, saying "I wanted to get the door, but Mama beat me to it." She beckoned me to come up with her. I told her about my plans for staying over for Rumi night and she became so excited that she jumped in my arms; twining her arms around my neck and locking her feet around my waist. She planted kisses all over my face and said "Do you know what you are doing to me?" I shrugged "Just look at what I am going through. I know it's been hard for both of us not seeing each other for three days."

Mahsa kissed me again and said lets go down, everyone will be here very soon." We went down to the kitchen and Mama gave me a glass of tea and asked me "Where have you been? She was like a zombie this morning and I was getting worried." I told Mama "She knows that my problem is that sometimes it's impossible to escape. These past three days were very hard for me to get away. I was like a zombie too both yesterday and today. It's hard for me too." Mama patted my cheek "I know baby you two are in a bad position. And I understand that it is very hard. I hope God helps you both because you are good people and I love both of you." Mama's eyes glistened "Mahsa is like my child, you know and I cannot bear to see her like that." I nodded "I know Mama; I will try to make it different from now on."

One by one, people started to arrive and when our teacher showed up, the session began. We had a nice night and the teacher suggested that I talk about Rumi for one of the sessions; I hesitated "Wouldn't it be better for you do it? You know so much more than I do." He said "That's not true, I think that you have a different perspective that I would like to hear." He went on encouraging me "Please do that on one of these nights, please?" "Okay" I said, "As you wish." I then asked everyone to choose a piece by Rumi so we could start a discussion on each one.

We dedicated the last fifteen minutes of our time for question and answer. During that time, I asked Mama if we could have the tea and coffee. She also brought out cookies with the tea and coffee. After everyone had left, Mahsa and I we went up to change. I sat on the bed, opened my book and began to sing for her. Mahsa quietly came to sit on the bed next to me, listening. Suddenly there was a noise at the bedroom door and I noticed Meetra standing there. Surprised, I stopped and Mahsa asked "Why did you stop?" Embarrassed, I said I was just singing to myself, I didn't expect an audience." Looking a little hurt, Meetra said "Okay, you don't want me here." I said Oh no, it is not that at all. Please come in but just promise me that you won't tell anyone about this." "Okay" she said "But waits a minute…" She ran to her room and came back with her guitar and said "Here's a deal, you sing and I'll play." I laughed "What a combo this is! A classic poem with classical guitar!" Clearing my throat, I started over and Meetra accompanied me very nicely. Our performance went on for more than half an hour until I got tired and stopped.

While I was singing, Mama had also joined the audience,

standing at the door. I really didn't mind though. Mahsa kissed me and said "Son of a gun! How come you never sang for me before? That was so beautiful and so romantic." Meetra also kissed me and asked "Why don't you want anyone to know that you sing?" I said "I have a million reasons…" and told her a couple. Then I asked her "How long have you played guitar?" Meetra shrugged "I started when I was seven." I said "So you must be a professional?" Meetra laughed "Oh no, I am not, I just play for myself and sometimes my friends."

I asked Meetra "Do you sing also?" She nodded "Yes, but only in English." "Would you mind singing us a song?" Meetra look at Mahsa who nodded. She picked up the guitar and sang quite beautifully. I found out later when I had moved to the US that she was singing country and western style with a classical guitar. Meetra performed for us until Mama announced that dinner was ready. After dinner, Meetra asked me "Can you do one more poem for us?" I sighed "My dear, we have a slight problem. I cannot memorize these poems because in school they forced us to memorize them and I fought against it. I lost interest in memorizing poetry altogether." But Meetra persisted; she wanted to hear one more poem! "I am going up to get the book." "Please" I said "Next time." But she ran and got it anyway.

I couldn't resist her begging, so I sang one more poem for her. Happy with that, she said good-night and went to her room. Mahsa and I took our tea up to our room. She hugged me and said "Are you really going to stay tonight?" I smiled at her "Yes, I'm really going to stay." She said "Ever since you arrived, I've been arguing back and forth with myself. One moment I was sure that you would stay and then the next moment I figured that by eleven-thirty you would say that you had to go. It's such a nice surprise to realize that I wouldn't have to be lonely tonight. I love that you are here with me with all my heart and with every inch of my body. I thank God you are with me tonight. If I didn't have to go to office every morning this week, I don't know how I would have gotten through it. I wrapped her in my arms and kissed her, saying "You know it's hard for me too. Actually it was very hard for me not to see you for three days. I was looking for any opportunity to stay with you for at least one night. After what my father said to me that night, I got really scared. I didn't know what to do and couldn't tell you about it either."

Mahsa continued "I prayed to God last night to help us find a way to be together. We are not criminals; we haven't done anything wrong, so why do we have to hide like this?" She sniffed "In every way, you are my husband and I am your wife; why are we so afraid? We didn't do anything wrong, we just love each other. Yes, there are some differences between us, but nothing that cannot be fixed." Mahsa looked at me with tears in her eyes and said "That dream of yours was so close to what

I really want to do. I want to go to your family's home, sit down with your father and talk to him. I want to tell him "Please either let us be together or kill us; just do something! I cannot take it anymore."

I kissed her again and said "I've been thinking about it too, but not quite that drastic, but close." With one swift movement, she pushed me onto the bed and said fiercely "You are mine and mine only! Nobody can take you from me, do you understand?" Breathless I replied "Yes and you are mine too." Satisfied, she said "Yes it's true, I am totally yours and nobody can change that either. Then she joined me in bed and…. Oh my God! What a passionate night that was. We were so, so hot. I couldn't imagine two people being that hot. We could have burned an entire city in a single moment with our combined passion.

We were wake for most of the night, neither of us getting any more than three hours of sleep. Before falling asleep, I begged her to please set the alarm for eight because there was no way I was going to get up at seven. She said "Fine, but with one condition: when I call you, just get up I will not have time to call you several times tomorrow. You remember that. "Okay!" I said "I will get up right away." I kept my promise and went off to school. But all day I was dying for want of sleep.

After morning classes, I went home and straight to bed. I

asked my mom to put my lunch aside saying that I would eat it before leaving for afternoon classes. She called me awake at a quarter to two. I reluctantly got up, ate my lunch and went back to school. After school I called Mahsa and she picked up, saying "You son of a gun, don't you ever keep me up that late again!" Laughing I said "Hi to you my Honey Bunch, did I really keep you up until five in the morning or did we do that to each other?" Her laugh rang out "Oh my goodness!" She said "I didn't crawl out of bed until one and I still feel tired." "Then go back to sleep." I suggested "And be sure to keep my pillow warm." "Is that right?" "Yes" I said "Unfortunately, I have to go somewhere with my mom later this afternoon." Mahsa said sadly "Well, in that case go and say 'hi' to her for me. Can you do that for me?" I said "For sure, with a kiss or without?" She laughed again "Now you're just teasing me! Ha, ha. Okay, next time will be my turn." She sent me a kissed and said "You take care of yourself, you hear that?" I said "I will don't worry." She said "I do...because..." and hung up; I caught a cab for home.

For the next four weeks that followed, Mahsa and I managed to see each other every day for at least an hour. There were even some days that I didn't go to school. One day I heard my parents talking about preparing for a pilgrimage to Mecca. Overjoyed, I asked them when they were planning to leave for how long they would be gone. They told me that they would be leaving in about two weeks. My father was suspicious "Where are you going?" Doing my best to look innocent, I said "I am not going anywhere." Then my mom added to the conversation "We cannot leave you completely alone." Dismayed, I asked "Why not? I was alone in Tehran but cannot be alone here? I am not going anywhere. I will be staying here!" My mother shook her head "I will ask the neighbor to stay here with you." I said "Fine, do whatever you want, but I am not going anywhere and that's that." She frowned at me "Okay, you spoiled boy, stay home."

The next day was a Rumi day, so after school, I went over to Mahsa's and took up her to the bedroom. I told her excitedly "Do you know what happened today?" Catching my excitement, she said "No what happened?" I replied "God gave us an answer; my folks going to Mecca for their pilgrimage. That means that we will be alone for nearly a month!" With a squeal of delight, she jumped on me. I knew that she would after I delivered my news, so that was the reason I took her to the bedroom. I spun her around as she kissed and squeezed me, asking "Is this for real?" I answered "Yes, it is for real; they are leaving in about two weeks." Mahsa sighed happily "May God blesses them twice. So now we will have some time together." She added "That means you will be coming to stay here, right?" I sighed "That's wishful thinking, my parents asked the neighbor to stay with me at night. But we can be together the rest of the time." Mahsa sat back with a sober look "Your folks are pretty smart, they put a watchdog on you. What did they do with you before when they would go to Mecca?" I shrugged "Nothing, they just want to do this now, figuring that I cannot be alone in the house. It's their rule." Then she said "What a good guy you are; following every rule like a good boy."

Then she started laughing "Goooooood boy follows the all rules is it?" We went down to wait for everyone to arrive.

When the session started, the teacher asked me "When do you think you will be ready to lead the session?" I swallowed the lump in my throat "I can do it next week. I made everything ready so next week would be perfect." "Good" he announced "Listen everybody next week, Yousef will talk about Rumi, who is he and why it's important to know him as a person and not just as a poet. We will also discuss why his poetry is different from any other poet."

Each person took turns reading their chosen poems and he explained each one to us. We went over four or five short ones and one was a little longer. It was a fantastic session. Our teacher answered everyone's questions and the session drew to a close. After everybody left we went to the kitchen for dinner and Meetra asked me "How long have you been studying Rumi?" "Not too long, almost two years. It started with one really short poem that I really loved. Then I wanted to learn what other works he had. I found myself getting deeper and deeper into his writings. It's like if you add a glass of water to the ocean; I was like that glass of water and Rumi's world is like the ocean. I have been swallowed up by the ocean of his writings." I continued "That's when I told myself that I have to be part of this ocean in order to understand the water. I started to go to my father's library and found a lot of books about Rumi and learned about whom he was and how he became a philosopher, a Gnostic and mystic poet, which is why he is so different from others."

Meetra then asked "Will you tell us everything that you learned next week?" Shaking my head, I said "No, not all of it but I will try to tell you who he was and how and why he became the person he was." I added "Then I will tell you who Shams was and the impact he had on Rumi's life. I will go over how they met and why Rumi, who was a very well respected scholar himself, eventually became one of Shams' most devoted followers."

At that point, Mahsa suggested to me "Can you give me your notes when you are done so I can keep them?" I said "Sure they are yours if you want them and if you need anything more let me know so I can add to them." Meetra excused herself and went to her room and Mahsa and I did the same. We always waited for her to go first before going up together and she knew that. As we got ready for bed, Mahsa said "I cannot be up until four or five. Do you remember the last time?" Indeed I did remember. Smiling, I said "I remember. All we did was holding each other and make love. How was that different from any other time?" But tonight we didn't have sex; we just loved each other and that in of itself was very enjoyable and satisfying.

Mahsa confessed to me later how much she loved the way we made love that night. It was a different kind of love; a love that included our hearts and souls and not just our bodies. We did it often after that; simply because there were times when neither of us wanted to have just sex, while loving each other was exactly what we both needed. That evening after we had made love, Mahsa turned to me "Yousef you know that I love you more than ever." I said "Why is that?" She said "It's because you showed me a completely different kind of life. You also showed me how I can be a better lover and that I can love somebody as much as I love you. You have no idea what you've done! And it's not just what you've done for me, but my whole family, even Mama!"

I replied "I didn't do anything that you didn't do as well. Maybe I was just a catalyst for these things. I needed them myself, so how could I change you? She said "One day I will show you all that you have done for us. And that day is not too far away. I know then that you will see it for yourself. I love you my Chubby and you really are my Chubby. That's a perfect name for you and I love you so much!"

We fell asleep and the next day was business as usual. Time flew by quickly until one afternoon I didn't have class, so I went over to the house and knocked at the door. Mama let me in and I found Mahsa in the kitchen, she was sitting at the table, but she didn't seem to have her usual spark that she always had. I looked at her carefully "What is wrong?" "It's nothing" she said "I just couldn't go into the office today, I don't know why." She looked up at me "I am sorry baby that I have put a lot on your shoulders and it's not fair for me to do that. You've been handling it so well with all your heart." I said "What are you talking about? I love 'handling' all this in my life. Somebody entrusted it to me and gave me opportunity and responsibility. And for that, I am very grateful. You know that nobody else has given me such an opportunity before. I really love it and I thank you."

She got up and took my hand, saying "Come with me." I followed her up to the bedroom and sat down. Mahsa took my hand again and said "Yousef, listen to me very carefully." She looked so serious that I started to get nervous. "Yousef that's your name, is it not?" I nodded "Yes it is." She continued "Yousef my dear love, we have known each other more than a year and a half. Is that correct?" "Yes. What is the meaning of all this?" She put her hand up to stop me "Just listen my dear; this is very important for me. In this past year and a half we have shared a life together; but today I have gotten to the point in which I have to do something. You see, all girls when they love somebody or they want somebody to love them will go to a certain point and then stop there. Sometimes, but not very often, one will pass that certain point and keep going and going. Once she reaches this level, the relationship must become different. I wanted to tell you about this before we got any further. You may not know this, but girls will often keep some feelings locked deep inside of themselves and normally won't share those feelings with anybody with the exception of a very special time with a very special person. Once these feelings are revealed to that special someone, it becomes a totally different world and hopefully love will open up for them."

"My dear, I never thought that we would ever get to this point because only a few people get to this point even after years and years of knowing each other. I guess it's because we moved too fast and we got to this point so quickly."

"My Yousef, my Chubby, my love and my life, listen very carefully. I am going to give you something today that I having waiting to do all my life. Oh my sweetheart you don't know how long I have been going back and forth with this decision. Now I have gotten to this moment which is very important in every girl's life, including me."

Mahsa took me in her arms and said "And this decision has been so much harder with you because you have so many different aspects at different times. I know Yousef from when he was two years old all the way up to fifty. But I have made up my mind that I will give this to all of them and I know each of them is an important part of me, so be it." Mahsa hugged me much tighter to herself. Her skin was so hot that I could feel the heat coming off of her in waves. She rested her head on my shoulder and I felt like I was going to burst into flames; my shoulder and chest got so hot and then she started to cry. Although I was confused, I didn't say anything. I just held her and stroked head, but I could feel something deep inside of myself, something that I've never felt before. After her tears had subsided, Mahsa sniffed and said "My dear I just gave you something that I hope you will keep for the rest of your life." Then she kissed me, took my hand and said "Come with me." But she stopped at a closet first then said "Come on." Obediently, I followed her back downstairs.

Once we had gotten to the kitchen, we sat down at the table and Mahsa asked Mama "Mama would you give me that small red box"? Then Mama said yes Maam then she brought that bex to her. She look at the box then she gave it to me. I look at the box I wanted to know what,s inside but seame to be Mahsa blocked me out and I couldn't see what is inside of that box.

Finally I opened the box ane as soon as I saw what was in it my eyes be come wide open and my jaws droped and become so heavy.

CHAPTER 16

Keys

That evening after we had made love, Mahsa turned to me "Yousef you know that I love you more than ever." I said "Why is that?" She said "It's because you showed me a completely different kind of life. You also showed me how I can be a better lover and that I can love somebody as much as I love you. You have no idea what you've done! And it's not just what you've done for me, but my whole family, even Mama!"

I replied "I didn't do anything that you didn't do as well. Maybe I was just a catalyst for these things. I needed them myself, so how could I change you? She said "One day I will show you all that you have done for us. And that day is not too far away. I know then that you will see it for yourself. I love you my Chubby and you really are my Chubby. That's a perfect name for you and I love you so much!"

We fell asleep and the next day was business as usual. Time flew by quickly until one afternoon I didn't have class, so I went over to the house and knocked at the door. Mama let me in and I found Mahsa in the kitchen, she was sitting at the table, but she didn't seem to have her usual spark that she always had. I looked at her carefully "What is wrong?" "It's nothing" she said "I just couldn't go into the office today, I don't know why." She looked up at me "I am sorry baby that I have put a lot on your shoulders and it's not fair for me to do that. You've been handling it so well with all your heart." I said "What are you talking about? I love 'handling' all this in my life. Somebody entrusted it to me and gave me opportunity and responsibility. And for that, I am very grateful. You know that nobody else has given me such an opportunity before. I really love it and I thank you."

She got up and took my hand, saying "Come with me." I followed her up to the bedroom and sat down. Mahsa took my hand again and said "Yousef, listen to me very carefully." She looked so serious that I started to get nervous. "Yousef that's your name, is it not?" I nodded "Yes it is." She continued "Yousef my dear love, we have known each other more than a year and a half. Is that correct?" "Yes. What is the meaning of all this?" She put her hand up to stop me "Just listen my dear; this is very important for me. In this past year and a half we have shared a life together; but today I have gotten to the point in which I have to do something. You see, all girls when they love somebody or they want somebody to love them will go to a certain point and then stop there. Sometimes, but not very often, one will pass that certain point and keep going and going. Once she reaches this level, the relationship must become different. I wanted to tell you about this before we got any further. You may not know this, but girls will often keep some feelings locked deep inside of themselves and normally won't share those feelings with anybody with the exception of a very special time with a very special person. Once these feelings are revealed to that special someone, it becomes a totally different world and hopefully love will open up for them."

"My dear, I never thought that we would ever get to this point because only a few people get to this point even after years and years of knowing each other. I guess it's because we moved too fast and we got to this point so quickly."

"My Yousef, my Chubby, my love and my life, listen very carefully. I am going to give you something today that I having waiting to do all my life. Oh my sweetheart you don't know how long I have been going back and forth with this decision. Now I have gotten to this moment which is very important in every girl's life, including me."

Mahsa took me in her arms and said "And this decision

has been so much harder with you because you have so many different aspects at different times. I know Yousef from when he was two years old all the way up to fifty. But I have made up my mind that I will give this to all of them and I know each of them is an important part of me, so be it." Mahsa hugged me much tighter to herself. Her skin was so hot that I could feel the heat coming off of her in waves. She rested her head on my shoulder and I felt like I was going to burst into flames; my shoulder and chest got so hot and then she started to cry. Although I was confused, I didn't say anything. I just held her and stroked head, but I could feel something deep inside of myself, something that I've never felt before. After her tears had subsided, Mahsa sniffed and said "My dear I just gave you something that I hope you will keep for the rest of your life." Then she kissed me, took my hand and said "Come with me." But she stopped at a closet first then said "Come on." Obediently, I followed her back downstairs.

Once we had gotten to the kitchen, we sat down at the table and Mahsa asked Mama "Mama, do we have an extra key for the house?" Mama said "Yes Ma'am." and retrieved it for her. Mahsa took the key and then opened a small box and took out a beautiful silver heart key chain. She placed the house keys on the key chain, saying "Yousef my sweet heart, my love, my life this is the key from my eyes, my lips and my heart. This key is for your eyes, lips and your heart. Hold on to it because this is also the key to your new home! Please know that we all are here for you at any time. Then she kissed me and put the key in my hand which I put inside my top jacket pocket. I said "This key given from the heart must be next to the heart. I kissed her and said "Thank you, I will keep it forever."

From that moment our relationship became stronger than steel. I stayed until six and went home early because the next night was our session and I had planned to stay that overnight.

I got home very early, went to my room and after an hour, I came back out with my book. I stepped into my father's study and he said "Aha you and your book again?" I said "Yes and I have some questions to ask you." My father seemed very pleased with this "God blesses you! Now what is your question?" Making myself comfortable, I asked him about Rumi and Shams. He looked at me closely with his one good eye and didn't say anything. He just sat there for a while as though thinking of an answer. Finally he spoke "Listen my son and listen carefully…" and he went on and on about the extraordinary lives of these two guys who were reputed to be lovers. My father spoke at great lengths for a couple of hours until he said "You must go, it's time for prayer." I went to my room and decided that I too would pray. I waited until my father finished his prayers and went back to him. This time, I read two poems of my choice.

He gave me a hint about them that I didn't pick up on that time; but it came to me a month later. My father did such a wonderful job explaining those poems to me and from time to time he would suggest different perspectives.

I spent most of the evening studying Rumi. After dinner I sought my father once more and brought my notes. After reading them to him, explained that I had to do a presentation tomorrow night about Rumi and Shams. "What you think?" Thinking for a moment, he replied "It is not a bad start. But you need to research more because his life and his writings are not just one thing, there are so many facets that you need to consider. You have to know all of them in order to gain a greater understanding of the man and his life. But there is still so much that you don't know yet, my son." He smiled at me "But you are off to a good start." Then he said "I hope you are studying your other subjects too." I promised him that I would.

I kept my promise and after leaving my father's room, I studied some of my subjects. Next day in school, all I could think about was the session later that day and my presentation. Finally afternoon classes let out and I went over to my 'home'. This time, I didn't knock; I opened the door with my key. Walking in, I said "Hi anybody home?" Mahsa's voice floated back to me "We are in the kitchen." She greeted me with a hug and a kiss and surprised me by saying "Thank you for what you've done." I shrugged "You're welcome but I didn't do anything." Mama asked me "What do you want "lovey" boy, coffee or tea?" I couldn't make up my mind "Well, both are nice. Give me whatever you have." Mama handed me a steaming mug of coffee. We sat and talked and I told Mahsa about the previous night with my father. She looked pleased "Good boy, you are doing the right thing by spending time with him. You should be close with your parents. Time is too short and precious and the feelings are too strong to ignore." Mahsa stood up and stretched, saying "I'd better go up and get ready because they will be here soon."

After Mahsa had gone upstairs, Mama came out and asked "Where is she?" I said "She went up to get ready." Mama looked at me sidelong "Are you sure?" I looked again and said "Yes, she's gone." Mama came close to me and said "Listen to me son. I came to work for this family when she was just a child and I too was very young, but I remember it like it was yesterday. She always was alone, but always had a good head on her shoulders even as a kid. When she got married, I went with her. Even as a teenager, she was a lot more mature than anyone else I knew at her age. But with you, she is a completely different person; she listens to you, she relies on you, she needs you in her life and finally she is very happy when she is with you." Mama continued "The last time I saw her that happy was when her father was still alive. But most of the time she hasn't been happy. I don't know why I am telling you all these things but I just want you to know and please don't do anything stupid to ruin what you have with her." I loved Mama for always being a straightforward person and I answered her honestly "I love Mahsa too much to do anything stupid. Okay? I got you." Mama nudged me in the ribs "This stays between you and me." I nodded "Of course Mama, my mouth is sealed."

Meetra arrived and Mahsa came down and people started arriving and the session was about to begin. I walked in and sat on the floor. We sat on the floor in a circle so everyone could see and hear well enough and to also have a sense of community between each of us.

Taking a deep breath, I began "This is a night dedicated to love and lovers...." "First we have to learn who Rumi was. He was the son of well-known scholar who was also a mufti. A mufti is a very high cleric, much like a bishop. Rumi grew up traveling with his father and throughout his early years, met many renowned Persian and Arabic philosophers and muftis, like Attar of Nishapur. Rumi became fascinated with teachings of his father other philosophers. One day, Attar told Rumi's father "You have to take very good care of your son because he has a fire inside and the brightness of his mind will burn the minds of millions and he will bring a revolution to our society." When Rumi was twelve, Attar gave him a book filled with his own secret writings, which Rumi kept his entire life. Rumi's father took Attar's advice and made sure to provide Rumi with the best possible education and sent him to study with the top scholars in Damascus, where he met and studied with Shams. After many years, Rumi became a well-versed scholar and mufti. At this point he began writing books and become very well known amongst his peers and a well-respected philosopher in the late thirteenth into the early fourteen centuries. Rumi also had a background in Gnosticism, Sufism and mysticism but these were not his areas of expertise."

"Then there was Shams, much older and very wise; he was a top scholar in Gnosticism, Sufism, mysticism, philosophy and religion. He lived very simply, much like a pauper. Shams knew Rumi and followed his works with great interest. In Shams' opinion, Rumi was not yet ready to delve deeply into mysticism and Gnosticism, so Shams waited patiently for the right time and then he started getting close to him. Shams had one simple objective and that was to turn the Rumi at that time into the Rumi we know and admire now. Shams was deeply spiritual and instantly recognized latent spirituality within Rumi. Once Rumi was ready, Shams began to teach him."

I became known and powerful, when I died from being an inanimate object.

Y. JOSEPHSON

Then I became brutal (animal) when I died from power and knowing.
After I died from my brutality, I became human.
So why must I be afraid of death, when death doesn't make me less.
I will finally die from being human.
Then I shall rise up and fly higher than the mightiest of angels.

~Rumi – Excerpt from Book 3 of the Masnavi

Translated by Yousef

"When Shams opened the first door of spirituality for Rumi, he grabbed a hold of these ideas and didn't let go. Rumi's readiness to learn all that Shams taught him added to his already strong convictions. Rumi wrote down everything so that future generations like ours could learn from him. The two men became so close that it seemed as though they shared the same mind. Rumi once said of himself 'I was young then I became wise then I died in order to become human.' Rumi refers to death because Shams taught him an Old Iranian belief that says 'In order to find the reality of life, we each must pass through death.' But Rumi is not talking about physical death, but instead a death of the spirit or what we know as ego. This is a battle in which you will kill the I, ME, MYSELF and what remains after that death is nothing but love. Jesus taught the very same thing."

The session was a huge success that ended with coffee

and tea. The tutor came up to me and whispered in my ear "Thank you!" I replied "You're welcome." Other people were crowding around me, asking questions and I excused myself, saying to him "I will talk to you later."

After everyone had left, Mahsa and I went upstairs to change and came back down for dinner. Meetra chattered excitedly "Oh my God you were very good! You took me so high that I felt like I had smoked something." Mahsa sharply turned to her daughter "And did you?" Meetra's cheeks turned crimson "Well, just a couple of times. I only had two puffs each time." Mahsa warned her "Be careful not to get hooked on that stuff. It is very bad for you." We finished our dinner and everyone said goodnight and went to their rooms. When I came to bed, I found Mahsa sitting on her side with her knees tucked under her arms like a little girl. She just sat there looking at me and finally spoke "Anybody else I can figure out, but not you and I am totally confused." I said "Why and what happened? You were okay before the session." She replied "I am okay now too. But you must tell me: who are you and how old are you really?" Now I was confused "What are you talking about?" Mahsa shook her head "No Yousef, I am serious, I know who I am and you know how old I am. There are sometimes when you put your head on my lap, I feel like you are two or three and when we are together, you are closer to me in age. But tonight you spoke in such a way that if I didn't know you or if I closed my eyes, I would think you were a fifty year old cleric. Really Chubby I am so confused as to whom I have to deal with! I love all of your many facets, but tonight you showed me yet another one. It is really hard to deal with."

I held her and said "I am sorry baby, I didn't mean to confuse you but that's the way I talk, when I talk about Rumi." She said "And it was absolutely amazing. I enjoyed it the same as how Meetra described it. You took me so high I didn't want to come down. The way you described Rumi's life to us, it was like you knew them personally. I looked around the room and everybody else seemed to have the same feeling. How could you know how to do that? You are just nineteen, my God, but you were so good!"

I gave her a hug then rested my head on her lap and she said "This is exactly what I mean. What am I going to do with you? Looking up at her, I said "It's because you are everything to me. You are my mom, sister, lover, wife and the most important thing is that you are my best friend, doing your best to understand me."

She kissed me and spent a long time just inhaling my scent and finally said "For a long time I wanted to tell you something that's been on my mind, but couldn't work up the courage because I thought it might make you angry. But after what you just said, let me tell you who you are to me. You are my father, brother, husband, lover and as you said most importantly, you are my best friend who understands me. I don't need to tell you what I want because you just seem to know and sometimes you will give me something before I even know that I needed it. Now I understand where you come from and who you are because we both have those things in common." She kissed me and said "I really can relate to you. You told me before how you felt that way, but it was hard for me to understand, but now I can feel it too."

We held each other so tightly and went to sleep, happy in the knowledge that our relationship was stronger than ever.

In the morning, I woke up to find Mahsa was already up and dressed. She beamed at me like a bright ray of morning sunshine, saying "Good morning!" I smiled back "Good morning my sweetie did you sleep well?" She replied "Yes thanks to you. I kissed her, got ready for school and said bye "I will see you later this afternoon." "See you later alligator. She said. On the way to school, I remembered how the older men would talk. One guy told the other "Do you know when the best time in a marriage is?" The other thought a moment and said "Yes, the morning after the first night of the honeymoon." The first guy nodded "Yes I wish I could go back to that special time." and the other guy said "Me too."

When I got to school, I wrote that down on a piece of

paper and put it in my pocket. After school let out that afternoon, I went to my other home and let myself in. Mahsa was in the kitchen. When I kissed her, I noticed that her face was absolutely beautiful and she looked so happy. I asked her "How are you?" She flashed me her gorgeous smile and said "I feel wonderful, like the first morning of honeymoon." Stunned, I grabbed her and kissed her again. "What was that for?" She asked. Not saying a word, I took out the piece of paper and handed it to her. "Oh myyy God!!!!" She cried, "Mama, look at this! I have finally found a guy who is always one step ahead of me." At that, Mahsa flung her arms around me and kissed me, saying "Mama what did I tell you? This is the guy for me, there can be nobody else." We sat down and Mama brought us tea and said to Mahsa "What a lucky girl you are!" But you have to take care of him and watch over him." I didn't know what Mama meant by that and still don't to this day. She and I studied some Rumi together for an hour and talked for a while until it was time for me to go home. Days passed quickly and it was finally time for my folks to leave for Mecca. After returning from the airport with my sister, I called Mahsa and we talked for about a half an hour, before hanging up, I said "I will see you tomorrow and I will bite you this time for real!" Laughing, she said "As if you could!"

I stopped by the next day and went to the kitchen and called out "Anybody home?" Mama came out and said "Mahsa is not home yet, have a seat. Do you want anything baby?" "What do you have?" She answered "Nothing yet." I said "Then if you can make me some Turkish coffee?" Mama got out the coffee "Do you want a single or double shot?" I said "Single is fine." She made the coffee and we chatted. Mama said "As I was saying yesterday please be careful with Mahsa, she is very sensitive. I forgot to tell you that she was very depressed for a year after her husband passed away. It got so bad that she had to see a doctor." I nodded "Yes, I knew that." Mama continued "It was a very bad time for her especially when her father died months after that accident. She was so bad that nobody could talk to her. I was the only one who could reach her. She was always so very good to me. I am telling you all these things because I love her and I don't want to see her get hurt. It would break my heart to see her like that again. You understand don't you?" I said "Yes Mama. It is very nice of you to tell me all those things. Now I can take care of her better." She said "That's way I am telling you because I know you love her so much; maybe even more than I do. I don't know." Mama went on to tell me about Mahsa's father and her relationship with him. She said "They were very close, so his death was very hard for her." I finished my coffee and she asked "Would you like another?" "No thank you." As Mama puttered around the kitchen, she continued "She really loves you. I have never seen her like this." I said "I know and I love her too, very much." There was a knock at the door and Mama went to open it. Mahsa was home! She followed

Mama into the kitchen and we kissed each other and she asked me "When did you get here?" I said "About an hour ago. Mama kept me company." Then she said "I'm sorry baby, I got stuck in the office. One day you will have to visit." "Yes" I said "For sure I would love to come. But I hope nobody will say 'who the hell this guy?'" Mahsa laughed "No, and that's none of their business, that's my business. It's my office and they just work there. So they won't have any questions about you." I said "Okay, one day we will go there, but I think we should go together, it might be better that way." She said "Yes I would love it."

Mahsa asked me to go upstairs with her. As she changed her clothes, she asked "Are you going to stay?" I said "No because it's the first night, so it's not a good idea. I hope you understand." She looked disappointed "You're right." "But" I said "I will stay until ten" Mahsa expression brightened a little "Very well Chubby very well." We went back down to the kitchen where Mama had tea waiting for us. We talked and went over more of Rumi's poetry. Meetra came home around nine and joined Mahsa and me. The three of us start talking about various topics. Meetra told us about her day at school and her boyfriend and Mahsa about her day at the office. It was getting late; I kissed Mahsa and said bye to everybody and Mama called a cab for me. I got home sometime after ten and thanked God that I didn't eat anything over at Mahsa's because the neighbors were waiting for me. I quickly changed clothes and ate dinner with them.

After school, I stopped by to find that Mahsa was already home, but she had gone upstairs to lie down. I went up to see her and asked if she was okay. She said "Yes I am just tired. I worked so hard today because we were behind on a project and we have to finish it by Wednesday. I asked her if I should bring some tea up for her. Stretching, she said "No we will go down, but first, come here." I lay next to her with my arms around her. I kissed her as we lay there holding hands. I stayed until eight-thirty and said to Mahsa "You are tired, so get some rest and I will be here tomorrow night." She kissed me and said "My God you are too good to me. Go my dear and I will get some sleep. You're right I am tired." I kissed her and went home.

At home, I sat down with my neighbor and her three daughters; the oldest one was the same age as me. We had a pleasant conversation about her job, my classes and other things. We had dinner and then I went to my room to study. Before leaving for school, I informed her that I would be going to my sister's for lunch and that I would not be home that evening either. I explained that friends and I had a gathering every week with a tutor to study Rumi. When I was at my sister's for lunch, she too asked me to go home that night. I shook my head "I cannot, I have to go somewhere." My sister asked where and I told her about the Rumi session every week. Satisfied that I would not be getting into any trouble, she let the matter drop.

I got in and went to the kitchen and found Mama there. I said hi to her and she said "Hi baby, what are you up to?" I said "Nothing, can you give me something cold to drink?" "Sure, what would you like?" Thinking, I said "How about some of that sour cherry drink?" I asked "How is Mahsa? Did she get some rest last night?" Mama said "I guess she slept very well, she was fine this morning when she went to the office."

Mahsa came in around six, carrying two plastic bags. She ran upstairs and came back down quickly. She came to me and said "I'm sorry baby, I didn't see you." I kissed her, saying "No problem. How was your day?" She said "It was good, things are moving along nicely." She saw the glass in my hand "What have you got there?" "It's that delicious cherry drink. Here, have some." She took my glass, took a sip and said "That's a good idea!" Meetra got home and joined us in the kitchen and we waited there until people started arriving.

The session started promptly at seven. A couple of people asked the tutor a few questions about materials from two weeks ago; he answered them fully. We start reading some poems and he explained each one to us. Time passed quickly and before we knew it, it was time for questions. One of the guys said "My question is silly…" The tutor held up his hand, saying "There are no silly questions here." And provided an in-depth answer to the question and added "Nothing is silly when it comes to Rumi because he didn't believe such things like questions are silly. That's why he wrote some poems that some people think are silly but each one has plenty of meaning. So nothing is silly in here at our session." With that, the session ended and Mama served coffee and tea.

I went up to change and when I came back down to kitchen Mahsa said "Ha you've changed." I said "Yes I did." Then she went up and she returned, I noticed a piece of paper in her hand which she put in her pocket. After dinner Meetra went to her room and we retired to ours.

Note: From this point going forward, whenever you see the word June, it does not refer to the month. It is a Farsi term meaning 'Yes Sweetheart' or 'Yes Honey'. Another meaning pertains to something precious a person's life, something that completes a person's entire world.

Mahsa called to me "Chubby" I replied "June." She had the piece of paper in her hand "Do you know anything about this paper?" I said "What paper?" She said "The paper that has your handwriting on it." I was perplexed "I don't know what you are talking about." She showed it to me and asked "What is this?" "Where did you find this?" "On the floor, but that doesn't matter. Tell me about it." Taking a deep breath, I asked her to sit. Mahsa did as I asked and I continued "Let me read it to you. It was meant for you but I couldn't seem to find the right time to read it to you." She gave it to me and I read it to her. After I finished, I went to the closet and took out another piece of paper and did read that to her as well.

Dawn candle / Dawn's lofty sigh
My dawn candle comes to me, as the sun warms my heart comes back to me.
The beauty of her heart and spirit came to me as hot as the sun when she comes back to me.

The light of my holy sun illuminates my soul and my spirit.
It burns my heart and gives the heat of love that comes back to me.

The fire that burns turns me to ashes.
All the while I want her, she will be in my head and came back to me.

I am hers with my heart and spirit; I will be the road for her feet.
She will walk on me and bring me Holy Spirit and love and come back to me.

Dawn's lofty sigh rests on my heart and my spirit.
Then I become alive again, because your sweet love comes back to me.

~Yousef

She just sat and stared at me for a moment; finally she said "Where did you get those?" I said "Those are mine, as you know. I wrote them for you. These poems are from me to you." She still sat as though in disbelief, then said "These, are, for, me?" I smiled "Yes they are yours." She took the papers from me and pressed them against her heart, saying "I have to find a professional to frame these for me so I can hang them in there where I can see them all the time." She turned to face me "But my sweetie, you went too far. I am none of those things you said!" I replied "They are my writings, from my feelings about you. To me, you are every single one of those things I mentioned." She kissed me and hugged me so tightly I couldn't breathe. She said "My God what should I do with you? You are going to kill me one of those days! And if the day ever comes when I am no longer any of those things, I'll kill myself." I laughed and said "Nobody going to kill anyone. We will be happy family after all." It was now her turn to laugh "Now you have a problem." I said "What?" She said "I can't help but feel that I am less than what you say about me, and it bothers me." I wrapped my arms around her "You are not less! And you can do the same for me. Here's what you can do; get a journal that you really like and you can write your thoughts about me in your own words. Then give it to me and I will write some things about you. We can go back and forth.

She kissed me and showed me a whole new road to love, saying "Chubby, there are a million ways to achieve love." Together we flew so high that we reached the center of the universe where only love exists. It sounds unbelievable, but when you are in love, you can get there together. It is only then you can handle the heat and the intensity of each other's emotions.

We held each other tight and went to sleep. Mahsa woke me up for school, saying "Come on, you have to go to school and I have to get to the office. We both have places to be." I told Mahsa "I will be going to my sister's house tonight because she wants to see me." She kissed me and said "You are the Chubby."

After school, I stopped at my sister's and went out with my nephews. When we got back, I said "I am going home now." My sister said "What for?" "I don't have my books with me." That made everybody laugh, they knew me too well. Someone said "But you've never bothered to carry those books before." I ended up staying there that night and went home for lunch next day. That night I went to my heart's home.

Around eight, Mahsa asked "Would you like to go out?" "Yes please!" I said "I am dying to get out of the house." "Okay" she said "Let's go!" We changed clothes and went out. We drove around through the western and northern neighborhoods of Shiraz, before ending up at

Táchira. We had a great time and got home after one and headed straight to bed.

I had another poem for her and it really turned her on. After I had finished reading, she took the paper from me and we made such beautiful love. She was so light, so soft, so tender and lovely that I could hardly believe that this is the same Mahsa I knew and loved.

We got up around ten and were so full of energy that we both practically bounced out of bed. After quick showers, we went downstairs. We wanted to go to the garden but instead went to the backyard and spent a beautiful Friday outside. In the late afternoon, Mahsa seemed to get bored and said "Let's go back inside." We both changed into jeans. Mahsa turned on the stereo and said "Would you dance with me Sir?" I replied "It would be my pleasure!" As we danced, Mahsa said "I am Mahsa, what's your name?" Playing along, I said "It's Yousef." We made some small talk until I said "My God you have beautiful eyes! I cannot stop staring at them. How did you get them?" Mahsa laughed and said "Why did you say that? You screwed it up!" I said "I couldn't control myself. You know that I am crazy about your eyes." She said "I know, but you are crazy anyway." But she hugged and kissed me, saying "That was very nice, we should do that more often," I agreed. Then the doorbell rang and she went to the window to see who it was. "Oh my God!" she exclaimed "It's auntie and she brought company." Mama let them in and escorted them to the living room and we ran downstairs to greet them. It was Mahsa's auntie, her son and two guys I didn't know. I greeted auntie and kissed her hand when she introduced the others, "These are my younger brothers." I shook hands with each and sat next to auntie's son and talked to him. Auntie turned to me and said "This is the guy Mahsa has chosen and he is very handsome." They stayed for about an hour. After they had left, I told Mahsa "You are playing with fire, don't do that. What if they go and say anything to someone? We will be screwed." She said "Don't worry; they don't know who you are." I said "It is still dangerous." She said "But I didn't know they were coming. It was only supposed to be auntie and her son." We went to the kitchen and she made tea. I said "I have to go home. You know that." That didn't improve her mood "Yes I know." But I said "I think it would be better if I left now." I kissed her and said "See you tomorrow alligator." Scowling at me, she said "I definitely bite you tomorrow!"

I spent most of the following week at Mahsa's. One day, however, when I approached the house, I saw the outside light was on, which wasn't good. That means danger and that I could not go in. I went back to the town square and called her, but nobody picked up. There was nothing else I could do, so I went home and called her later that night. Mahsa told me everything that had gone on that day "My brother was here. I will tell you later about him.

Where are you?" I said "I am at home waiting for you." She said "I'm sorry baby but that was a family matter." I was concerned "Is everything okay?" She sounded tired "Yes everything is good. I guess I will see you tomorrow?" I said "Yes, I hope so."

I stopped by the next two days and on Wednesday night to my sister's. On Thursday night we went out again and got home around midnight. I read another poem to her and she got so hot and horny that she took me up to a wonderful place neither of us had ever known before. We got up earlier than ever on Friday; we were so full of energy again. Whatever she did, she did it again and I still don't know what it was. That morning she said to me "Let's go somewhere, it will be a nice surprise for you." When she told Meetra about it, she became excited and said "I want to come too!" That was the first time we went someplace together as a family in Shiraz.

I found out later that Mahsa's brother stopped by the house to ask her about selling the garden next to the house. Mahsa was reluctant to part with it and told him that she would have to think about it. Mahsa confided in me that she wanted to talk to some people about it. But I wasn't sure what her plans were for it.

The three of us got to the car and I suggested that Meetra sit in front but she refused and sat in the back. We drove west out of town, on the way to Táchira. But Mahsa turned down a road then she stopped at a place and we went in. We waited inside the family room next to the kitchen and two beautiful girls came out to greet us. They took turns hugging Mahsa and then she introduced me to them, saying "This is the guy I told you about." The sisters both looked me up and down and told Mahsa "He's young. Isn't twenty-seven or eight too young? Mahsa smirked "You don't know him; he can be as old as fifty." One of them looked at her sideways and asked "What are you talking about? How he can do that?" Mahsa replied "You will see it for yourselves." They invited us to sit and we talked for a while. One of the girls asked her how we met each other. Mahsa told them how it happened, telling them every detail. She also mentioned Assa's accident and that she had to go to London to see him. Then one of them said "I have a very personal question to ask." Mahsa narrowed her eyes "Just how personal? "Very!" "Okay, go ahead and ask." The girl blushed and asked "So, how was the first night?" Mahsa crossed her arms "First of all, that's none of your damned business!" She jerked her head at Meetra and me. "Let's go to the kitchen and I will tell you." The three of them went to kitchen and I could hear her voice telling them something, but I couldn't tell what. Meetra and I were left sitting there with our drinks. Meetra asked me "What do you think she is telling them?" I shifted in my seat; I was feeling very uncomfortable with the whole thing. "I don't know." I replied "But we have to end it somehow. Then I said very loudly "What time will lunch be ready?" I heard one girl say to Mahsa "He's good he doesn't act like he's feeling out of place." She said "Yes he is like that." Then someone called "Lunch will be ready in a minute. They set the table and called us in.

Lunch was very good and all in all, we had a nice afternoon. We went back to Mahsa's then I went home around seven. I spent a little time talking with the neighbor and then went to my room. She made dinner and after eating, I went to my room again. The next morning, she was knocking on my door for school.

CHAPTER 17

Mama

After school I went to Mahsa's and found Mama in the kitchen as usual. I said hi and she replied "Hi baby have a seat and let me bring you something. What do you want; tea or a cold drink? I said "Tea or coffee is good." She brought me tea. She said "Meetra is home but madam is not home yet." I said "I will stay here and keep you company. I like talking with you Mama." She refilled my cup and continued her story from the last time about how she got involved with Mahsa's family.

"I was very young, only fourteen when I came from my little village to here in Shiraz. Mahsa's mother had her about a year ago, so Mahsa was still only a baby. My duty was mostly to take care of Mahsa and I really grew to love her as my own. I was married once but the marriage didn't last and I never had any children of my own. After that, I decided never again to get involved with anyone and I never did. Mahsa grew up into a beautiful young woman and her parents decided to send her to school in London. She came back, got married and they went back to London together. After about four or five months, Mahsa and her husband sent for me to come live with them. At first I didn't like there, but Mahsa sent me to school to learn English. I learned enough to get by and it made things a little better. Mahsa then had Meetra and I was happy to have a baby in my life again. A year later, she had Assa. He was very hard to handle but mostly was a good boy. I stayed with them until they decide to come back here to Iran. Personally I was very happy to be back. I never really liked it over there that much. But now I am here in this house since they built it."

I said "My goodness you have been with Mahsa since she was one. No wonder she loves you like a real mother; but then again, you are her mother. Mama nodded "Yes she grew up with me." She poured more tea and said "It's really nice to have you here because I see that she is very happy with you. This is the first time on her life somebody can handle her. Her father couldn't do that and her husband, not at all. I think she has always been looking for someone like you. Where have you been all this time?" I said "Sorry Mama, but I wasn't born yet and after that I was too small. Maybe still I am too young."

Mama shook her head "No you are mature enough for her. I love you both."

At that point, Mahsa came in and said "Good afternoon guys. I am so tired! Mama, can you bring me something?" "Yes baby just sit down and relax and I bring you coffee." An hour later, Mahsa told me "We have to go to a party tonight and tomorrow as well. You don't have school, right?" I wanted to lie "I don't know." She laughed and said "From that answer, I gather that you have school. When everybody else has school, you don't. When everybody doesn't, you do. I am going to kill you one of these days!" To that I shot back "When will you do it because I would love that. I can see the newspaper headlines now: 'Dies by lover's hand'. I love it!" She threw a playful punch at my arm "Shut up! You know how to do that, right?" and she laughed.

I kissed her and said "I love you anyway. But tell me when are you going to kill me?" "Right now!" She said savagely "This is a perfect time. No question about it." I lunged at her faking an attack, saying "Should I get a knife?" "No thank you. I need you for right now. But I will kill you later." I said "That's fine baby any time you feel like it. I am here." She said "Okay, now let's go up and get ready to go." We each took a shower and Mahsa suggested that I wear my fitted jeans with a sports jacket. She wore jeans too; my God, anytime she wore them, I couldn't stare at her enough. I loved that look so much.

Around eight-thirty we went downstairs and Mahsa called out "We're going now, see you there." I was amazed, Meetra was coming too. We arrived at a beautiful house with a very large garden. We saw Mo and Mary and the two sisters from the other day, but Ali wasn't there. We sat down and the owner of the house came to greet us; hugged Mahsa and shook hands with me. She said "What would you guy like to drink?" Mo said "Mahsa will have wine and Yousef will have a double scotch." He winked "Am I right?" I said "Yes, you are. Thank you." The hostess brought our drinks and we enjoyed the time talking to the others. A half an hour later, Meetra arrived and called out "Hey gang, let's dance!" and went from person to person getting everyone up and out on the dance floor.

After a short while, Meetra joined us. She said hi to everybody and sat down next to me. Peering into my glass, she asked "What you have got there?" I said "Scotch." Meetra made a face and said "Avouch!" Turning to Mo, she said "I would like some wine." and Mo got a glass for her.

I whispered in Mahsa's ear "Let's go with Meetra and dance; the three of us We tried coaxing Mary, Mo and the sisters to join us as well, but they were content to stay put with their drinks. Mary said "I will tell her to put on some oldies." Meetra, Mahsa and I danced a couple of songs until the oldies came on and we were finally joined by Mary and Mo. We went back to our place and Meetra thanked me for the dance and said "Promise me, Yousef that we will dance later." I said "Sure dear." and she went off somewhere.

Dinner was served and consisted of mostly cold items like salads and cold cuts. But there was lasagna as well. We were asked if we wanted wine with dinner; and I got some white wine. After dinner Meetra asked me for another dance; I looked over at Mahsa and she nodded. I took Meetra's hand and lead her out to the dance floor. As we danced, Meetra asked, "Why you did look at mom?" I replied "I just wanted to make sure she was okay with us dancing together." Meetra thought about it for a little while then said "I wish I could meet someone like you, but just a little thinner." I said "I am chubby aren't I?" Blushing, she said "It's not that, but I like guys a little skinnier than you." I said "You will find your guy, don't worry. When the time comes, you will know it. Just don't lose faith." Meetra smile "I won't, that I promise you. When I see you and mom together now, I know that love can come in an instant. I hope I won't miss it. I keep my eyes and heart wide open."

We stayed until around one when Mahsa asked me if I was ready to go, I said yes. I found Meetra and asked her if she was ready she said yes as well. We said bye to everybody and gave hugs to those we knew. As we headed to the car, I grabbed the keys from Mahsa so I could open the doors for the ladies. Again, I asked if Meetra would like to sit up front but again she refused, saying "That's your seat." On the way home, the three of us talked about the party. Mahsa asked me what I thought of the party and I said "I thought it was great, I had such a good time!" Catching Meetra's eye in the rearview mirror, she asked her if she had a good time. Meetra replied "It was wonderful. I haven't had that much fun in one place in a long time." I joked "So you missed him, ha?" She smirked "No, not really. Every time we go to a party, he drinks too much. He thinks he won't get drunk, but he's wrong; every time he gets drunk and I end up having to drive him home." Mahsa became concerned about this and said "You have to be very careful. Situations like that can be very dangerous. You should do something about that before something happens." Meetra shrugged helplessly "But what can I do?" Mahsa replied "We will talk about it when we get home. I am driving now, but I will tell you later."

We got home and I ushered them in, saying "Please ladies first!" I followed them inside and locked the door behind me. We said good night and went to our rooms.

Mahsa and I had another romantic night together; making love without sex. Believe me, lovemaking can be so much more fun and satisfying when you are with someone you love so much. That alone can get you to the point of needing sex anymore in order to be satisfied.

Mahsa and I were at that beautiful point. We spent hours just enjoying each other and we fell asleep holding each other face to face and heart to heart. Next thing I knew, she was nudging me to get up. I did but not until after her second kiss. After breakfast, we went to side garden and walked for a while. As we headed back to the house, I told her "Let's do something crazy!" Mahsa laughed "Everything you do is crazy." I persisted "I know, but I really want to do this!" Intrigued, she asked Okay, what do we have to do this time?" I grinned at her "Let's go to my place!" Stopping short, she said "Are you crazy?" "I warned you that I wanted to do something crazy. And yes, I am! I want to do this now, because they are not home and the neighbors are away as well." Mahsa looked doubtful "And how do you know?" I replied "Because I know and you know that I know." Sighing helplessly, Mahsa turned for outside support "Mama what do you think?" Mama too shrugged "I really don't know baby. Yousef is the one who knows better." Mahsa could be so stubborn "He doesn't know anything! He just wants to do it, that's what it is. I know him too well already!" Finally Mahsa relented and asked "What do I have to do and what should I wear?" I instructed her on what to do and what to wear but first I called home to make absolutely certain that no one was home. The coast was clear! We headed over to my parents' house around four-thirty.

We parked the car a safe distance away and agreed to

meet at the house. I asked "Do you remember how to get there?" Mahsa nodded and I added "I will see you there." She replied "See you there." As soon as I got home I checked again to make sure that nobody was around. A few minutes later, there was a knock at the door. I opened the door and Mahsa stepped inside. We went straight to my room. Looking around, she said "My God, this is a pretty room." She hugged and kissed me, saying "I know where your father's office is, but where is your mom's?" I showed her around the house and we returned to my room and lay on my bed. I went to kiss her and open her blouse, when she stopped me short, saying "No, not in here! We are not going to make love here. This house is holy for me and I will not do it, so don't even try." Disappointed, I said "Okay, but this is my room." Mahsa flatly refused "Yes, but this house belongs to somebody very holy. I follow him and have too much respect for him. I will not do it; if you don't like it, then tough luck!"

We lay on the bed, just being with each other when suddenly phone rang, disturbing our peace and quiet. It rang and rang, until Mahsa said "Damn it Yousef, answer the damn phone already!" "Okay!" I launched myself out of bed and picked it up. It was my older nephew asking where I was. I answered "I cannot talk right now; I will call you later." Mahsa asked "Who was that?" "It was my older nephew." "Why you didn't talk to him? It's never good to ignore family like that. Don't do it." I answered "I don't know what might happen here. Someone could walk in unexpectedly and if I'm on the phone, I wouldn't be able to act quickly...." I didn't finish my sentence because I heard a sound. I grabbed her hand "Let's go – quick!" I took her to my father's study and said "I will take them to my room. Once we are inside, then you must quietly go down, get back to the car and wait for me. I won't be long, I promise." We put my plan into action, but once I got back to the car, she hit me on the back and started yelling at me "Don't ever force me to do these crazy things again! Do you have any idea how dangerous that was? That was foolish of you to pull a stunt like that." Without another word, we headed home and as soon as we got back Mama asked us what happened and Mahsa exploded all over again. "Mama this guy is absolutely crazy! I don't know what to do with him. You have to help me Mama." She told Mama what happen and the older woman doubled over in laughter. She laughed and laughed until tears streamed from her eyes. Wiping her eyes with one hand and patting Mahsa on the cheek with the other, she said "Oh my dear, try not to be so upset. He's young and wants adventure." Shaking her head, Mahsa growled "Not with me. I was never so close to having a heart attack and he just doesn't understand why I am so upset. What can I do?" I chipped in, saying "You can love me more and more." Mama shrugged "I told you, he's young and needs some adventure that's all."

I ventured over to Mahsa, kissed her and said "I will see you later Honey Bunch." "Where are you going now?" she demanded. I replied "I'm going to my sister. You know that my nephew called, so it's better that I go there tonight and check in before things get out of hand." Mahsa kissed me, saying "Please be careful! You know I need you now more than ever." I promised that I would and added "I'm sorry baby, sorry about today. But the neighbors weren't supposed to be home until later. We did have a good hour together though. You see? It wasn't such a big risk my love." Mahsa gave up the argument and called the cab. I kissed her again and left.

As soon as I got to my sister's house, she began to give me a hard time. She wanted to know where I was, what I did and why I haven't stopped by. It was the same old drill and I had an answer for everything. I stayed over that night which helped cool everything back down to normal. The next day I went to school, home for lunch and then to Mahsa's after school. I stayed for a couple of hours. Mahsa asked "Would you like to get out of town this weekend?" I said "Sure, why not Saturday is a holiday." When I got home, I had a chat with one of the neighbor's kids who was the same age as me. After laying my plans for the weekend, I had dinner and went to my room to study a little.

The days passed quickly and I did all I could to keep myself out of trouble; including not staying over on the session nights. I learned that my folks would be returning home early the following week. I also made sure to spend some time at my sister's house; that included having lunch and staying overnight a few times. But I made sure that I saw Mahsa every day even if it was just for two hours. On Thursday morning I arrived at school very early which surprised everyone. I went to the principal and informed him that I would be leaving town to visit some relatives in a certain city. He knew for a fact that my family does have a lot of relatives there, but he still had his suspicions and said "Fine, but you have to be here in school Sunday morning!" I agreed "For sure I will be here, don't worry." Scowling at me, he snapped "I am worried." I let his remark slide as I thanked him and left for my other house. On my way, I stopped at a shop in the market place where I had left a small suitcase. I didn't want to show up at school with it. That would lead to too many questions. When I stopped in the store, the shopkeeper said "Good luck and have fun!" I thanked him and got to the house by eleven o'clock.

Mahsa informed me that we had to pick up the sisters because they didn't have a car that day. We picked them up and went to the City Gate to meet Mary and Mo. (City Gate, also known as Qur'an Gate, is an ancient gate that leads into the city of Shiraz. It is a great archway surrounded by a park. The gate is about eight hundred years old dating back to one of the great Persian

Dynasties.)

We then headed northwest until the asphalt gave way to a dirt road and we continued along that for about half an hour. We finally reached our destination around two in afternoon. Mahsa handed me the keys to open the door and let everyone in. Once inside, Mo and I went through the place checking the heaters in each room. The place was rather chilly, so we made sure all the heaters had enough kerosene and turned them all on and loaded up the fireplace in the main room. Mahsa showed each party to their rooms while Mo started bringing out sandwiches for lunch. Mahsa informed us that we could go to the local village to pick up more food. We cut the sandwiches into three pieces, so that everyone could have one of each.

After lunch, everyone was tired after the long drive and went to their rooms to nap. We got up sometime in the late afternoon. Mary and I went to kitchen to fix some tea. At that time, one of the villagers stopped by to see Mahsa. He had noticed smoke coming from the house and was concerned. "Why didn't you send someone to let us know you were coming?" She said "I'm sorry, but we just decided to come only yesterday. But everything is okay. The only thing we need is food for dinner; can you bring us some things?" The man replied, "Absolutely, we will bring you dinner from the village and also my wife would love to see you. I will tell her to take care of dinner for you guys." Mahsa thanked him and gave him some money and our plans for dinner were taken care of.

A few hours later, he came back with some others and brought us the most amazing dinner. Everything was freshly homemade and delicious. We put blankets down in front of the fireplace and ate dinner picnic style. After dinner, Mahsa asked "Who is playing? You guys can choose or I'll say who does what." Mary then asked "What do you have here?" Mahsa thought for a moment then went upstairs and brought down a guitar and gave it to Mary. Mary played and sang a couple of early Beatles tunes.

Some of us took turns playing and/or singing songs. After a while Mahsa couldn't stop from yawning and said "I am tired so I am going to bed. You guys can stay up if you like." Everyone else said no, it was time to turn in. We turned off the heaters, banked the fire and one by one went up. As Mahsa and I got ready for bed, Mahsa said "Leave the drapes open so we can see the mountains in the morning. If they have snow on the peaks, it will be beautiful to see."

The next morning, I awoke to the sound of Mahsa calling me to see the mountains. We held each other as the sunlight beamed down on the snowy peaks, making them sparkle and glisten. It was so beautiful and peaceful that we could have lain there all day. But Mahsa said

"We should go down and join the others." Mahsa sent the gardener's son down to the village to buy more food and supplies. He returned a short while later and by that time, the others were getting up and coming downstairs.

Meetra was also going to join us that day as she had to be somewhere the previous night, so we were expecting her at any time.

The guy came back with freshly baked bread, eggs, cheese and butter all made from the local farms. We devoured breakfast like pigs and almost ate everything he had brought. Around noon, some people brought horses and offered us an afternoon ride. Mahsa, hold one horse for me, saying "She will be perfect for you. Mahsa knew that I had never ridden a horse before. They tried to instruct me how to mount the horse by putting my right foot in the right stirrup and swing my left foot over the horse's back which I could not do. The gardener went and brought a stool and that helped a great deal. I was finally on that horse and his son held her by the bridle for me until everybody else got ready then he walked my horse out to the field. Mahsa was giving me instructions about the horse and how to control her. After a while, I got the hang of it and Mahsa was proud of me for being such a good student. Then we left the stables.

The others raced with each other and galloped their horses pretty fast and I did okay, taking my time, riding slowly. Once I gained enough confidence, I let my horse pick up the pace, but nowhere near as fast as the others. We were then lead to a hill and everybody went up ahead of me. I was so afraid of going uphill, but I followed along. I guess that poor horse knew that I was a beginner and she was very gentle and patient. She really helped me to stay in the saddled and gave me a nice ride too. On our way back, we had to go back down that hill. I just sat there, unsure of how I was going to do this. Mahsa called back to me "What about you?" A little shamefaced, I said "I'd love to but I don't know how to get the horse down the hill without falling off." She said "You're right, just stay there, I will come and help you down." One of the sisters asked the group "Who wants to race me down the hill and back to the stables?" But nobody wanted to; even her sister refused. Mahsa told her "Don't even try it! You could hurt the horse and yourself!" I asked Mahsa if she would ride back with me. I wanted to go a little faster and she cautioned me to be careful. We rode at a brisk pace; fast for me, but not so fast for Mahsa. But she stayed with me, without complaint until we got home.

When we got home, Meetra was there waiting for us. She was disappointed that she had missed the horseback riding and said "I'm sorry I got here so late"! She looked up at me and smiled "Oh my God, you rode Blackie! She is a very good lady." When I got down the guy gave me a carrot to give to her. I gave her the carrot, which she seemed to enjoy greatly. I stroked her neck and head while she rubbed her face on my arm. Mahsa laughed and said "Oh, she likes you!" I pet her again and gave her another carrot; then someone took the horses away.

We went in and Mahsa asked the guy to pick up some lunch for us. He returned with some meat stew. After lunch, we went into the village and bought some items for dinner later. This time, I prepared a stew with rice.

As we waited for dinner to cook, we gathered around the fireplace and got comfortable. Mahsa asked me "Do you 'smoke'?" I didn't understand at first "What?" She nudged me "Weed" "Oh that!" I said "That's okay. Who has it?" Mahsa replied "Mo brought some but he asked me to check with you if it's okay." I said "Why ask me?" "Because" she replied "You are the head of my family." I said "Sure, go ahead. I've smoked weed before, but I can't do too much." Mo then brought out a small bag, rolled a joint and passed it around. I took a couple of puffs and passed it to the person sitting closest to me. Mahsa even allowed Meetra to smoke a little as well. On the second pass, I declined as did Mahsa and Meetra. The joint got passed around a few more times and I indulged in another puff followed by Mahsa and Meetra.

By now, we were all high and in a good mood. Mary handed the guitar to Meetra to play; but Meetra shook her head "While you are here, why should I play? You are the teacher and much better than I." Smiling, Mary started to play and sang a song. She was then followed with a song from one of the sisters. I asked Meetra "Do you have any poetry books with you?" She said "Yes but not Rumi." I said that's okay; let me see what you have." She brought me the book that had many new poems but that was okay with me. I asked Meetra "Can you play for me?" She gave me a wide-eyed looks "My God, you want to sing?" Winking at her, I said "Maybe" She asked for the guitar, started to play and I began to sing. Mahsa just sat there shocked, but I guess that was a side effect of her being high. I sang a couple of poems, but inspiration seized me, or maybe it was the pot. I sang one after another until I had sung all of them. Everybody gave me a hand and Mary asked Mahsa "Is there anything he cannot do?" Mahsa laughed "I really don't know. There are some times that he surprises me too!"

Then Mahsa said "What happened to our dinner?" I said "It should be ready by now." I went in and checked the simmering pot. "Yes it is ready." Everyone pitched in setting the table while I brought out the food. After dinner, we went back to flop down next to the fireplace and Mo rolled another joint. I only took a couple of puffs. Mahsa kept a sharp eye on Meetra and they only had one puff each and we let the others smoke the rest.

Mary and one of the sisters took turns playing guitar and singing songs. Mo asked me if I could read more poems from that book. "Okay" I said "This one is a very lovely poem…" Meetra picked up the guitar and played while I sang. But somewhere in the middle of that poem, my emotions got the best of me and I broke out into tears. I looked around to find that some of them were crying too. "I am so sorry!" I sniffed "I just couldn't control it. The tears just came." From the corner, Mo said quietly "It's okay, Yousef, I cried too."

We stayed up until one in the morning, laughing, talking and telling stories. Finally one by one we said goodnight and headed to our rooms; but not before debating about where Meetra was going to sleep. I offered to sleep on the sofa and she could share the room with Mahsa. Mo disagreed, saying "No, I will sleep here and she can share the room with Mary." Mahsa stepped in and said "Nobody has to stay on the couch; Meetra will stay in our room." That settled everything and everyone went to bed. The three of us got into our room, only to have another debate between me and Meetra. I offered to stay on the floor and Meetra refused, saying that she would sleep on the floor. Exasperated, Mahsa said "Shut up both of you! All three of us can sleep in the bed. There's room enough for everyone." She looked over at me and said "Yousef, you have your side and I will be in the middle and she gets my side. End of conversation." We couldn't say anything after that, there was no use arguing with her. Whenever Mahsa said 'end', that end meant *the* end. So the three of us climbed into bed with

Mahsa in the middle. To say that made for an awkward night would be an understatement.

Mahsa woke me up in the morning so we could gaze at the mountain scenery again. "This is the last day." She said "I want to see the mountains with you one more time." I wrapped my arms around her and kissed her, saying "Thank you for everything and I do mean everything." Smiling at me, she replied "You're welcome."

After breakfast, Mahsa announced to everyone "I don't have any plans for today, but we can go to the river and see the waterfall." Everybody said "That would be great." Mahsa then said "It would be best if we cleaned up quickly and leave soon." After a short drive, we arrived at the spot; my God what a beautiful place it was! Two rivers came rushing down from the mountains, met and become one river that tumbled down a great cliff to create a fantastic waterfall. I dipped my hand in the water and pulled it quickly back out. My God, that water was freezing cold!

We stayed for a while, taking in the scenery. Some of us wanted to fish, but were told that the fish was not good for eating. I wasn't sure whether they just wanted to keep the fish for themselves or they really were bad. But I kept my thoughts to myself. We returned to the house and had a light lunch. We spent the afternoon cleaning up and helping Mahsa close up the place, making sure that everything was turned off. She asked the gardener to check the place after we had left. It was time to go; the sisters went with Mo and Mary and Meetra rode with us. We followed Mo's car along the dirt road until we finally got onto the asphalt road. Mo sped up and quickly left us behind. I told Mahsa "Are we in a rush?" She said "No, I am not going any faster than we need to."

It was late in the afternoon by the time we got home. The first thing we all did was jump in the shower. After feeling clean and refreshed we went downstairs and said hi to Mama. Mama asked "How was your trip?" I said "It was wonderful, couldn't have been better!" Meetra added "It was such fun!" she continued "Oh Mama, Yousef sang some of the poems for us and I played my guitar. It was all very romantic." Meetra turned to me "Assa was right your voice is wonderful. One day I will have to record you singing and me playing. We will also have mommy reading some Rumi as well. I'll send it to Assa, he would love it!" Mama asked us what we would like to have for dinner. Meetra said "Something light like sandwiches." Mahsa and I both agreed.

Mama busied herself making us cold cut sandwiches, which made for a perfect dinner. Meetra excused herself and went to her room to study. Mahsa and I went to our room and got ready for bed.

As we got into bed, I said to Mahsa "Thank you very much for that lovely trip. I really enjoyed it." She said "I hope we will be to go to those places more often. I'd love to go everywhere with you, but we have these problems to deal with right now. But one day we will get to do all the things we want. But in the meantime, I am really proud of us to be like this; to be a married couple. I just want us to be free of all these stupid restrictions put on us by everyone else." I kissed her and said "I love you no matter what." Mahsa replied "I love you with everything I have in my body and especially with all my heart." Then she kissed me back passionately. I said "Oh yes, that's the one I have been waiting for at least the past four or five days! You just made my day. Thank you and I love you so much." We curled up together, holding each other tightly.

The next morning woke me up for school. The next day, after school I had to go with my sister to pick up our parents at the airport.

While we were waiting to meet them, I stole away telling my sister that I needed to use the men's room and called Mahsa. She asked "Where are you, the airport?" I answered "Yes, I just wanted to call you and give you a kiss from here. I wish I could make love with you right here while I am waiting." Mahsa laughed "You know what you are?" "No, I don't know, but you can tell me." She laughed again "You are absolutely crazy and you should be institutionalized!" Now I was laughing "That's okay, only as long as I can make love with you while I'm there." She laughed "My God, you are something!" I kissed her and said "Well at least I can do this." She said "Okay, fair enough. When can I see you again? I guess we won't be able to see each other for the next three or four days." Sadly, I said "Yes dear, I will have to be home during this time. But I will call you the first chance I can get." She too sounded sad now "Take care of yourself, will you?" I promised her that I would "I will see you soon." She replied "I want to be you." then she hung up.

CHAPTER 18

Nasty Business

My parents arrived and we headed home. I went to my room and waited until after eleven and then called her again. When she picked up, she asked "Are you home now?" I answered "Yes I am and I miss you, I wish I could go there and be with you." She said "That's my wish too." We talked for about ten minutes and hung up. I went to my father's study and after a little while, I said goodnight and went back to my room and to bed. I was so tired that I fell asleep in no time. The next day, I chose to stay home because we were going to have a lot of people coming and going at the house. That was normal after a cleric like my father returns from Mecca. I was busy all day but in late afternoon I got a chance to call her again.

When she picked up the phone, I said "It's me!" "I know." She sounded very serious and said "Listen very carefully Yousef, I will not be able to see you for at least two weeks. I will call you when I can. Do you understand? I will call you." Then she said goodnight and hung up, leaving me standing there feeling stunned.

I had no other choice but to involve myself with dinner and family stuff so I didn't have to think about what just happened. I went into the kitchen and the cook said "What are you doing in here?" I said "I'm just checking on things." Giving me a sideways look, he said "Checking things or do you want something? I put your stuff to the side." I repeated stiffly "No I've just come to check." I guess he noticed that I was not in a good mood and kept his remarks to himself. Instead, he went to the back and brought out a plate of crusty rice that comes from the bottom of the pot with some stew over it and said "Here, this is for you." I thanked him and went to the corner and ate in silence.

As I ate, thoughts whirled through my head. Maybe Assa come home without telling her and that's why she cannot see me. Then I thought back on our conversation; why did she say goodnight? We never said that to each other in the last year and half. This was the ultimate torture; maybe it was this or maybe it was that. All I knew was that I would have to wait as she instructed until she called me. Four days went by and I dragged myself to school and home again. One day I asked one of my guys to bring me some opium. Surprised, he said "What do you want that for?" I snapped at him "To smoke, what do you think what I want it for?" When I refer to 'my guys', I had a gang of about ten guys who were in charge of controlling our area from another gang from a different neighborhood. A day later, he brought me some and warned "Be careful, don't use too much." I said "I know what I'm doing." I went home that night and smoked a small piece and then stole a couple of my father's valium, took one and fell asleep. The next day was worse; I couldn't do anything. I walked through the day feeling numb and there was nobody I could talk to. One miserable day followed another and I was in hell, there was nothing I could do about it. One afternoon, I found Meetra and asked about her mother. All I got was a cryptic response "She is okay, everything is fine." That made me feels a little better knowing that at least Mahsa was okay. I kept turning my thoughts over and over in my head, trying to figure out what I might have done or said to make her so angry with me. But I couldn't figure out what it could have been. In the meanwhile, on some nights I would smoke some opium and pop a valium.

Well into the second week of my horrible isolation, I went to see Meetra again and all she told me was "She is okay! Don't you understand that? But you have to wait." She said "It's better that you wait a little longer." So that's how the second week passed and I was smoking more and more opium which made me even more crazed. One day during a school break, I went to the market and bought some cigarettes. I left the shop and lit a cigarette when suddenly a car horn blared. I quickly turned to say something rude to the driver when I saw her across the street. I ran to her heedless of the traffic and came very close to getting hit by an oncoming car, but I didn't care. I jumped in and she sped off as fast as she could. I said hi and she said hi and nothing else until we got home. We went in and I went to the kitchen and said hi to Meetra and Mama. They said hi back, but this time, it was much different. They actually didn't seem happy to see me. Sharply, Mahsa called my name; something she had never done before so I quickly went up. Quick as a cat, she grabbed me and shoved me against the wall and said "You son of a bitch! Why have you brainwashed me? WHY? Why did you do that?" She repeated the same words over and over again. I was confused, she wasn't making any sense. Then she shoved me again and shook me hard and kept repeating "You son of a gun! Why have you brainwashed me? Why did you do that?" She screamed at me "What was it? I wasn't enough for you sun of a bitch! I'd like to kill you right now!!!!" Confused and terrified, I started crying loudly and repeating my own words "Please tell me what I did! I don't know what I did! Just tell me what I did, please someone tell me!" I was screaming too "What's going on and what did I do wrong because I don't know what I did wrong! Please tell me please tell me!!!" Mahsa herself was in tears and continued pushing me between the wall and the door, again and again, repeating herself. I couldn't talk anymore, I was just crying and sometimes whispering "Please tell me, please tell me." Shaking, I begged her to tell me what was happening. She screamed at me to shut up and began repeat herself over and over again. Sobbing, my knees gave out and I sank to the floor, all the while begging her to tell me what happened. Finally, she stopped speaking and opened a drawer of the night stand and threw something at me. As it fluttered past my face, I realized that it was a picture. Mahsa screamed at me again "Why did you do it? Why? Why did you lie to me? Why did you lie to me! Why did you brainwash me? You son of a bitch, everything you said was a lie."

By that time, I had stopped crying, leaned over and picked up the picture to get a good look at it. I looked and looked, but didn't see myself there. Then I realized that it wasn't me. I held the picture up for Mahsa to see and said "This is not me, this is not my picture!" She sat in front of me, her eyes narrow "Are you saying that this is not you?" I nodded "Yes, this is not me." She hesitated and then demanded "Look me in the eye and say it." I looked intently into those gorgeous ocean blue eyes, but all I saw was hate and anger. I burst into tears again, blinked through my tears and locked eyes with her again and said "This is not me; this is a picture of my brother." She spat out her words "Do you think I am an idiot; that I cannot see? No you are the idiot!" I said "Look again. Do you really see me there?" She grabbed the picture and stabbed the image with an angry finger, saying "Yes here you are, you fucking moron! Do you think I am blind or an idiot? I got news for you, I am none of those, you are." I took the picture from her hand and looked at it again. "Okay" I said "If you think that this is me, give me one hour. I will bring you proof that this is not me." Turning her back on me, she said "You had better bring proof! You have two hours to come back and don't even think about coming back without it."

I went back downstairs on shaky legs and asked Mama to call a cab for me. As soon as we got to my home, I left my jacket on the seat and told the driver to wait for me "I will be back in half an hour and I left. I ran straight to my room, opened a picture box and found envelop of those pictures. Luckily, the negatives were there as well. I grabbed them and ran downstairs. Just as I was heading out the door, my mom called "Where are you going?" I said "I have to go and show this to someone. It is very important. I cannot wait and neither will they. My mom said "Now wait just a minute, who are *they*? What are you doing to yourself? Don't go." I held my ground "Mom, I cannot wait. I must go. It's a matter of life and death!" Without another word, I left the house. I jumped in the cab and headed back to Mahsa's. I knocked on the door and was let in. Mahsa came down to meet me. I showed her the original picture with the date on it. Then

I showed her the doctored photo and explained how someone could remove the date and fix the picture to look like me. But she cut me short, saying "Then why did I get this one? Your proof is not enough for me." I asked her "Who gave you this picture?" She said "That does not matter." "But it does matter!" I exclaimed. I kept asking over and over "Who gave you this picture? Tell me!" Finally Mahsa got mad and exploded "Who gave me this picture? Meetra gave it me!" I looked at both Mahsa and Meetra in disbelief as Meetra wailed "Mommy, now look what you did." I held up my hands in surrender and said "Okay, now I understand what's going on. O.K. I got it." Meetra pleaded "But is not what you think!" "Fine" I said "Then please tell me what is going on." Meetra said "There's nothing going on. A guy gave me that picture." I said "Just like that?" She nodded "Just like that." "Who is he?" Meetra shook her head "That I cannot tell you. I promised not to say." I stared at her "Are you kidding me? You two just killed me on the spot. Now you don't want to tell me the guy's name who's responsible for all this." I flung my hands into the air again "That's just beautiful! It's okay! I am a dead man anyway. She broke my heart and killed me upstairs. So now it really doesn't matter anymore. I won't survive this. That is a promise, but after I'm gone, you can blame yourselves."

I grabbed the envelope and the pictures and without looking at anyone, I said "Bye. See you someday in the place all we go." I opened the door and walked out. Meetra came running after me with tears in her eyes, saying "All I can do is showing you who he is." I said "That's all I need. Call me and let me know when and where." She said "I will do that. Either tonight or tomorrow night. I will call you." I had one more dig "Be sure to ask your mom that's it's okay for you to call me." Defeated, Meetra looked down at her feet and said "Fine, just don't do anything crazy. Everything will be okay. I know that she is angry now, but that will change. Now go."

I don't remember how I got home but I do remember that I cried all the way. I went to my room, locked the door and dumped myself on the bed and fell asleep out of sheer exhaustion. When I got up in the morning, my mother was so upset with me for running out of the house like I did. She asked me a million questions. I told her that there was nothing she could do to help that she should just leave me alone was the best.

The next day, Meetra called and told me to meet her tomorrow at the university by noon at a certain place. I thanked her and said that I would be there.

I went to school early that day and sneaked out for a smoke and headed straight for the university. It was only eleven and I knew that I was very earl, but I couldn't wait. I got myself a coffee and took two valium to help me relax. I found the spot where Meetra told me to be and waited. Meetra said that she would signal by moving her purse up and down like a yoyo. I spotted her coming from a building and a minute later a guy showed up, walking toward her. I knew that son of a zombie. There was the signal! Before he took another step, I pounced on him and grabbed him by the neck. I called him by mane and I told him how much I wanted to break his neck. He squirmed "Yes, you could do that, but then you will go to jail!" I squeezed harder "Don't worry about that." I said "Now tell me who's behind this and why." He said "If I tell you, will you let me go?" I said "Let me hear what you have to say first." Meetra stepped closer to witness the conversation as he told us everything about his uncle. "He is in love with her." He jerked his head at Meetra. "Then he found out that you were going to her house too often and Meetra had already turned him down, so he started putting things together and come up with a plan to get you out of the picture." He winced "So to speak." I told Meetra to search him and she did. We found a bunch of things including drugs.

I released my grip around his neck, but held his arm and told him "Where did you go to make such a nasty job of that photo?" I twisted his arm "Just tell me the truth." He told us where his uncle had gone to get the photo altered. Then I asked him "How the hell did you guys get that picture?" He said "I really don't know. My uncle just gave it to me and said "Go get that son of ...." Once I had gotten all useful information from him, I said "This day never happened. Do you understand? I have pictures too; with you, your father and uncle together in front of a whore house. If any of you come near any of us again, I will destroy all of you and I can if I send it to the newspaper. Now do you understand how important this is?" Visibly shaken, he said "Yes Yousef." I said to him again to make my point "Now go tell that bastard that if he ever comes near her that I know what to do." Then I added "You must promise me and swear that you will do as I say." Nodding, he said "I promise and I swear. I will tell him what you said. And I will forget today altogether. But please promise me that my mom won't find out." I said "I promise you as long as your uncle doesn't do anything stupid." I released him, saying "Now you go." He hesitated "Could you give me back my stuff?" I shook my head "Just get out of here! Go, GO!"

As he turned to leave, Meetra called out "Just tell your uncle that he is pathetic and I don't ever want to see him – ever!" Also be sure to tell him that his mind is so small and works only from the gutter. That's why I said no to him in the first place! Please tell him so he knows that he's nothing, not even a man. A man doesn't do these things!"

After he had gone, I asked Meetra if she would come with me to where they had doctored the photo. She said

"Yes, but I have to get back here. I said "I will bring you back, don't worry." We got a cab and went to that place. Thank God the owner wasn't there. We went in and I told the guy behind the counter "I just wanted to let you know that your little business is going to be out in the street." Shocked, he asked "Why, what happened?" I handed him the doctored photo "Did you do that? Why in the name of God? How much do you charge for such a lousy job?" He said "Two hundred rials. That's the best it gets." I told him "Do you have any idea what you are doing?" No, what?" Trembling with rage, I said "Your lousy job just killed me, that's what it is." I continued "Don't do this man! It's not worth it. You could kill somebody doing this. If I see your work one more time, no matter where, I will tell your boss what you're doing; then you will be back on the street. I will make sure of that." Then I demanded that he give me everything they gave him. Without a word, he handed everything over to me and we left the shop. We got another cab and we went to her house.

Meetra opened the door and let me in. She called for her mother who came down and met us in the kitchen. I laid out all the evidence on the table and told her everything. Meetra nodded "That's the whole story. He is clean like before." I took out the key hanging from the silver heart and put it on top of everything and said "Okay, now I am clean. What is next? I am giving you back your key and until you trust me two hundred percent, I don't want it. You said upstairs that you wanted to kill me." My eyes filled with tears "Trust me you succeeded with what you said to me. I am a dead man with broken heart. My heart has a leak in it and I don't think I will be around much longer. As I said before, I'll see you there." I turned toward the door. Mahsa said "Wait a second, please!" "What for? So I can make you angrier? I don't want to see you angry and hurt like that. So long my love." And I left. I could hear her shouting for Mama to stop me, to bring me back. Her voice carried itself to my ears, wailing "Please somebody, bring him back!" Then I heard Mama calling after me "Yousef, Yousef baby, baby...." Reluctantly, I stopped and she finally caught up to me, panting, she said "Please come back baby." I looked at her sadly "What for Mama? You didn't see what she did and what she said. I wasn't kidding, Mama, when I said that she really killed me. Why would I come back when the woman that I love is gone? The Mahsa I knew who was full of love and kindness is now a woman who has no trust, only anger. How can I come back to that? You be the judge and tell me what to do." Mama's eyes glistened with tears as she kissed me and said "God bless you my son and God help you both!" There was nothing more for me to do, but leave. I walked home and believe it or not, I made it. I will never know how I got there, but I did. However there was nothing left of me; I was just a body without a soul.

Life or destiny tries to teach us lots of things, but sometimes we don't want to hear and accept them. We want to continue our way without any thinking. I never thought I could live without Mahsa but it did happen! Life and destiny showed me what they meant, but still I refused to accept their fact and continued with my thoughts. They showed me how poor I am before them and they have full power. They also showed me how I can work with them in becoming a successful person in future. But I had to pass the test to be accepted by life and destiny. That afternoon, I walked home while my life was getting upside down. I was confused as to why. I got home my mother was in the yard, I said hi and went to my room and I got to my bed and went to sleep. My mother knew something was wrong but she waited till I woke up. She came to my room with glass of tea and asked me, what was wrong? I told her, I had a headache and she got me couple of tablet with water. I took them and then my mother left me alone, because she knew I was not going to talk about the things she wanted to hear. But who could give me a tablet for my broken heart? Absolutely, positively nobody, of course. My face and my body were so cold but I didn't say anything to anyone, because passing a huge test was in front of me. I had to pass that test no matter what. I got myself couple of Valiums and went to sleep again waiting to see if I would pass the test.

Life speeds up on me like speed of light. I couldn't do anything to stop it. Life and destiny showed me I don't have anything in my power, but instead they had full power in my life, as I said before. I was still confused about my life while the country suddenly went upside down and full of mess. My father and my brother somehow got me a passport and kicked me out and in no time I found myself in the U.S.A. I thought I could play with life but I was dead wrong. I started working in Los Angeles in 1982 and had to deal with an enter-family marriage in 1987. I was dead wrong again. Marriage became so messy and ended in 2007. For me a new life began. The new life had to be different because life by itself is love; and love could make your life up and down time and time again.

I still believe in love and its power. Because, I know what love can do to anybody's life. I believe love will knock on my heart again and, I am hoping this time, I will keep love as tight as I can. I better not miss the opportunity. After all love is life and life is love.

Y. JOSEPHSON

www.ingramcontent.com/pod-product-compliance
Lightning Source LLC
Chambersburg PA
CBHW051931290426
44110CB00015B/1942